ENVIRONMENTAL

INTERPRETATION

A Practical Guide for People with Big Ideas and Small Budgets

ENVIRONMENTAL INTERPRETATION

A Practical Guide for People with Big Ideas and Small Budgets

Sam H. Ham

Professor
Department of Resource Recreation and Tourism
College of Forestry, Wildlife, and Range Sciences
University of Idaho
Moscow, Idaho

North American Press
Golden, Colorado

Library of Congress Cataloging-in-Publication Data

Ham, Sam H.
    Environmental Interpretation: a practical guide for people with big ideas and small budgets / Sam Ham.
        p.   cm.
    Includes bibliographical references and index.
    ISBN 1-55591-902-2
    1. Natural areas – Interpretive programs. 2. Environmental education. 3. National parks and reserves – Interpretive programs.
    I. Title.
    QH75.H36 1992   92-17212
    333.7'014 – dc20   CIP

Printed in the United States of America

0 9 8 7 6 5 4 3 2

North American Press
350 Indiana Street
Golden, Colorado 80401-5093
USA

For Jared and Alison:

Sorry this took so long. You were *always* number one.

CONTENTS

FOREWORD

I have always considered environmental interpretation to be a craft of special importance. Like all crafts, it requires technical skill, wisdom and purpose. Its special importance lies in the economic, environmental and political crises that threaten the quality of life and landscape over much of our planet. If these crises (from local issues like preserving a neighborhood stream to global issues like ozone depletion) are to be solved, they will be solved in place by empowered and informed citizens who understand their relationship with nature. The craft of environmental interpretation can contribute to this empowerment, and *Environmental Interpretation: A Practical Guide for People with Big Ideas and Small Budgets* is a book on how to accomplish it.

As the subtitle suggests, the interpretation profession is increasingly composed of people with big ideas and small budgets. The big ideas are partly a response to the environmental issues that assault us—parks are encircled, forests deforested, open space developed, water, food, and soil tainted or threatened. These issues cry out for interpretation, as do the underlying natural systems in all their complexity and beauty. The big ideas are also the product of increased education, including the rise of professional training in interpretation, and the emerging global communication network, creating a global culture we only now dimly can foresee. The phrase, "think globally, act locally," becomes increasingly meaningful. From it, big ideas readily emerge.

The small budgets are meaningful, too. As a new century dawns, a budgetary crisis confronts social services at all levels of government, in the United States, in many countries of Europe (East and West), throughout much of Latin America and Africa, and in the new republics of the former Soviet Union. It is unlikely to disappear any time soon. One of the most common (and sincerely felt) complaints of interpreters is that they are unable to do their jobs without more money. Small budgets are relative (even the interpreter with a $100,000 operating budget can feel strapped for funds), yet lack of money should not be an obstacle to practicing the craft of environmental interpretation. That is a central theme of Sam Ham's book: good interpretation is not resource-dependent, but craft-dependent. This is a unique, valuable, and in these days of high-tech (and high cost) solutions to contemporary problems, almost a revolutionary perspective.

Environmental Interpretation is built like a good manual should be (and here I'm thinking of Persig's *Zen and the Art of Motorcycle Maintenance)*: it tells us not just how to do things, but the deeper (and ultimately more important) rationale of *why* these things work. As Ham demonstrates, the collecting of techniques or "gimmicks" is not the true mark of a profession. If it were, I doubt we would be comfortable about going to our family physician, or for that matter, calling the local plumber. We expect them to be professionals at their craft, not amateurs. Professionals understand why successful methods work, not just how to apply them. That way, when the methods don't work, they know the implications and can decide on alternative courses of action.

Hence, this book's foundation is a solid understanding of communication, primarily from the perspective of cognitive psychology. The early chapters describe the important qualities of effective interpretation. These qualities—that interpretation is pleasurable to the audience, relevant to their lives, organized, and has a central theme—transcend culture and class and serve as essential principles of environmental interpretation wherever it is practiced. The later chapters apply these principles to the major tools of the environmental interpreter—talks, guided walks, exhibits, community outreach programs, and so forth. The case studies demonstrate that these qualities matter, and that while the basic communication principles are always the same, their application can be substantially different depending upon the medium or the message.

While the foundation is communication theory, the brick and mortar of *Environmental Interpretation* are the techniques, carefully described and amply illustrated. This is a catalogue of appropriate technology, and as the book makes clear, the search for such technology often leads us to the past. In its pages are described a wealth of low-cost methods—some old and forgotten and others simply

obscure. Ham has pulled little known and little appreciated gems from unlikely places (such as audiovisual aids books written for teachers in the 1950s and manuals on how to teach medicine and health at the village level to nonliterate people). Appropriate technology can also be new, and the reader can find a practical discussion of how to use computers for exhibit labeling as well as a revival of "pounce drawings," a method old-time teachers used to transfer drawings and artwork to chalk boards. Readers can learn how to create low-cost but sophisticated colored background slides with superimposed titles in the same chapter in which they learn how to make flannel boards that use pieces adhered with homemade glue and rice chaff.

This range of technology is presented not as interpretive folklore (which would be fascinating in its own right), but for a real and strategic purpose. One of the most unusual features of *Environmental Interpretation* is its simultaneous release in English and Spanish versions. The case studies for each version vary somewhat, yet they demonstrate that interpreters can learn from a broader range of examples than they might at first expect. A big idea to one interpreter may be a new museum pamphlet or an improved park map, to another it may be an extensive community education program. Small budgets in one context may mean shooting your own background slides; in another it may mean mixing your own glue. We all have something to teach and learn from one another.

Although cultural and political realities can vary dramatically, interpreters throughout the Western Hemisphere share some of the same basic challenges—to do more with less, to communicate well, to empower the public to understand

and thereby, possibly, deal wisely with the environmental crises of our time. The readers who turn these pages will find themselves immersed in the passing on of an important craft and enriched by skill, wisdom and purpose. May they make the most of it.

Gary E. Machlis
Sociology Project Leader
National Park Service,
Cooperative Parks Studies Unit
University of Idaho, Moscow

Ask any conservationist to list the top three problems facing the world today, and one of them is certain to be the lack of public support for conservation. This is often said with a rather plaintive tone, almost as if the public were somehow at fault. After all, isn't it already obvious to everyone that the environment holds the key to our future?

It may be more productive to look at this problem as essentially one of ignorance, or lack of information. If only people were made more aware of the values of their environment, then they would rally to the cause. This is the "big ideas" that Sam Ham addresses in *Environmental Interpretation: A Practical Guide for People with Big Ideas and Small Budgets.* "Environmental interpretation" quite simply means making the environment understandable to lay people—whether they are farmers, politicians, or visitors to forests, parks, and museums. With this book, Sam Ham has produced a much-needed practical guide for building public appreciation of the environment. It is aimed at the practitioner who wants to reach people visiting protected areas, people living in and around them and people living in cities whose political support is essential to conservation.

This is a particularly timely book, coming out shortly after the IVth World Congress on National Parks and Protected Areas, held in Caracas, Venezuela, in 1992. That gathering, which brought together more than 1,800 conservation leaders from 133 countries, was very clear about the urgent need for building public support for the environment in general, and for protected areas more specifically. Two workshops related to this book were held at the two-week Congress, one on using education to build greater involvement in environmental and protected area issues, the second on how to provide information to people visiting protected areas. Both of these workshops considered drafts of *Environmental Interpretation* and discussed them with Sam Ham. There was unanimous agreement that this book has saved the workshops a tremendous amount of work, because the workshops at the Congress were aimed at developing precisely the practical tools that are so carefully described in *Environmental Interpretation.* This enabled participants at the workshops to focus instead on how to put into action the tools that Ham has developed. Even before it was published, this book was already developing a foundation for action by protected area managers, conservation organizations, tourism agencies and interpreters all over the world. Teachers, extension specialists and educators at museums, aquaria and botanical gardens will find this volume pertinent and valuable to their work. And its focus on low-cost communication methods will make it doubly valuable to most of the world's interpreters who, sadly, must work within extremely tight budgets.

Environmental Interpretation quite rightly leaves the content and subject matter of specific interpretive programs to the people developing them; each site has its own special characteristics and calls for its own content. That said, I would like to suggest that most interpretive programs can build upon an almost counter-intuitive duality—that even though modern civilization is dependent upon global cooperation, local self-reliance is a value to be maintained, and if possible, nurtured.

It might seem strange that someone working for the International Union for Conservation of Nature and Natural Resources suggests a focus on people rather than nature. But most of the conservation problems our world faces are *human* problems. Almost all protected areas were formerly occupied by people, and their historic influences on the environment contributed to the species and landscapes that people admire today. Building support for protected areas might be best based on showing what they mean to people today, both those who live in and around them and those who visit them.

It might also seem strange to advocate internationalism in national parks and forests. But once you have an audience (whether it is seeking shelter from rain in a visitor center, hiking in the sunny hills, or simply carrying out daily sustenance activities), you can make a fair assumption that the audience already senses something about the values of unspoiled land. This provides an excellent opportunity for the skilled interpreter to address issues extending far beyond the boundaries of a specific area—provided, of course, that these broader issues can be tied back to the immediate setting. For example, global phenomena such as climate change and air pollution have direct effects on protected areas, and these can be demonstrated to visitors. How much carbon does the area contain in its living matter? What changes in vegetation and fauna can be expected if the climate changes? What influences of industrial pollution are being felt by the area and by the people who live nearby?

On the other hand, most protected areas have been established because they have not been radically changed by industrial society. The ecological harmony such areas represent provides a very effective background for teaching self-reliance.

How did pre-industrial populations earn a living from the resources in the area? What mechanisms did those people use to prevent over-exploitation of their resources? What are the relationships between the natural resources being managed today and people living on surrounding lands, and how sustainable are these relationships in the long term?

Those of us living in the developed world need not romanticize self-reliance. Our dependence on the rest of the world is what makes us wealthy, gives us automobiles and computers and chocolate. But this dependence is not free. One of its costs has been our links with nature. So let's use our natural resource lands and protected areas to teach people worldwide about the trade-offs between dependence and self-reliance, between ecosystems where people are functioning parts and ecosystems where people dominate through tools and energy brought from far afield. And let's make sure that people are aware of the fragility of wealth brought by dependence and that they appreciate the durability of the material poverty of self-reliance.

Building on the practical advice contained in this important book, almost anyone can become far more effective at conveying a theme crucial to human civilization. The well-being of humanity depends on a harmonious relationship among people and the rest of nature.

Jeffrey A. McNeely
Chief Conservation Officer
International Union for Conservation of
Nature and Natural Resources (IUCN)
Gland, Switzerland

PREFACE

INTERPRETATION IN NATURAL RESOURCES, AGRICULTURE, AND THE ENVIRONMENT

This is a book about interpretation in natural resources, agriculture, and the environment. It is also a book about being resourceful and how to communicate well, even when money and materials are limited. The book is intended for people who work in forests, parks, protected areas, extension sites, zoos, museums, and other settings in which there is a need to communicate technical information to nontechnical audiences. If you want to communicate better with your audiences but feel frustrated because you don't have access to expensive equipment and materials, this book is written for you.

I've been an "interpreter" since about 1970. That was the year I got my first real job in the interpretation field. Well, it was sort of the interpretation field. Although I was working in a park, I never made any real presentations or led any real tours, but I did think about doing them. Some days, when I was lumbering up the trail to dig a new post hole or check for litter, I would fantasize about leading real people up that trail to show them the wonders of nature. Thanks to an enlightened boss and park board, a few years later I was doing exactly that, and my career in natural resources has never been the same.

The park was called Kamiak Butte. It was a state park then, but later it was converted to a county park—the first one ever in Whitman County, Washington. Technically it was state forest land. In fact, the main trail was nothing more than an old logging road. The park was, and still is, surrounded by private farms that extend right up to the perimeter fences. Looking back on it now, I feel lucky to have worked at Kamiak Butte. It was a microcosm of the real world of natural resource conservation, preservation and multiple-use management. I couldn't have had a better classroom.

Because of its setting, Kamiak Butte is a biological island harboring native plant and animal communities that are hard to find in Whitman County. It's a biodiversity preserve located in the heart of one of the world's largest agricultural regions. Since the term "biodiversity" wasn't used in those days, we just called the place a "park." And it was there that I developed my philosophy toward interpretation's role in land management. The park's logging history and agricultural setting offered outstanding opportunities for natural resource interpretation. Its namesake, Chief Kamiakin, was a famous native American who led a confederation of Indian tribes against the white army in the late 1850s. His story, along with the region's natural resource and farming heritage, gave me an early education about the complicated relationships between people, nature, natural resources, and the environment. Human ideologies, religions, value systems, and moral codes have been, and continue to be, at the heart of Kamiak Butte's story—just as they constitute the story all over the world whenever people differ in opinion about their natural resource lands and how they should be used and managed. Unraveling and accurately repackaging these complexities can be both the challenge and joy of an interpreter's job. In the two decades since working there, I've had the great fortune to teach interpretation in many countries. But everywhere I go, I see the Kamiak Butte story being retold. The language, music, and customs are different, but the story is undeniably the same.

Interpretation Is Communication

It has bothered me that the word "interpretation" is sometimes used to refer only to educational programs in parks and recreation settings. Even though I've worked in a lot of parks and now make a living teaching in an academic department of natural resource recreation and tourism, I've always taken a much broader view of interpretation. It seems natural that interpretation would grow out of the recreation field because it is the recreationist's freedom of choice, perhaps more than any other trait, that best defines the pleasure-seeking audiences most park interpreters have to reach. But I've never felt that parks and recreation settings were the only places interpretation should or could be practiced.

The best teachers, salespeople, lawyers, and cab drivers I know are *interpreters*. So are the best extensionists, museum curators, zoo educators, and mass media personnel. Despite obvious differences in the range of topics a professional communicator might treat, good communication (by that I mean communication that captures attention and makes a point) always seems to have the same qualities regardless of who's doing it or the subject matter being addressed. Being an "interpreter" doesn't just mean learning forestry or agriculture or botany or zoology. Depending on the interpreter's occupation, it could also mean learning about arithmetic, shoes, legal statutes, or how beer is made. Beyond acquiring advanced knowledge in some subject area, being an interpreter first means knowing about *communication*, and being able to recognize and explain the qualities that make it work best. Simply put, that's what this book is about. And it's aimed at anyone who wears, or would like to wear, the "interpreter" label, regardless of his or her occupation.

Big Ideas and Small Budgets

If you're around interpreters a lot, you start to hear some of the same frustrations over and over. Probably the most common complaint among some interpreters is that they just can't do their jobs without more money. The funny thing is, I hear this as much from people who have six-digit budgets as I do from people who have only two-digits to work with. While the desire for larger budgets is understandable (and there's no denying that money helps an interpretive program), I'm troubled when lack of money is used as the reason for doing nothing at all. My philosophy is that true "professional" interpreters are like liquids—they take the shapes of their containers. Whatever the constraints are, they acknowledge them and simply get on with their work inside the boundaries and limitations they have to deal with. Their work is too important to let anything get in the way of it. To them, lack of money isn't an obstacle to doing their jobs, nor to doing them well. It's merely an inconvenience.

More than mere money, it is an understanding of how communication works, and practical knowledge of how to apply it, that are at the root of most effective interpretive programs. Certainly, financial resources permit us to hire specialists and to use flashier and more durable materials (and these are nice). But in twenty years of thinking about interpretation, observing it, and practicing it, I don't recall even one instance in which a mediocre communication strategy was saved from mediocrity by flashiness. I do, however, remember *many* captivating programs that required nothing more than an interpreter's time. And I recall many low-budget exhibits, low-budget audiovisual programs and low-budget self-guided trails that were truly excellent. The biggest difference between interpreters who achieve excellence and those who achieve mediocrity seems to be in their knowledge of *how* to communicate, not in the size of their budgets. This is the philosophy that has guided my work on this book since its inception more than three years ago.

As the subtitle suggests, the focus of this book is unmistakably on low-cost communication methods. Much of the resource material available to interpreters today presents a money-dependent model that low-budget operations simply can't attain—and this is as true in countries like the United States as it is in the so-called "developing" world. Recognizing this, I began a search for low-cost methods that sometimes led me to forgotten and even "home-spun" communication technologies. This has been part of the fun of writing the book. The result, I hope, is a stimulating blend of old and new. Resisting the temptation to describe more advanced technologies, particularly in audiovisual production, has been a daily challenge because they're fun for me. But through the course of researching this book I've discovered a new kind of fun in being able to communicate well with limited resources. As I stress in almost every chapter, this is something anyone can do if he or she first knows the principles underlying effective communication.

How This Book Is Organized

The book contains eleven chapters, each focusing on a different aspect of interpretation. Most chapters contain guidelines for developing some form of interpretive device (for example, a talk, an exhibit, an audiovisual program, etc.) and include both illustrations and photographs to make understanding easier. Following each chapter is a list of the references cited, and for those wanting more information, additional readings in English and Spanish. Offering readers a selection of the best information available in both languages has been a goal from the outset. Despite what federal and state governments may think, it's clear that Spanish has become a bonafide second language in the United States, and many readers may want to consult the Spanish-language references. In fact, American society (and here I mean all of the Americas, not just the United States) is increasingly bilingual. I just don't think it makes sense to keep English- and Spanish-language literatures separate any longer.

At the end of each chapter are one or more case studies related to that topic. These case studies (twenty-nine in all) were written by people, like you, who needed to communicate but had limited resources to do it. In most of them, how the authors overcame the limitations and produced an effective communication device is highlighted. The case studies come from five different countries in North, Central, and South America, the Caribbean, and Europe. Although our cultures vary, you will find that the need to communicate better about natural resources is something that binds us together professionally. Solutions to communication problems, regardless of where they originate, are relevant everywhere at some level. And this is the level at which the case studies focus.

The chapters are organized into three main divisions. Part I is entitled Important Concepts. Here we learn how easy it is to apply the four basic qualities of an interpretive approach to communication, and how to distinguish interpretation from other forms of information transfer. We briefly review the common interpretive media, contrast voluntary and involuntary audiences and consider some important conceptual tools which will be referred to throughout the book. Despite its title, Important Concepts is intended to be very practical. It will be well worth your effort to consider the ideas presented in these chapters before going on to Parts II and III. Especially important is the concept of thematic communication. Mastering this valuable, yet simple idea will not only make the rest of the book easy to use, it may change your whole approach to everyday communication.

Part II looks at "conducted activities" presentations that are delivered or led by an interpreter. We will consider proven methods for developing effective talks, tours, guided walks, and special activities such as puppet shows, living history demonstrations, and others. In addition, we'll review the qualities of successful "roving" or impromptu interpretation, as well as how to organize and operate an effective information center. One of the five chapters in Part II shows how to design and use inexpensive visual aids in oral presentations. Among the visual aids discussed are slides, overhead transparencies, flip charts, flannel boards, chalkboards, and props. At the end of the chapter are step-by-step instructions for making your own drawings and illustrations. The final chapter of Part II is entitled Case Studies on School and Community Programs. It is built around eight specially invited case studies, each dealing with a particular kind of program aimed at local communities, school groups, or both. Some of the authors tell how they developed successful, low-cost programs; others tell how they acquired funds to do something more elaborate; and all of them highlight successful techniques of building and maintaining environmental awareness in local communities.

Part III, Self-Guided Media, deals with communication devices that do not require the presence of an interpreter. Some of the most common self-guided media in natural resources interpretation are exhibits, signs, trails and audiovisual programs. Chapters on each of these topics are included, and as in every chapter, the focus is on low-cost methods and materials. Although there are many factors to consider, an attempt has been made to present them step-by-step in order to guide the reader's thinking and to make understanding easier. (Perhaps conspicuously absent is a chapter on interpretive publications. Although the original plan was to include such a chapter, so many excellent references on designing publications already exist that duplicating them here would have been redundant.) The final chapter discusses ways to take care of interpretive resources such as outdoor signs, photographic

prints, slides, negatives, and video- and audiotapes. Special attention is given to protecting these interpretive resources from the damaging effects of heat and humidity.

The book concludes with four appendices. Appendix A includes a glossary of 136 important terms that are used throughout the book. Appendix B (Models) is included as a source of ideas for those readers who can build whatever they can visualize. It contains drawings and sketches of many types of interpretive structures (such as exhibits, signs, benches, etc.) and interpretive installations (such as trailside improvements and outdoor amphitheaters). Also included are the plans for constructing a simple, low-cost copystand for photography (courtesy of Eastman Kodak Company). Appendix C contains lettering aids including letter templates and a tracing grid. Appendix D lists the names and addresses of key organizations and other sources of information on interpretation and related matters. The book concludes with a subject index to help those in need of quick and specific information.

ACKNOWLEDGMENTS

It is insufficient to say that this book is the product of a team effort because it required an *extraordinary* team. The job was too big for me, alone. Although my name appears on the cover, it means only that I'm responsible for any shortcomings in the manuscript. Any accolades rightly belong to a number of others. First among them is my wife, Barbara, who spent countless hours reading and critiquing drafts that were still too rough to show to less compassionate reviewers. Her many nights and weekends at the computer page-pouring the Spanish version of the book were uncompensated and crucial to meeting the deadline. She also rendered many of the illustrations and worked hand-in-hand with artists, photographers, translators and a sometimes difficult author. Barbara's professional touch and constant eye for quality are evident throughout this book. A limited production budget required creative ingenuity, sometimes daily. Barbara was always the first source.

Gerry Snyder, Manager of the University of Idaho's Natural Resources Communication Laboratory, is responsible for at least half of the photographs in this book, undoubtedly the better half. His careful eye and outstanding technique have improved many times over the book's visual quality. Besides shooting and developing photographs for the manuscript, he also wrote a case study for Chapter 4, reviewed Chapters 4 and 10, and did original research for part of Chapter 11. Assisting Gerry was Jared Juusola, also a skilled photographer and a talented darkroom technician. Jared's hard work is evident in every chapter of the book.

Assistants Claudia Charpentier, Silvia Sigcha, Nina Chambers, and Jeannie Harvey also deserve special recognition. All helped where needed on many facets of the book, but especially in readying the Spanish version for publication. Claudia's superb translation and Silvia's careful proofreading created an easy-to-read manuscript. Nina coordinated communication with case study authors in eight different countries and edited some of their manuscripts. Jeannie helped in translating some of case studies for the Spanish version of the book and worked tirelessly inputting changes as they were edited. Having such dedicated and versatile assistants was an unexpected and fortuitous advantage.

A special debt of thanks goes to John Hendee and Leon Neuenschwander, respectively dean and associate dean of the College of Forestry, Wildlife and Range Sciences at the University of Idaho. They were behind my original decision to write the book, and repeatedly offered support and encouragement during my work on it. I am especially grateful to Gary Machlis who wrote one of the forewords and to my friends and colleagues in the Department of Resource Recreation and Tourism who were exceptionally supportive even though my absences meant extra work for them. Drs. Jim Fazio, Chuck Harris, John Hunt, Ed Krumpe, Bill McLaughlin, Wej Paradice, Nick Sanyal, and secretary, Jana Schulz, time and again provided encouragement when it was needed most and a level of understanding only friends could give. Thanks also to the students who had to tolerate my absence from the classroom, yet had only encouragement to offer.

Three other people deserve special recognition for their contributions to the book. First is former graduate student, Nancy Medlin, who reviewed drafts of a number of chapters. Besides her helpful critiques and constant support, Nancy's other contribution was that she coined the term "theme title" one day when I was trying to explain the concept to a group of students but lacked a succinct label for it. Her term has since become a standard part of my vocabulary and is used extensively in Chapters 8 and 9. Scott Fedale, Head of Washington State University's Information Department, spent hours researching and voluntarily writing parts of the section on video tape protection that appears in Chapter 11. I also am grateful for his careful technical review of that entire chapter. Jeff Egan, former student and now successful architect and cartoonist, created the caricatures in Chapters 1, 4, 5 and 8. Despite his demanding schedule, Jeff responded enthusiastically to my request for the drawings. The lighthearted tone of his characters was exactly what was needed to soften the potentially esoteric ideas they illustrate. His talent speaks for itself.

Many people have made unusually significant contributions. Some of them helped convince me to write the book in the first place; others provided timely encouragement to stay with it once I began; and others took such an interest in the book that they provided a level of assistance far beyond what I ever could have asked. For this and their many kindnesses, I want to thank my good friends and colleagues: Jim Barborak (University for Peace, Costa Rica), Jorge Betancourt (U.S. Peace Corps/Honduras), Dick Bottger (University of Idaho), Claudia Charpentier (Universidad Nacional, Costa Rica), Juana María Coto (Universidad Nacional, Costa Rica), Scott Eckert (U.S. National Park Service), Rich Fedorchak (U.S. National Park Service), Jim Gale (U.S. Forest Service), Neil Hagadorn (U.S. Forest Service), John Hendee (University of Idaho), Glenn Hinsdale (U.S. National Park Service), Jon Hooper (California State University, Chico), Sergio León (Costa Rican National Park Service), Bill Lewis (University of Vermont), Craig MacFarland (Charles Darwin Foundation), Rich Meganck (U.S. Environmental Protection Agency), Yadira Mena (Costa Rican National Park Service), Zulma Mendoza (El Salvador Ministry of Culture), Kathy Moser (The Nature Conservancy), Leon Neuenschwander (University of Idaho), Jim Pollock (U.S. Forest Service), Arturo Ponce (Fundación Natura, Ecuador), Eliane Reggiori (Alternative Travel Group, Ltd., London), George Savage (University of Idaho), Ray Tabata (University of Hawaii), Jim Thorsell (International Union for Conservation of Nature and Natural Resources, Switzerland), Isabel Valencia (Center for World Environment and Sustainable Development, North Carolina State University), Francisco Valenzuela

(U.S. Forest Service), John Warren (U.S. Agency for International Development/ Honduras), and Phil Young (Development Alternatives, Inc.). I also want to acknowledge several former students for their hours of good company and resonant responses to many of the ideas presented in this book: Amy Adams, Bruce Andersen, Mary Bean, Brian Carroll, Lizeth Castillo, Neemedass Chandool, Dave Dankel, Elmer Diaz, Mary Dresser, Scott Eckert, Marianne Emmendorfer, Rich Fedorchak, Sheri Fedorchak, Brian Gilles, Robin Hartmann, Dottie Kunz-Shuman, Terry Lawson, Nancy Medlin, Dan Ng, Bob Ratcliffe, Mary Rellergert, Laura Rencher, Jaime Schmidt, Daphne Sewing, Sarah Sheldon, David Sutherland, Doris Tai, and Dan White.

I am deeply grateful to the USDA Forest Service, Tropical Forestry Program for its support in publishing the Spanish-language edition of this book. Through its tropical forestry initiative, the USDA Forest Service is making worldwide contributions to the sustainable management and use of tropical resources. I am honored that this book has become part of this important effort.

The International Union for Conservation of Nature and Natural Resources (IUCN) has been a constant source of moral support and technical assistance since the inception of this book. Jim Thorsell, M.A. Partha Sarathy, Wendy Goldstein, Bing Lucas, and Vivienne Solís have all contributed time, energy or information. I am especially indebted to Jeffrey McNeely, IUCN's Chief Conservation Officer, for writing one of the forewords.

Several other institutions and organizations have assisted in this effort including the U.S. Forest Service, U.S. National Park Service, U.S. Fish and Wild-life Service, U.S. Bureau of Land Management, U.S. Army Corps of Engineers, Idaho Department of Parks and Recreation, Utah Department of Natural Resources, Washington State Parks and Recreation Commission, Wildlife Conservation International, New York Zoological Society, The Nature Conservancy, National Wildlife Federation, World Wildlife Fund, World Resources Institute, National Association for Interpretation, John Veverka and Associates, the Caribbean Conservation Corporation, Eastman Kodak Company, and Dahn Design.

Many dedicated employees of the U.S. Agency for International Development in Honduras, Costa Rica and Guatemala, and the agency's Bureau for Latin America and the Caribbean in Washington, D.C., helped time and again with technical reviews, case studies and information for the Spanish edition of the book. The U.S. National Park Service's Division of International Affairs provided important training information. Its *Manual para la Capacitación del Personal de Areas Protegidas* constitutes one of the important authoritative works in protected area management in the Spanish language, and is cited in several chapters. The U.S. Peace Corps contributed in many ways. Several volunteers and their in-country counterparts gave me time in the field to explain projects and generally show me around. Professional staff in the Office of Training and Program Support cheerfully offered advice and technical information whenever I asked for it. The Office of Information Collection and Exchange was extremely cooperative, running down publication titles and in providing prompt written permissions for use of certain materials. In addition, a very special note of thanks goes to the Costa Rican National

Park Service and Ministry of Natural Resources, Energy and Mines for its technical assistance during my field work in Costa Rica in 1990.

I want to mention a number of other people whose help was particularly valuable. These are the people who wrote case studies, provided key information, reviewed draft chapters, offered photographs or made other special arrangements in behalf of the book. I am deeply indebted to every one of them: Bob Adams, Bruce Andersen, Lora Anderson, Wilma Baker-Nelson, Jim Barborak, Gary Bartlett, Gerald Bauer, Jorge Betancourt, Sarah Bevilacqua, Andy Boyd, Corky Broaddus, Celese Brune, Bruce Burwell, Beth Case, Bob Carlson, Kevin Carson, Jim Case, Luis Diego Castillo, Neemedass Chandool, Claudia Charpentier, Dick Clifton, William Cordero, Gerry Coutant, Paul Cowles, Todd Cullings, Richard Dahn, Scott Eckert, Jeff Egan, Jim Fazio, Rich Fedorchak, Scott Fedale, Pamela Finney, Paul Frandsen, Mike Freed, Jim Gale, Judy Giles, Shelly Gradwell, Michael Gross, Neil Hagadorn, Jared Ham, Alison Ham, Carlos Roberto Hasbún, Mary Beth Hennessy, Bill Hinkley, Glenn Hinsdale, Evan Holmes, Jon Hooper, Chris Hudson, Tom Hudspeth, Susan Jacobson, Denver James, Cindy Johnson, Susan Jurasz, Jared Juusola, Alan Kaplan, Natalie Kruse, Sam Kunkle, Leonardo Lacerda, Terry Lawson, Sergio León, Bill Lewis, Craig Mac-Farland, Gary Machlis, Juan Ramón Martinez, Colin McEwan, Jeffrey McNeely, Rich Meganck, Yadira Mena, Zulma Ricord de Mendoza, Kenton Miller, Larry Mink, Kathy Moser, Lezlie Murray, Ralph Naess, Lewis Nelson, Roger Norton, Tom O'Brien, Brian O'Callaghan, Wej Paradice, Peg Paradice, Sue Perin, Mike Pierce, Randy Pitstick, Jim Pollock, William Possiel, Jim Quiring, Susan Reel, John Robinson, George Savage, Jaime Schmidt, Daphne Sewing, Grant Sharpe, Sarah Sheldon, Silvia Sigcha, María-Isabel Silva, Pete Slisz, Michael Smithson, Betsy Snyder, Wendy Snyder, Vivienne Solís, Steve Sorseth, David Sutherland, John Swallow, Doris Tai, Rodolfo Tenorio, Keith Thurlkill, Fred Tracy, Pat Tucker, Isabel Valencia, Francisco Valenzuela, John Veverka, Don Virgovic, Wendy Walker, Steve Wang, John Warren, Bill Wendt, Christopher Whinney, Dan White, Gary Williams, Joy Passanante Williams, Kathleen Williams, and Dave Wolfe.

Last, I want to express my deep appreciation to the International Wilderness Leadership (WILD) Foundation and its executive director, Vance Martin, for taking such an interest in bringing this book to print. Vance is one of the world's tireless leaders in environmental conservation and a staunch supporter of efforts to educate people about their natural heritage. His encouragement, careful management, and cheerful disposition have made working with him and the WILD Foundation an absolute pleasure. I am flattered that this book is embraced by an organization whose work I hold in such high regard. A final note of thanks goes to Shirley Lambert, Jay Staten, and others at North American Press and Fulcrum Publishing. Their hard work and commitment to quality are a winning combination and evident throughout the book.

Sam H. Ham
Department of Resource Recreation and Tourism, College of Forestry, Wildlife and Range Sciences, University of Idaho, U.S.A.

Part One

Important Concepts

CHAPTER ONE

WHAT IS INTERPRETATION?

Interpretation is simply an approach to communication. Most people think of it as the process through which a person translates one language into another, for example Spanish to English or English to Spanish. At its most basic level, that's exactly what interpretation is, translating. Environmental **interpretation** involves translating the technical language of a natural science or related field into terms and ideas that people who aren't scientists can readily understand. And it involves doing it in a way that's entertaining and interesting to these people. Simply put, that's the topic of this book.

The first author to define interpretation formally was Freeman Tilden (1957). He wasn't a scientist, a naturalist, a historian, nor a technician of any kind. Rather, he was a playwright and philosopher. He was not well grounded in the biological or physical sciences—frequent subjects of interpretive programs—but he was an unusually sensitive person with a profound intuitive understanding of how humans communicate best. This understanding guided his view of interpretation which he defined as, "An educational activity which aims to reveal meanings and relationships through the use of original objects, by firsthand experience, and by illustrative media, rather than simply to communicate factual information."

As his definition suggests, Tilden saw interpretation as an approach to communicating which stresses the transfer of ideas and relationships rather than isolated facts and figures. Although an interpreter may use factual information to illustrate points and clarify meanings, it's the points and meanings that he or she is trying first to communicate, not the facts. This is what distinguishes interpretation from conventional instruction. In the classroom, the teacher's goal often is to communicate facts alone, a process necessary in the long-term education of students. In interpretation, we present facts only when they help the audience understand and appreciate what we're trying to show or explain. In instruction, presenting facts may be the teacher's ultimate objective; in interpretation it never is. Carefully selected facts can be supportive, illustrative and illuminating—but they're never ends in themselves. In interpretation, as we'll see shortly, the goal is to communicate a message—a message that answers the question "so what?" with regard to the factual information we've chosen to present. In this respect, there's always a "moral" to an interpreter's story.

Interpretation Versus Formal Instruction

One of the difficulties many interpreters have is understanding that their job is not to "teach" their audiences in the same sense they were taught in school. Many interpreters enter their jobs without formal training or prior experience, and they are unsure just how they should approach their role as communicators. The only role models that many interpreters have are their former teachers. There is nothing inherently wrong with this because there are some very good teachers; but as we shall see, communication methods appropriate in the classroom may not be acceptable to audiences outside of the formal education system.

Look at the example in Figure 1-1. Mr. Jones is a high school science teacher during the school year and an interpreter at a nature reserve in the summers. He's fascinated with rocks and minerals and tends to emphasize them in his science classes as well as in his talks at the nature

reserve. Notice Mr. Jones' classroom teaching methods. He tells his students to read from a geology book so that they'll learn terms he feels they should know in order to identify several kinds of rocks. Among these terms are cleavage, silicates, tetrahedral bonding, volcanism, metamorphosis and sedimentation. Whether you know much about rocks, you might agree that these are important terms for Mr. Jones to teach his students. He also gives lectures using his extensive notes, and writes and draws a lot on the blackboard. The students, on the other hand, know it's their role to copy the material from the blackboard and to take notes on everything Mr. Jones says during his lectures. There will be an exam soon and they'll be expected to know everything they've read and everything Mr. Jones has said. In other words, the students will have to demonstrate to Mr. Jones that they remember the facts he taught them about rocks. But they don't mind; although Mr. Jones demands a lot of work from them, he's a nice man, he tells a lot of jokes in class, and he gives fair exams. Most students enjoy his classes.

Now look at Mr. Jones, the interpreter. He likes to give talks about geology to visitors at the nature reserve. He photocopies pages from the geology book, the same pages his students read, so that the people in his audiences can learn terms like cleavage, silicates, tetrahedral bonding, sedimentation, and the rest. He passes these out to the visitors and then presents his talk using a portable blackboard that he borrowed from the school. He didn't have to work too hard preparing the talk because he was able to rely on some of the lecture notes he uses in his classes at the high school. The only trouble is that, unlike his students who usually enjoy his lectures, the people

Figure 1-1. Contrasting formal education and interpretation. (Drawings by Jeff Egan)

attending his talks always seem bored. Mr. Jones can't understand why. He decides that people who visit the nature reserve simply aren't interested in rocks, and he considers changing the topic of his talk to something they'd be more interested in.

The problem, of course, wasn't with the visitors and certainly not with the topic. No topic is inherently boring or interesting. There are only people who make them that way. Mr. Jones' problem was that he failed to understand that what made Mr. Jones, the teacher, effective would not necessarily make Mr. Jones, the interpreter, effective. He needed a different approach for the nature reserve visitors. As we will see, they were a different kind

of audience than his students, and Mr. Jones needed to change his communication methods to suit his audience.

Captive Versus Noncaptive Audiences

Let's further analyze the problem in Figure 1-1, this time in terms of the audience Mr. Jones is trying to communicate with in each setting. It's probably already clear to you that his error at the nature reserve was that he treated his audience like students. Why should this make a difference? Are his students different kinds of people than visitors at the nature reserve? If some of his students attended his talk at the nature reserve, would they be interested in his presentation even when the rest of the audience wasn't? The answer is probably not.

People act according to the environment or situation they're in. Where we are influences much of our behavior including how we talk, how we conduct ourselves, what we're interested in and what kinds of behavior we expect from other people. If you and a close friend were at the beach together you'd behave and expect others to behave much differently than if the two of you were in church, at a restaurant or at a wedding. Your ideas about what's interesting, funny, out-of-place, etc., would probably be very different in each of these settings. What might seem funny at the beach or restaurant, for example, might seem terribly inappropriate at church or the wedding. In the classroom, Mr. Jones' students expect certain kinds of behavior from him, behaviors that are consistent with his role as "Mr. Jones, the teacher." At the nature reserve, they'd expect a different Mr. Jones, not the teacher. The reason is that at the nature reserve the students probably don't see themselves as "students," but rather as visitors.

Interpreters who understand why and how audiences such as these differ, and even more important, how to tailor communication methods to suit them, have a distinct advantage over interpreters who don't. Although there are many physical differences in the two settings, there's one overriding psychological difference. The classroom is a setting in which the audience has to pay attention. The nature reserve or park is one in which it doesn't. Boiled down to a single defining characteristic, it may be said that the students in the classroom are a **captive audience** because they're forced to stay

and pay attention if they want to get good grades or avoid the trauma of getting poor ones. They've come to expect and to accept certain forms of information transfer that they associate with the classroom setting. On the other hand, the visitors at the park are a **noncaptive audience** because they don't have to worry about grades. If they decide to stay and pay attention, it will be only because they want to. If the presentation isn't interesting, if it seems too academic, or if it requires too much effort to follow, they probably won't pay attention. In the classroom, students will try to pay attention regardless of how boring or difficult the information is. They have to. There will be an exam.

Figure 1-2 lists the key differences between captive and noncaptive audiences. Although the most common captive audience is the student in a classroom, there are many kinds of noncaptive audiences: visitors in forests, parks, zoos, museums, botanical gardens, etc., participants in extension programs and people who read magazines and newspapers, watch television and listen to radio. As Figure 1-2 suggests, any audience that has the option of ignoring the information without punishment or loss of a potential reward is a noncaptive audience. Noncaptive audiences are driven to pay attention not by some external reward (like a grade), but rather by their own intrinsic satisfaction with what they're hearing, seeing or reading. The only reward noncaptive audiences seek is internal. As long as the information they're receiving continues to be more interesting and entertaining than other things around them, noncaptive audiences will pay attention to it. However, if the information loses its interest or entertainment value, the audience

Differences Between Captive and Noncaptive Audiences

Captive Audiences	**Noncaptive Audiences**
▮ Involuntary audience	▮ Voluntary audience
▮ Time commitment is fixed	▮ Have no time commitment
▮ External rewards important	▮ External rewards not important
▮ Must pay attention	▮ Do not have to pay attention
▮ Will accept a formal, academic approach	▮ Expect an informal atmosphere and a nonacademic approach
▮ Will make an effort to pay attention, even if bored	▮ Will switch attention if bored
▮ Examples of motivations: • grades • diplomas • certificates • licenses • jobs/employment • money • advancement • success	▮ Examples of motivations: • interest • fun • entertainment • self-enrichment • self-improvement • a better life • passing time (nothing better to do)
▮ Typical settings: • classrooms • job training courses • professional seminars • courses required for a license (e.g., driving)	▮ Typical settings: • parks, museums, reserves, etc. • extension programs • at home watching television, listening to radio, reading a magazine

Figure 1-2. Typical characteristics of captive and noncaptive audiences.

will switch attention to something more immediately gratifying. This response may be overt as when someone puts down the magazine, switches the television channel, turns off the radio, or walks out of the movie theater early. It may also be quite involuntary, as when we find ourselves daydreaming in the middle of a conversation.

The mind tends to go where it finds the most gratifying information. Psychologists have linked this tendency to two kinds of chemicals called endorphins and dopamine that the brain produces. Some of these chemicals are a lot like morphine in their chemical makeup, and like morphine, they're addictive. Pleasurable thought stimulates the brain to produce endorphins and dopamine. Boring or excessively difficult information causes the brain to look for more gratifying information elsewhere. This is essentially what happens when we daydream. Consider the student, part of a captive audience, who knows he must pay attention in a class on a certain day because the next exam will stress the information that will be covered. Subconsciously, perhaps, he's saying to himself, "Okay, brain. We've got to pay attention today. *Please* pay attention today, there's going to be an exam!" With determination to commit to his notes every piece of information the teacher presents, our student finds himself an hour later being awakened from one of his better daydreams by the sound of his own name. It's his teacher telling him that he should pay better attention if he wants to do well on the exam! The brain is in control of our attention. So powerful is its tendency to find pleasure that even a student consciously trying to pay attention to an important lecture is unable to do it if the presentation isn't interesting. Going

back to Mr. Jones' experience at the nature reserve, it's easy to understand why the people in his audience weren't able to pay attention. They didn't even try; they didn't have to.

The Interpretive Approach to Communication

If Mr. Jones had been aware of the differences between his captive classroom audience and his noncaptive nature reserve audience, what changes might he have made in his approach? What might he have done to hold his audience's interest and make them want to pay attention to his talk? Although there are many possible answers to these questions, all of them would boil down to four general qualities that Mr. Jones should try to give his presentation. Taken together, these qualities distinguish interpretation from other forms of information transfer and define the **interpretive approach** to communication. They are:

1. Interpretation is pleasurable.
2. Interpretation is relevant.
3. Interpretation is organized.
4. Interpretation has a theme.

Quality 1:
Interpretation Is Pleasurable

Interpretation is entertaining. Although entertainment isn't interpretation's main goal, it's one of its essential qualities. All good communication is entertaining in the sense that it holds its audience's attention. As Mr. Jones discovered, if noncaptive audiences aren't entertained, they're likely to switch their attention to something more interesting.

Figure 1-3. Interpretation is enjoyable. Children in an environmental education program have fun searching for seeds in a friend's sock. Parque Residencial del Monte, Costa Rica. (Photo by Sam Ham)

As explained earlier, this may be an involuntary action such as daydreaming, or it can be more blatant such as getting up and walking out in the middle of a presentation; audiences viewing exhibits or signs may simply stop viewing them; boring publications may end up in a garbage can, or worse, on the ground.

How to make learning fun will vary depending upon the communication medium one is using. Entertaining exhibits, for example, have different qualities than entertaining audiovisual programs or entertaining talks. Yet one thing which seems to stand out in all successful interpretation is that it's informal and not classroomlike.

Interpreters can create an informal atmosphere in many ways. For example,

a speaker like Mr. Jones could use a conversational tone of voice, rather than the artificial and stuffy tone that some academicians and politicians are known to use, especially when they read from notes. (A good speaker avoids reading from notes. In fact, most interpreters don't use them at all; referring to notes creates a formal or even academic atmosphere.) Also, research on exhibits has shown that people will pay less attention if the exhibits utilize media or communication strategies that remind them of formal education, such as Mr. Jones' portable blackboard. Generally, the best exhibits are those that are gamelike, participatory, three-dimensional or which contain movement, changing scenes or lively colors—all characteristics more commonly associated with entertainment than with traditional classroom media. Likewise, talks, tours and other kinds of presentations have been found to attract greater attention if they incorporate humor, music, or two-way communication. For similar reasons, an audiovisual program containing background music will usually hold an audience's attention longer than one containing only a narrator's voice; and a publication which has illustrations or which uses colors other than just black and white is more likely to be read than one which has only text photocopied on white paper.

Contrary to some people's opinion, you don't have to be a gifted communicator to be entertaining. In fact, there are a number of straightforward techniques that anyone can use to increase the entertainment value of technical information. Some of these are listed in Figure 1-4.

There Are Many Ways to
Make Technical Information More Entertaining

Smile: A smiling face indicates pleasure in most cultures. An old saying goes: "When you're smiling, the whole world smiles with you." This means that your audience will take its cue from you. If you look like you're relaxed and having fun, they'll begin to feel that way too. Being too serious can create a formal atmosphere.

Use Active Verbs: Verbs are the power in any language. Don't take away their power by making them passive (e.g., "The bat pollinated the tree," not "The tree was pollinated by the bat.") Academic writing stresses passive verbs too much. Use powerful, active verb forms.

Show Cause-and-Effect: People like to know what things cause other things to happen. Try to show direct relationships between causes and their effects.

Link Science to Human History: Research shows that nonscientists are more interested in science if it can be related to people from a different time. For example, weaving information about plants into a story of how indigenous people utilized those plants in their diets, art, religion, etc., may be more entertaining than the same information would be by itself. Telling about any aspect of a natural or physical science through the eyes of those who explored it, discovered it, described it, wondered about it, overcame it, succumbed to it, worried about it, died from it, were saved by it, empowered by it, hindered by it, or who otherwise affected or were affected by the thing in question, will generally make it more interesting to nonscientists.

Use a "Visual Metaphor" to Describe Complex Ideas: A visual metaphor is an illustration which shows visually what might be difficult to describe convincingly with words alone. For example, one way to describe the rich diversity of tropical invertebrate species would be to show a map in which the sizes of countries and continents were based on the number of invertebrate species they contained. As Figure 1-5 shows, the countries in the tropics would be much larger than those elsewhere. The small island country of Cuba, for example, contains more invertebrate species than all of North America.

Use a "Vehicle" to Make Your Topic More Interesting: A vehicle is part of a communicator's strategy to make a topic more entertaining by telling about it in the context of some overriding scene, setting or situation. Examples:

• **Exaggerate Size:** "If we were small enough to actually walk inside of a wasp's nest, you'd be amazed at what you'd see."

• **Exaggerate Time Scale:** "If time were speeded up so that a thousand years went by every second, you'd be able to stand right here and watch continental drift for yourself."

• **Use an Overriding Analogy:** That is, an analogy that your entire presentation revolves around (e.g., likening the earth to an onion's layered skin in order to tell about certain geologic processes; comparing a volcanic landscape to an ocean; relating forest succession to the construction of a house; or comparing natural resource management (use and protection) to a person with a split personality.

• **Use a Contrived Situation:** Demonstrate the need for forest conservation by making up a story about a town in which there is no such thing as wood or wood products; go forward or back in time; pose a hypothetical problem or set up an illustrative situation (e.g., "What would life on earth be like if its average temperature increased just 5° C?" or "What if there were no predators?"

• **Use Personification:** Give selected human qualities to nonhuman things (e.g., "What might trees say if they could talk?" or "How might ants view humans?") Give the narrator of a slide/tape program an animal's identity or point of view. Walt Disney made personification famous in his many movies about animals and stories in which the audience experienced certain adventures through the eyes of the animal characters. This technique has been criticized (sometimes rightly and sometimes not) by biologists, because it involves giving human qualities to animals that are not human. Be careful when using personification. Don't imply that animals and plants really think and act like humans.

• **Focus on an Individual:** That is, make up a fictitious but scientifically accurate story about one particular person or object (e.g., an animal, plant, rock, water molecule, ice crystal, etc.). Give an account of what this person or thing experiences in terms of the technical information you are trying to get across to your audience. [Examples: Follow a single water molecule as it goes through the entire water cycle, or a mass of rock as it gets changed from sedimentary to metamorphic to igneous states; describe what happens to a particular parrot after it is taken from its tropical forest home and transported with other birds to a pet store in another country; tell about the final days of the last individual of a particular species; describe a specific smuggler's attempt to transport ocelot skins out of a country; follow the mishaps of a particular bear that had to be killed by park rangers because it had become dependent on park visitors for its food, etc.] Sometimes, giving the individual a name or other identity adds to the entertainment value of the story (e.g., Walter Water Drop, Bear Number 74, Smuggler Smith, etc.).

Figure 1-4. Examples of ways to be more entertaining.

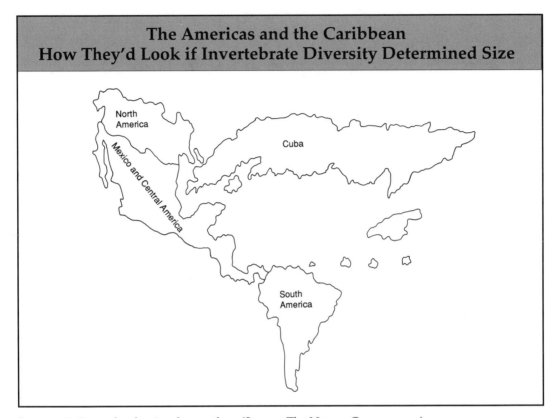

**The Americas and the Caribbean
How They'd Look if Invertebrate Diversity Determined Size**

Figure 1-5. Example of a visual metaphor. (Source: The Nature Conservancy)

Quality 2: Interpretation Is Relevant

Information that's **relevant** to us really has two qualities: it's **meaningful** and it's **personal**. Although related, being meaningful and being personal are different things. As we'll see, information that's meaningful isn't necessarily personal. When we succeed in giving interpretation both of these qualities, we've made it relevant to our audiences.

What Does Being "Meaningful" Mean?

When information is meaningful it's because we're able to connect it to some-

thing already inside our brains. Meaningful information is said to have "context" since we understand it only in the context of something else we already know. Some psychologists say that we humans have a lot of words floating around in our heads, and that when something we hear or see reminds us of one or more of them, we attach a meaning to it that's based on the words it awakened in our minds. When something we hear or see doesn't connect with anything we already know, it's meaningless to us. The trouble with a lot of interpretation is that it's meaningless to its audiences. Mr. Jones could probably do at least two things to

Figure 1-6. Interpretation is meaningful. An interpreter compares the eruption of a volcano with a pot of percolating coffee. University of Idaho. (Photo by Gerry Snyder)

make his talk more meaningful to the visitors at the nature reserve. First, he could avoid using technical terms unless they're necessary for his audience to understand some important concept or idea he's trying to get across. In this case, however, it appears that Mr. Jones is simply trying to teach his audience the terms, just like he teaches his students the same terms. Since few nongeologists have words in their heads that would be awakened by terms like tetrahedral bonding, silicates, or sedimentation, these words probably aren't very meaningful to Mr. Jones' audience. Second, he could try to **bridge** the unfamiliar world of geology to things that his audience is likely to already know something about. He might do this using **examples**, **analogies**, and **comparisons**. Common everyday things make the best "bridges" (see Figure 1-7).

In his first principle of interpretation, Tilden captured the essence of this idea when he said, "Any interpretation that does not somehow relate what is being displayed or described to something within the personality or experience of the visitor [audience] will be sterile." By this he meant that interpreters must not only find a way to link the information being presented to something their audiences know about, but to something they care about. With noncaptive audiences, this is especially important because they'll almost always ignore information that seems unimportant, even if they understand it perfectly. Consequently, we can understand why it's hard to sit through presentations we've heard before, or to read something we've read before. Although the information is very meaningful, it lacks the promise of new insight, and is therefore unimportant to us.

The reverse is also true. That is, noncaptive audiences can be expected to switch their attention to any information that is highly personal. Highly personal things include ourselves, our families, our health, our well-being, our quality of life, our deepest values, principles, beliefs and convictions. As we'll see, any communication that connects itself to this inner circle of our lives will capture and hold our attention more so than other kinds of information. In fact, our tendency to pay attention to personal information is so powerful that we do it even when we're consciously trying not to.

What Does Being "Personal" Mean?

Being meaningful is only half the challenge if interpretation is going to be relevant. The other half is being personal.

"Shadowing" and the Power of Being Personal

The best communicators always try to connect their ideas to the lives of their

Examples, Analogies, and Comparisons
Three Ways to Bridge the Familiar and the Unfamiliar

Examples: Quickly refer to something or someone that is like or in some way represents that kind of thing or person you are talking about.

• "These orchids are a good example of a plant that grows on other plants."

Analogies: Show many similarities of the thing you are talking about to some other thing that is highly familiar to the audience.

• "To understand how volcanoes work, think of a covered pot of boiling water."

Comparisons: Show a few of the major similarities and/or differences between the thing you are talking about and something else which can be related to it. The result is that one or both of the objects becomes clearer in relation to the other.

• "These two pine trees are a lot alike. Both have three needles to a group, and they grow in the same kinds of places. But if you smell the bark, you'll notice that one of them smells like vanilla and the other like turpentine!"

Two Special kinds of Comparisons: Similes and Metaphors

Similes: Compare some characteristic of two things using the words "like" or "as."

• "This tree has spines like daggers on every limb."

• "At this stage of their development, the spiders are as black as coal."

Metaphors: Describe something with a word or phrase usually used to describe something very different.

• "The canoe *plowed* through the rapids."

• "It was as though every tourist on the bus decided at that moment to throw what was left of his lunch out the window. For 10 minutes, it *rained* garbage."

Figure 1-7. Techniques for making information more meaningful.

audiences. The power this gives their presentations has been shown repeatedly in laboratory experiments utilizing a technique called **shadowing**. In these experiments, a person wears stereo headphones and is given very different tape recorded messages in each ear. In the left ear the person might hear a story about some city, for example Paris while simultaneously hearing a description of a complex process in the right ear, for example photosynthesis. The person is told to pay attention to the message about Paris, and to ignore the message about photosynthesis. This is a difficult task in itself, but there's more. Besides having to listen to only one of the two messages, the person is told to "shadow" or repeat back the message he or she is listening to as it is heard, all the while trying to ignore the other message. Few mental tasks require as much concentration and sheer effort as shadowing.

Moray (1959) and Cherry (1966) conducted shadowing experiments and found that not only was it difficult for their subjects to shadow, but when they tested their recall of the information they were supposed to pay attention to, the subjects could remember very little. Of course, when the researchers tested their recall of the ignored message (in our example, the description of photosynthesis), the subjects remembered even less. In Cherry's experiment, they didn't even notice a switch from English to German, and in Moray's experiment, they didn't recognize that some words were repeated thirty-five consecutive times! In both studies,

however, when the researchers prefaced some part of the ignored information with the subject's name, the subjects were able to remember it later, even though they remembered nothing else! Studies like these dramatically show why interpretation needs to be personal. We will pay attention to information we care about, even if we're trying to concentrate on something else.

As Solso (1979) pointed out, most of us have experienced this kind of thing at one time or another: You're at a noisy party or social gathering and someone on the other side of the room says, "I heard that George and Alice … ." Until then completely involved in their own conversations, every George and Alice in the room turns an attentive ear to the speaker. Consider also how well parents can distinguish between their own children's shouting and that of other children at a noisy playground. Psychologists call this **selective attention**, and it's something that all audiences have. They'll predictably switch their attention to things they care about, and as we saw, even when they're consciously trying not to.

But how could Mr. Jones make his presentation on geology more personal? Certainly, he couldn't mention the names of all the people in his audience. Even if he knew them, there'd probably be too many. But he might try two other simple techniques that are almost as effective. These are self-referencing and labeling (see Figure 1-8).

Self-Referencing and Labeling
Two Ways to Make Communication More Personal

Communication that appeals to those things we really care about—such as ourselves, our loved ones, our strongest beliefs, values and deepest convictions—attracts our attention. Information which is somehow related or connected to this inner circle of our lives will seem more important to us than it otherwise might. That's because it's more personal, and therefore, more relevant. Interpreters can make their communication more personal in many ways. Two simple techniques are self-referencing and labeling.

1. *Self-referencing* means getting people in your audience to think momentarily about themselves as you give them some new piece of information. This makes them relate to that information at a personal level and, according to research, increases the likelihood that they will pay attention to it, understand it, and be able to remember it later. You can use self-referencing by issuing a simple phrase (the self-reference) and then relating to it the information you want your audience to remember. For example:

• "Think of the last time you … "

• "Have you ever … ?"

• "How many of you have ever … ?"

• "At one time or another most of us have … "

• "How many of you can remember the very best teacher you ever had? Think about that person for a second. What do you suppose made him or her such a good

teacher? One thing you probably noticed was that … etc."

2. *Labeling* is classifying people (or kinds of people) in either a positive, negative or neutral way. When the label is issued, most people in your audience will either associate themselves with it, or disassociate themselves from it. Either way, they'll have to identify themselves in relationship to the label. Information that you relate to the label therefore seems more personal to them.

• Examples of positive labels: "People who understand the value of a forest know that … ," "If you're the kind of person who cares about wildlife, then you probably … ," "The most advanced farmers around here are doing a lot to control … ," "Parents who care about … ," "Choosy mothers choose Jif!"

• Examples of negative labels: "The worst criminals are the ones who commit crimes against nature," "The biggest headache for land managers are those people who think that … ," "If you don't care about protecting endangered species, then you probably don't believe that … ."

• Examples of neutral labels: "People who live in the Northwest … ," "We Oregonians … ," "Children … ," "Parents … ."

Warning: Be careful using labels. They classify (stereotype) people. Even positive and neutral labels have the potential to offend.

Figure 1-8. People pay attention to things they care about.

Self-Referencing

Self-referencing is getting people in the audience to think about themselves and their own experiences as you give them new information. This causes them to connect the new ideas you're giving them with something they already care about, themselves. Mr. Jones could do this by using simple phrases like, "Think of the last time you ... ," "Have you ever ... ?," or "At one time or another, most of you have probably...." Self-referencing phrases are simple, and research has shown that using them will considerably increase the interest level of your communication, as well as what people will understand and remember from it.

As you may have noticed, self-referencing often utilizes the word "you." This is a powerful word in all languages, and the best interpreters use it frequently. But variations can also be effective. For instance, try substituting other words for "you" in the previous examples. You'll see that although the effect is different, the new phrases still help to personalize the information which follows them. For example, "Think of the last time a person you know did such and such ...," or "Have your kids ever ...," or "At one time or another, most of us have probably ... ."

How could Mr. Jones use self-referencing to make his talk on geology more personal? If he were trying to explain the process of sedimentation, for example, might he say something like:

"How many of you like to skip stones across water? Have you ever noticed that the best skipping stones are found near rivers? Why is that, do you think?

That's right, they're smooth and polished from the water's current ... just the way wood is smooth after you rub it with sandpaper. And if you've ever used sandpaper on a piece of wood, you know that all that rubbing can cause quite a mess. 'Sediment' is just another word for the mess. In a river, the mess comes from small particles of rock that have been rubbed off by the water, and, of course, all the soil and other material that washes in from the sides of the river. Over time, the mess piles up, and the whole process is called 'sedimentation.' If you're like me, you're thinking that one of the best things about rivers is that you don't have to clean up after them. Or do you? Where do you suppose all the sediment goes?"

In this statement, Mr. Jones did two important things to make his description of sedimentation more personal to his audience: he used three self-referencing phrases, and he used the word "you" ten times. He also made sedimentation more meaningful to his audience by using an analogy (comparing wood sanding to sedimentation), and he tried to be light-hearted and informal in his tone. It appears that Mr. Jones is more interested in helping his audience understand how the process of sedimentation works than he is in teaching them the terminology and facts he might expect his high school students to know. Contrast the above description with the more formal definition Mr. Jones gives to his students from his lecture notes:

"Sedimentation is the process by which particulate matter is freed from parent material by the erosive power of water, and subsequently deposited as strata at a point downstream directly proportional to the mass of the particles and the velocity of the stream."

Had Mr. Jones, the interpreter, relied on his class lecture notes instead of on his knowledge of techniques like self-referencing and analogies, his audience would have received a very different presentation. Yet something you might be thinking, and which school teachers everywhere should consider, is whether the interpretive approach would be better even in the classroom. If teachers want their students to be interested in their subjects and to feel that what they're learning is really important in their lives, they would be well served to think more like interpreters than some teachers currently do.

Labeling

A second technique for making interpretation more personal is **labeling**. It's based on the idea that people will pay attention to things that remind them of themselves. Used frequently in advertising, a "label" is simply a statement that's made about a "kind" of person or group of people in relation to some idea, point, or object that the communicator is trying to describe. A successful peanut butter advertisement seen in many countries states, "Choosy mothers choose Jif." This message says that mothers who really care about their children will select the brand, Jif, presumably because it is better. The label is "choosy mothers." Since most

mothers like to think of themselves as being careful about the food they give their children, they pay attention to the advertisement. An extensionist once said to his audience, "If you really care about the water, air and soil you'll leave for your children, then you'll be very interested in what I'm going to show you this afternoon. If these things don't interest you, then you might leave now and send me your children, instead. Certainly, *they* will care."

Although it was probably too strong a statement, you can see in the latter example that labels can be negative as well as positive. The idea is that people like to see themselves as having good qualities, and they'll often pay attention to a negative label in order to reassure themselves that they're not like the people being described. Another example is a ranger at a campfire program in Grand Teton National Park in the United States who told his audience, "The worst criminals are the ones who commit crimes against nature."

Labels can also be neutral and nonjudgmental: "People who live in a warm climate…," "Most Hondurans…," "We Ticos…," "People from the United States … ," "Trinidadians over the age of thirty … ," etc. As in the case of positive and negative labels, neutral labels can help the interpreter personalize the information he/she's presenting because when the label is issued, most people will either associate themselves with it, or disassociate themselves from it. In either event, the label requires them to identify with something personal as the information is presented. A frequent result is that the information is more interesting to them.

Be thoughtful when using labels. They classify people, and therefore have the potential to offend if they're not chosen carefully. In addition, you should be

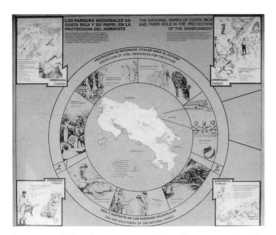

Figure 1-9. Interpretation is organized. Although it's a little busy, this bilingual interpretive sign has four conspicuous main ideas. Volcán Irazú National Park, Costa Rica. (Photo by Sam Ham)

Quality 3: Interpretation Is Organized

That is, it is presented in a way that is easy to follow. Another way of stating this idea is that interpretation, at its best, does not require a lot of effort from the audience. Noncaptive audiences will switch attention if they have to work too hard to follow a train of thought. In advertising, this relationship is well known. Mass media experts have even developed a formula to express it:

$$\frac{\text{Probability that}}{\text{a noncaptive audience will pay attention}} = \frac{\text{Reward (potential benefit)}}{\text{Effort (amount of work required)}}$$

The formula, developed in 1971 by Wilbur Schramm, says that audiences that don't have to pay attention, won't, if they have to work too hard. As the amount of work they have to do increases, the likelihood that they'll continue to pay attention decreases. Put another way, the best interpretation is highly entertaining and easy to follow.

What Does Organization Really Do? An Example

Think of the last time you entered a movie theater late. If you're like most people, your first concern was trying to figure out what was going on in the movie so that you could make sense out of what you were hearing and seeing on the screen. If you weren't too late, you were probably able to figure things out pretty quickly. But if you missed more than fifteen minutes or so, you probably missed the introductions of the key characters, and even more important, the plot.

careful not to exclude part of your audience with a label that's too restrictive, unless, of course, that's your intention. Finally, try to select labels that are important to people in your audience. An extension specialist might be more effective using the label, "People who want to make sure they'll still be able to grow crops five years from now … ," than if he/she simply said, "People who have farms around here … ." Both are good labels, but the first one's better because it refers to something that's probably more important to his or her audience. Likewise, an interpreter at a zoo might say, "All of us who care about preventing the extinction of this animal believe that … ," instead of just "A lot of people think that … ." Practice using labels and self-referencing. The better you get at recognizing and capitalizing on opportunities to use them, the more personal your communication will become.

Undoubtedly, you then spent the next several minutes trying to piece things together. When you thought you'd finally figured it all out, you probably felt you could relax; that is, until one of the characters said something or did something that didn't fit with what you thought was going on. Then you had to start all over again trying to figure things out.

If you paid a lot of money to see the movie, you probably continued this trial-and-error process as long as it took to get things straight. However, if you were home watching television free of charge, you probably switched channels or turned off the set long before you spent a lot of effort. Likewise, if you were at a park viewing an exhibit, reading a brochure, watching a slide program, or listening to a talk, you probably either started to daydream or just got up and left altogether. Why?

The reason, of course, is that noncaptive audiences won't spend a lot of time and effort to follow a difficult presentation. As our formula suggests, they usually decide early on whether the benefits of paying attention are going to be worth the effort it will take; and a major factor in their estimate of the effort is how well the message is organized. If the ideas being presented follow a logical train of thought, little effort is needed to keep things straight. A movie's plot, the introduction of a talk or audiovisual program, and the title, headings and subheadings of an exhibit or brochure, all help to provide this logic. The result is that the information presented is easier to follow because it can be put into categories, and therefore, not seem like so much. But, as in the example above, if the ideas being presented can't be attached to some organizational framework, they become mere isolated facts. And, as we shall see, humans have definite limits in their ability to keep unorganized information straight in their minds. If too much information builds up out of context, we become hopelessly confused and eventually quit trying to sort it out. With noncaptive audiences, this can happen in a matter of seconds.

Organizing information is like putting a piece of tape or "Velcro" on every idea and fact that you're presenting, and then sticking each one to some larger idea. When we can connect a piece of information to some idea (like a plot or major point) that we already have in our memory, that information seems easier to remember. If we keep the main ideas to a manageable number, we can present an amazing amount of information within them. But what exactly does a "manageable number" mean?

The Magical Number Seven Plus or Minus Two

The answer to the above question is five or less. That is, talks, exhibits, publications, audiovisual programs, etc., that try to present five or fewer main ideas, will be more interesting and more understandable than those which try to communicate more. The number "5" comes from studies on just how much information we humans are capable of handling all at one time. The most famous of these studies was done by George Miller in 1956. His article, "The Magical Number Seven, Plus or Minus Two," demonstrated a principle that still stands: on the average, we humans are capable of making sense out of only 7 ± 2 separate and new ideas at one time. Therefore, it makes sense that the number of main ideas in a presentation of information unfamiliar to an audience ought to be limited to 7 ± 2. But since some of us can handle only as many as 5 (that is 7 minus 2), the actual number of main points should be five or fewer (see Figure 1-11).

This important guideline applies to all types of presentations whether they be spoken or written, auditory or visual. The only requirements are that: (1) the audience can easily distinguish between the main points and the subordinate information you attach to them, and (2) the number of main points you present doesn't, in fact, exceed five. Intelligently applied, this principle will help make any factual presentation easier to follow, more understandable and more memorable.

In our example, how could Mr. Jones improve the organization of his talk on geology so that his audience could follow him more easily? Besides keeping the number of main points to five or fewer, the key will be that Mr. Jones selects them carefully, based upon the main message or **theme** he wants to get across to his audience. This leads us to the final quality of interpretation.

Quality 4: Interpretation has a Theme

Interpretation is thematic if it has a major point. As we'll discuss in Chapter 2, a theme is not the same as a topic, even though the two words are often used interchangeably in English and Spanish. Virtually any presentation of ideas can (and should) have both a **topic** and a **theme**. Their major difference is that the topic is merely the subject matter of the presentation, whereas the theme is the main point or message a communicator is trying to convey about that topic. Experienced interpreters will tell you that there are few, if any, concepts more

important than "theme" when it comes to selecting and organizing ideas for a presentation. How you can put this important idea to use is the subject we now consider.

The Story's the Thing

In discussing the characteristics that make interpretation different from other ways of communicating, Tilden (1957) said: "The story's the thing." By this he meant that presentations, whether written, spoken or conveyed by electrical devices, should have the qualities of a **story**. That is, they should have a beginning, an end,

Figure 1-10. Interpretation has a theme. The theme of this old sign is obvious: Only you can prevent forest fires. Apparently, thematic communication is nothing new to natural resource managers. Gifford Pinchot National Forest. (Photo by Sam Ham)

In Interpretation, It Pays to Keep Your Main Ideas to Five or Fewer

People have definite limits in their ability to make sense out of new information. Research has shown that the sheer amount of information, as well as how it's organized, make a difference in how well we're able to sort it out and use it. Studies have shown that most people are capable of handling about "7 ± 2" different pieces of information at a time. That is, some people can keep as many as nine different ideas or facts straight in their heads, whereas others can only deal with five or fewer. This relationship has less to do with the person's intelligence than it does with the amount of prior experience he or she has with the topic at hand. It stands to reason, then, that since some people in your audiences will have difficulty when the number exceeds five, you should limit the number of main ideas in your presentations to five or fewer. Doing so will make it easier for people in your audience to follow your ideas, and this will increase the likelihood that they'll continue paying attention to you.

Some examples:

If you limit yourself to no more than one second, which group is easier to count, A or B?

A	B
* * * *	* * * * * * * * *

How about this one, A or B?

A	B
* * * * * * * *	+ + + + * * * *

Notice how organization can make a difference. Even though B has the same amount of information as A, it's easier to sort out because it's organized into two easy-to-see categories. So actually, there are only two pieces of information in B (two groups of four), whereas A contains eight. In communication, good organization reduces effort. Remember, though, that the audience is likely to remember the categories later, but not all of the information contained in them.

Now try this one.

A	B
TWAFBIPHDIBMCIA	TWA FBI PHD IBM CIA

Obviously, if our ideas are organized around things the audience already can relate to, our presentation will be that much easier for them to follow.

Figure 1-11. The "magical number, seven plus or minus two."

and most of all, a message or moral. The message may be short and simple: "Water pollution is getting to be a serious problem." Or it may be more involved: "Water pollution threatens both our health and our economy, and there is something we can all do about it." As you probably noticed in the two examples, each theme requires its own set of facts, concepts and main points. This is because every theme involves telling a different story than other themes would tell, even if they share the same topic. Although both of the above themes stemmed from the topic "water pollution," the development of each would require a fundamentally different approach. With a theme clearly in mind, a communicator enjoys the luxury of knowing exactly what he/she needs to say, write or show in order to get that message across to the audience. Obviously, a mere topic does not provide that kind of insight.

The trouble with a lot of interpretation is that it has only a topic (for example, "soil erosion," "birds," "ecology," etc.), and since there's almost no limit to the number of themes that one could develop around a given topic, such a presentation proceeds without focus or direction, as if it were trying to say everything and nothing at the same time. Think of the teachers you've had in school. Were there any that you just couldn't seem to take notes from? Were you ever frustrated because you would sit for an hour, listening and understanding what you were hearing, but still unable to write it in your notebook? Did you walk out some days asking yourself "so what?" after listening to what seemed to be an endless list of unrelated facts? Contrast those teachers with the ones you found it easy to take notes from. What do think accounted for the difference?

Presentations which don't have themes beg the question, "so what?," and unfortunately, most of us have read or listened to information that has left us asking this question. But presentations which do have themes seem to be "going somewhere," and it's easy for us to organize all the facts and supportive details in our minds because we can "stick" them to the theme. This is what the plot does for a movie or story, as we saw previously. And as we noted, when audiences don't know where a presentation is going, they have nothing to "stick" all the facts to, and they become lost in a sea of irrelevance. The theme of a presentation and the five or fewer main ideas used to develop it, provide the "adhesive." In this important respect, themes not only help interpreters select from their wealth of knowledge which few facts and concepts to put into their presentations, but if they reveal in advance what the theme is, and how it will be organized, their audiences also benefit in terms of understanding and comprehension. As Figure 1-12 illustrates, there are many ways to do this, and they vary depending upon the form of your presentation (i.e., whether it's a talk, exhibit, brochure, sign, trail, etc.). For this reason, we'll give separate attention to organizational techniques in each of the chapters on interpretive media.

All presentations ought to be able to stand up to the question, "so what?" Good stories, poems, songs, dramas, and classroom lectures offer an answer. So do good talks, exhibits, brochures, signs and other interpretive media, if they have a message. You may know it by other words: the big picture, the moral to the story, the punchline, the main idea, etc. But all these words mean about the same thing, and regardless of which term you prefer, you

Some Ways to Show Audiences Your Theme and Organization	
Type of Interpretive Presentation	**Example Applications**
Talks, scripts, etc.	Tell your audience in the introduction what the theme is, what the main points are, and the order in which you will present them. (See Chapters 2 and 3.)
Guided walks, hikes, tours, excursions, etc.	Tell your audience in the introduction what the theme is, what the main points are, and a little about the key stops you will be making. (See Chapters 2 and 5.)
Brochures and publications	Indicate in the title or subtitle what the theme is. Use headings within the text to show the main points, and subheads and paragraphs to show the subordinate information. (See Chapter 2.)
Exhibits	Indicate in the title or subtitle what the theme is. Use headings within the text to show the main points. Break up main points with illustrations, photographs or three-dimensional objects. Use subheads, paragraphs or illustrations to show subordinate information. (See Chapters 2 and 8.)
Signs	Indicate in the title or subtitle what the theme is. If appropriate, use headings within the text to show the main points. (Signs usually contain only one or two main ideas.) (See Chapters 2 and 8.)
Self-guided trails	If you're using a brochure, consider an opening paragraph that states the theme of the trail and that briefly tells about some of the most interesting stops. If you're using signs, consider installing an introductory sign at the trailhead which tells what the theme is, and which briefly tells about some of the most interesting stops. (See Chapters 2 and 9.)

Figure 1-12. Techniques for revealing the theme and organization of main points in several kinds of interpretive presentations.

should make sure your presentations have one. In Chapter 2, you'll see how easy this is to do and just how important the placement of the theme can be in an oral, written, visual or audio presentation.

Going back now to Mr. Jones, what might he do to make his talk on geology more organized and thematic? By now the answer is probably obvious: he should select a theme from his topic, decide which five or fewer main ideas he should present in order get the theme across, and then, at the time of presenting his talk, reveal the theme and main ideas to his audience, so that they can follow him without a lot of effort. Although as we'll see in Chapter 3 there's more to consider in developing a talk, having a theme and an organization to support it is critical to the success of any interpretive device.

Recall the segment of Mr. Jones' talk that we looked at earlier:

> "Sediment' is just another word for the mess. In a river, the mess comes from small particles of rock that have been rubbed off by the water, and of course, all the soil and other material that washes in from the sides of the river. Over time, the mess piles up, and the whole process is called 'sedimentation.' If you're like me, you're thinking that one of the best things about rivers is that you don't have to clean up after them. Or do you? Where do you suppose all the sediment goes?"

His topic seems to be geology, and more specifically, soil erosion and sedimentation. But what do you think his theme might be? Of course, it's hard to tell

from such a small piece of his talk, but Mr. Jones seems to be building up to the idea that we do, in fact, have to "clean up" the mess that sedimentation can cause. His statement about the "soil and other material that washes in from the sides of the river," and the question he poses to his audience at the end of the paragraph, provide a clue to his thinking. Where's he taking us with this question? Perhaps to the realization that the sediment ends up in the river where it fouls and contaminates our drinking water, spoils our fisheries, and potentially blocks shipping channels. If so, Mr. Jones' theme is easy to see. He's trying to tell his audience that *soil erosion not only threatens agriculture, it threatens our water, fisheries and major shipping corridors.*

If this were Mr. Jones' theme, what five or fewer main ideas might he want to include in this talk? What other information would he want to include under each of these points? This would depend on Mr. Jones' interests, knowledge and beliefs about the topic he's dealing with, wouldn't it? If three different people were independently developing this talk, they'd probably come up with three different ways to do it, and all three would probably be different from Mr. Jones' approach. For the sake of example, however, let's assume Mr. Jones settled on the outline of ideas in Figure 1-13.

What's important to notice about Mr. Jones' outline is that he obviously selected his main points based on the theme he wanted to leave with his audience. Having done this, he then asked himself what subordinate information (facts, concepts, anecdotes, analogies, etc.) he'd need to include under each main point in order to get it across. His approach makes a lot of sense because it capitalizes

Outline of Mr. Jones' Talk on Sedimentation and Erosion

Topic: Soil erosion and sedimentation

Theme: Soil erosion not only threatens agriculture, it threatens our water, fisheries, and major shipping corridors.

I. Soil erosion and sedimentation are natural processes that humans can affect.
    A. Soil erosion
        1. How it happens and what causes it
        2. Where the run-off goes
    B. Sedimentation
        1. Sand paper analogy
        2. Rubbing makes a mess.
        3. The mess piles up

II. Soil erosion affects agriculture.
    A. Story about my grandfather's farm
        1. Didn't terrace, didn't seed vulnerable areas
        2. In two heavy rain years, lost top soil, no crops
        3. Went broke, lost his farm
        4. My father grew up poor and under fed
    B. Our future depends on agriculture

III. Sedimentation affects our drinking water.
    A. Run-off carries dirt and contaminants
        1. Dirties the color of our water
        2. Chemicals and bacteria in the run-off poison our water
            a. Story about the Lopez family
            b. Story about the Anderson's baby
    B. Statistics about diseases and deaths due to water contamination

IV. Sedimentation affects fish habitat.
    A. Fish have to "breathe" clean water
    B. Fish eggs need clean water to develop and hatch
    C. Death rates and survival of fingerlings in certain rivers
        1. Clean rivers
        2. Dirty rivers
    D. Importance of fish in many people's diets and economy

V. Sedimentation affects shipping canals.
    A. How sedimentation builds up in the channel
        1. The Panama Canal problem
        2. The Columbia and Mississippi Rivers in the United States
    B. Costs of dredging are enormous

Figure 1-13. Example of the outline of a thematic talk.

on the fact that people learn big ideas (like themes) by combining smaller ideas (like main points and subordinate information).

Little Meanings Add Up to Big Ones

Think of the last time you were standing around with a group of friends telling jokes. Probably, one person's joke reminded someone else of a joke, and that joke reminded someone else of another joke, etc., until finally, you were reminded of a joke that you decided you'd tell the others. Of course, before you could tell the joke (that is, before you could tell it well), you had to reconstruct it in your mind and silently rehearse it.

Think about how you did this. If you're like most people, you probably thought first of the punchline. If you couldn't remember the punchline, you probably couldn't tell the joke. Why? Because everything you'd say in recounting the joke would have the single purpose of building up to the punchline. If you didn't know the punchline, you didn't know where you heading.

Let's say that you were able to recall the punchline. What did you think of next? Obviously, you began to think about the individual pieces of information that you'd have to give so, at the end of the joke, the people would see (and hopefully appreciate) the humor in the story. It's almost always important that you remember to tell all of the things that lead up to the punchline, isn't it? Have you ever gotten to the punchline of a joke only to realize that you'd earlier left out a crucial piece of information? Have you ever had to say: "Oh, I forgot to tell you that ... ," right as you were about to surprise your audience with the punchline?

Of course, as any good joke teller knows, the order or sequence in which you give the individual pieces of information can also be critical. How many times have you been in the middle of telling a joke and realized that you'd revealed an important piece of information too soon? This mistake usually causes the joke teller to say something clever like, "Oh, I shouldn't have told you that yet!" or "Pretend I didn't say that, OK?" By then, of course, it doesn't much matter; the joke has been spoiled.

If you've been in situations like these, then you already understand why thematic communication is so important, and you understand very well just how little meanings add up to bigger meanings. There's really not much difference between the way you remembered your joke and the way you should plan an interpretive talk, script, or other presentation which will be heard by an audience. In most presentations, of course, you won't want to wait until the end to reveal the "so what?," as you do when telling a joke. In fact, as we'll see in Chapter 2, thematic interpretation is usually most effective when the audience knows at the very beginning what the theme and five or fewer main ideas are. (An exception might be presentations on controversial topics.) We'll also see that how we apply this idea in preparing an oral presentation is different from the way we apply it in written presentations.

In our joke example, the punchline can be thought of as the theme, because when it's heard by the audience, it answers the "so what?" question with respect to all of the information that preceded it. That is, after hearing the punchline the audience will understand immediately why you said everything that you said in telling the joke. If you gave them a lot of information that didn't relate to the punchline, they probably didn't laugh at the joke. This is because they tried to connect everything you said to the punchline, and any information which didn't relate served only to confuse them. It's our nature to try to connect little pieces of information to some larger idea, and the audiences that you'll encounter everyday in your work are no different. They'll try to connect every piece of information you give them to a theme. In other words, they'll always be asking themselves, "so what?" even if the question is posed subconsciously.

Going back to the joke, you've probably already noticed that the information you had to give the people before revealing the punchline is nothing more than the five or fewer main ideas we've been talking about in this chapter. With the theme (punchline) in mind, the interpreter selects the main ideas that he/she considers most important to get the theme across to the audience. Remembering our upper limit of five, it's important that we include in these main ideas those facts and concepts that we think are crucial to understanding the theme. Underneath these ideas, we can include whatever other details (including facts, concepts, comparisons, analogies, etc.) we think will add color, interest, and meaning to the story. But we should do this with full knowledge that our audience is not likely to remember much about them later. Usually, however, they'll remember the theme and the five or fewer main ideas used to support it. We'll return to this idea in Chapter 2.

Finally, as our example illustrated, the order in which we present our ideas can determine whether the audience will understand the theme. With some themes,

the sequence may not be particularly important. But with others, the train of thought you're trying to establish en route to the theme may depend on a logical sequence. Most jokes are like this, as are interpretive strategies which show cause-and-effect, or which present concepts that build upon one another. Mr. Jones is presenting such a talk. Before his audience can understand his theme, they must have a pretty clear idea of: (1) what soil erosion and sedimentation are, and how they're related; (2) how soil erosion affects agriculture; (3) how sediment affects drinking water; (4) how sediment affects fish habitat; and (5) how sediment affects shipping canals. The order in which these main ideas are presented here, and in Figure 1-13, makes sense because before Mr. Jones' audience can appreciate the effects that erosion and sedimentation have on agriculture, drinking water, fish habitat and transportation, they must first know what he means by these terms, and how erosion accelerates sedimentation. These ideas presented, Mr. Jones can then call his audience's attention to the problems that erosion and rapid sedimentation can cause. On the face of things, the order in which he presents these four problems doesn't really matter, but since "threats to agriculture" appears first in his theme statement, followed by "drinking water, fisheries and major shipping corridors," it makes sense that he'd also present the problems in that order.

Glossary terms: analogy, bridge, captive audience, comparison, example, interpretation, interpretive approach, labeling, magical 7 ± 2, meaningful, metaphor, noncaptive audience, personal, relevant, selective attention, self-referencing, shadowing, simile, story, theme, topic.

Good Interpretation's Worth Money: Financing Programs with Donation Boxes

Todd Cullings, Lead Forest Interpreter
Mount St. Helens National Volcanic Monument,
Amboy, Washington

Your budget's been cut. You don't have enough funds to meet visitor needs. These are common problems that all managers face sometime during their career. I faced these same problems one season when my budget was reduced by more than half. The impact of the budget cuts was devastating and I needed creative solutions to serve the 650,000 visitors who travel every summer to the field interpretive sites. We had to conduct fewer programs per week, but it was important to us to still maintain the quality and diversity of our programs.

One way to raise money is through partnerships. Chief Naturalist Jim Gale, Naturalist Ralph Naess and I sought out partners and successfully established $18,500 in partnership funding. We then looked at other possible funding sources. As managers, we didn't think twice about establishing donation boxes in visitor centers. Although we were uncomfortable with the idea of establishing donation boxes at live interpretive program sites, we believed this might be the solution we needed. We felt strongly that visitors would support quality interpretive programming at Mount St. Helens.

We approached the Monument's Public Service Assistant, Reed Gardner, regarding the legality of donation boxes and our concern about being able to apply the funds where they were needed most. He informed us that the Forest Service Manual permitted the collection and expenditure of donations. We quickly developed the following message for the donation boxes: "Your contributions support interpretive services at Mount St. Helens." The message was placed next to the Forest Service shield to identify the agency and beneficiary of the contributions. We then developed criteria for the fabrication of the boxes. We determined that the most important criteria were that they be secure yet transparent for visitors to see what had been contributed. They also needed to be compact for easy installation and transport, and mounted on an interpretive/ managerial message which would be there when the boxes were removed. We decided on a strong plexiglass design and had five boxes and their mountings made for $103 per set.

One donation box was set up at Windy Ridge viewpoint, which receives an annual visitation of approximately 320,000 visitors. Interpretive programs about the May 18, 1980, eruption and current biological events are conducted in a 150-seat amphitheater. Initially, most naturalists were uncomfortable about asking visitors to donate to the interpretive program; most of us felt this was a service that visitors' tax dollars already should have paid for. As their supervisor, I felt uncomfortable pushing them on this issue, so during the first two weeks of operation, we didn't promote the donation box program. I was disappointed with the amount of funds being donated ($35 per day), because I felt that we were offering excellent interpretive programs.

The Forest Service was concerned that naturalists would sound as if they were begging for money, and they didn't want visitors to feel that they were obligated to donate to the program. I felt that it was critical to develop sincere, service-oriented messages about the donation boxes. That's when I decided to enlist the help of a veteran naturalist who I knew dearly loved the interpretive program at Mount St. Helens. As an experiment, I instructed him to present the following message at the end of each of his programs: "Due to budget constraints, we are conducting twenty-nine less interpretive programs per week, but we feel that we are providing you (the visitor) with an important service. If you feel that this service is important to you and would like to see more interpretive programs offered for you and future visitors, you can help support the interpretive program." (I asked the naturalist just to point to the donation box without mentioning the word.) That evening, the naturalist returned with the donation box stuffed full. He had conducted three programs and received $119.51 in donations. The cost of his salary to the Forest Service was $67.20.

I instructed each naturalist how to present the donation message in a positive, heartfelt manner, and then carefully worked with them to develop smooth transitions from the conclusions of their interpretive programs to the donation box message. Some naturalists even incorporated the donation message into the theme of their program. Within a week, the single donation box was being stuffed so full that visitors had difficulty pushing money into the slot on the top of the box! A second donation box was set up on the opposite side of the amphitheater.

Due to the success of the donation box program, we were able to hire two naturalists solely from the money generated. Creative energy and a $206 investment generated over $11,000 in less than three months. The interpretive program was self-supportive (operating without any government funding) for an entire month. Why was this program so successful? Because visitors gladly donated $5, $10, $20, and even $50 bills for quality interpretive services. And we have a quality interpretive program because we diligently practice the basic principles of thematic interpretation. Does good interpretation pay? We think so!

References

Bradford, H.F. 1986. *Chemical Neurobiology: An Introduction to Neurochemistry.* New York, NY, USA: W.H. Freeman and Company.

Cherry, C. 1966. *On Human Communication,* 2nd ed. Cambridge, Massachusetts, USA: Massachusetts Institute of Technology.

Ham, Sam H. 1983. Cognitive Psychology and Interpretation: Synthesis and Application. *Journal of Interpretation* 8(1):11-27.

Lewis, William J. 1980. *Interpreting for Park Visitors.* Philadelphia, Pennsylvania, USA: Eastern National Park and Monument Association, Eastern Acorn Press.

Miller, George. 1956. The Magical Number Seven, Plus or Minus Two: Some Limits on Our Capacity for Processing Information. *Psychological Review* 63(2):81-97.

Moray, N. 1959. Attention in Dichotic Listening: Effective Cues and the Influence of Instructions. *Quarterly Journal of Experimental Psychology* 11(1):56-60.

Schramm, Wilbur. 1971. *The Process and Effects of Mass Communication.* Urbana, IL, USA: University of Illinois Press.

Solso, R.L. 1979. *Cognitive Psychology.* New York, NY, USA: Harcourt Brace Jovanovich, Inc.

Tilden, Freeman. 1957. *Interpreting Our Heritage.* Chapel Hill, North Carolina, USA: University of North Carolina Press.

Additional Reading

In English:

Boulanger, F. David and John P. Smith. 1973. *Educational Principles and Techniques for Interpreters.* Portland, Oregon, USA: USDA Forest Service, Pacific Northwest Forest and Range Experiment Station, General Technical Report PNW-9.

Dick, R.E., D.T. McKee, and J. Alan Wagar. 1974. A Summary and Annotated Bibliography of Communication Principles. *Journal of Environmental Education* 5(4):8-13.

Fazio, James R. and Douglas L. Gilbert. 1986. *Public Relations and Communications for Natural Resource Managers.* Dubuque, Iowa, USA: Kendall-Hunt.

Field, Donald R. and J. Alan Wagar. 1973. Visitor Groups and Interpretation in Parks and Other Outdoor Leisure Settings. *Journal of Environmental Education* 5(1):12-17.

Gelder, E.S., R.A. Winett, and P.B. Everett. 1982. *Preserving the Environment: New Strategies for Behavior Change.* New York, New York, USA: Pergamon Press.

Ham, Sam H. and Richard L. Shew. 1979. A Comparison of Visitors' and Interpreters' Assessments of Conducted Interpretive Activities. *Journal of Interpretation* 4(2):39-44.

Krumbein, W.J., Jr. and L. Leyva. 1977. *The Interpreter's Guide.* Sacramento, California, USA: California Dept. of Parks and Recreation.

MacKinnon, John, Kathy MacKinnon, Graham Child and James Thorsell (eds.). 1986. *Managing Protected Areas in the Tropics* (Chapter 7). Cambridge, United Kingdom: International Union for the Conservation of Nature & Natural Resources and the United Nations Environment Program.

Regnier, Kathleen, Michael Gross and Ron Zimmerman. 1992. *The Interpreter's Guidebook: Techniques for Programs and Presentations*. Stevens Point, Wisconsin, USA: UW-SP Foundation Press, Inc.

Sharpe, Grant W. 1982. An Overview of Interpretation. Chapter 1 in Sharpe, G.W. (ed.), *Interpreting the Environment*. New York, New York, USA: John Wiley & Sons.

Shiner, J.W. and Elwood L. Shafer, Jr. 1975. *How Long Do People Look At and Listen to Forest-Oriented Exhibits?* U.S. Department of Agriculture, Forest Service Research Paper NE-325. Upper Darby, PA, USA: Northeastern Forest Experiment Station.

Washburne, Randall F. and J. Alan Wagar. 1972. Evaluating Visitor Response to Exhibit Content. *Curator* 15(3):248-254.

In Spanish:

Ham, Sam H. 1992. *Interpretación Ambiental: Una Guía Práctica para Gente con Grandes Ideas y Presupuestos Pequeños*. Golden, Colorado, USA: North American Press/Fulcrum Publishing.

MacKinnon, John, Kathy MacKinnon, Graham Child y James Thorsell (eds.). 1990. *Manejo de Areas Protegidas en los Trópicos* (Capitulo 7). Cancun, Quintana Roo, México: Amigos de Sian Ka'an A.C.

Miller, Kenton. 1980. Planificación de Parques Nacionales para el Ecodesarrollo en Latinoamérica. Madrid, Spain: FEPMA.

Moore, Alan, Bill Wendt, Louis Penna e Isabel Castillo de Ramos. 1989. *Manual para La Capacitación del Personal de Areas Protegidas* (Modulo C: Interpretación y Educación Ambiental, Apunte 4a). Washington, D.C., USA: Servicio de Parques Nacionales, Oficina de Asuntos Internacionales.

Morales, Jorge. 1987. *Manual para la Interpretación en Espacios Naturales Protegidos*. Anexo 3 del Taller Internacional sobre Interpretación Ambiental en Areas Silvestres Protegidas. Santiago, Chile: Oficina Regional de la FAO para América Latina y el Caribe, 7-12 de diciembre de 1988.

Morales, Jorge. 1983. *La Interpretación del Medio Ambiente en el Ambito de la Educación Ambiental No Formal*. I Jornadas sobre Ecologa y Medio Ambiente. España: Parque Nacional de Doñana, 9–10 de abril.

Tobin, Kenneth. 1989. La Metafora. Presentación en el Taller de Enseñanza de las Ciencias, Centro de Investigación y Docencia en Educación (CIDE). Heredia, Costa Rica: CIDE, Universidad Nacional.

CHAPTER TWO

PRACTICING THEMATIC INTERPRETATION

As we saw in Chapter 1, when interpretation has a theme it has a **message**. We call this thematic interpretation. When our communication isn't thematic, it seems unorganized, difficult to follow, and less meaningful to our audiences. This is simply because they can't easily see where the communication is going, and they don't know how to connect all the information they're receiving. But when the information we present is thematic—that is, when it's all related to some key idea or central message—it becomes easier to follow and more meaningful to people.

Most people practice thematic communication every day. Think of what you do when you call someone on the telephone. Usually, you say hello and then tell the other person why you're calling. Generally, the reason you give for calling will carry some kind of message or theme. For example, you might say, "I'm calling

because I'm going to be near your office next week, and I'd like to see you if you'll be available." In another call you might say, "I'm calling just to say thanks for the nice birthday card you sent me." When we give statements like these at the beginning of the conversation, they help the listener connect all the information that follows to our main message. Rarely do we make a call and then just start talking—giving information, facts, etc.—without first saying something that helps the person listening put it all into perspective. In other words, we naturally assume the listener will be confused if he or she can't connect the information we're giving to some central message. So practicing thematic communication is something most of us do every day, more or less intuitively.

Although preparing an oral or written presentation differs from making a telephone call, the notion that we should try to connect the information with a theme is the same. Research has shown that when audiences know the theme in advance, not only are they more apt to pay attention to the rest of the presentation, but they'll remember more of it later. Interpreters who think thematically therefore have a distinct advantage over those who don't. They can more easily decide which facts and supportive information to include in their written and oral presentations, and even more important, their presentations will be more interesting and memorable to their audiences. How to think thematically is the subject of this chapter.

Topics Versus Themes

In Chapter 1, we saw that even though a lot of people use the words **topic** and **theme** interchangeably, they're quite different. The topic of a presentation (whether written or oral) is simply its **subject** matter, whereas the theme of the presentation is the specific message about the subject we want to communicate to the audience. In other words, it's the story we've decided to tell. As Figure 2-1 illustrates, an interpreter could select any number of themes from a single topic. But since any one theme constitutes a different story, the interpreter will find that different kinds of information will be needed to develop different themes. For example, Figure 2-1 lists eight different themes that an interpreter might develop regarding the single topic "birds." Look at the first two themes listed. The first one says: "Birds are a very interesting group of animals because of their special adaptations for flight." The second theme is: "Native birds in this country are rapidly disappearing." Even

though both themes have something to do with the topic "birds," they focus on very different stories, and therefore would require very different kinds of information.

You could probably add to the list of themes in Figure 2-1. Think of what you'd like other people to know about "birds" or a particular species of bird that lives near you. Is there some message about birds you think is important for everyone to hear? How many ways can you complete the following sentence?

"When it comes to birds, I think it's important for people to understand that ... "

Try it. When you're finished filling in the sentence, you'll have written a theme. Try writing themes for some of the other topics listed in Figure 2-1. Remember to write them in complete sentences. After you've written each theme, ask yourself what kinds of information you'd need to present in order to get the message across to an audience. You'll discover that once you have a theme in mind it's surprisingly easy to select the needed information—much easier than if you had only a topic in mind when you started. At this point, you'd be able to outline the presentation (whether it be a talk, an exhibit, a publication or an audiovisual script) in a relatively short period of time. In communication, things always seem clearer when you know ahead of time what you want to say.

How to Write a Theme Statement

Interpreters who are just beginning to think thematically sometimes have trouble writing themes, even though they

Thinking in Terms of Themes—Not Topics

The *topic* of an oral or written presentation isn't the same as its theme. The topic is simply the subject matter of the presentation. The theme, on the other hand, is the principal message about the subject that you want to get across to your audience. The theme always answers the question, "so what?" with respect to the topic.

Look at the following list of topics. Notice that each topic is a sentence *fragment*. It tells the *subject matter*. Now look at the list of themes. Even though each theme relates to the topic "birds," it suggests a very different approach from all the other themes. That's because any topic can have many themes depending on what the interpreter wants to communicate to the audience.

Examples of Topics

1. Birds
2. The forest
3. Volcanoes
4. Competition between plants
5. Animals that live in the desert
6. Nocturnal snakes
7. Rivers
8. Erosion
9. The importance of tree planting
10. Maintaining water quality

Examples of Themes for the Topic "Birds"

Obviously, it would be possible to develop any number of themes for each topic. The following eight themes, for example, correspond to the first topic listed above, "Birds." Notice that the themes are expressed in *complete* sentences. They each have a subject, a verb, and a period at the end.

1. Birds are a very interesting group of animals because of their special adaptations for flight.
2. Native birds in this country are rapidly disappearing.
3. Hummingbirds are a lot like helicopters. Their special wings allow them to fly backwards or hover in the air.
4. Cattle egrets play an extremely important role in rural areas.
5. Eagles and falcons help humans.
6. The turkey vulture fulfills the role of "garbage collector," which is an extremely important, though undervalued, ecological function.
7. Studying how birds fly led to the invention of early airplanes.
8. Because they're rarely seen, nocturnal birds are the subject of many superstitions and potentially threatening misconceptions.

Figure 2-1. Examples of topics and themes.

understand what a theme is. Usually, the problem is that they forget to write their themes in complete sentences. Sentence fragments (e.g., "adaptations for flight" or "native birds that are rapidly disappearing") express topics, not themes. They describe the subject matter of a presentation, but not the central message that the interpreter wants to communicate to the audience. Therefore, they provide few clues to the interpreter about what kinds of information to include, or how it should be organized. Such statements are good in that they help the interpreter to narrow the topic. But they fall short of answering the question "so what?" with respect to the topic.

Figure 2-2 presents three easy steps for writing theme statements. To help you see the difference between topics and themes, you're first asked to describe the topic in general terms (Step 1), and then to say it in more specific terms (Step 2). Sometimes, new interpreters think that the specific topic in Step 2 is a theme statement. But as Step 3 shows, the theme needs to be written in the form of a complete sentence. In order to fill in the sentence in Step 3, you'll have to write a complete sentence which expresses the message you want to get across to your audience. Notice how much clearer and more informative your theme statement in Step 3 is, compared to the comparatively vague descriptions of the topic in Steps 1 and 2. The theme tells what's important about the topic, and having this clearly in mind before you start to develop the presentation will make your job much easier and your communication more effective. The best interpreters will tell you that as you get better at writing theme statements, you'll become a better communicator. As an aid to beginners,

additional examples of themes are listed in Figure 2-3.

Why It Helps to Build Your Presentation Around a Theme

In Chapter 1, we emphasized that thinking thematically helps a communicator in two important ways. First, with a theme in mind, you'll know almost immediately what kinds of information will be needed to get the theme across to the audience, including the five or fewer main ideas and all the supporting information. This gives you a big advantage because it also helps you see what *not* to include. In this way, starting with a clearly defined theme simplifies not only your planning and design of a presentation, but also the research and information seeking you'll have to do. Put differently, thinking thematically focuses your attention and therefore reduces your work.

The second advantage is that most audiences find thematic communication easier to comprehend and more interesting than communication which isn't unified by a clear theme. In Chapter 1, we noted that when audiences know in advance what your theme is going to be, they're able to see the relevance of the rest of the information you give them. Educational psychologists like David Ausubel (1960) call this an "advance organizer" because when we know in advance where a presentation is going, it's relatively easy for us to connect other information to it. This makes it easier for us to store that information in our minds and keep everything sorted out. So themes not only help interpreters by focusing their attention on the few facts and concepts that will be needed to present the theme,

In Three Steps, Anybody Can Write a Theme

Sometimes interpreters have difficulty writing good themes simply because they aren't yet used to thinking thematically. Expressing a theme is easy, however, if you remember the difference between the topic (subject matter) of the presentation and the theme (the principal message you want to communicate to your audience about the topic). As a communicator, your task is to relate *themes* to your audience, not just information about the topic.

Steps in Theme Writing—An Example

1. Select your general topic (for example, "our soil") and use it to complete the following sentence:

   "Generally, my presentation (talk, exhibit, etc.) is about
   _____our soil_____."
   (put your general topic here)

2. State your topic in more specific terms and complete the following sentence:

   "Specifically, I want to tell my audience about
   the importance of conserving our soil."
   (put your specific topic here)

3. Now, express your theme by completing the following sentence:

   "After hearing my presentation (or reading my exhibit, etc.), I want my audience to understand that it's necessary to conserve our soil in order to increase our crops and to protect the quality of our water."
   (put your theme here)

Figure 2-2. An example of thinking thematically.

What Is a Theme?

A theme is the central or key idea of any presentation. When a good presentation has been completed, the audience should be able to summarize it in one sentence. This sentence would be the theme. Development of a theme provides organizational structure and clarity of understanding. Once the theme of a presentation has been decided, everything else usually falls into place. Themes should:

1. Be stated as short, simple, complete sentences.
2. Contain only one idea.
3. Reveal the overall purpose of the presentation.
4. Be specific.
5. Be interestingly worded (if possible using active verbs).

Examples of Themes

1. Our children depend on us to take care of their natural resources.
2. Preserving biodiversity is like having a life insurance policy.
3. Three kinds of frogs live in this forest, and knowing which is which could save your life.
4. Some species are capable of adjusting their behavior to conserve body heat.
5. All life is dependent on the sun.
6. Energy is found in various forms, some very surprising.
7. Energy flows in only one direction, and is neither created nor destroyed.
8. Blue grass makes our water cleaner.
9. Everything is on its way to becoming something else.
10. Careless spelunkers can upset a delicate balance of life.
11. Exploring caves is a sensuous experience.
12. Everything in life is related to everything else.
13. The mosquito plays an important role in nature.
14. Underneath the ground is a fantastic plumbing system.
15. Mosquitos are fascinating insects once you get to know them.
16. Three main factors determine how geysers work.
17. The grizzly bear is a doomed species.
18. Lincoln's life was often marred by tragedy.
19. Charles Manson is a lunatic, but a brilliant one.
20. Much of the literature about the Mayan culture is incorrect.
21. To understand the Mayans, one must understand their fascination with the stars.
22. Robert E. Lee was a famous soldier, but his personal life is poorly understood.
23. Knowing a foreigner's culture is the fastest road to friendship.
24. A tiny rare plant in Mexico saved the U.S. corn crop.
25. Baseball is America's greatest gift to the world.

Figure 2-3. More examples of themes. (Adapted in part from Lewis 1983.)

but if they tell their audiences in advance what the theme is, most people will find the presentation easier to follow and comprehend.

Experiments by Thorndyke (1977) show why thinking thematically makes such a difference, and how a smart communicator can take advantage of it. Thorndyke developed four different versions of the same story and presented them to different people. The four versions were all basically the same with one key difference: one version of the story told the theme in the beginning; another version gave the theme just at the end; a third version told the theme in the middle of the story; and in the final version, no mention of the theme was made at all. After presenting the different versions of the story to many different people, Thorndyke gave them a test to see how much of the story they comprehended and how much they remembered. You probably won't be surprised to learn that the version people comprehended and remembered best was the first one, the one in which the theme was given at the beginning. The next best version was the one in which the theme was given at the end. (Like the punchline of a joke, hearing the theme at the end naturally causes us to try to connect everything we've just heard to it. However, as Thorndyke's results suggest, we may forget a lot that we wouldn't have forgotten if we'd known the theme in advance.)

The least comprehended and remembered of the four versions in Thorndyke's experiments was the one in which no theme was ever given. Thorndyke wondered just how bad the no-theme story was, so he did an interesting follow-up experiment. First, he created a new version of the story—this time by randomly ordering the sentences of the story so that it was completely jumbled and mixed up. Next, he presented the jumbled story to some new people and then gave them the same tests to determine what they comprehended and remembered. What Thorndyke found says something important about thinking thematically: he discovered that the jumbled version was no less comprehensible nor any less memorable than the no-theme version. In other words, even though its sentences were presented in a normal sequence, *the version without a theme still was no more easily understood or recalled than a completely jumbled story comprised of unrelated sentences.*

People Remember Themes— They Forget Facts

Another important lesson from Thorndyke's experiments has to do with what audiences remember—and what they forget—after hearing or reading a presentation. When he tested to find out what people remembered from his stories, he discovered that they tended to recall the plot structure and the main ideas, but that they tended to forget the subordinate facts and details. This is typical of how humans learn, and it's why we stress thematic communication. That is, most audiences will remember the theme, along with the five or fewer main ideas used to present it, but they'll forget most of the rest (recall the "Magical Number 7 ± 2" from Chapter 1). For this reason, in interpretation it's important that everyone in the audience comprehends the theme. And since some people may not pay attention for very long, they need to learn the theme *quickly*—before they switch attention or leave. If you practice this idea, you can be fairly sure that everyone in your audience will get the same message regardless of how much time they actually invest reading, viewing or listening to your presentation. Of course, someone who pays attention longer will get more details and a fuller explanation of your theme, but with time, most people will forget the facts and remember only the theme.

So having a theme, and then sharing that theme with your audience at the very beginning of a written or oral presentation, makes a lot of sense. How to apply this important idea is the topic we take up next.

Being Thematic in Oral and Written Presentations

Since audiences listen differently than they read, techniques for communicating thematically depend on whether you're preparing a presentation that audiences will hear (such as a talk, a tour, a script for an audiovisual program, etc.) or one that they'll read (such as an exhibit, sign, brochure, etc.). As we'll see shortly, the strategy in both cases is to make sure that our audiences learn the theme as quickly as possible, but how we accomplish this in **oral presentations** isn't the same as our approach in **written presentations**. Let's consider oral presentations first.

Thematic Oral Presentations

Oral presentations are those in which *spoken words are heard* by an audience. They include talks, demonstrations,

tours, guided walks and hikes, narrated audio recordings, and soundtracks for slide and video programs. What makes them different from most other kinds of presentations is that *the interpreter controls the order* in which the audience receives ideas and information. This is fundamentally different than an exhibit, for example, because in an exhibit people can start reading anywhere they choose, and they can finish reading anywhere they choose. But in an oral presentation, it's the interpreter, and not the audience, who controls the sequence. In this important respect, oral presentations are **linear** because they proceed in a definite sequence which is defined by the person speaking.

Being thematic in an oral presentation is easy, whether it's a personal presentation like a talk or tour or a non-personal presentation such as a narration recorded on tape. All that's necessary is that we put into practice what we learned from Thorndyke's (1977) study. Recalling that he found the best stories were those in which the theme was given at the beginning, and that the second best were those in which the theme was given at the end, imagine how much better any oral presentation would be if the interpreter told the audience the theme in *both* places—that is, at the beginning and again at the end. Although we'll return to this idea in each of the chapters in Part Two (Conducted Activities), the approach will be basically the same regardless of the kind of oral presentation you have to prepare. Simply put:

In oral presentations, you should reveal the theme to your audience at the beginning of the presentation, and then reinforce it at the end.

Thematic Written Presentations

Written presentations are those in which *printed or written words are read* by an audience. They include exhibits, signs, most brochures, and just about any presentation that requires an audience to read. With the possible exception of short stories, novels and other sequential, book-length manuscripts (topics we won't cover in this book), it's the *audience*, and not the writer, who controls the order in which the information is read. In this sense, written presentations are **nonlinear**. In an exhibit, for example, there's no definite sequence the audience must follow in looking at it. Viewers can start reading anywhere they wish, and they can decide to read some things while choosing to ignore other parts of the exhibit. This makes it more difficult for an interpreter to establish a logical sequence of ideas as he or she can in an oral presentation. A written presentation requires a different approach because all people probably won't read the text in the same order, and research has shown that most of them probably will read only a fraction of the information that's presented. As we'll see in Chapter 8, one of the most common errors interpreters make in preparing the text for an exhibit is that they try to write a linear, sequential presentation of ideas. But exhibits, signs and most brochures don't lend themselves to that approach because the interpreter can't control the order in which different parts of the message will be read.

You may already be thinking that there's one major exception—*the title*. In most cultures, people will predictably read the title of a written presentation first. Although there are many possible reasons for this, one thing is clear: if you give an audience the theme in the title of a written presentation, virtually everyone is going to get the main message regardless of how much time they might spend reading the rest of it. This is a powerful technique, and it's easy to apply for anyone who understands the difference between a theme and a topic. Most titles (especially in exhibits, signs and brochures) give only the topic—for example:

"Agriculture"
"Soil Erosion"
"Benefits of Trees"
"Medicinal Plants"

But when a title goes beyond the topic to communicate the theme, it ensures that the central idea of the exhibit, sign or brochure will be read by people, even if they read nothing else. In addition, titles based on themes are often more interesting to audiences because they express a complete *idea* rather than just a topic. For example, which titles do you think are more interesting, those above that are based on topics, or those following that are based on themes?

"Our Lives Depend on Agriculture"
"We Are Losing Our Soil"
"Trees Help Us"
"This Forest Is Your Pharmacy"

Although we'll return to this idea in Chapter 8 (exhibits), the approach is basically the same for almost any written presentation:

In written presentations, you should reveal your theme in the title.

Glossary terms: linear, message, nonlinear, oral presentation, subject, theme, topic, written presentation.

Thematic Interpretation– The Price Is Right!

Jim Gale, Chief of Interpretation
Mount St. Helens National Volcanic Monument
Gifford Pinchot National Forest,
Vancouver, Washington

Meaningful interpretation doesn't cost anything; it only requires a theme.

At Mount St. Helens National Volcanic Monument we've found that the interpretive programs people enjoy most are thematic—that is, they have something clear and important to say to our audiences. Whether we're communicating orally or with exhibits and signs, everything we do is guided by a single, simple objective: to communicate a theme as forcefully as possible. In 1984, we adopted a policy that requires all interpretive efforts to be thematic, conveying a complete, identifiable message that is easily understood by the visitor. For our seasonal interpreters, this requires an annual intensive training program built squarely on a thematic approach. We start with an understanding of how to communicate to a noncaptive audience, combine it with research on how the human brain works, and help our interpreters apply this knowledge in designing their own programs. Lectures and field trips led by scientists and indigenous people are then held to provide the subject matter expertise the interpreters will need.

This formula has worked well for us over the past eight years and our interpreters are lauded as being among the best in the country. We believe our thematic approach makes the difference.

During the summer, each interpreter develops a theme with three to five supporting concepts for each program. Programs include talks, walks, hikes, car caravans and evening programs. We provide an average of six talks and six walks daily, with an additional campfire program, two hikes and a car caravan on weekends. Complementing our conducted activities are more than fifty interpretive signs, dozens of brochures, thirty-eight information boards, two videos and an auto cassette tour. Every one of these has been developed using the thematic approach presented in this book, and although we continually make changes and improvements, we are immensely satisfied with the results. Over 90,000 people attended our live programs in the summer of 1992, and we have been overwhelmed by the number of verbal and written compliments we have received about the quality of our interpretive programs. We believe this is due to the fact that they leave each of our programs not only with the satisfaction of having had a fun time, but with something far more enduring—a theme.

Enduring messages are organized and conveyed thematically using the interpretive approach outlined in the first chapter of this book. After eight years, it's clear that the interpreters at Mount St. Helens have truly internalized this philosophy, not only by practicing it, but by teaching and mentoring each other in the techniques of thematic interpretation. Through this coaching process, interpreters have their activities evaluated throughout the summer, with priority given to how well the theme was communicated to the audience. Video recording of interpretive programs is also used to allow interpreters to see themselves in action and to determine for themselves how well their audiences are grasping their themes.

Since we began in 1984, we have grown into a strong and innovative interpretive team bonded by our focus on the thematic approach. As one who has been with the team since its inception, I am absolutely convinced that what we are doing at Mount St. Helens is applicable everywhere there are interpreters. Whatever stories you interpret, no matter what kind of ecosystem or technical subject matter you must explain, no matter where you are or how big or small your program is, you should be practicing thematic interpretation. Artfully carried out, the results are undeniably positive. And the best part is that a good theme doesn't cost a penny.

References

Ausubel, David P. 1960. The Use of Advance Organizers in the Learning and Retention of Meaningful Verbal Material. *Journal of Educational Psychology* 51:267-272.

Lewis, William J. 1983. Identifying a Theme. *The Interpreter* 14(1):i.

Thorndyke, P.W. 1977. Cognitive Structures in Comprehension and Memory of Narrative Discourse. *Cognitive Psychology* 9(1):77-110.

Additional Reading

In English:

Ausubel, David P. 1968. *Educational Psychology: A Cognitive View.* New York, USA: Holt, Rinehart and Winston.

Ham, Sam H. 1983. Cognitive Psychology and Interpretation: Synthesis and Application. *Journal of Interpretation* 8(1):11-27.

Lewis, William J. 1980. *Interpreting for Park Visitors.* Philadelphia, Pennsylvania, USA: Eastern National Park and Monument Association, Eastern Acorn Press.

Regnier, Kathleen, Michael Gross and Ron Zimmerman. 1992. *The Interpreter's Guidebook: Techniques for Programs and Presentations.* Stevens Point, Wisconsin, USA: UW-SP Foundation Press, Inc.

In Spanish:

Ham, Sam H. 1992. *Interpretación Ambiental: Una Guía Práctica para Gente con Grandes Ideas y Presupuestos Pequeños*. Golden, Colorado, USA: North American Press/Fulcrum Publishing.

Moore, Alan, Bill Wendt, Louis Penna e Isabel Castillo de Ramos. 1989. *Manual para La Capacitación del Personal de Areas Protegidas* (Modulo C: Interpretación y Educación Ambiental, Apunte 4a). Washington, D.C., USA: Servicio de Parques Nacionales, Oficina de Asuntos Internacionales.

Part Two

Conducted Activities

CHAPTER THREE

HOW TO PREPARE AND PRESENT A TALK

In interpretation, we use the word **talk** instead of **speech** because it captures the spirit of informality that we discussed in Chapter 1. Put another way, saying that "I'm going to give a talk today" expresses an image of a speaker chatting with an audience, more or less in a conversational tone. Saying that "I'm going to give a speech today" conjures up the idea of a speaker standing behind a podium or lectern, half reading notes that have been carefully prepared. The main difference between a talk and a speech is that even though both have been carefully prepared, the talk sounds more spontaneous and informal to the audience, in part because the speaker usually doesn't use notes, and in part because he/she consciously tries to be more conversational in tone. Speeches, on the other hand, tend to be more structured and they seem more formal to their audiences. Politicians give speeches because of the formal ceremonies in which they usually have to present them. Interpreters give talks because of the informal circumstances in which they usually have to present them. This chapter is about preparing and presenting talks. (Since we will emphasize thematic talks, you should review Chapters 1 and 2 if you're not yet familiar with themes and thematic interpretation.)

Types of Talks

There are many types of talks, and interpreters can present them in many different kinds of settings and to different kinds of audiences (see Figure 3-1). For example, an employee at a park might tell visitors about things to do and see in the area; a nursery manager might explain to a group of school children how seedlings are planted and cared for; a museum worker might explain the significance of something in one of the exhibits for an

There Are Many Kinds of Talks

Talks can be presented almost anywhere there is something important to talk about. Following are some common examples of different kinds of talks, their settings, audiences, and typical purposes.

Type of Talk	Typical Audience	Typical Purposes	Typical Settings
Orientation Talks	Visitors, tourists, school groups, organized tours, field trip groups	To orient people to a place and to tell them what they can see and do there	Visitor centers, museums, zoos, gardens, nurseries, demonstration areas, stops on a field trip, ships, buses, cars
Site Talks	Visitors, tourists, school groups, organized tours, field trip groups, extension audiences	To explain or show the importance of what is occurring or has occurred at a natural, historic, or demonstration site	Forests, parks, botanical gardens, zoos, nurseries, demonstration areas, stops on a field trip, ships, buses, cars
Exhibit Talks	Visitors, tourists, school groups, organized tours, local community residents	To explain or show something related to an exhibit the audience is looking at	Visitor centers, museums, zoos, botanical gardens, nurseries, demonstration areas, fairs, celebrations, community events
Skill Demonstrations	Visitors, tourists, extension audiences, school groups, organized groups	To demonstrate to people how to do something, or to show how people in the past did something	Extension program sites, forests, parks, visitor centers, farms, classrooms, museums, zoos, nurseries, demonstration areas

Classroom Talks	Students and teachers	To explain concepts related to a topic of interest, to prepare students for a field trip, or to reinforce what was learned during a previous exercise or field trip	Schools, classrooms, auditoriums
Campfire Talks or Evening Outdoor Talks	Visitors, tourists, campers, local community residents, organized tour groups, school groups	Any of the above, although the tone is often more philosophical or inspirational because of the time of day and setting	Amphitheaters, campgrounds, campfire circles, or other open-air location which is comfortable and safe after dark
Other Talks	Any audience listed above	To develop conceptual awareness or appreciation of an idea or topic of interest	Meeting room, classroom, auditorium, amphitheater or other location with chairs or benches for seating

Figure 3-1. Examples of different kinds of talks.

organized tour group; or a forest ranger might gather campers around a fire and tell them a story about conservation. All that's required to give a good talk is a theme, solid preparation, and enthusiasm.

As Figure 3-1 suggests, talks can have very specific purposes (such as teaching a skill, orienting visitors to a place, explaining a scene or object on display, etc.). Or they may have more general purposes—creating awareness, building appreciation, or suggesting new ways of thinking or looking at something. Your objective, and the theme you've selected to help you accomplish it, will guide your approach. For example, if you want your audience to be familiar with the medicinal uses of local plants, you'll probably want to focus attention on specific plants. But if your aim is to raise awareness about the value of conserving nature, you may want to talk in more general terms, appealing more to feelings than to logic. In practice, however, most good talks have qualities of both approaches.

Talks can be presented in visitor centers, at zoos, museums, parks, forests, botanical gardens, nurseries, demonstration and research sites, classrooms, auditoriums, meeting rooms, amphitheaters, aboard ships, in buses or cars, or in other settings. As Figure 3-1 shows, where a talk is presented usually has something to do with its purpose and with the kind of message you want to get across. But how you prepare and present an effective talk will usually be the same regardless of the setting in which it will be given.

Qualities of a Good Talk

Good talks have the qualities that we outlined in Chapter 1. That is, they're interpretive; they're entertaining to their audiences; they present information in a way that makes it meaningful and relevant; and they're well organized around a central theme with five or fewer main ideas. As any experienced interpreter will tell you, the best way to tell whether a talk is good is to watch the audience. If the people's eyes are focused on the speaker, and they seem interested and involved, then the talk is doing what the interpreter wanted it to do—hold the audience's attention.

Since holding attention is the biggest challenge you'll face as a speaker, you should think carefully about how you're going to accomplish this each time you plan and prepare a talk. Maybe you'll want to create some kind of vehicle or other scenario as we discussed in Chapter 1. Maybe it would be best to link your topic to human history, or to relate a cause-and-effect story. Maybe your topic lends itself more to role playing, or perhaps to a more straightforward presentation. Whatever approach you use, you should decide upon it at the earliest stages of planning and then build your talk around it. The best speakers spend as much or more time planning how to maintain their audience's interest as they do planning

the information content of the talk, itself, and that's why their audiences pay attention to their talks.

Of course, many factors combine to make a successful talk. Smiling and facial expressions, eye contact with the audience, appropriate inflection and variation of speaking tempo are just a few examples. Although we'll come back to these and other considerations later in this chapter, it's important for you to know that they're mere mechanics. Although they're important, what is most important in presenting an effective talk is your attitude. If you're preparing a talk that you really want to present, then many of these mechanics will come naturally to you—especially after practicing the talk and presenting it a few times to different audiences.

Freeman Tilden (1977) called this kind of attitude "the priceless ingredient." He argued that interpreters who really care about their subject matter, and who really want to communicate its importance to other people, will be more successful than interpreters who aren't driven by such deep desires. In Tilden's viewpoint, possessing this priceless ingredient is even more important to capturing an audience's attention than advance preparation. Speaking from the heart is almost always more powerful than speaking only from the mind. That's why even the most boring speakers suddenly become interesting when they get excited or emotional about something. All of a sudden they're driven by a deep desire to make themselves understood—to communicate—and they instinctively look you in the eye, raise their voices, express their inner feelings with their faces and their bodies, and seem to change personality before your very eyes. Under these circumstances, they don't need their notes because their feelings guide their thoughts and their words.

Has this ever happened to you? If it has, you probably noticed how much easier it was to find the words you wanted to say—and how good it felt. The best speakers have learned how to get themselves excited before every talk, even talks they've presented many times before. They know consciously or subconsciously that this feeling, even more than their practice and preparation, will make the crucial difference in their performance. But imagine how much more effective you could be if you had both this feeling and the advantage of advance preparation.

Unfortunately, the feeling can't be taught; it must come from within you. Each interpreter develops the feeling within himself or herself, or it simply doesn't occur. When it does occur, however, you'll find that your words come easily, and that even though you may forget to say something you had planned to say, it usually won't matter—it didn't fit what you were feeling at the time. Trust your feelings; let them guide your communication approach. If you do, you'll probably find yourself more comfortable speaking in front of strangers because they'll respond like friends to your message.

A Note About Personal Style

Most good speakers have studied the techniques of other good speakers, but they copy nobody. In other words, good speakers usually model their approach after other speakers they've watched and heard, but the style they use is their own—it's unique. Have you ever watched a speaker you think is particularly good and silently wished that you, too, could make presentations like that? Have you ever tried to copy a technique and found that it just didn't work for you the way it worked for the person you borrowed it from? The reason is probably that you were trying to mimic a **style** that wasn't "you." Style is a very personal thing, and it's molded more by your personality—and what feels comfortable to you—than it is by any list of communication "rules" or standard techniques. Some speakers feel comfortable with an animated, energetic style. They seem to bounce off walls and burn a lot of calories when they're speaking. Other speakers seem calmer and more composed when they talk in front of an audience. Still others are able to practice both styles, each reserved for different situations. And, of course, there are many more possibilities—each a matter of personal style. The important thing to remember, and this is especially true for less experienced interpreters, is that no style is inherently more effective or better than any other style. The best style for you is your style.

Each of us is unique. We come to our jobs with our own personalities, our own knowledge, our own attitudes, values, and beliefs, and with our own faces, voices, bodily features and posture. Yet all of these things are an inseparable part of our personal style. To expect a different speaker's style to always work for us ignores this fact. Regrettably, inexperienced interpreters sometimes become discouraged when a technique or approach they've borrowed from someone else doesn't work well for them. They lose confidence in their ability because they expected the impossible—to be someone they're not.

More likely than not, techniques which we've borrowed and used successfully were borrowed from people who are similar to us in personality, appearance, or attitude. Hundreds of body movements, facial expressions, and barely perceptible fluctuations in voice and demeanor all come together at precise moments throughout a presentation, and collectively they achieve a desired response in the audience. It's enormously difficult to plan and consciously orchestrate each of these minute details—or even to be aware of them as we carry them out—much less to copy them from another person. For this reason, the more like "us" the other person is, the more likely we'll have success using aspects of that person's style.

The best style for you is the one you feel most comfortable with. It's your unique approach to communication, one that fits your personality, features and attitude; it's how you communicate naturally, even though it may be carefully planned; and it's an approach or series of approaches that will develop and change over time—as you change. The best advice for the inexperienced interpreter is "just be yourself." Pay attention to what others are doing and learn from their example, both good and bad. But keep in mind that their successes may not fit your style, and that what failed for them may work well for you.

How to Plan and Prepare a Thematic Talk

Fortunately, although it's generally not possible to teach an interpreter the "feeling" part of effective speaking, it is possible to teach the preparation part. Dozens of good books exist on this subject, and our purpose here won't be to duplicate them. Instead, our approach will be to reconsider the purposes of different parts of a talk (the **introduction, body,**

and **conclusion**) and, by way of an example, to suggest how you might use this knowledge in planning your own talks. In doing this, we'll consider a simple approach, which we'll call the **2-3-1 Rule**, as a method for guiding our thinking and decision making as we develop a talk. Since we'll stress the preparation of thematic talks, you should review the appropriate sections of Chapters 1 and 2 if you're not yet familiar with the development and use of themes.

Parts of a Talk and Their Purposes

Although most people know that every talk should have three parts—an introduction, a body and a conclusion—too many of us think of them as being simply the beginning, middle and end. The best speakers, however, know that there's much more to the parts than that. And, to a large degree, it's their ability to understand and accomplish the different purposes of the three parts that makes their talks seem more interesting and easy to listen to. Fortunately, anybody can do this.

There is wide disagreement over how long each part of the talk should be. A lot depends on how long the talk, itself, is. For example, in a twenty-minute talk (a common length when the audience is seated), the introduction should probably account for about 25 percent (five minutes), the body for about 50 to 60 percent (ten to twelve minutes), and the conclusion for about 15 to 25 percent (three to five minutes). In a shorter talk (five-minute orientation talk), the introduction may account for only 5 percent (roughly fifteen seconds), the body for 90 percent (four-and-a-half minutes), and the conclusion for 5 percent (fifteen seconds). But

Figure 3-2. Planning a talk starts with research. (Photo by Gerry Snyder)

these are just averages, and there is no evidence to suggest that any part of any talk should be a certain length. Beware of "experts" claiming to know the "rules" about such things. Communication is rarely so simple.

But if there are no firm rules, then how do we know just how long an introduction, body or conclusion should be? The answer is: each part of the talk should be as long as it needs to be in order for it to accomplish its purposes. Knowing what each part should do, we can then prepare it in such a way, and at such a length, to do precisely that and nothing else. Having done this well, you'll then know how long each part needed to be. It needed to be the length that you've made it.

An old adage in speech communication goes: "Tell them what you're going to say, say it, and then tell them what you said." Although you probably know that preparing a good talk takes a little more technique than just this, you probably also agree that it's pretty good advice. Roughly speaking, introductions tell the audience what you're going to say; bodies tell them what you said you would talk about; and

conclusions often summarize or reinforce what was said in the body. But in thematic communication there's more still to these three parts of a talk. Compare the different purposes of the introduction, body and conclusion as they're shown in Figure 3-3. Notice that although they do indeed correspond to the beginning, middle and end, they each have a specific task with respect to the theme of the talk.

The Introduction

A good introduction does at least two things very well. First, it creates interest in the talk. It doesn't just make the audience willing to listen to the talk—the best introductions make them want to listen to it. As we saw in Chapter 1, this is essential for noncaptive audiences, because very early in the presentation they'll decide whether it's going to be worth their time to pay attention to it. For this reason, many speakers start off their presentations with a provocative statement or an interesting question. For example, in a talk whose theme is "If the world is actually getting warmer, the lives of future generations will change dramatically," the speaker might begin by posing the question: "What would you do if tomorrow you woke up in the middle of an ocean?" Another example is a talk about the growing number of visitors in protected areas in which the interpreter's first words were, "A lot of people don't know it, but we're about to love our wilderness to death!" Grater (1976) described a similar beginning in a talk about Giant Sequoias. His advice is to "strike a spark with the opening sentence."

The second thing a good introduction must do is orient the audience to the theme, and tell generally how the talk is going to be organized. In Chapter 1, we saw how important organization can be. When audiences know ahead of time how you're going to organize the information you'll give them, it's easier for them to keep it straight in their heads later. This makes listening to your talk easier, and increases the likelihood that the audience will pay attention to it. As we noted in Chapter 1, if you keep the number of main ideas to five or fewer, most audience members will be able to follow your train of thought quite easily—that is, as long as they can see the relationship between the theme of your talk and each of the main ideas. Different speakers accomplish this in different ways. In our talk on global warming, we might begin as follows:

"What would you do if tomorrow you woke up in the middle of an ocean? As unbelievable as this sounds, some scientists are telling us that future generations may actually have to face a very different world than the one you and I live in. The cause, they say, is that the world is getting warmer. In the next few minutes, I'm going to tell you about global warming and why scientists think it's happening. We'll look briefly at its causes and how it can affect not only the oceans, but agriculture and forestry. Most of all, we'll look at how it might affect people all across the world—including us, our children and their children. I think you'll see that if the world is actually warming, sooner or later people everywhere will have to change the way they're

living—and they'll have to change it dramatically."

Two things are clear in this introduction. First, the theme is obvious: "If the world is actually warming, sooner or later people everywhere will have to change the way they're living—and they'll have to change it dramatically." Second, it's clear that the speaker is going to talk about four main ideas with respect to the theme: (1) the reasons scientists have come to believe that the earth is getting warmer, (2) global warming's effect on oceans, (3) its effect on agriculture and forestry, and (4) its effect on people. Although you might introduce this talk differently, your introduction should try to accomplish the same two things.

Not all talks will use a vehicle or overriding scenario as discussed in Chapter 1. Those that do, however, should use the introduction to prepare the audience for it. For example, suppose we were going take the audience into the future, to a hypothetical place in the northern latitudes, where an Eskimo family was sitting under a shade tree during an exceptionally hot summer day talking about the "old days" when their ancestors had to bundle up to stay warm against the freezing wind. With this vehicle, we could present the four main ideas of our talk through the conversation of the family. If we were going to do this, we might add the following to the above introduction:

"Nobody really knows for sure exactly what's in store for future generations. At this point, we have only some general ideas. But to give you a feeling for them, I'm going to ask you to use your imagination a little, and come forward in time with me—say about 100 years or so—to the home of the Chilkoot family, a group of Eskimos who live in the northernmost part of our planet. How might the Chilkoot family be living in comparison to their ancestors a century before?"

Of course, there are many possible vehicles for any talk, and many talks won't include one at all. The important thing to remember is that if you decide to use a vehicle, you should explain it in the introduction so that the audience will be prepared for it when you get to the body of the talk. Often, the vehicle is the final part of the introduction, as in our example above.

Finally, many speakers use the introduction to set the stage for a maximum impact conclusion. There are many ways to do this—a key phrase or sentence that's spoken in the introduction and repeated again in the conclusion, part of a story that's begun in the introduction and finished in the conclusion, a major idea that's given in the introduction and repeated in the conclusion, "flashback" slides (slides which are shown in the introduction and again in the conclusion), etc. And as we've stressed repeatedly, the theme of the talk, itself, should always be given both in the introduction and conclusion.

The Body

A good body tries to accomplish just one purpose—to develop the theme. "To develop" means to present the information that's needed to get the theme across to your audience. This information should be organized around the five or fewer main ideas that you mentioned in the introduction, and it should include no other information. Facts, concepts, examples, comparisons, analogies, anecdotes, and other illustrative material should be included as needed in order to make the body entertaining, meaningful, personal, and informative to the audience (see Chapter 1 for a review of these principles.) A very general outline of the body of our talk on global warming might look something like this:

> I. There is evidence that the earth is getting warmer
>
> II. Global warming could affect the oceans
>
> III. Global warming could affect agriculture and forestry
>
> IV. Global warming could severely affect people

Under each main idea there might be subheads (A, B, C, etc.) that will include the facts, examples, anecdotes, and other illustrative information referred to above. This "color" is usually important because it helps make the information we're presenting more interesting and more relevant to the audience. The best interpreters recognize this and use it to advantage, but they also recognize that what people will remember from their talks will be the five or fewer main ideas and the theme, not the color (see Chapter 2). For this reason, they're highly selective in choosing which subordinate information to include in their talks.

Since ending one main idea and beginning the next often involves a conspicuous change of topic, you might want to include **transitions** between them.

A Good Talk Has a Good Introduction, a Good Body, and a Good Conclusion

In every good talk, there is an introduction, body, and conclusion—each of which accomplishes a different set of purposes. Preparing an effective talk is simple if you think of it as developing these three different parts, and if you concentrate on designing each part to accomplish its specific purposes.

Part of the Talk	Purpose(s)
1. The Introduction	• to create interest in the theme, and to make your audience want to hear more about it. (Remember, they're a noncaptive audience.) • to orient the audience to the theme, and tell them how your talk is going to be organized. (Remember the "Magical Number 7 Plus or Minus 2.") • to establish the conceptual framework that you rely on in the body, and to introduce the vehicle (if you're using one). • to set the stage for the conclusion.
2. The Body	• to develop the theme, organized just as you said it would be organized, and using whatever facts, concepts, analogies, examples, comparisons, etc. that are needed to make the information entertaining, meaningful, and relevant to your audience.
3. The Conclusion	• to reinforce the theme—to show one last time the relationship between the theme that you revealed in the introduction and all the information you presented in the body. Many conclusions summarize the key points that were made earlier, and some offer ideas about the larger meaning of the theme (e.g., what the "bigger picture is" or "where we go from here").

Figure 3-3. Purposes of the three parts of a thematic talk.

Transitions, like the one we included at the end of the introduction of our talk, don't need to be complex. In fact, the best ones are short and simple. Their purpose is merely to indicate to the audience when you're going to quit talking about one main point, and begin talking about the next one. For example, after talking about the evidence for global warming (Part I in our outline above), we might use a transition like the following to begin talking about global warming's effect on the oceans (Part II):

> "So as you can see, there's some pretty strong evidence that the world really is getting warmer. And if this is true, it's probably going to affect us in a lot of different ways. Let's talk first about how it might change the earth's oceans… "

This transition says to the audience: "Okay, we're done talking about the reasons that scientists think the world is getting warmer, and we're now going to talk about how global warming could affect us. We'll start with its effect on the oceans." Similarly, once we finish talking about Part II, we might use the following transition to introduce Part III:

> "But global warming could affect more than just our oceans, it could have far-reaching effects on agriculture, and on our forests."

Transitions are easy to include in any talk. They're simple statements that serve only to remind the audience when you're going to change topic. Many speakers memorize their transitions. This helps

them to remember the rest of the talk, principally because it's much easier to remember the "color" underneath each major idea than it is to remember the entire body as one big narrative. In our global warming talk, it is as though we're telling four small stories held together with transitions, rather than one big story. Less experienced interpreters sometimes forget to plan their transitions, and their talks suffer as result. If you have trouble remembering talks, or feel you must rely on notes to do it, try using preplanned transitions between your main points. Chances are, you'll find that using them makes remembering what you want to say much easier.

The Conclusion

A good conclusion is like both the punch line of a joke and the final note of a song. It serves as a "punch line" because once people hear it, they can clearly see the relationship between the information you've presented and the theme or "so what?" of your talk. A conclusion is like the "final note" in the sense that a good one signifies a sure and unambiguous end to the presentation. As we'll see shortly, after a good conclusion, the audience is so full of thought that no additional words are needed.

The main purpose of the conclusion is to reinforce the theme of the talk. The best interpreters know this and almost always repeat the theme—sometimes verbatim—in the conclusions of their talks. Beginning interpreters sometimes have trouble knowing exactly how to do this. Many find that their conclusions improve simply by using the following transition between the last sentence of the body and the conclusion:

"So I hope you can see that ..."
(followed by the theme).

or

"At this point, you probably can see that ... " (followed by the theme).

For example, we might begin the conclusion of our talk on global warming by saying:

> "So I hope you can see that if the world really is getting warmer, sooner or later people everywhere are going to be living very differently than the way we live today."

Many speakers like their conclusions to include a summary of the five or fewer main ideas that they presented in the body. For example, we might say:

> "At this point, you probably can see that there are good reasons for scientists to believe that our planet is getting warmer. And if they're right, future generations can expect a lot of changes. The oceans will spread due to the melting of the polar ice caps, and forests and food crops in some parts of the world may be devastated. Nobody can say for sure exactly what's going to happen, but one thing is certain: If the average temperature of our world increases even just a little, people everywhere will be in for some dramatic changes in the way they live."

Notice how this conclusion briefly reminds the listeners of what they've heard, and then reminds them of what it means—the theme. Although there are many ways to conclude any talk, the best conclusions are usually those which try to do both of these things. Many go on to suggest an even larger significance—such as what the audience can do to act on its new knowledge (e.g., "Where do we go from here?"), or to ponder a philosophical question related to the theme of the talk. An example might be:

> "Above all, I hope you leave here today thinking about whether we have a responsibility to give our children, and their children, a chance to have the kind of life they want—rather than the kind of life scientists are telling us they will have if all the evidence about global warming is correct."

Whether you include this sort of appeal in your conclusion will depend on the theme of your talk, and even more on your personal style.

Earlier we noted that many speakers like to use the introduction to prepare the audience for a more powerful conclusion. Several methods for doing this were discussed including the reiteration of key phrases in both parts of the talk, the use of "flashback" slides, leaving a half-finished story or anecdote for the conclusion, and other techniques. We emphasized also that all thematic talks should include a statement of the theme in both the introduction and conclusion.

The reason audiences seem to respond well to this kind of design—talks which have interrelated introductions and conclusions—has to do with an idea some psychologists call **pragnänz**. Pragnänz is a German word which means roughly "wholeness," "completeness" or "unity." Psychologists believe that people like completeness in their world because it gives us order and predictability. In a talk, completeness occurs when the audience senses that everything has come "full circle"—or when there's **closure**, as educational psychologists call it. When a key idea or scenario is introduced early in the presentation, and then occurs again at the end, it seems to bring everything you've been talking about back to the beginning; it gives the talk a quality of being complete and whole, rather than only partly finished; and it reassures the audience that it now has the whole story and that there are no "loose ends." Audiences who've just listened to a good talk, usually feel this sense of closure or pragnänz, just as they feel it at the end of a good book, movie or play.

As we suggested earlier, good conclusions are like the final note of a song because they signify a clear and certain end to the talk. Have you ever heard what you thought was the last sentence of a talk, only to have the speaker continue with some extra information? These are called "false endings" because, until the speaker began talking again, it seemed as though the talk was finished. Usually the additional information didn't help much, and if you're like most people, you probably were a little bothered by it. The reason is that you were feeling pragnänz—you felt for a moment that there was closure, and that additional words were unnecessary. Often, these additional words spoil the ending of what might have otherwise been a very good talk. Avoid false endings.

Another common problem with conclusions is that sometimes the speaker's last sentence doesn't seem like the last sentence—often because of the speaker's inflection, or because in making the closing remarks he/she suddenly introduces a completely new idea—and so the audience is left expecting more. Usually, after a prolonged and awkward period of silence, the people in the audience begin to figure out that the speaker is finished talking, they gradually start leaving, amidst scattered applause and muffled pleas for reassurance like: "Is it over? Is that the end?"—believing the talk was somehow incomplete—thinking more needed to be said. Sometimes, the speaker senses the awkwardness and utters something like: "That's it" or "It's over." But statements like these only remind everyone that the ending was awkward. This problem usually occurs not because more information was needed—though that would certainly be the case if the body of the talk weren't well developed—but rather because of the speaker's tone or inflection as the last sentence was spoken.

A simple and effective technique to avoid awkward endings is to make the final two words of every talk "thank you" (though some speakers prefer "goodbye" or "good night"). Such words really say very little; but they're phrases that can rarely be followed by other words at the end of a presentation, regardless of how they're said. Therefore, when you say "thank you" or "goodbye," you're really saying to your audience:

> "This is the end of my talk and I will say no more now. If you've enjoyed my talk, you may now applaud or come forward to talk privately with me.

Or you may get up and leave. In any event, I'm finished."

And of course, after saying "thank you" or "goodbye," you really should be finished. Following these words with any others will do exactly what you had hoped to avoid by using them—it will create a false or awkward ending.

Putting It All Together Using the 2-3-1 Rule—An Example

Planning and preparing a thematic talk is simple if you really appreciate the different purposes of the introduction, body and conclusion. In the example which follows, we're going to see just how easy it can be. We'll start at the very beginning with a general idea of the topic that we want to talk about. Then, using our knowledge of thematic communication and how the three parts of a talk work together, we'll separately develop an introduction, an outline of the body, and a conclusion. The order in which we do this will be guided by a simple procedure called the "2-3-1 Rule" (body-conclusion-introduction) which will be explained shortly.

In our example, we're going to go step-by-step, making various decisions about the talk as we plan each of its parts. Although different authors might organize these steps differently, we're going think in terms of ten:

1. Choose a general topic.

2. If necessary, choose a more specific topic.

3. Choose a theme based on the topic of your talk.

4. Summarize your entire talk in a short paragraph whose first sentence is the theme.

APPLY THE "2-3-1 RULE"
5. Prepare an outline of the body.

6. Prepare the conclusion.

7. Prepare the introduction.

8. Rearrange the order and tie your talk together.

9. Practice your talk.

10. If appropriate, choose a title for your talk.

Our Scenario

Suppose you're in charge of managing a forest, and that a recent study has shown a dramatic decline in certain species of native birds in your forest—especially some of the nocturnal species

Figure 3-4. Enthusiasm and body language helped this interpreter capture his audience's attention. Mount St. Helens National Volcanic Monument. (Photo by Sam Ham)

like owls and nighthawks. Having determined that a community education program was needed, you decide to prepare a twenty-minute talk about nocturnal birds that you'll give at schools, clubs, and other places over the next several weeks in order to raise community awareness of the problem. You proceed as follows:

Step 1: Choose a general topic.

Choose a topic you think will interest your audience, and one which you're interested in and know something about.

> *Our general topic:* "Birds which live in the forest"

Having determined the general subject matter of your talk, you should do your "homework." Research your topic, searching not only for factual information but for ideas which can help you make the talk more entertaining, meaningful, personal and organized. If you have trouble understanding something you read, chances are your audience will have even more trouble understanding that information. Most of the difficult material probably won't be necessary in your talk, but if some of it is, you'll certainly want to be thinking of "bridging" techniques (see Chapter 1) in order to make it meaningful to your audience. Also, your research may give you ideas for a vehicle or other "creative packaging" for your talk.

Most of all, your research will probably help you narrow the topic. At this point, you should already be thinking: "What story do I want to tell about this topic?" If you aren't yet able to answer this question, your topic is probably too general or too vague. If so, try narrowing it further.

Step 2: If necessary, choose a more specific topic.

Select a specific aspect of the topic that interests you and which you can treat in the amount of time available for your talk.

> *Our specific topic:* "Nocturnal birds which live in this forest"

When the topic of your talk is too general you run the danger of presenting an oral catalog of facts. You want your talk to have a message, that is, a theme. To have a thematic talk, you'll first need a well defined topic.

But it's also possible to have a topic which is too specific. Very narrow topics are fine as long as you have the depth of knowledge they require, and the communication ability to make such an extensive treatment of a limited subject interesting to a noncaptive audience.

Step 3: Choose a theme based on the topic of your talk.

As we saw in Chapters 1 and 2, the theme is your message—the important idea you want your audience to understand or appreciate after listening to your talk. Selecting your theme is the most important decision you'll make in developing your talk because everything you say will somehow be related to the theme. The theme statement answers the question "so what?" with respect to your talk.

> *Our theme:* "Our misunderstanding of nocturnal birds is leading to their disappearance from this forest."

Step 4: Try to summarize your entire talk in a short paragraph in which the first sentence is your theme.

Besides helping you determine how your talk might begin and end, this short synopsis will focus your attention on the kind of information that will be needed to develop your theme. In other words, it will help you identify what to include in your talk, as well as what not to include. Putting the theme in the first sentence of the paragraph forces you to think thematically as you write the rest of it. As accomplished speakers will tell you, having this clarity of focus at the outset is an amazing advantage. If you can't find the words to write this paragraph, then you probably need to spend more time thinking about your theme because you're not yet sure what message you want to communicate to your audience. But once written, this thematic paragraph will make development of your talk a lot easier.

Our thematic paragraph: "Our misunderstanding of nocturnal birds is leading to their disappearance from this forest. Nocturnal birds are one of the most interesting groups of animals because they don't become active until it's dark. Many of them, such as the owls and nighthawks that live around here, have unusual adaptations for this kind of life. Unfortunately, because of their secretive habits and period of activity, we rarely get a chance to see these birds. And because of our lack of familiarity with how they really live, people have created many superstitions and legends about them. We need to remember that even though we can't see them, these birds are an interesting and important part of the natural community in this forest. The future of these birds may well depend on you and me."

The "2-3-1 Rule"— Body, Conclusion and (Then) Introduction

At this point, you're ready to think about the words you'll actually say in presenting your talk. A common mistake is trying to prepare the introduction first. The reason this is a mistake has to do with the purposes of the introduction: to create interest in the talk, and to tell the audience the theme and how you're going organize your presentation of it. Obviously, you can't do this until you know what the talk will include and how it will be organized. And you really can't know these things until after you've outlined the body. So even though the body is the second part of the talk you'll present, it's the first part to be developed. Likewise, since good introductions are designed, in part, to prepare the audience for the conclusion, it makes sense to prepare the introduction last— even though you're going to present it first.

This approach is what we'll call the **"2-3-1 Rule."** The name comes from the order in which the different parts of a talk are developed: 2 (body), then 3 (conclusion), and then 1 (introduction). This rule stems from the fact that it's simply not possible to know what needs to be concluded in the conclusion, nor introduced in the introduction, until you know what you're going to present in the body of the talk. In other words, what approach should you use in the introduction in order to prepare people for the body and conclusion? How can you plan the introduction if you don't yet know what's going to follow it? Most likely, your experience tells you that you can't. And that's why the "2-3-1 Rule" makes sense—especially for people who don't yet have a lot of experience developing talks.

Step 5: Prepare an outline of the body of your talk.

Following the "2-3-1 Rule," prepare an outline of the body first. This could simply be a list of the five or fewer main ideas, and under each, the selected facts, concepts, and illustrative information you think will help you to communicate your theme clearly and in an interesting or entertaining way. Of course, the outline should show the sequence in which you plan to present these ideas. Some speakers like to plan their transitions at the same time they prepare the outline, but others prefer to wait until Step 9. It really doesn't matter when you develop them as long as you do it at some point. Especially important are the transitions that will take you from one main point to the next, and from the body to the conclusion of your talk. The following outline includes these transitions.

Our outline for the body of "Wings of the Night:"
I.   Many kinds of birds are active after dark.
    A. Where they stay during the day.
    B. Many "replace" diurnal birds which have similar roles.

(Transition: "You may be wondering at this point just how these birds get along at night. For example, how do they fly in the dark, and how do they find food? Well, the answer is that they have some special features and abilities that other birds don't have. In other words, they're adapted to a nocturnal way of life. Let's talk about some of these adaptations.")

II. Nocturnal birds are adapted to night life.
    A. Specialized eyes for seeing in the dark.
    B. Specialized wings of owls and how they fly silently.
    C. Rudimentary feet of nighthawks.
    D. Development of song instead of brightly colored plumage.

(Transition: "Well, we've talked about how these birds are adapted to living in the dark. But just exactly what do they do that we can't see?")

III. Nocturnal birds have unusual lifestyles and habits.
    A. Habitat and places where they can be observed.
    B. How they feed and care for their young.
    C. What they eat and where they find it.

(Transition: "As fascinating as nocturnal birds are, they're a misunderstood group of animals—mainly because we can't see them very often. Over the centuries, this has led to a number of legends and superstitions about them. I'd like to tell you about a few of them.")

IV. Legends and superstitions cloud our understanding of nocturnal birds.
    A. How legends originate.
    B. Owls and nighthawks are common subjects.

(Transition: "Although these legends and superstitions are interesting and even fun to hear, they sometimes cloud our judgments about nocturnal birds. That is, we sometimes think of them as just unseen, mysterious creatures rather than as important parts of nature's design. And a good example are the owls and nighthawks that live around here.")

V. Owls and nighthawks are useful in nature.
    A. How owls help control rodent populations.
    B. How nighthawks help control insect populations.
    C. How misconceptions of their roles are threatening these birds.
        1. Indiscriminate killing and poisoning.
        2. Habitat loss due to cutting, plowing and elimination of food.

Take a moment to compare this outline with the short paragraph we wrote in Step 4. Notice that what we wrote in the paragraph helped us determine the main ideas to include in the body of the talk. Notice also that each of the five main ideas is essentially a little theme, each an important part of the overall theme of the talk. As we saw in Chapter 1, in interpretation little meanings "add up" to big ones.

Step 6: Prepare the conclusion of the talk.
    With an outline of the body, you should now think about how you want to conclude your talk. Remember that the purpose of the conclusion is to reinforce the theme. You should develop your conclusion following the train of thought you established in the body. What can be concluded from these ideas? The answer, of course, is your theme. The theme, and

therefore the conclusion, should always answer the question "so what?"

Frequently, the conclusion is the most difficult part of the talk to develop. As we discussed earlier, the ending must be final, yet smooth, and it should fit your entire presentation. Your conclusion is your last opportunity to leave a lasting impression with the audience. Make the most of these few minutes. It could be a brief summary of your five or fewer main ideas, or a recapitulation of the logic that you established in the body. Many times the conclusion suggests "where we go from here." Others assume an inspirational or philosophical tone, but these are more difficult to handle—depending on your personal style. But no matter which technique you use to conclude your talk, the objective should be to reinforce the theme, and to show one last time its relationship to the information you've chosen to present during the rest of the talk.

Our conclusion: "As you're probably already thinking, it's very easy for us to damage or even destroy those things we don't understand. And maybe first among these are the things we can't see. Because they can't be observed very often, nocturnal birds are the subject of many superstitions and misconceptions—and our difficulty in understanding and appreciating their natural roles is beginning to put them danger. The owls and nighthawks in this forest are good examples of nocturnal birds which need our help. Their habits and adaptations teach us how animals are molded to the environments they live in, and that each one of these animals has a vital function in nature's design—even though we don't always see it. Only if we understand the important roles they play—roles which almost always affect our well-being too—can we appreciate why it's important to preserve them. Their future really does depend on us—a future that all of us can share. Thank you."

Step 7: Prepare the introduction.

The introduction is the last part of the talk you'll develop, even though it's the first part of the talk you'll present. Remember that its purposes are to capture the audience's interest, reveal the theme, and tell how the body will be organized. As we discussed earlier, it's often a good idea to begin with a jolt—a "grabber" which commands attention. There are many techniques which have been used successfully: an interesting but brief story, a rhetorical question, a vivid example of something you're going to talk about, a colorful statement, etc.

> *Our introduction:* "Did you know that nighthawks used to warn people around here when witches were in the vicinity? If the buzz of a nighthawk was heard at twilight, parents got very concerned about their children's well-being until about midnight. Many parents wouldn't let their kids leave the house at such times. And abnormal behavior was to be expected from kids until the danger subsided."

Having attracted our audience's attention, we now need to tell them about our theme and how the talk is going to be organized:

> "Nighthawks and owls are two birds that live in this forest, and they're a part of a special group of creatures called nocturnal animals—animals that become active when other animals, including humans, are just settling in for the evening. But because these birds carry out their lives in the dark, few of us actually get the opportunity to see them, and no doubt that's why we've created so many legends and superstitions about them.

> "In the next few minutes, we're going to talk more about these interesting birds, and their future. We'll explore their adaptations for a nocturnal life; we'll talk about their habits, and we'll see that the very things which used to cause parents to worry so much are really just behaviors that these birds have developed in order to cope with their life in the darkness. We'll see that their habits and special adaptations can show us a lot about how nature is able to mold animals into filling specific roles in the natural community—that is, in nature's design. But we'll also see that these fascinating birds need our help. Their secretive, nocturnal life hides them from us, and this makes it hard for us to know and understand

them the way we understand other animals. Because of this, their future may be in jeopardy.

"Let's talk first about what it's like to live without light, and about the variety of nocturnal birds that live around here."

You've probably noticed several things about our introduction. First, it's designed to create interest, to reveal the theme, and to tell how our presentation will be organized. You may also have noticed that the theme statement is near the end of the introduction. Although this isn't always necessary, it's often easier for the audience to remember the theme if it's the last thought you give them before beginning the body of your talk. Notice also that the final statement of the introduction is really just a transition to the first main idea in the body. Finally, notice that the words "nature's design" are emphasized, as they were in the conclusion we developed in Step 6. This is a simple example of how to tie the introduction and conclusion together by building an identical phrase into both. The phrase adds little in the way of substance, but it helps the audience to feel closure, or pragnänz, when it recognizes that it has heard it a second time.

Step 8: Rearrange the order and tie your talk together.

At this point, we've prepared (1) an outline of the body of our talk, (2) a conclusion, and (3) our introduction. We now must meld these pieces into a logical order, refine the introduction and conclusion so that they connect well, plan any transitions that we haven't yet prepared, and develop the body in more detail—

deciding more precisely what we want to say about the main points in our outline. Chances are by now you already have a pretty good idea of the words you would use, but it's still better to think them out more carefully before you try to present the talk to a real audience. If you don't, you may find that your talk is too long. This often happens when we feel confident and comfortable with a topic—so comfortable that we end up talking about it in excess. It's usually better to think ahead of time about the words you'll use. In this way you'll know right away whether you need to limit your explanations, delete something, or even revise the body to include fewer main ideas.

Many speakers like to write their words out in a complete narrative, pretty much exactly as they plan to say them. Writing the words helps them get a feeling for their talk, and helps them to get excited about the talk and enthusiastic about presenting it. It also helps them to further improve the talk because, by writing out their words, they're forced to think everything through in the same detail with which it will someday be presented to a real audience. The only drawback of writing out your words is that it can tempt you into trying to memorize everything. But as we'll discuss shortly, you should resist this temptation. It almost always hinders more than it helps a talk.

Step 9: Practice your talk.

You're now ready to present your talk—or are you? Up to this point, developing the talk has probably been a silent exercise. You've probably been "saying" the words in your mind, but that isn't the same as saying them aloud. Practice doing this. Some speakers say that talking to themselves in a mirror helps. Others prefer to stand alone in a room. Others like to take a walk while they're practicing. And others like to be doing something altogether different—cooking, driving, etc. Whichever way you prefer, the important thing is that you be able to imagine yourself in front of the audience you'll be speaking to, and that you say the words at the volume you would normally use were the people actually there. Volume and inflection have a curious relationship. What sounds appropriate at a low volume may not sound quite right when the same words are spoken at a louder volume.

Many speakers like to record themselves because listening to the tape helps them identify the parts of the talk that need improvement. Video taping is also valuable if you have access to the equipment. Generally, it's a good idea to try your talk out in person with a group of friends. But you may have to ask them to be critical. Friends usually like to tell us how good we are, not how we can improve. If they can find no fault in your talk, ask them if they have any ideas about how you could make your presentation even better.

Keep looking for ways to improve your talk. Besides making your presentation better, making small changes will also prevent you from becoming bored with your talk. This is especially important after you've given it several times. Obviously, however, you shouldn't change something that doesn't need to be changed. In other words, if it's not broken, don't fix it.

Step 10: If appropriate, choose a title for your talk.

Not all talks need a title. But if your talk will be advertised ahead of time, it's a good idea to have one. Try to make your title attractive but at the same time descriptive of your topic.

Our title: "Wings of the Night"

Adding Visual Aids

At last our talk, "Wings of the Night" is developed. If we were planning to present this talk using slides or other visual aids, we would now (and only now) begin thinking about them. We've developed a thematic talk that will stand by itself, and although adding a visual dimension will probably make it even better, our talk doesn't depend on visual aids. Good talks are like this. If this were a slide talk, for example, we could still present it even if we lost our slides or the projector broke. We'll come back to this idea in the next chapter. For now it's enough to say that if you've developed a talk in which each of the three parts is designed to accomplish its specific purpose, you've probably developed a talk that can hold attention and clearly communicate a theme. There's little else you could ask a talk to do. Judged against these two criteria, a poor talk will usually be a poor talk regardless of the quality or quantity of visual aids you use to present it. The same is usually true for a good talk, too.

To Memorize or Not to Memorize?

Don't be tempted to memorize your entire talk. Writing out your talk is a method to help you tie its three parts together, and to help you to get a better feeling for how you want to present it. And although writing may help you to

Figure 3-5. The final step in preparing a talk is selecting visual aids. Natural Resources Communication Laboratory, University of Idaho. (Photo by Gerry Snyder)

remember things later, trying to memorize every word you've written can hurt your talk in two important ways. First, most people sound unnatural when they're reciting something from memory—they sound memorized, more like they're reading than speaking, memorizing puts you in the dangerous position of having to remember everything when you're speaking. If somewhere in the talk you forget what the next words are "supposed" to be, you'll essentially have forgotten the remainder of the talk. This is because we tend to memorize words sequentially. When we can't remember the next words in the sequence, we can't remember what follows them either. Many speakers are unable to recover from these "mental blocks," as we sometimes call them, and both they and their audiences suffer.

If you feel you need to memorize something, memorize the following:

- The very first thing you'll say when you greet your audience
- The outline of the body
- The first sentence of your introduction
- Your theme statement in the introduction
- Every transition
- The first sentence of your conclusion
- Your theme statement in the conclusion
- The last sentence of the conclusion

With these parts of your talk firmly in memory, you'll never be far from something you can remember, even if you momentarily forget what comes next. If you're extremely worried about remembering parts of your talk, it probably wouldn't be too distracting to have a note card containing your theme and main headings. But keep it tucked away in a pocket, and use it only in an emergency. Above all, don't hold it in your hand in full view of the audience. Keep it out of sight unless you really need to refer to it.

A Word About Stage Fright

Stage fright is normal, and fear of speaking in front of strangers is something we all share. Even the most experienced speakers get sweaty palms and a nervous stomach before giving a talk. But their experience has taught them an important lesson: stage fright is a friend, not an enemy. Although fear never feels good, research has shown that moderate fear (such as stage fright) actually helps us perform. This kind of "arousal," as psychologists call it, makes us more alert, more focused and less likely to forget— even though we feel just the opposite. High levels of arousal (such as the kind William Tell must have felt aiming his crossbow at the apple on his son's head!) can impair our ability to perform. But stage fright is a much lower form of arousal. It can enhance our ability to think and speak, and experienced speakers take advantage of it. Good speakers often claim that their worst talks were the ones they were not nervous about giving. Remember this the next time you feel ready to succumb to the clutches of stage fright. It may not make your stomach feel any better, but it may well help your attitude.

What to Do If You Forget What to Say

One of the biggest causes of stage fright is the haunting thought that you're going to forget what to say when you're in front of the audience. If you've memorized your talk, you've greatly increased the likelihood that this will happen to you. But even if you're not reciting your talk from memory, you may momentarily lose your train of thought. Fortunately there are a few easy things you can do to recover. If you're using visual aids, you can simply advance to the next one to jog your memory. And if that doesn't work, try the next one, and so on. If you're not using visual aids, don't panic. Simply pause and think about your outline. If you

still can't recall where you are, go to the next transition and it will take you to the next main idea. Even though you may be disappointed that you forgot to say something you had planned to say, your audience may not even realize it. Besides, if what you forgot was really that important, you'll probably remember it later and still be able to "work it in."

In the worst scenario, you may have a complete lapse of memory. If this happens, remember one thing: the people in your audience are your friends; they want you to succeed. Most of them have had to speak in front of a group at one time or another, and they can empathize with you. To some extent, they feel your pain, and they're pulling for you. Knowing this, you should say simply that you've momentarily lost your train of thought. If you have a note card containing your theme and main headings, take it from your pocket and look at it, determine where you are, and continue. Some speakers like to break the nervous tension by adding something humorous—for example, by making a joke about themselves and their inability since childhood to remember things, or by asking a person in the front row of the audience if he/she remembers what is supposed to come next in the talk. Whatever fits your personal style is what you should do. At the very least, you can do what was recommended above—just continue your talk at the next transition. Later, if you remember whatever it was you had forgotten earlier, you can always say: "Oh, now I remember what I forgot earlier. It was … " But if it is too late to work it in, or if it really wasn't that critical to the talk, let it go. Maybe you'll remember it the next time you give the talk. And if you discover over time that you keep forgetting the same piece of information, you should consider deleting it from your talk altogether. Chances are, if you keep forgetting it, it's not that important to the theme you're trying to get across to your audience.

Tips for Better Speaking

Presenting a good talk requires, first and foremost, good planning and intelligent design of the introduction, body and conclusion. Having accomplished this, however, there are a number of "mechanics" which can help make your presentation even better. Some of these mechanics are things you can do with your body, eyes and face; others are communication strategies or techniques that you can build into your presentation. Following are six ideas you should consider.

1. Stand in front of the room and face your audience when you're speaking. Even when you're using a slide projector it's better to stand in front. Sometimes the remote control cord won't reach to the front of the room and you're forced to present from the back. If that's the case, make an effort to get a remote control extension cord for your projector. In Chapter 4 you'll see how easy it is to make such an extension cord yourself.

2. Look at your audience while you're speaking. In most cultures, eye contact is basic to good communication and the best speakers consciously use it to make what they're saying seem more personal to their audiences. Some speakers pick out three or four people in different places in the audience and concentrate on having eye contact with them. Even better, however, is to train yourself to look all around your audience, and to alternate momentary glances at different people throughout your presentation. A powerful

technique is to occasionally give prolonged eye contact to an individual in your audience. This technique works especially well when you want to emphasize something, but it can be used just about any time in a presentation. Ordinarily, speakers have only momentary eye contact with audience members. So when you extend your eye contact (to say two or three seconds) with any one individual, it's as though you're talking, at that particular moment, to just him or her. To the person you're looking at, and to others nearby, it seems that you're having a personal conversation. Because of the prolonged eye contact, what you're saying seems more important, more sincere, and more personal. If you make frequent use of this simple technique, you may find that your audiences pay better attention to what you're saying.

3. Practice smiling. As we saw in Chapter 1, smiling tells your audience that you're having a good time—that you like being there with them. Many speakers feel so nervous that they have a hard time smiling. And speakers trained in the sciences

Figure 3-6. Constant eye contact creates a personal atmosphere. Mount St. Helens National Volcanic Monument. (Photo by Sam Ham)

may have actually been trained not to smile when they're speaking because any show of emotion detracts from the "scientist's" image of being objective and rational. This may be reasonable advice when you're giving a technical presentation to a group of other scientists, but it's certainly not the way you should present yourself to other audiences. If your goal is to make your message seem important and interesting to your audience, smiling will help you. It will make you seem friendly and approachable. An expressionless face will make you seem formal and less approachable. Like any facial expression, smiling can be overdone. Use a variety of facial expressions that are appropriate to the mood you're trying to establish.

4. Use active verbs. If you were trained in the sciences you probably were told to use passive verb forms. This was because it allowed you to make the thing you were describing (rather than you) the subject of the sentence. For example, in science we're taught to say "The seedling was planted"—rather than "I planted the seedling." Fortunately, the latter form is becoming more accepted in technical communication today, but still, many of us can't break the habit of using passive verbs. This is unfortunate because active verbs are generally more interesting to people than passive ones. Consciously practice using active verbs. Try to catch yourself slipping into the old fashioned passive mode, and change those verbs to their active form. Even if you don't appreciate the difference, your audiences will.

5. Make use of **foreshadowing**. Foreshadowing is simply a way to prepare your audience for something that's going to come later in your presentation. It could be a subtle hint about a topic you're going to discuss, or it may simply be an advance notice of something you're going to talk about in a later part of your presentation. For example, after telling the audience about a certain thing, you might say something like, "But in a few minutes I'm going to tell you about an interesting exception to this." The following use of foreshadowing might be incorporated in our talk on nocturnal birds:

> "One of the interesting things about owls is that they get most of their food through surprise attack. I'll tell you exactly how they do this when we talk about the ways they've adapted themselves for nocturnal living."

Foreshadowing gives your audience something to do besides listen. Done well, a foreshadow causes the audience to think, anticipate and therefore, pay even closer attention to what you're saying— and to what you're going to say. It actively involves the audience in your talk by bringing them into the thinking process with you, and by alerting them to watch for ideas you've not yet presented.

6. Incorporate **mystery** into your talk. Using mystery is similar to foreshadowing in that it engages your audience, but it does it by giving them a problem to solve, or a riddle to figure out. For example, the way we foreshadowed the owl's ability to get its food through "surprise attack" could be changed slightly to make use of mystery:

> "One of the interesting things about owls is that they get most of their food through surprise attack. But can you guess how?

Their bodies and wings are so big that you'd think the animals they're hunting would be able to hear them in time to escape, wouldn't you? Ah, but this is just one of the many ways owls have adapted to their life in the dark. As we talk about these adaptations, see if you can figure out which one gives them this important ability."

Another way to use mystery has already been suggested. In your introduction, you might begin a story or anecdote related to the theme of your talk, and then tell the audience that you'll reveal later how the story ends (usually in the conclusion of your talk). Regardless of how you use it, mystery will motivate your audience to pay attention. Of course, what you say between the time you introduce the mystery and the time you resolve it has to be interesting enough that your audience

is willing to wait for the answer. And remember that a good mystery creates high expectations in the audience about the ending. Make sure the ending justifies the expectations you've created.

"By the way, owls don't make a lot of noise when they fly. Even though their wings are large, their feathers have soft edges and are hooked together in a way that softens the sound of the air passing through them. Consequently, owls don't make the loud 'whooshing' sound that other large birds make when they fly."

Glossary terms: 2-3-1 Rule, body, closure, conclusion, foreshadowing, introduction, mystery, pragnänz, speech, style, talk, transition.

Talks Afloat—Mobile Interpretive Programs for Tour Boat Passengers in Misty Fiords National Monument

Jim Case, Wilderness Ranger
Misty Fiords National Monument,
Tongass National Forest, Alaska

In 1991, in an effort to improve visitor services at Misty Fiords National Monument, a new interpretive program began. The decision was made to station two wilderness rangers in a temporary camp at the mouth of one of the more frequently visited fiords in the central part of Misty. That's when Rudyerd Bay became a summer home for me and John Wooton. Beginning in May, our main duty each day was to paddle out to different tour vessels as they entered the Bay. Once alongside the vessel, we'd board and begin a series of informal talks about the magnificent land and seascape the passengers were seeing. We didn't know it at the time, but we were beginning a new tradition of interpretation.

Our day begins at 5:00 a.m. when John and I, clad in Forest Service uniforms, paddle the kayaks from our camp in the forest, out into the mouth of Rudyerd Bay. Our tools include a map of Misty Fiords National Monument, a portable VHF radio, a pair of binoculars, and a copy of the latest

color map of the Tongass Land Management Plan. From our kayaks we see the tour vessel Spirit of Alaska as it rounds Point Eva, headed our way; we've been in radio contact with them since 4:15 a.m., confirming our rendezvous. The one-hundred-and-forty-seven foot vessel idles as we paddle up to the fantail. Two crewmen from the ship come aft to help with our bowlines as we climb out of the kayaks. We climb aboard and haul the kayaks onto the fantail, securing them for the trip into Rudyerd Bay.

When the passengers emerge, we are at the head of Rudyerd Bay and they are greeted by the sight of a two-thousand foot waterfall, cascading down a slender notch in the nearly vertical granite cliff. The early risers scan the sedge grass meadows with binoculars, hopeful of brown bear sightings. A member of the crew hands me a cordless microphone as the sleepy passengers gather about on the outside foredeck. For the next hour and a half, as we cruise slowly back out of the bay,

John and I use the microphone and the changing scenery to relate some of the stories of this part of America's magnificent Wilderness Preservation System.

Misty Wilderness Ranger program began in 1989 when, acting as the Resource Assistant, I created that seasonal position. The first two rangers were women and they began backcountry patrols early that summer. The main impetus of their work involved traveling the coastline of Misty in kayaks, inventorying accessible campsite areas, recording wildlife data, looking for archaeological sites and making informal contact with visitors they encountered along the way. The two rangers camped along the way for ten days at a time, with four days off at the end of each hitch. Kayaks were selected as a mode of transport because they're practical and comply with local Forest Service policy of non-motorized use in the Monument. (Not even chainsaws are allowed. Cabin and trail maintenance in Misty are accomplished with use of hand tools, such as the old two-person crosscut saw.) Since 1990, four different rangers have done seasonal work in Misty.

Over the winter of 1990-91, three tour companies signed contracts with the Forest Service, requesting us to present interpretive talks on their vessels in the Rudyerd Bay area. All three companies have small vessels (each carrying about ninety people). In addition, all have their own naturalists aboard, specialize in getting passengers to remote locations in Southeast Alaska, and sail as close to the shoreline as possible to enhance wildlife viewing. We wilderness rangers augment these tour programs by adding some "local flavor" and Forest Service recreation information to the passengers' experience. Depending on the tour vessel, we may describe the local geology, wildlife, ecology, marine biology, history, or recreational opportunities in the area. Our programs were well received by the tour companies and by the public. We improved on our communications skills and gained new knowledge through our in-house training and by listening to a variety of professional "ships' naturalists." We keep learning and we keep getting better.

This summer, we made contact with more than 2500 tour boat passengers and seventy-five kayakers in Rudyerd Bay. A few times we helped the campers by providing a place to dry their gear and giving them specific information about trails, campsites and safety; on a couple of occasions, we gave campers spare food when their pickup boat canceled due to weather. When we're not giving talks or helping campers, we sometimes assist the Alaska Fish and Wildlife Division in field work, help out our trail crews, give assistance to the archaeologists working in the area, or collect information for trail inventories and daily weather reports.

A final aspect of our interpretive work involves the staff of the Tongass National Forest. We made an offer to any U.S. Forest Service employee across all disciplines of forest management to come stay with us so that we could share information. Two volunteers stayed with us in camp and two members of the Cultural Resources staff came out. These four people all boarded the vessels with us and gave their particular stories to the passengers; we enjoyed having the company and the passengers were delighted with the special insights they could provide.

We're proud of our interpretive program and grateful we were able to be part of a new tradition. Outside of our time and the handouts we give to passengers, the cost is relatively low. All it takes is a spirit of cooperation among the tour companies and the Forest Service, and of course, a belief in the inherent value of timely and tasteful interpretation.

References

Grater, Russell K. 1976. *The Interpreter's Handbook: Methods, Skills and Techniques.* Globe, Arizona, USA: Southwest Parks and Monuments Association.

Tilden, Freeman. 1977. *Interpreting Our Heritage* (2nd ed.). Chapel Hill, North Carolina, USA: University of North Carolina Press.

Additional Reading

In English:

Boulanger, F. David and John P. Smith. 1973. *Educational Principles and Techniques for Interpreters.* Portland, Oregon, USA: USDA Forest Service, Pacific Northwest Forest and Range Experiment Station, General Technical Report PNW-9.

Fazio, James R. and Douglas L. Gilbert. 1986. *Public Relations and Communications for Natural Resource Managers.* Dubuque, Iowa, USA: Kendall-Hunt.

Ham, Sam H. 1983. Cognitive Psychology and Interpretation: Synthesis and Application. *Journal of Interpretation* 8(1):11-27.

Hubbard, Douglass and William W. Dunmire. 1968. *Campfire Programs: A Guide for the Leaders of Campfires in the National Parks.* Washington, D.C., USA: U.S. National Park Service, Visitor Services Training Series.

Krumbein, W.J., Jr. and L. Leyva. 1977. *The Interpreter's Guide*. Sacramento, California, USA: California Dept. of Parks and Recreation.

Lewis, William J. 1980. *Interpreting for Park Visitors*. Philadelphia, Pennsylvania, USA: Eastern National Park and Monument Association, Eastern Acorn Press.

Regnier, Kathleen, Michael Gross and Ron Zimmerman. 1992. *The Interpreter's Guidebook: Techniques for Programs and Presentations*. Stevens Point, Wisconsin, USA: UW-SP Foundation Press, Inc.

Risk, Paul H. 1982. The Interpretive Talk. Chapter 9 in Sharpe, G.W. (ed.), *Interpreting the Environment*. New York, New York, USA: John Wiley & Sons.

Thompson, David D. Jr.. 1968. *Talks: A Public Speaking Guide for National Park Service Employees*. Washington, D.C., USA: U.S. National Park Service, Visitor Services Training Series.

U.S. Forest Service. No date. Campfire Program Sense. *Interpretive Services Guideline Series*. Washington, D.C., USA: U.S. Department of Agriculture, Forest Service.

In Spanish:

Ham, Sam H. 1992. *Interpretación Ambiental: Una Guía Práctica para Gente con Grandes Ideas y Presupuestos Pequeños*. Golden, Colorado, USA: North American Press/Fulcrum Publishing.

Moore, Alan, Bill Wendt, Louis Penna e Isabel Castillo de Ramos. 1989. *Manual para La Capacitación del Personal de Areas Protegidas* (Modulo C: Interpretación y Educación Ambiental, Apunte 4a). Washington, D.C., USA: Servicio de Parques Nacionales, Oficina de Asuntos Internacionales.

Morales, Jorge. 1987. *Manual para la Interpretación en Espacios Naturales Protegidos*. Anexo 3 del Taller Internacional sobre Interpretación Ambiental en Areas Silvestres Protegidas. Santiago, Chile: Oficina Regional de la FAO para América Latina y el Caribe, 7-12 de diciembre de 1988.

CHAPTER FOUR

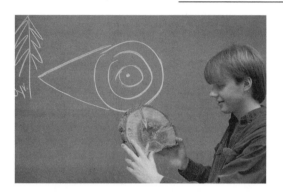

TIPS ON USING VISUAL AIDS

There are many kinds of **visual aids**. Some of the more common ones are **slides**, **overhead transparencies**, **props**, **flip charts**, **chalkboards**, and **cloth boards**. Depending on the kinds of presentations you give most often, some of these may be more useful to you than others. The kind of visual aids you use most probably has a lot to do with their availability and the kinds of situations you work in. The country or region in which you work, and the tastes and customs of your audiences are also important. Therefore, we won't be advocating the choice of any of these media over others, nor will we discuss which are "better." This is a very subjective thing, and usually depends more on situations and individual speakers than on anything else.

What does seem clear, however, is that the effectiveness of any visual aid has a lot to do with the skill of the person using it. For this reason, we'll be focusing on how to use different visual aids in order to make your presentations clearer, more understandable and more entertaining to your audiences. First we'll discuss the role of visual aids in interpretation, and then we'll turn our attention to a few basic guidelines for using them effectively. Useful English-language discussions of the advantages and disadvantages of different visual aids can be found in Bajimaya and Fazio (1989), Bunch (1982), and Bunnell and Mock (1990). In Spanish, Enríquez (1987), Ham and Enríquez (1987), Moore et al. (1989), Morales (1987), and Muñoz and Peña (1990) are recommended.

The Role of Visual Aids in Interpretation

In Chapter 3 we saw how to develop a thematic talk. In developing a talk, good communicators often take into account the kind of visual aids they're planning to use—but it's not their main concern, that is, not yet. Their most important concern is to first develop a good talk. Good talks, as we saw in Chapter 3, are those that can stand alone without visual aids.

Having accomplished this important task, we would then turn our attention to visual aids. We'd ask ourselves: "Now that I've developed a talk that's good enough to present without visual aids, would adding a visual dimension make it even better?" If the answer is yes, we'd then decide what kind(s) of visual aids to use. In short, this is the role of visual aids. As the word "aids" implies, they're "helpers." The best communicators know that it's better to first develop a talk and then to select visual aids to help illustrate their words, than it is to develop the visual aids first and then start searching for words to illustrate them. As Grater (1976) advised: "Develop a talk that can be illustrated; not illustrations that are looking for a talk."

Some presentations can't incorporate visual aids. For example, we might have to prepare a talk on a moment's notice or the electricity may not work to run a slide projector. Furthermore, some presentations involve ideas that are difficult or even impossible to illustrate visually (e.g., talks which pose highly subjective or philosophical questions). Talks which don't involve the use of visual aids are called **nonillustrated talks**. Nonillustrated talks can be just as effective as **illustrated talks**, even though they sometimes require a little more skill on the part of the speaker. But planned well, words alone can paint vivid pictures in our minds because they capitalize on the power of an audience's imagination. For this reason, you shouldn't necessarily assume that

every talk you give has to involve visual aids; but you should also remember that good visual aids do enhance most presentations.

So when should you decide to use visual aids in a talk? By now, the answer is probably obvious: Use visual aids when they'll make your presentation even better—when they'll make the information you present clearer, more interesting and easier to comprehend. But don't use them if the visual aids, themselves, will need a lot of explanation—that is, if they're too complex, or not clearly related to your commentary. You'll only add to the amount of work your audience has to do, and increase the likelihood that it will switch attention.

Think of visual aids as helpers that come and go, as needed, throughout your presentation. When one is needed, you bring it into your talk at the precise moment it's required. And when it ceases to help illustrate what you're saying, you take it away or replace it with a new one that helps to illustrate your next point.

How Does the Brain Utilize a Visual Aid?

Figure 4-1 presents a simplified view of what happens when a person listening to a talk is suddenly presented a visual aid. Notice that what the person is doing is listening. That's the brain's primary activity at the time. Listening means hearing the words that are being spoken (or played back on a tape), thinking about them, and trying to keep the information straight in our heads. Our focus on listening will not change, even when the speaker uses a visual aid.

At the moment the visual aid is presented, our natural tendency is to look at

In an Illustrated Talk, Listening Comes First

Figure 4-1. How humans respond to visual aids during a talk. (Drawings by Jeff Egan)

it, but this doesn't mean that we stop listening. On the contrary, the visual aid may even intensify our desire to hear the speaker's words. This is because we'll automatically try to relate what we're seeing with the words we're hearing. Put a different way, when you show a visual aid during a talk, the people in your audience will quite naturally try to relate it to what you're saying—whether or not you instruct them to do so. That's why you usually don't have to **reference** your visual aids—for example, by saying things like "As this slide shows … ," or "This is a picture of a pine tree … ," or "This flip chart has a list of … ," etc. If you're talking about a pine tree as you show a slide of a tree, you may rest assured that most people in your audience will assume it's a

pine tree, even if it's not. If you begin talking about something as you turn to a list on a flip chart, you can be certain that people in your audience will assume that the list pertains to the things you're talking about, even if it doesn't.

Using visual aids effectively is easier when you understand this tendency in your audiences—they'll always try to relate what you show them to what you're telling them at the time. As long as the visual aid is being shown to them, they will try to make connections between it and your commentary.

But what happens when the visual aid stops giving the people in your audience new information, or when they can no longer see the connection between it and your words? Let's say, for example, that you're presenting a slide talk on pesticide danger. At a certain point in the talk, you're telling how to use a spray can safely, and at the same time you're showing a slide of a spray can. Next you begin telling about safety equipment such as gloves, masks, and boots. But, unfortunately, since you don't have any slides of this equipment, you simply leave the slide of the spray can on the screen. What happens?

One possibility is that some people, perhaps those especially unknowledgeable about such things, might try to connect the slide of the spray-can to your commentary on safety equipment. Clearly, this would only confuse them. Another (and perhaps more likely) result, is that once the people conclude that there's no relationship between the slide and your words, they'll begin to analyze the slide, to notice fine details on the can, the color of the sky, the bird on a distant tree, and other features in the picture that have little to do with your commentary on safety equipment. As long as the visual aid was presenting information that was consistent with your commentary, your audience could take in the words and the visual aid simultaneously, more or less as a unit. But when they became unrelated and inconsistent with one another, people in the audience had to work a lot harder. Put in such a position, almost any audience (and especially a noncaptive audience) will pay more attention to the slide, and eventually tune out your commentary—it simply can't compete with a visual. And although our example has pertained to the use of slides, the same thing can be expected when you're using any kind of visual aid.

Although the mental process of connecting words and visual aids is actually a little more complex, this description of it helps us to see how to use visual aids more strategically in our presentations. And it leads us to four basic guidelines that apply to our use of all visual aids:

1. *Simplicity, Clarity, and Legibility:* A visual aid can't help you communicate if it's too complex, unclear or unreadable. Try to include only as much information as you need to illustrate the point you're making. As a general rule, it's usually better to use a greater number of simple visual aids than it is to use a fewer number of more complex ones. And, of course, drawings, illustrations and written words in a visual aid should be legible to everyone in the audience, even those seated farthest away. Although there are many ideas to consider in designing a visual aid, you can use the chart in Figure 4-2 as a general guide for determining the sizes of letters that need to be viewed from different distances.

2. *Consistency and Support:* Make sure that the information in the visual aid corresponds to what your words are saying. That is, make sure it's consistent with and supportive of your commentary. When it's not, take it away or replace it with a new one that is consistent. Remember, you don't have to have a visual aid for everything you're saying. Even with slides, it's possible to darken the screen (either by turning off the projector or by using a "black" or colored acetate slide), thereby freeing your audience from having to look at a slide that no longer supports what you're saying. (How to prepare black and colored acetate slides is explained later in this chapter.)

3. *Duration:* A visual aid should be shown only for as long as it provides new and relevant information with respect to your commentary. As long as your visual

Words in a Visual Aid Must Be Readable		
VIEWING DISTANCES AND MINIMUM HEIGHTS OF LETTERS		
Viewing Distance	**Main Headings**	**Subordinate Text**
5 m (16 ft.)	2.5 cm (1 in.)	1.25 cm (0.5 in.)
10 m (32 ft.)	5.0 cm (2 in.)	2.5 cm (1 in.)
15 m (48 ft.)	7.5 cm (3 in.)	5.0 cm (2 in.)

Notes: The heights shown are the minimum sizes of letters as they should appear on the viewing surface (such as a flip chart sheet, chalkboard, projection screen or some other surface). In the case of projected images such as slides and overhead transparencies, the figures refer to the size of the letters once they've been projected onto the screen. Don't use this chart if you're making letters for an exhibit or sign. A different set of rules apply (see Figure 8-17). (Sources: Hooper 1987 and Sanchez 1990.)

Figure 4-2. A guide to minimum letter height for visual aids in oral presentations.

aid does this, you can continue to show it. But once the visual aid stops providing new and relevant information, you should remove it or replace it with one that does. Much has been written about how long a given visual aid should be shown to an audience. In the case of slides, for example, many authors have claimed that this many seconds or that many seconds is the absolute maximum, and some have even given a minimum time that they should be shown. We will not concern ourselves with such "rules" here, simply because there's no clear evidence to support them. At best, they reflect a particular author's personal style or preference, or what has proven to work best for him or her. But the fact is that no research suggests that a given time interval is best for all situations. Highly sophisticated subliminal cues (measured in microseconds of dura ful ways. And extended viewing of a single slide (even two or three minutes or longer) can hold an audience's attention in some situations. There's great variation in how long a visual aid can or should be shown, and still do its job. Be wary of rules about such things; they rarely tell the whole story. The best guideline is to show a visual aid only as long as it continues to provide information relevant to your commentary.

4. *Referencing:* **Referencing** means calling unnecessary attention to a visual aid through statements such as "Here we have a ... ," or "This is a ... ," etc. Try not to reference a visual aid unless it's really necessary or helpful in your presentation. Since your audience instinctively tries to relate each visual aid with your commentary, you usually won't have to call attention to it. Sometimes, however, referencing actually helps to reference a visual aid, such as when you need to point out a small detail that might otherwise go unnoticed, or when you're showing more than one visual aid and wish to call your audience's attention to a particular one, or

when you want your audience to compare one thing to something else and need to point both out. But outside of such circumstances, it's probably best to avoid referencing your visual aids. Although no known research has been done on this topic, many experts agree that frequent referencing becomes repetitive and even annoying to an audience.

These **four guidelines** pertain to all visual aids. As guidelines, they represent an approach to using visual aids. But they're not necessarily hard fast rules. Although guidelines give us general direction and a point of view, there may be times when you'll want to "violate" one or more of them. If doing so would make your use of the visual aid more effective, then that's exactly what you should do. Ordinarily, however, following these guidelines is a good idea.

Generally, it's good practice to use different kinds of graphics in a presentation (e.g., don't show only bar graphs, or only line graphs, or only pie charts, etc. if it's not necessary), but try to adopt a consistent design for each kind. Unless varying part of a design is necessary to emphasize something or to highlight a key difference, you'll usually want to use the same basic colors and type styles for each type of graphic (e.g., blue and yellow pie charts, red and black line graphs, etc.). Don't use more than two or three colors or type styles in any one graphic.

Remember, if you're going to photograph the artwork (e.g., for a slide or exhibit illustration), you'll need to leave space around the border to make sure your picture doesn't show the edges of the paper. (Most cameras photograph slightly more than you see through the viewfinder. If your artwork is too close to the edge of the paper, your picture may show

the paper's edge and the table or easel it was photographed on.)

Using Visual Aids in a Talk

Many kinds of visual aids are available to interpreters, and we're going to look in more detail at six of them: slides, overhead transparencies, props, flip charts, chalkboards, and cloth boards. These were selected because of their wide availability and relatively low cost, and because in the Western Hemisphere they're among the most common visual aids used by speakers in natural resource and agricultural fields. In addition, the techniques for using them pertain to a number of other media as well. If you're using a visual aid that isn't included here, look carefully at the guidelines for those you think are most similar to it. Chances are, you'll see a lot of ways that those procedures can be applied to the visual aid you're interested in using.

Slides

Slides are one of the most common visual aids used in natural resource fields today, and much is known about how to utilize them effectively. Although they lack the movement and dynamism of video or motion pictures, they offer two very important advantages to environmental interpreters: portability and large image size. Since you can take slide projectors just about anywhere, delivering stimulating presentations to all kinds of audiences is possible. Special batteries and portable generators allow the use of slide projectors even in remote areas where electrical current is unavailable. With slide projectors, it's easy to project larger images than are normally possible with

Designing Effective Visual Aids

Although experts say that visual aids can increase our comprehension and retention of information by as much as 50 to 200 percent (Bunnell and Mock 1990), this is true only when the visual aids are well designed. Poorly designed or overly complex visual aids are more likely to confuse than clarify, and often can reduce comprehension. Following are a few simple guidelines for designing effective visual aids. Although there may be exceptions, following these guidelines will almost always improve your ability to communicate visually. English-language readers interested in more advanced techniques should consult Hooper (1987), Meilach (1990), Bunnell and Mock (1990), and Eastman-Kodak (1982). Good Spanish-language references are Muñoz and Fonseca (1990), Muñoz and Peña (1990), and Pino (1989).

1. Keep each visual simple both in design and in the amount of information it presents. Generally, each visual aid should present only one thought or main idea related to your commentary. If the audience can't easily see the relationship within one or two seconds, the graphic is probably too complex.

Bad   Better

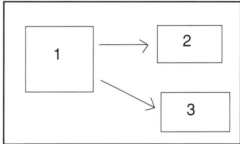

2. Limit line graphs to three or fewer curves, tables to five or fewer columns and rows, and lists to six or fewer lines of text.

Bad   Better

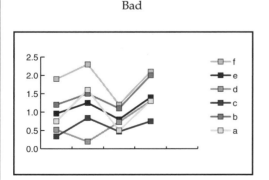
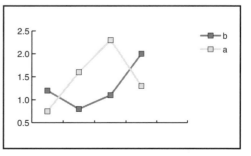

3. Be conservative with type styles and lettering. Avoid fancy, decorative type styles; block style is almost always more readable. As much as possible, arrange lettering horizontally so that people can read left to right. Vertical lettering is hard to read unless the reader can turn or reposition the surface it's printed on. This is relatively easy with a piece of paper (such as a brochure), but not so if the words are printed on a flip chart, chalkboard, exhibit, or in a projected image such as a slide or overhead transparency. Except for titles and one or two-word labels, avoid using all capital letters.

Bad   Better

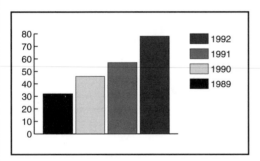

4. Use labels instead of legends and keys.

Bad   Better

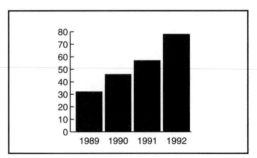

5. Present images that your audience can relate to. For non-technical audiences, use two-dimensional rather than three-dimensional graphics. (Since most people aren't accustomed to looking at three-dimensional bar graphs, they might spend more time trying to understand the graphic than listening to your commentary.)

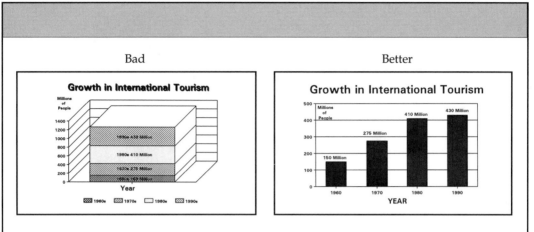

6. Break complex information (like graphs, charts and tables) into parts, using a series of simple visuals rather than a single, complicated one.

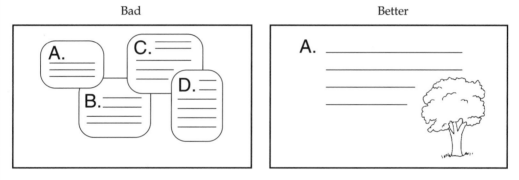

7. Balance the design. Don't crowd too much into any one part of the visual, and be sure to put plenty of space between things.

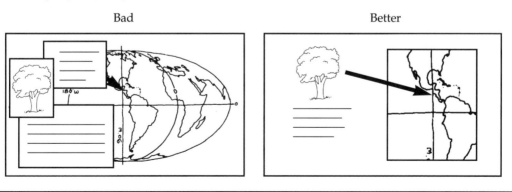

Figure 4-3. Some guidelines for designing better visual aids.

video and motion picture projection equipment. For most audiences, the large image, itself, has entertainment value; and for some audiences, slide presentations may still be a novelty. For example, extension specialists in Central America believe that large-format slide presentations have great potential in their work, mainly because many rural audiences rarely get to see projected slides, even though they're often quite familiar with television and radio (Ham 1990). In addition, slides have the advantage of being more easily changed, rearranged and replaced than videos and motion pictures.

Kodak Slide Projectors

Although there are many brands of slide projectors, those made by Kodak are best for most situations. They're far more durable than most other brands, and because of their superior cooling systems they're especially reliable in warm climates. Kodak projectors are easy to use, even by someone completely new to slide projectors. In addition, they're designed for easy maintenance (such as changing bulbs, cleaning lenses, etc.), and for quick minor repair (for example, when a slide jams in the projector or the carousel won't advance). Kodak projectors are found all over the world. Not only is it easy to find stores which sell them, but useful accessories (such as carousels, bulbs, remote controls, remote control extensions, lenses and lapse dissolve units) are also easy to order. Most important, finding maintenance and spare parts for Kodak projectors is relatively easy in most large cities in the Western Hemisphere and Europe. No other brand of slide projector offers these advantages, despite what eager salespeople may tell you.

Figure 4-4. Common Kodak slide projectors. From left to right: Ektagraphic, Ektagraphic-III and Carousel. (Photo by Gerry Snyder)

There are two main kinds of Kodak slide projectors, the Ektagraphic and the Carousel. Both kinds come in many different models. Of the two, the Carousel is less expensive though slightly less durable. It's designed primarily for home uses. Ektagraphic projectors, on the other hand, cost more but they can stand much heavier use. Either kind is recommended over a non-Kodak brand, but if you have the extra money to spend on an Ektagraphic, the added durability may well be worth it. A comprehensive comparison of different models of Ektagraphic and Carousel projectors can be found in an annual publication called Kodak Sourcebook (Kodak Publication No. S-74) which is available at most audiovisual stores.

In the Ektagraphic line, Ektagraphic-III models contain a number of useful features that the conventional Ektagraphics don't have. Among other things, these include access to the lamp and lenses from the rear of the projector rather than the bottom, and a manual "select" button allowing free turning of the tray without electricity. In mid-1992, Kodak released a new line of projectors called "Ektapro."

According to Kodak, the first two Ektapro models represent the most significant advances in slide presentation technology in twenty-five years, yet they're as easy to use as the more conventional Ektagraphic and Carousel models. Because they're controlled by microprocessors, Ektapro projectors are more precise and more dependable than earlier models. They also can be connected directly to computers, and thereby easily integrated into computer-aided multimedia presentations.

Four Myths About Using Slides in a Talk

Much has been written about using slides in a talk, and lists of good and bad techniques abound. Although most of the advice contained in these lists is quite useful, some "myths" about slide presentations have been created. Over the years, some of these myths have been repeated by so many of us that they've now become unquestioned "truths," even though there's little evidence to support them. In most cases, the advice they offer isn't necessarily wrong; it simply applies to very limited circumstances or to a very specific situation. The problem is that some of these myths have now come to be accepted as standard procedures. Four of the most common myths are shown in Figure 4-5. Be suspicious of such "rules" and lists of "Do's and Don'ts." As we've repeatedly seen, communication is rarely so simple.

Following are some guidelines for using slides in a talk. Although many more advanced techniques are possible, any speaker who pays attention to these guidelines will be able to present smoother, more interesting slide presentations. There are many excellent references on presenting slide talks, and readers

interested in additional information should consult them. The most complete technical reference in English is Jon Hooper's (1987) *Effective Slide Presentations* produced for the California Department of Forestry and Fire Protection. Podracky (1983), Bishop (1984), Stecker (1987), Lewis (1980), Grater (1976), and Regnier et al. (1992) are also valuable references. Some good Spanish-language sources are Muñoz and Peña (1990), Moore et al. (1989) and Morales (1987).

Guidelines for Using Slides

1. Be sure to have the things you'll need in order to present your talk, and to solve any problems that might arise with your equipment. At a minimum, you might consider:

- A slide projector with lens (or two projectors if you're going to use lapse dissolve)

- If you have one, carry an extra projector in case one breaks

- A screen or something which can be used as a screen (white sheet, white board, etc.)

- Your carousel (with slides already cleaned, in the correct sequence and oriented properly in the tray)

- Electrical extension cord (the longer the better) or a charged battery or generator if local electricity is unavailable

- Electrical adaptor for the wall outlet (3-pronged type)

- An extra projector bulb

- A pointer if one will be needed

Beware of Four Myths About Using Slides

Myth 1: *Never show a vertical slide.* Some authors claim that alternating horizontal and vertical slides is distracting to an audience, but there's no evidence to support this claim. A better rule would be to show the slide which best illustrates the idea you're talking about (regardless of whether it's horizontal or vertical on the screen). If you have only a vertical slide which illustrates something well, it's better to use the vertical slide than to substitute a horizontal one which doesn't really illustrate what you're talking about. If, however, you have a horizontal slide which illustrates the idea just as well as a vertical one, it's probably better to use the horizontal one. In fact, you'll find that it's possible with most screens to get a larger image size if you keep all of your slides horizontal. This is because most screens aren't square, but rectangular in shape. Therefore, if you adjust the projector for the largest possible horizontal image, you'll find that your vertical slides are chopped off at the top and bottom. To get both horizontal and vertical slides to fit on a rectangular screen, you'll have to reduce the size of the image. If you use a lot of vertical slides, it's a good idea to make or buy a square format screen so that you can project larger images.

Myth 2: *Never show any slide unless it's of the highest photographic quality.* If all speakers followed this advice, they'd present few slide talks. Most of us aren't professional photographers, and we have to rely on less-than-perfect photographs for our slide talks. A better rule might be to use the highest quality slides you have which illustrate the ideas you want to illustrate, and make plans to replace mediocre slides with better ones as soon as possible. Clearly, if a mediocre slide illustrates an idea better than some other slide, we'd be better off using the mediocre slide regardless of how pleasing the other one was. Remember, the purpose of the slide is to illustrate our words, not to demand its own attention. Usually, it's the combination of our words and the slide that communicates to the audience, not the slide alone. Of course, we don't want to use slides of such poor quality that they fail to illustrate anything, but at the same time, we don't want to delay presenting the talk simply because every slide isn't a perfect photograph.

Myth 3: *Never show a slide for more than a certain period of time.* As discussed earlier, a better rule would be to show a slide only as long as it continues to illustrate what you're saying. If you have a lot to say and you sense that the slide is being projected too long, try showing different views or different angles of the scene or object. As Risk (1982) and Kenny and Schmitt (1981) suggested, this will keep your presentation "moving."

Myth 4: *Never reference a slide.* Although it's generally good technique to avoid slide referencing, there are times when referring to something on the screen is necessary. A better rule would be to avoid referencing your slides except when it helps your audience to understand something better.

Figure 4-5. Rethinking some "rules" related to slide talks.

• A small coin or screwdriver to release a jammed slide (see Chapter 10)

• A soft cloth for cleaning lenses

A good idea is to prepare a small case or "kit" that already contains the small items. Then you won't have to spend time finding everything the day of your presentation.

2. Be sure to arrive at least an hour early in order to prepare the room, set up your equipment and test its operation. The first thing to do is make sure the electricity works. Then check to make sure the room is dark enough for your slides to be seen. If there are problems with either of these requirements, you'll need time to solve them. Once you've taken care of the electricity and operation of your equipment, arrange the room the way you'd like it.

3. Make sure the bottom of the screen is at least 1.2 m (4 ft) above the floor so that everyone can see it easily.

4. When setting up the projector, make sure that you fill the screen with the image. If you have both horizontal and vertical slides, make sure that both fit on the screen (see Myth 1 in Figure 4-5).

5. Don't put objects under the front leveling foot of the projector in order to raise the image higher on the screen. An image projected at such an extreme angle looks distorted on the screen (an effect called "keystoning"). If the screen is too high for the projector, either lower the screen (see Guideline 3 above) or elevate the entire projector by using a box or higher table.

6. Be sure the first slide is focused.

7. When speaking, stand at the front of the room and face your audience. Although you'll want to glance briefly at each slide just to make sure it's the right one, you should concentrate on speaking to your audience and not to the screen. Be sure to stand well to one side of the screen so that you don't block your audience's view.

8. Your remote control cord will need to reach all the way from the projector to the front of the room. Since the standard cord is only about 12 feet long, you'll need a remote control extension cord for many situations. You can buy one from a store which sells Kodak slide projectors, or you can make your own (see Figure 4-6). If you buy one, remember that they only come in 25 feet lengths; buy two if necessary. It's best to run the cord next to a wall so that people don't trip over it, but this takes a lot more cord. If your cord is not long enough, at least tape the cord to the floor and wrap it once around one of the projector table legs to avoid an accident.

9. Ask someone to be responsible for turning off and on the lights. Rather than having to say "lights please" at the beginning and end of your talk, a smoother alternative is to tell this person what you'll be saying at the beginning when you want the lights to be turned off—that is, give him or her a "cue." When he/she hears the cue, the lights will be turned off. Inform the person that at the end of your talk, the words "thank you" ("goodbye," "good night," etc.) will be the cue for turning the lights on again.

10. Before starting your slide talk, make a few introductory remarks with the lights on. This helps establish rapport because it allows you and the people in your audience to see each other clearly before the room is darkened.

11. Remember that the people in your audience can see your face even

when you can't see theirs. Once you begin showing slides, the main source of light will be the projector—which will be illuminating the backs of people's heads, but not their faces. Some speakers think that since the audience's faces are dark, their face must be dark too. Not true. Although your face may not be well illuminated, there'll probably be enough light for people to see your eyes and facial expressions. Continue to look at your audience, just as if the room were fully illuminated.

12. Start and end with a blank or dark screen. To do this, make your first and last slides **black** or **colored acetate slides**. A black slide could be a commercially made plastic slide or simply a 2 by 2-inch (3.7 x 3.7 cm) piece of cardboard or other stiff, heat-resistant material. Just insert the black slides into the desired slots of your carousel. Whenever the tray reaches one of those positions, the cardboard will fall and block the projector's light. The effect is a dark screen. (The newer models of Ektagraphic slide projectors automatically block light from reaching the screen whenever there's an empty slot in the slide tray. In older models, an empty slot will create a blinding flash on the screen as described next.) Alternatively, you can make colored acetate slides simply by putting a piece of colored acetate (it comes in many colors) into a regular slide mount. It's usually not a good idea to tape anything (e.g., acetate or paper for a black slide) on to the outside of a slide mount. Although it may work fine in an emergency, over time the tape will soften in the projector's heat and could cause your projector to jam.

13. Avoid showing a blinding white screen (a "polar bear in a snow storm," as some have called it). Unprepared speakers sometimes arrive at what they think is the

last slide, and then advance the projector one more time "just to make sure." On older projector models, this would create the familiar blinding white screen. Know when you have reached your last slide. When you advance the projector again, it should be to a black or colored acetate slide. This darkens the screen and creates a pleasant ending to your talk. (An effective alternative is to end your talk with a slide showing the logo (or identifying symbol) of your organization.)

14. Try not to "announce" each slide change with an unnatural pause or through conspicuous display of the remote control. Memorize the location of the advance (forward) button on the remote control. This will keep you from having to stop and search for it each time you want to change slides. Try to keep the remote control out of the audience's view. A mistake that some speakers make is holding the remote control directly in front of them, and then dropping their arm conspicuously as they push the advance button. This effectively announces to the audience that the slide is about to change, and gives the presentation a choppy, less spontaneous look. Professionals put the remote control in one hand which is lowered to the side or held behind the back, and simply push the button whenever the next slide is needed. This frees the other hand for gesturing and pointing, and avoids calling attention to the remote control, itself.

15. Know the order of your slides. This is surprisingly easy, even when you have a lot of slides. If your talk has been prepared as recommended in Chapter 3, you'll find that your slides are so closely associated with your words that one automatically suggests the other. You'll know which slides will be shown during

Making a Remote Control Extension Cord Is Easy

If your remote control cord isn't long enough to allow you to stand in front of your audience when showing slides, you can easily make your own extension. Cut the remote control cord in the middle and connect a 25-foot (8 m) or longer piece of similar wire between the two ends. For Kodak remote controls there will be five different wires to connect. Just twist the end of each small wire to one end of your extension, and make sure that you connect that wire to the same wire on the other end of the original remote control cord. If you have a soldering tool, it's a good idea to solder each connection. But even if you don't, a firm twist and a piece of electrician's tape will last quite a while.

Tips: If the individual wires aren't colored or numbered, you might have trouble determining which ends go together. You can use the following simple technique to verify which wire is which: (1) hold two of the wires with your thumb or finger onto opposite terminals of a common 9-volt (transistor radio type) battery; and (2) on the other end, touch different combinations of wire ends to your tongue. When you feel a tingling sensation on your tongue you can be sure that you've found the ends of the same two wires. Through the process of elimination you'll be able to identify which wire is which. Once you have successfully located the first wire end, connect it to the corresponding wire on the original remote control cord. Repeat this procedure with the rest of the wires. Be sure to wrap plenty of tape around everything when you're done.

Kodak remote control extension cords can also be purchased. Almost any audiovisual store will have them or be able to order them. Kodak's cords come in 25-foot (8 m) lengths. To make a 50-foot (16 m) extension, simply connect two cords together. You may add more than two, but the extra length creates a noticeable delay in the time it takes for each slide to change. With practice, however, you can easily accustom yourself to the delay.

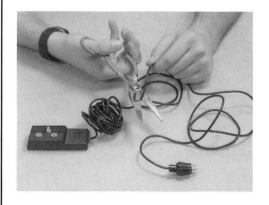 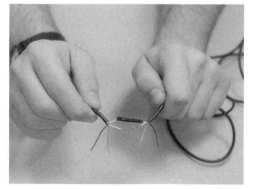

Figure 4-6. Instructions for making a remote control extension cord for a Kodak slide projector.

different parts of your presentation, and which words you'll use when different slides are being projected. As we saw in Chapter 3, this can be especially useful if you momentarily forget what comes next in your talk. In such a situation, you can simply advance the slides until one reminds you of where you are.

16. Anticipate the next slide, and push the button early enough that it's already on the screen when it's needed. Except at transitions, most slide changes will probably come in mid-sentence rather than at the end of sentences. For example, "One of the most common kinds of trees around here [push remote control button] are the pines." Notice that although the word "pines" wasn't said until the end of the sentence, the button was pushed early enough to bring the slide (a picture of a pine tree) to the screen at the precise moment it was needed. Can you see how the effect would have been different had we waited until the end of the sentence to push the button? Anticipating slides creates continuity and fluidity in a slide talk.

17. Use **progressive disclosure**, when you want to gradually add detail to some basic idea. Progressive disclosure is simply showing a series of related slides which build upon one another, each one adding a little more information. For example, if the first slide in a sequence is a simple base map showing only the outline of some area, subsequent slides might add the locations of main cities, then rivers, then mountains, etc. Another example would be a series of slides, each one adding a new line to a list. Using progressive disclosure allows you to talk at length about something without having to show the same slide all the time. It also allows you to gradually reveal the complexity of something, rather than overwhelming the audience with all the details in a single slide.

18. Use close-ups as often as possible. People are generally more interested in things they can see in detail. A common technique is to show a distant view followed by a close-up view of the same thing. This gives the audience a feeling both for its size as well as its details. A more dramatic effect is created by starting with a distant scene of something, and then showing two or three slides which get progressively closer, the final slide being a close-up.

19. Make sure that all your slides will be projected on the screen just as they were photographed. Left should be left, top should be top, etc. Although upside down slides are obvious, those reversed from left to right aren't (unless they show words, numbers or scenes that are familiar to you). The problem with reversed slides is that they focus differently on the screen than slides that are correctly projected. To avoid the need to continually refocus, you'll need to make sure that all of your slides are inserted into the carousel correctly. This is easy if you remember that each slide should be put into the tray upside down with its emulsion side toward the screen. As Figure 4-7 shows, if you hold a slide parallel to the ground at eye level, you'll notice that it bows slightly. The side that bows inward (i.e., the concave side) has the emulsion on it. Usually, but not always, this is the side with the film company's name on it. Today, many commercial slide mounts include the words "this side toward the screen" on the emulsion side.

Overhead Transparencies

Like slides, overhead transparencies are used extensively in natural resource

How to Put Slides Into a Carousel Correctly

The right hand above is showing the emulsion side of the slide.

The emulsion side is slightly concave.

Figure 4-7. Correct way to put a slide in a tray (upside down with the emulsion side toward the screen). The emulsion side is always a little duller than the nonemulsion side. Usually (but not always) the brand name of the film is printed on the emulsion side. Note for advanced readers: if you're using a rear-screen and either no mirrors or an even number of mirrors, you'll need to have the nonemulsion side facing the screen. (Photos by Gerry Snyder)

communication and extension programs. They are especially useful when a speaker wishes to interact extensively with the audience or when being able to write or draw on projected images is necessary during the presentation. In this respect, overhead transparencies have the advantage of being interactive like flip charts and chalkboards. The main trade-offs between overhead transparencies and slides are shown in Figure 4-8. Generally, slides are preferred when audiences are too large for extensive interaction or when the speaker needs to show a lot of "real world" (in-the-field) scenes. But in other situations, overhead transparencies are often better because of their flexibility and interactive nature.

Following are some guidelines for using overhead transparencies in a talk. Although many more advanced techniques are possible, any speaker who pays attention to these guidelines will be able to make better presentations. English-language readers interested in additional information should consult Bunnell and Mock

(1990) and Brown et al.(1989). In Spanish, Muñoz and Peña (1990) is highly recommended.

Guidelines for Using Overhead Transparencies

1. Stack your transparencies in the sequence in which you plan to use them.

2. Have two piles—one containing the transparencies you have not yet shown, and in the other the ones which have been shown.

3. Transparencies which are used a lot should be mounted in cardboard frames and sandwiched between sheets of clean paper to protect them from light, heat, dust and moisture.

4. Before the presentation begins, position and focus your first transparency on the screen. That way, when you begin the presentation you can simply turn the projector on and the first visual will be properly projected on the screen.

5. At the end of your presentation, turn the projector off before removing the last transparency. This avoids having a glaring white screen.

6. When a transparency no longer pertains to your commentary, either replace it with one that does or darken the screen (either by turning off the projector or covering the transparency with a piece of paper.)

7. Know the order of your transparencies and anticipate each one. If possible, have it in your hand, ready to change slightly before you actually need it. In this way, you minimize the amount of time it takes to change transparencies and avoid making your audience wait for you. It gives your presentation more fluidity because you're able to change visuals quickly and more precisely in time with your commentary.

8. At different points during the presentation, you may want to talk for a while without a transparency being projected. Two techniques work best. The first is simply turning off the projector and then turning it back on once you've said what you wanted to say. (Of course you would have changed transparencies before resuming unless you intended to use the same one.) Though workable, some speakers claim that the sound of the fan going on and off and the "clicking" of the on/off switch can be distracting. The second technique is probably a little smoother and requires only that you plan ahead. By having a piece of blank paper over the next transparency (perhaps labeled "transition" as a reminder), you can simply place the next transparency (with the paper still covering it) on top of the one being projected and then pulling the bottom piece of acetate out. This leaves the next visual ready for unveiling. Yet because the transparency is still covered, the screen is dark, allowing you to continue talking without anything showing on the screen. When you're ready to show the next transparency, you simply remove the paper cover.

9. Some speakers prefer to change every transparency as described above, thereby avoiding the distraction of a glaring screen between transparencies. To do this, it helps to already have a piece of paper between every transparency and the next. Then whenever it's time to change transparencies, you can simply: (1) grab the next paper-covered transparency in the pile, (2) place it on the projector, and (3) remove the paper cover, allowing the transparency to be viewed on the screen. This makes changing transparencies much

smoother than many people think it can be.

10. Don't look at the screen when you're pointing to something or trying to write on a transparency. Look instead at the actual transparency. Remember that what you see is identical to what the audience is seeing on the screen.

11. When pointing, just lay your pointer (or pen, pencil, etc.) directly onto the acetate and turn it to point at whatever you wish to emphasize. This keeps the pointer in sharper focus leaving little doubt about what you're pointing at.

12. With overhead transparencies, "progressive disclosure" is easy. Simply tape successive transparencies together (preferably in a cardboard frame) so that when each is laid down it adds something to the illustration that's being projected. Bunnell and Mock (1990) have called this method of gradually revealing information the "additive technique." It's also called "sandwiching" because the individual acetates are arranged in layers like a sandwich. Taping the layers firmly together is important so that the separate sheets don't move, changing the position of the details each shows. Another technique is to use a piece of paper to hide sections of the transparency and then to reveal the whole a little bit at a time (line by line or section by section). If the paper is thin enough, it will allow you to see what is covered at the same time preventing the image from reaching the screen. According to Bunnell and Mock, however, some audiences resent the "hiding" technique because they don't like being told how fast to read. As is so common in communication, each speaker needs to decide which technique is best for him or her based on what is known about the audience that will hear and see the presentation.

13. Many speakers like to write their outlines or lists of key ideas on acetates before a presentation and then project them as they speak. Each transparency helps the audience see what the speaker is talking about at the same time providing notes for the speaker.

14. Use a colored marker or "grease" (wax-based) pencil to add color, words or drawings directly on to the transparencies as they're being projected. Be sure to wipe them clean with a soft cloth afterwards. If you don't want to take a chance of permanently marring a transparency, simply place a clean piece of acetate over it, and write on the top piece rather than on the original illustration.

15. Many photocopiers will accept acetate sheets, making the transfer of printed material onto overhead transparencies easy and relatively inexpensive.

16. You can make your own transparencies by writing directly on sheets of clear acetate, or by preparing artwork on paper and then photocopying the results onto acetate sheets.

17. Many of the guidelines for using slides also apply to overhead transparencies, especially numbers 2-7 and 10.

Props

Props are objects, either the real thing or representations (like models and drawings), which a speaker can show to an audience during a presentation. Although the word "prop" includes several kinds of visual aids, they're used in very similar ways. Props have been classified differently by various experts. For example, Muñoz and Peña (1990) divide them into four categories: unmodified real objects, modified real objects, specimens and models. Fazio and Gilbert (1986), on

Overhead Transparencies or Slides?		
Type of Visual Aid	**Strengths**	**Limitations**
Overhead Transparencies	Interaction with audience is easier and speaker can change or add to projected images. Can be used in partial light; a totally darkened room isn't required. The speaker can easily change the sequence of a presentation, or return to a previous visual.	Because the projector is in front, blocking the audience's view can be a problem (along with noise). Using real world (field) scenes is very expensive and usually impractical.
Slides	Real world (field) scenes can be used easily and cheaply. Better image quality, especially with fine details. Since the projector can be positioned behind the audience, it doesn't block people's view or interfere with their hearing as much.	Interacting with the audience is more difficult because the room is dark and the sequence of the slides can't be changed easily. Can't be used well in partial light. The sequence of the presentation can't be changed easily. Adding to or changing a visual is impossible during a presentation.

Figure 4-8. Some strengths and limitations of overhead transparencies and slides (adapted from Bunnell and Mock 1990).

the other hand, refer to them as: actual objects, static graphics, models, and active graphics.

Generally, props may be: (1) real things, objects that are taken from their customary settings and shown to an audience (e.g., seedlings, animal specimens, rocks, soil and water samples, etc.), (2) models, three-dimensional representations of real things that would be impractical to transport or difficult to see when life-size (e.g., a building, a human lung, a bacterium, etc.), or (3) graphics, two-dimensional representations of real objects that would be impractical or impossible to transport (e.g., a map showing the world, a drawing of an extinct species, a photograph of a field, etc.).

Use of props may be passive or active, depending on what the speaker does with them. According to Fazio and Gilbert (1986), **passive props** are shown or displayed by the speaker, but they're not actively manipulated nor moved during the explanation. For example, an interpreter may refer to a map that's hanging on the wall; a different speaker might explain something about a graph or chart that's mounted on an easel; or another person might use a scale model of a tropical forest to show where different animals live in the canopy. What makes these props passive is their use. In all three cases, once the speaker began to show them, they remained stationary. Once they were in place, the speaker could refer to them as needed in the presentation, but he/she didn't actively manipulate them.

By contrast, **active props** are those which the interpreter actively manipulates. There are many ways to use a prop actively. For example, a speaker may pass around a particularly aromatic leaf and tell his audience to smell it; he/she might

Figure 4-9. Active use of a prop. An interpreter demonstrates antler growth using a real elk antler. Olympic National Park. (Photo by Sam Ham)

pour water onto a homemade model of a farmer's field in order to demonstrate soil erosion; or he/she might gradually disassemble a model of a tree in order to show the bark, cambium, xylem and phloem. In this sense, changing slides in a talk is an "active" use of a visual aid, whereas projecting only one slide which remained unchanged for the duration of the talk would be a "passive" use. As we'll see, flip charts, cloth boards and chalkboards are visual aids that are especially well suited to active uses.

Following are some guidelines for using props in a talk. English-language readers interested in additional information are referred to Brown et al. (1989) and Fazio and Gilbert (1986). In Spanish, Muñoz and Peña (1990) is recommended.

Guidelines for Using Props

1. Make sure the prop is visible to everyone in the audience. If the prop is too small for everyone to see (such as a seed, cone or pebble), you should have enough of them to distribute throughout the audience. A quick way to distribute

things is to ask the person sitting at the end of each row to do it for you. If you can't obtain a sufficient number, consider using a large drawing or model instead of the real object.

2. When you're holding the prop, hold it high (at or above the level of your ear). Stand close (but not too close) to the first row of your audience, and alternately turn to the left and right sides, pausing so that everyone has a chance to see the object clearly.

3. Try not to talk to the prop. Maintain eye contact with the audience except when you must look at the prop in order to point to some precise location or specific feature.

4. Not everyone in the audience will be looking at you at every second of your presentation. When pointing to something, do it slowly and deliberately so that everyone can clearly see where you're pointing. When showing a general area (as opposed to a specific point), make slow, exaggerated circular motions around the area you want your audience to see.

5. Props can be used as analogies. As we found in Chapter 1, analogies help to bridge the unfamiliar with the familiar, and the best analogies involve everyday things. Regnier et al.(1992), for example, suggested assembling a common flashlight and batteries to show how different parts of an ecosystem are interdependent.

6. Whenever it's possible, make active use of props. Even a two-dimensional graphic can be active. For example, can you write on it? Can you stick something else to it? Can you pick it up, hold it in your right hand, and then in your left hand? Can you invite an audience member to come forward to hold it for you?

7. When possible, encourage your audience to use additional senses. Will touching, handling, smelling or even tasting or listening to the prop help people to understand your point? Remember, though, that giving your audience something to do will focus its attention away from you. You'll need to take this into account in planning your presentation. A good technique is to simply pause until everyone has had a chance to do whatever it was you asked them to do. With large audiences, this may not be feasible because of the amount of time it could require. In such a case, having many examples of the object to pass around would be helpful (see Guideline 1).

8. Rehearse how you'll use each prop in your presentation. Try to plan the exact moment at which you'll reveal each one, remembering that the words you use to introduce it will influence how your audience looks at it, and how interested they'll be in it. Unless you're going to pass the prop around, you might want to tape a small note card containing a few key words on the back of it to remind you of what you want to say. With props, referencing usually isn't a problem. For example, it seems quite natural to say "This is a cone from a lodgepole pine … ," or "Now I want to show you … ." Still, it may sound more interesting to your audience to say, "A good example of a fire species is the lodgepole pine … " (just as you reach for the cone). Be sure to plan not only how you'll introduce and use each prop, but how you'll conclude your use of it.

Flip Charts

Flip charts usually consist of large sheets of paper mounted on a free-standing easel or attached to a wall or board. The sheets on most flip charts are stacked on top of one another so that only one sheet at a time is showing, and when removed, exposes the next sheet for viewing. Depending upon your needs, however, it's possible to arrange the sheets in other ways. For example, some speakers like to arrange their sheets on a wall in horizontal sequence so that all of them can be seen simultaneously. This format can work well if it's necessary to refer back to previous sheets during your presentation. Some speakers accomplish the same ends by taping each sheet to a conspicuous place on the wall once they remove it from the easel. This gives them the flexibility to refer back to previous sheets while allowing them to keep subsequent sheets hidden from view until it's time for them to be used. In this respect, the sheets of a flip chart are a lot like slides, each one projected in a desired sequence and hidden from the audience's view until the speaker decides it's time to expose it.

Like slides, previously prepared flip chart sheets are very portable and adaptable to different locations and settings. The sheets can be used over and over again, and individual sheets can be easily modified, updated or replaced at little expense. Because of the widespread availability of paper and colored markers (including refillable or "rechargeable" markers), creative and colorful illustrations are easy and inexpensive to produce. As we'll see at the end of this chapter, there are a number of inexpensive methods that non-artists can use to create their own illustrations. An important advantage of flip charts is that they're interactive, allowing you to add details to an illustration as you're talking about it.

Following are some guidelines for using flip charts in a talk. In English, Brown et al. (1989) is recommended to readers especially interested in the use of

Figure 4-10. Once removed from the easel, flip charts sheets can be taped to a wall for easy reference and reinforcement. La Selva Biological Station, Costa Rica. (Photo by Claudia Charpentier)

flip charts. Arévalo (1990) is a good Spanish-language reference.

Guidelines for Using Flip Charts

1. Locate the flip chart easel in front of the audience. It's best to put it in the center so that it can be seen by everyone and not just by the people on one side of the audience. Make sure that the bottom of each sheet is at least 1.2 m (4 ft) above the floor so that it won't be blocked by the heads of those seated in the first row.

2. Pre-crease the top edge of all the sheets so that they won't wrinkle when they're turned.

3. If you're right-handed, stand to the audience's left side of the flip chart; if you're left-handed, stand to the right side. This will allow you to write or point to the sheets without blocking the audience's view.

4. If you have a pointer, use it gracefully—without a lot of unnecessary movement or exaggerated motions, such as twirling it or slapping at the paper.

Simply put, try not to draw attention to the pointer. Don't hold the pointer except when you need to use it. Put it down after each use.

5. Try to always be aware of where you're standing in relation to the flip chart. It's especially important not to block your audience's view of the sheets. In addition, you might sometimes want to walk to a position well away from the easel in order to focus attention on yourself rather than on the flip chart.

6. In planning the sequence of your sheets, remember that you can include blank sheets in places where no illustration is needed. Blank flip chart sheets serve the same purpose as "black" slides (that is, they avoid making your audience look at a visual aid which no longer corresponds to your commentary, or at a subsequent illustration for which you aren't yet ready). As Arévalo (1990) advises, avoid "showing one thing and talking about another." Some speakers like to use blank sheets between every illustration and the next. This prevents the details of the next sheet from showing through on the one that is currently being used.

7. In preparing your sheets, write carefully, using letters that are easy to read. Some speakers like to draw a series of very light pencil lines on each sheet to use as lettering guides. This helps to keep their words and sentences etc., level on the sheet. A useful technique is to first prepare each sheet entirely in pencil. This allows you to make corrections and improvements in each illustration before using permanent markers. Once you're satisfied with the design of a given sheet, you can then write over the pencil with colored markers, and erase any unwanted pencil marks. Use the table in Figure 4-2 to determine the minimum size of your letters.

8. Don't try to crowd too much information onto a single sheet. Put plenty of space between things. You can always use additional sheets of paper.

9. Use emphasis to highlight major points or to draw attention to different parts of each sheet. Color, size of letters, capital versus lower case letters, underlining, and numbering main points are examples of ways to show emphasis. Emphasizing titles, main headings, and key points helps your audience to quickly see the organization of the sheet, and to make sense of it without a lot of effort. Remember, though, that all emphasis equals no emphasis. That is, highlighting too many things has the effect of emphasizing nothing. For example, <u>you</u> <u>probably</u> <u>can't</u> <u>say</u> <u>which</u> <u>word</u> <u>in</u> <u>this</u> <u>sentence</u> <u>is</u> <u>most</u> <u>important</u>. That's because every word is underlined and so none of them looks more important than the others. It's probably <u>much</u> easier to tell what is more important in <u>this</u> sentence, right? The same precaution applies to any emphasis technique. For example, a single word

Figure 4-11. An example of good flip chart technique: (1) written words are legible; (2) the speaker stands to the side to avoid blocking her visual aid; and (3) she maintains eye contact with her audience rather than talking to the flip chart. (Photo by Gerry Snyder)

written in red will stand out much more on a sheet that otherwise contains only black lettering than it would if all or most of the other words were also red.

10. Reserve capital letters for main titles, subheads or key ideas that you want to emphasize. It's usually not a good idea to capitalize everything, especially on a sheet containing a lot of written words. (The reasons for this are discussed in Chapter 8.) Written text is almost always easier for people to read if both upper and lower case letters are used. For example:

CAPITALIZED TITLES
ARE FINE

BUT PARAGRAPHS THAT ARE WRITTEN IN ALL CAPITAL LETTERS ARE MORE DIFFICULT TO READ. IN PART, THIS IS BECAUSE EVERYTHING IS EMPHASIZED. WHEN BOTH UPPER AND LOWER CASE LETTERS ARE USED IN A PARAGRAPH, IT'S EASIER FOR THE READER TO SEE WHERE ONE SENTENCE ENDS AND THE NEXT ONE BEGINS. ALSO, BECAUSE OF THE WAY THEY ARE DESIGNED, CAPITAL LETTERS TEND TO CROWD TOGETHER MORE THAN LOWER CASE LETTERS. AS THIS PARAGRAPH SHOWS, LETTERS THAT ARE CROWDED ARE MORE DIFFICULT TO READ.

However, paragraphs that are written in both upper and lower case letters are easier to read. This is because not everything is emphasized. When both upper and lower case letters are used in a paragraph, it's easier for the reader to see where one sentence ends and the next one begins. Also, because of the way they're designed, capital letters tend to crowd together more than lower case letters. As this paragraph shows, letters that aren't so crowded are easier to read.

11. Maintain eye contact with your audience. Remember, your audience is primarily concerned with listening to you. Your flip chart sheets are not the presentation; you are. They're just helpers. Be familiar enough with what's on each sheet (and the next one) that you won't have to look constantly at the flip chart. Avoid reading to your audience from the flip chart. Encourage them to look at you as much as possible. This makes your presentation more personal and allows you to use your face and body to make your presentation more enjoyable and entertaining for them (see Chapter 1). The best way to get the people in your audience to look at you is for you to look at them.

12. Always rehearse your presentation before giving it. In particular, make sure you know the sequence of your flip chart sheets. As you rehearse your use of each sheet, try to predict what's going to be on the next sheet. When you can do this successfully for all of the sheets, you'll find: (1) that you'll have little trouble remembering your talk (in fact, you probably won't even need notes); (2) that your talk will become smoother (largely because your transitions between the flip chart sheets will improve); and (3) that

your self-confidence as a speaker will increase (because your flip chart sheets will help not only your audience, but you).

Chalkboards

The term "chalkboard" really refers to a wide range of devices. The traditional chalkboard is a piece of black or green slate on which a speaker writes using white or colored chalk. There are also plastic and metal boards designed for colored felt-tip markers. Because of the kind of surface these boards have, markings can be erased using a piece of cloth just as chalk can be erased from a traditional chalkboard. In addition, small magnets can be used to attach illustrations to metal chalkboards. In effect, this gives them some of the qualities of cloth boards which we discuss later in this chapter.

The main advantage of chalkboards is that they allow you to write or draw as you're speaking. Elaborate illustrations such as drawings, charts and tables can be drawn ahead of time and then referred to repeatedly during the presentation. As the presentation unfolds, you can add details to illustrations when they're needed, and erase details that are no longer needed. Such uses make chalkboards a more dynamic visual aid than many communicators think they are.

Chalkboards are probably the most common visual aid used by classroom teachers today, and this has given them a reputation for being an unexciting and purely academic medium. But this undeserved reputation is probably more a result of unimaginative uses of chalkboards than it is of the nature of the medium, itself. Still, it's true that they remind of us school and formal instruction, and for this reason, they may not be the best visual aid to use in many kinds of speaking situations. For example, they probably seem more acceptable to audiences in extension programs than they do in parks, museums and other places people go for recreation. When using chalkboards, be careful that you don't create an unnecessarily formal or academic atmosphere. As we saw in Chapter 1, this makes communicating with a noncaptive audience more difficult.

Following are some guidelines for using chalkboards effectively. Readers interested in further information are referred to Muñoz and Peña (1990) in Spanish, and Brown et al. (1989) in English.

Guidelines for Using Chalkboards

1. If the chalkboard is large enough, divide it into two sections—a "work space" where you'll alternately write and erase words, ideas, etc., and a "prepared" space which contains more elaborate illustrations which you prepared earlier. In this way, you can avoid making your audience wait while you draw complicated illustrations or write detailed information on the board. Use the work space for information that is needed only temporarily, and the prepared space for information that you'll use for longer periods of time.

2. Work from left to right and top to bottom. Besides keeping you more organized, this will make it easier to refer back to previous points without having to search for them.

3. Write large enough so that everyone in the audience can easily read even the smallest detail. Don't say things like, "I know those of you in the back probably can't see this, but ... ". If it's worth seeing,

then everyone should be able to see it, not just people in the front row. A general guideline is that a letter has to be at least 1 inch (2.5 cm) high to be read by someone 32 feet (10 m) away, and 2 inches (5 cm) high to be read by someone 48 feet (15 m) away. Beyond this distance, using a chalkboard probably isn't a good idea. Use the table in Figure 4-2 to determine the minimum size of your letters.

4. If you have trouble writing sentences in a straight line, try putting a small chalk mark on one side of the board, and another at the same level on the other side of the board. As you write, start at the level of the left mark and then use the right mark as a target.

5. When you must stop talking in order to write something on the board, do it as quickly as possible. That way, you'll minimize the interruption in your presentation.

6. Write legibly. Although writing speed is important, legibility is essential. If what you have written or drawn is unintelligible, it can't help your audience understand what you're saying.

7. When you use an important term that's likely to be unfamiliar to your audience, write it on the chalkboard as you use it the very first time. This satisfies your audience's need to visualize the word, and allows them to more easily concentrate on what you're saying. (Writing words, of course, presumes that your audience can read. If your audience is illiterate and the term really is important, simply repeat the word slowly. If possible, have a picture to show or refer to a previously prepared illustration on the board which helps them understand the term.)

8. Erase frequently. Try to keep your work space looking neat and uncluttered, and avoid crowding too much informa-

tion into it. The best way to accomplish this is to erase information as soon as it's no longer needed. As you're erasing that part of the board, make your transition to the next topic. For example, as you erase the information you've just finished using, you might say something like, "Now let's spend a little time talking about such and such … ." Doing this helps to tie your presentation together and avoids awkward periods of silence as you turn your back on the audience to erase.

9. You can create a sense of mystery by using "progressive disclosure." There are at least three ways to do this. First, you can tape paper over prepared illustrations (or various parts of them) and unveil them as you need them in your presentation. A second way to use progressive disclosure is to gradually add details to prepared illustrations as you talk about them. Third, some speakers like to prepare ambiguous beginnings of illustrations in the work space and then, at some carefully planned moment, add the remaining details to complete the picture (see Figure 4-12).

10. If you're not good at drawing, try using one of the methods shown in Figures 4-15, 4-16, and 4-17 at the end of this chapter. One of the "dot-tracing" methods in Figure 4-15 is especially suited to chalkboards. It requires only a drawing or picture that you want to copy, a sharp pointed instrument, some chalk dust, and some time. If you have access to a projector (slide, opaque or overhead), the **projection method** in Figure 4-17 is even easier to use.

11. When appropriate, use color and other techniques for adding emphasis. Colored chalk and colored markers are commonly available in stores which sell art supplies and books. If you use markers a lot, consider buying rechargeable

You Can Build Mystery Into Chalkboard Presentations

1. Unveiling

2. Gradually adding details to prepared illustrations

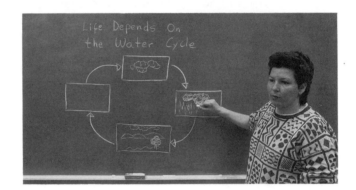

3. Completing ambiguous beginnings

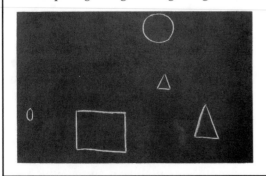

Figure 4-12. Three ways to build a little mystery into chalkboard presentations. (Photos by Gerry Snyder)

(refillable) ones. In the long run they'll be more economical than disposable markers.

12. Effective uses of chalkboards and flip charts are similar in some ways, and many of the guidelines we discussed for using flip charts could also apply to using chalkboards (especially Guidelines 1, 4-5, and 9-12).

Cloth Boards

One of the oldest visual aids is the cloth board. You may know it by other names such as "flannel board," "felt board," or "Velcro board," depending upon the kind of material it's made of. They're also called "slap boards" because of the way some speakers slap illustrations onto them during a talk. Although they're probably best known as story-telling devices for children, cloth boards can be used effectively in almost any kind of presentation and for many kinds of audiences. Cloth boards are a common visual aid in many countries, especially in school and extension programs. Fazio and Gilbert (1986) have argued that, because of their novelty, cloth boards can be surprisingly effective even in countries like the United States and Canada where they are used less frequently.

Cloth boards offer a number of advantages. They're, by nature, an "active" visual aid. Speakers add illustrations to the board at the precise moment they're needed, and then take them away when they're no longer needed. Depending on the situation, there are several ways to involve people in the audience as part of the presentation. As explained later, members of the audience can even be used as "walking" cloth boards. Creating a sense of mystery and anticipation is easy in cloth board talks because the audience is always wondering what the next illustration will be and when it will come. Cloth boards lend themselves to explaining things step-by-step. Attaching real objects to the board is possible (as long the objects don't weigh too much for the kind of material on the board), and very attractive illustrations can be used, increasing the entertainment value of the presentation.

Although commercially made Velcro ("hook-and-loop") boards can be expensive, they're the strongest and most reliable kind of cloth board. Good hook-and-loop material can hold very heavy objects (even tools, typewriters, and medium-sized rocks will adhere to them). However, presentations which rely mainly on lightweight illustrations (such as drawings or pictures mounted on cardboard) don't require this kind of holding power. In most presentations, flannel or felt will work just as well.

Of these two materials, flannel is usually less expensive, but felt is more durable and may be available in more colors. Besides flannel and felt, other materials (such as corduroy, coarse sandpaper, fuzzy yarns, cotton balls, spun wool and other soft, textured materials) will stick to the flannel board (Brown et al. 1989). By gluing patches of one of these materials to the back of a photograph, magazine picture, drawing, graphic, word card, or other light-weight object, the object can be attached to a cloth-covered board, making possible an active and entertaining illustrated talk.

Flannel and felt boards are inexpensive and easy to make (see Figure 4-13). Since both materials come in a variety of colors (available at fabric stores), attractive backgrounds can be created, and different

Cloth Boards Don't Have to Be Elaborate

Figure 4-13. Examples of simple cloth boards: (a) a cloth board on a simple easel made of three sticks and some string; (b) a large outdoor cloth board (the fabric is attached to a permanent board and removed when not in use); (c) a wool blanket over the back of a chair can even be used; (d) an indoor cloth board on a simple but sturdy stand; (e) wrapping and nailing cloth board material around the back side of a frame; (f) applying masking tape to hide the nails and give the board a smoother edge.

Use a Cloth Board That's Big Enough to Be Seen		
Recommended Dimensions for Several Audience Sizes		
Dimensions of the Board	Size of Audience	Maximum Viewing Distance
1 by 1.5 feet (0.30 x 0.50 m)	1 to 10	6 ft (2 m)
2.5 by 5 feet (0.75 x 1.25 m)	10 to 40	16 feet (5 m)
4 by 7.5 feet (1.25 x 2.25 m)	40 to 75	23 feet (7 m)
5 by 9 feet (1.5 x 2.75 m)	75 to 100	30 feet (9 m)
Notes: Dimensions given are the minimum for each viewing distance. To use the smallest cloth board, hold it on your lap and gather the audience around you. [Sources: Adapted from Muñoz and Peña (1990) and Brown et al. (1989).]		

Figure 4-14. Approximate dimensions of cloth boards for various audience sizes and viewing distances.

backgrounds can be used for different presentations. Black, blue, green, brown, and various pastels seem to make the best backgrounds, depending, of course, on the colors used in the illustrations (Muñoz and Peña 1990).

If your budget is severely limited, you could even use a wool blanket or flannel sheet—either mounted loosely on a board or wall, or simply draped over the back of a chair (Werner and Bower 1986). Another way to save money is to make your own backing material for the illustrations. Simply smear homemade glue (made of flour and water) on the back of each illustration, and then sprinkle some sand or wheat chaff (rice chaff or other grain husks will also work) onto the wet glue. According to Werner and Bower, once dried, the tiny barbs of the chaff are actually superior to flannel, felt or sandpaper in adhering to the board. It's a good idea, however, to first mount the illustrations on a stiff backing (such as cardboard or stiff paper) and then apply the glue to the backing. Still another option is to attach rolled pieces of tape to the backs of illustrations and simply stick them to a piece of painted, relatively smooth board.

The size of the board you need for any presentation will be determined by the number of people in your audience and how close they are to you. You can use Figure 4-14 as a rough guide. Obviously, for larger boards you'll need larger illustrations.

Following are some guidelines for using cloth boards in a talk. English-language readers interested in more information are referred to Fazio and Gilbert (1986), Werner and Bower (1986), and Brown et al. (1989). Spanish-language readers should consult Muñoz and Peña (1990) and Werner (1986).

Guidelines for Using Cloth Boards

1. With very small groups, position the people around you and hold a small cloth board in your lap. Be sure to have your prepared materials close-by on a small table or chair, or involve an audience member by giving him or her the stack of illustrations (face down, of course) and asking for each one as it's needed.

2. With larger groups, be sure your board and the prepared materials are big enough and high enough to be seen. The bottom of the board should be at least 1.2 m (4 ft) above the floor. Large cloth boards can be put on an easel or hung from a wall, if necessary.

3. Keep your illustrations simple. Silhouettes showing only a few key characteristics of the subject they represent are often sufficient. Remember, the people are listening to you. An illustration which merely symbolizes what your words are describing will usually be quite clear.

4. Avoid what Fazio and Gilbert (1986) called "the seven sins" of cloth board use:

- Digging: having to shuffle through your illustrations because you don't have them arranged in the order that you intend to use them.
- Waving: holding an illustration in your hand while you're gesturing or pointing at something else.
- Exposing: showing the back side of an illustration.
- Petting: repeatedly running your fingertips over an illustration to make sure it's stuck to the board.
- Blocking: blocking your audience's view of the board.
- Speeding: putting an illustration on the board before you're ready for it.
- Creeping: putting an illustration on the board too late, after you've already presented what it was supposed to illustrate.

5. Don't allow your audience to see your illustrations until you place each one on the board. Keep them face down on a table, chair, or in a box, and take only one at a time from the pile.

6. If you want to briefly review or summarize what you've just finished discussing, do it illustration-by-illustration as you remove the pieces from the board, starting with the first item you put up. When you're done reviewing, the board will be blank and you can begin applying illustrations for the next topic or idea.

7. Cloth boards invite active movement by the speaker. Emphasizing an idea by occasionally pointing directly at a related illustration makes it even more interesting to the audience. Still greater emphasis is created if you continue to look directly at the audience as you're pointing to the object. Muñoz and Peña (1990) have found that a speaker can make a particularly strong point by removing an illustration from the board and then moving toward the audience showing it. Still another idea is to create "walking flannel boards" by putting flannel shirts on selected audience members and attaching illustrations to them (Freed 1991).

8. Try animating stories, chronologies and cause-and-effect relationships. According to experts, these kinds of presentations not only capture interest, but audiences understand and remember them better than other kinds of presentations (Brown et al.1989).

9. For some audiences, it may be appropriate to ask the people to make their own illustrations and to give their own presentations. For example, a local farmer might tell how he got better crops after trying a soil conservation method. Children might tell stories about the kinds of trees or wildlife they saw on a field trip. Or a nursery manager might show good and bad ways to plant container seedlings.

10. Protect your illustrations. Keep them in labeled envelopes away from extreme temperatures and humidity. This will keep them from peeling and warping.

11. Refer to our guidelines for using flip charts. Many of them also apply to cloth boards, especially Guidelines 1, 3, 5, and 8 through 12.

Creating Your Own Illustrations

Contrary to what many people think, you don't have to be a professional artist to create certain kinds of illustrations. Although artistic ability certainly helps (and is even essential when truly professional results are required), there are many kinds of illustrations that almost anyone can produce easily and cheaply.

Four methods for creating your own illustrations are shown in Figures 4-15 through 4-18. All of them can be used to make illustrations for each of the visual aids discussed in this chapter—slides, overhead transparencies, props, flip charts, chalkboards, and cloth boards.

You'll also find that variations on these methods can be used to create illustrations for exhibits (see Chapter 8) and publications. With the exception of the "projection method" (Figure 4-17), they don't require special equipment, and none of them is expensive. When you try them, don't be discouraged if your first attempt isn't perfect. With a little practice, you can master all four methods in a short period of time, and soon you'll be producing more attractive illustrations than you might have guessed you could create.

A number of companies produce booklets of generic illustrations called "clip art." The booklets contain drawings (of plants, animals, people, cities, rivers and many other subjects) which you can "clip" out and use. Instead of cutting up your booklet, you should first photocopy the page containing the drawing you want to use, and then cut out the photocopy. Most art supply stores and many book stores sell clip art, or have information on how to order it. When you buy clip art, you also buy the right to copy and use it.

Always know and respect copyright laws pertaining to the use of printed illustrations. Although the laws vary greatly from country to country, it's generally a good idea to ask permission before "borrowing" an illustration from a copyrighted source (such as a book or magazine). Often, permission is freely granted for nonprofit, educational uses. But it's still safer, and certainly more courteous, to ask.

Readers interested in slightly more expensive illustration techniques should consult Hooper (1987), Meilach (1990) and Brown et al. (1989) in English. In Spanish, Muñoz and Peña (1990) and Pino (1989) are recommended. Each of these references contains a number of additional illustration methods that are only slightly more complicated than the ones included in this book.

Glossary terms: active prop, black slide, chalkboard, cloth board, flip chart, grid technique, guideline, illustrated talk, lacquer thinner transfer, non-illustrated talk, passive prop, progressive disclosure, projection method, prop, referencing, slide, tracing, visual aid.

Do-It-Yourself Illustrations: Method One—Tracing

Tracing is probably the easiest way to create your own illustrations. Following are five different tracing techniques. The first four are for tracing from original artwork such as a drawing, photograph or other existing illustration. The last method is for "tracing" drawings from real-world scenes. Any of these methods could be used to create slides, overhead transparencies, props, flip chart sheets, chalkboard drawings, or cloth board illustrations.

1. *Carbon Paper Tracing:* Simply put a piece of carbon paper between the original artwork and a sheet of blank paper (or other surface you wish to trace on). With a pen, trace the outline and other details directly on the original. A carbon copy will be produced on the blank sheet. Unless you're willing to mark on the original, it's a good idea to first photocopy the original and then trace the copy. It's important to use a pen because it allows you to press firmly enough to cause the carbon transfer without tearing the original, and the ink tells you where you have already traced. It's best not to retrace your lines, so trace carefully.

Tips: If you plan to make silhouettes on colored paper (e.g., for a cloth board presentation), it's usually best to trace onto white paper, attach that piece of paper to a piece of colored paper, and then cut out the image along the carbon lines. This method is also useful for making your own letters for an exhibit or display.

Dot tracing on paper.

2. *Dot Tracing on Paper:* Using an original or photocopy, carefully punch small holes (1.5 to 3 mm or 1/16 to 1/8") along the outline of the image you want to reproduce. Although a sharp instrument such as a nail, awl or ice pick works best as a hole punch, a sharp pen knife could also be used. Be sure to place something soft (such as a thick newspaper or soft piece of wood) underneath the original before punching the holes. Once the holes are punched, clip or tape the master to the piece of paper you want to trace on, and carefully make a small pencil mark through each hole. When you remove the original, you'll see a dot outline of the image. Use a pen to connect the dots, and erase unwanted pencil marks when you're finished.

Tips: Depending on the thickness of the master, it might help to first glue it to another piece of paper (the sturdier the better) before punching the holes. If you plan to photocopy the tracing, use a light blue (often called "non-photo blue") pencil to make the dots. Since light blue pencil marks don't photocopy, you won't have to do any erasing once the dots are connected. "Fill-in-the-dot" drawings for children can be created if you darken and number the pencil dots instead of connecting them yourself.

Dot tracing on chalboard.

3. *Dot Tracing on a Chalkboard:* Punch holes in the original as you would for dot tracing on paper. (For chalkboard tracing you'll need to attach the original to a stiff backing before punching the holes. The backing could be a piece of construction paper, window shade material, or simply two or three pieces of regular writing paper that have been laminated together.) Tape the punched outline at the desired location on the chalkboard. With a very dusty chalk eraser (or a rag that has been heavily dusted), pat firmly along the punched outline. The result is a dot outline on the board. As with the pencil-dot drawings above, you can now fill in the dots to complete the drawing.

Tips: Use colored chalk to embellish parts of the drawing. Once the basic illustration is on the board, you can gradually add details to it during your presentation.

4. *Backlighted Tracing:* Lay a piece of white paper over the original artwork and place them together against a strong light source. A light table or window work best as light sources. You could also draw on the flat surface of an overhead projector, if you have one. The backlighting reveals enough detail in the original that it can be traced onto the white sheet of paper.

Tips: The stronger the light source, the easier it will be to see the image you want to trace. Since the image has to show through the top piece of paper, lighter weight paper will be easier to trace on. A bright flashlight will even work as a light source if the top paper is not

Tracing on a light table.

too heavy. Usually it will be best to photocopy the results. Remember that it's possible to photocopy the illustration onto colored paper, perhaps for a brochure or exhibit illustration.

Tracing real-world scenes.

5. *Tracing Real-World Scenes:* With some patience, you can draw real-world scenes almost as well as a trained artist. You'll need a piece of clear acetate, a window, and either a grease pencil or an overhead transparency marker (for writing on the acetate). Simply tape the acetate to a window that looks out to the scene you want to draw. Try to position the acetate on the window so that you can look directly through it to the desired scene (at a 90° angle). Trying to draw at any other angle may distort the scene. With the grease pencil or marker, carefully trace the lines in the scene that you want to show. Remove the acetate from the window. Since the drawing can easily smear, you should cover it with a piece of clean paper to protect it. Your drawing can be photocopied to white or colored paper for use in an exhibit or publication, as artwork for a slide, or used as an overhead transparency. If you now want to transfer it to a flip chart sheet or chalkboard, use one of the other four tracing methods. If you want to enlarge the drawing, use the grid technique explained in Figure 4-16, or one of the projection methods in Figure 4-17.

Tips: Try making your drawings either in the morning or afternoon of a relatively sunny day when there are strong shadows. This will help you see which lines need to be traced from the scene. At mid-day and on cloudy days, things tend to look flatter because shadows aren't very pronounced. The result is that you can't see the depth in the scene, and therefore have trouble deciding which lines will be important to trace.

Figure 4-15. Five ways to trace artwork. (Photos by Gerry Snyder)

Do-It-Yourself Illustrations: Method Two—The Grid Technique

The **grid technique** is especially useful when you want to make an enlarged drawing of almost any kind of existing artwork (drawing, map, magazine picture, photograph, etc). It can be used to prepare the artwork for a slide, to prepare an illustration for a poster or exhibit, or simply to transfer artwork to a flip chart sheet or chalkboard. All you need is the original that you want to enlarge, a ruler, a pencil, and a little time. In five easy steps you can create your own enlarged drawing at almost no cost.

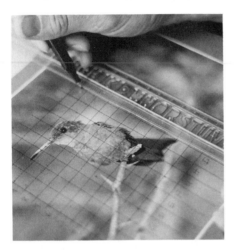

The Five Steps

1. Select the original artwork that you want to copy (a drawing, map, photo, etc.). If you don't want to mark on the original, make a photocopy, and continue with steps 2 through 5.

2. With your ruler and pencil, draw a small but uniform grid directly onto the artwork. Assign numbers to the spaces between the horizontal lines, and letters to the spaces between the vertical lines. This will create a grid comprised of small squares (1A, 2B, 3C, etc.). Generally, it's best to draw your lines about 0.5 inch (1 cm) apart, but this depends somewhat on the size of the original.

3. Decide how big you want the enlargement to be, and then prepare another grid (at the desired scale) on whatever material you want to draw on (e.g., a flip chart sheet, a piece of paper, poster board, etc.). If you're going to create a chalk enlargement, you should first clean the board with a damp sponge or rag (not paper) and allow it to dry thoroughly. Make paper grids with a pencil and chalkboard grids with chalk. (In both cases, be sure to draw very lightly since you'll want to erase the lines later.) To make a 200 percent enlargement, make your squares two times the size of the squares in the original grid; for 300 percent make them three times larger, etc. (If you're going to photocopy the drawing later, use a light blue pencil to draw the grid. Since photocopiers don't reproduce the color blue, you won't have to worry about erasing the lines when the drawing is completed.)

4. Now draw in each square the corresponding part of the original artwork. For example, what's in square 5C in the original should be drawn in square 5C of the enlargement; what's in F6 should be duplicated in F6, etc. At this stage, it's best to draw lightly in pencil (chalk if you're working on a chalkboard). That way, you can erase mistakes cleanly and make any fine corrections you think are necessary. When you're satisfied with the results, carefully retrace your pencil lines with a dark pen or marker (chalk, if using a chalkboard). This completes the enlargement.

5. Carefully erase the grid (unless it's drawn in blue pencil for photocopying). If you're going to be erasing a chalkboard grid, use a slightly damp sponge or rag (not paper).

Figure 4-16. Instructions for making grid drawings. (Photos by Sam Ham)

Do-It-Yourself Illustrations:
Method Three—Projection

If you can project an image onto a piece of paper or a chalkboard, then you can draw it. There are three ways to do this, each requiring a different kind of projector. The method(s) you use will be determined by the kind of projector(s) you have and the kinds of original artwork you want to draw from. The procedures, however, are the same for all three methods. Other ways to use the **projection method** are described in Chapter 8 (Exhibits).

1. In a darkened room, project your original artwork onto the desired surface (e.g., piece of paper, flip chart sheet, chalkboard, etc.). Move the projector further away from the surface if you want a larger drawing, and closer if you want to make it smaller.

If your original is:	Then you'll need:
• on a slide	• a slide projector
• on paper (in a book, magazine, etc.)	• an opaque projector
• on acetate or clear plastic	• an overhead projector

If you're going to be drawing on a chalkboard, you should first clean the board with a damp sponge or rag (not paper) and allow it to dry thoroughly.

The three alternatives.

2. With a pencil (or chalk if you're drawing on a chalkboard), carefully trace the details you want to include in the illustration. Remember, you don't have to include everything. Trace only those parts of the projected image that will be helpful and meaningful in your presentation.

3. Once you've finished, you'll want to check the drawing in full light. Turn the projector off (being very careful not to move it even slightly). Turn the room lights on and check your work. Make any additions or erasures you think are needed. You can do this with or without the projector on, depending on your skill and the kinds of corrections you need to make. If you turn the projector on again, be careful not to move it. Continue this process until you're satisfied with your drawing. Turn the projector off and the room lights on.

4. Using a dark pen (or chalk), retrace the details in your drawing. Consider adding color, shading, etc. to liven the illustration.

Low-Cost Variation: You can sometimes trace the outline of an object by mounting a flashlight behind it and casting its shadow onto the drawing surface. If you don't have a flashlight, try a candle, lantern or some other reasonably strong light source. Flickering candles are hard to work with. Try to find one that gives steady, even illumination.

Figure 4-17. Instructions for making projection drawings. (Photo by Gerry Snyder)

Do-It-Yourself Illustrations:
Method Four—Lacquer Thinner Transfers

If your original artwork can be photocopied, you can **transfer** the general details of the photocopy to a desired background using **lacquer thinner**. Since lacquer thinner is a solvent, it dissolves the ink (toner) on a photocopy and makes the image momentarily transferable. But don't expect a complete transfer. This method is most useful when you want a general, partial or stylized image. If what you really want is an exact copy, make another photocopy.

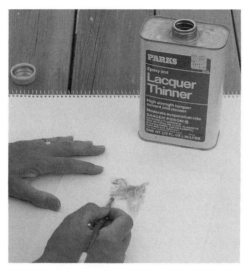

Apply thinner to the back of the photocopy.

Burnishing using the blunt end of the brush.

The Procedures

1. Select the image you want to transfer and the background material you want to transfer it to (paper or other porous material works best). If the original image is not already photocopied, do so.

2. Place the original *face down* on the background material and in the location you want it to appear. (Applying lacquer thinner directly to the photocopy ink will cause it to smear.)

3. Apply a small amount of lacquer thinner to a broad artist's brush (about 1/2-inch wide) and very lightly and quickly brush the back side of the artwork. To ensure complete coverage, make horizontal strokes followed by vertical strokes over the entire area to be transferred. Be careful not to use too much lacquer thinner; it can cause the image to "run." If necessary, experiment with different amounts of thinner until you get desired results.

4. Using the butt end of the wooden brush handle (or any blunt object such as the bottom edge of a jar or a piece of smooth, rounded wood), immediately burnish the image onto the background by rubbing firmly over the entire image area. Again, using both horizontal and vertical strokes helps to ensure a complete transfer. Once the lacquer thinner is applied, you have to work quickly in order to transfer the image before the thinner evaporates. Burnishing causes the image to be imbedded into the surface of the background material.

Results: On left is original photocopy. On right are three of the transferred images.

5. Carefully peel the original off the background and view the transferred image. Evaluate the results, and if necessary, try again using a different amount of lacquer thinner or a different burnishing pressure.

Tips: With some experimentation, you can also transfer color photocopies using the lacquer thinner method. Although there is inevitably some shifting and fading of color, the results can be extremely satisfactory for certain uses. (The image in the above photographs is a color photocopy of a plate from a birding guide.) Depending on the type of ink used in printing, color magazine photographs can sometimes be transferred directly using this method.

Figure 4-18. Instructions for transferring photocopies using lacquer thinner. (Photos by Sam Ham)

The Idaho Natural Resource Education Traveling Trunks

Larry Mink, Interpretation Program
Coordinator, Idaho Department
of Parks and Recreation,
Boise, Idaho

The Idaho Department of Parks and Recreation has a mission to provide quality environmental education for park visitors as well as for Idaho school children. By 1986, environmental education was conducted by individual state parks on a limited basis, but the effort was sporadic. Some state parks were carrying out excellent programs with a high volume of local students; some were doing nothing. There was a concern of successfully reaching the very rural areas of Idaho with our environmental education program, especially those areas situated far from our parks and organized programs. Staff was limited and we could not afford the personnel, nor travel time, necessary to reach these audiences. An environmental education outreach program that took minimum time, staff and budget was needed. Was there such a program available with all these attributes? Yes!

An idea was initially established: gather an array of environmental education materials—from plants and trees, to wildlife and soils—add a teacher's guide with suggestions for use, throw all this into a durable trunk and mail it to schools which have a desire to use it. This initial idea became the seed for the establishment of a new program we now call the "Idaho Natural Resource Education Traveling Trunks" (INRETT).

After further discussions with other Idaho resource agencies, six trunks, each focusing on a different topic, were selected rather than one "variety" trunk. The six topics were: 1) wildlife; 2) forestry; 3) soils; 4) water; 5) outdoor recreation; and 6) botany. The idea of sending six the trunks across the state of Idaho was accepted, but three important questions needed to be answered: 1) Who would select and put the trunk materials together? 2) Who would coordinate the entire program? and 3) What should be included in each trunk? After sorting out these details, we began the INRETT in earnest.

The INRETT became a cooperative agreement between the Idaho Department of Parks and Recreation, Idaho Department of Fish and Game, U.S. Forest Service, U.S. Soil Conservation Service, the Idaho

Botanical Gardens, and the Idaho Department of Education. Each agency was responsible for purchasing a trunk and the educational material to fill the trunk. The Idaho Department of Parks and Recreation agreed to coordinate the partnership effort through its central office in Boise. The cooperative team needed to decide what materials should be included in each trunk. School teachers who would use the trunks were asked what materials they would like to see inside of them. The overall consensus was "hands-on" material/objects, touch-and-feel items, and audio-visual programs. The traveling trunks program was well on its way.

The cooperative team established the following goals for the INRETT:
1. To enrich the current curriculum which is based on textbook topics.
2. To provide hands-on materials for teachers in order to enhance the learning atmosphere.
3. To prepare students for field trips and further study of the selected topic.
4. To provide educational materials that will pique student curiosity in the subject matter.

5. Overall, to provide teachers with additional resource material to better teach students about Idaho's natural resources.

Each traveling trunk is made of a durable, heavy duty material. Each measures 12" high, 20" wide, and 28" long. Each trunk is supplied with an array of hands-on environmental education materials. For example, the Forestry Trunk contains approximately fifteen tree cross sections (or "tree cookies") of various Idaho tree species, a variety of pine cones, color photographs of trees, a slide show on the biological diversity within a forest, and much more. The wildlife trunk consists of animal skins, skulls, fish eggs, video cassettes, posters, and more. All trunks come with a teacher's guide and at least one audiovisual program. The materials are carefully arranged in the trunk with a liberal amount of foam padding to protect fragile items.

The cost of preparing the trunks was minimal. Each heavy-duty trunk cost $150.00. The educational materials that were selected to fill the trunks cost anywhere between $150.00 to $400.00, depending on the trunk's contents. So, for a total of $300.00 to $550.00, a successful education kit was produced.

We advertise the INRETT each year during September by sending a brochure and sign-up form to every elementary and junior high school in Idaho. Teachers fill in the form indicating which trunk they would like on which date. Trunks are scheduled for a period of one week in each classroom. Schools may request as many of the six trunks as they wish. After their time has been confirmed, a confirmation letter is sent with an invoice for $15.00 per trunk which covers the cost of round-trip shipping by United Parcel Service (UPS). Since they're local, Boise area teachers may pick up the trunks and use them for one week at no charge. The trunks are automatically picked up by UPS on a predetermined date and delivered back to Boise. When a trunk arrives back in the office, it is checked, cleaned and restocked, if necessary, and immediately sent to another school.

The INRETT was an instant and overwhelming success. Demand for the trunks far exceeded the supply almost from the beginning. After the first year of operation, additional Forestry, Wildlife and Outdoor Recreation trunks had to be added. The third year, yet another Wildlife trunk was added. Wildlife and Forestry are the most requested trunks.

The trunks are shipped to all corners of the state, from large cities to rural, isolated towns. Each year the trunks are sent to over fifty different Idaho towns and over 10,000 students per year are reached through INRETT. This program is very successful in reaching communities that are unable to find other environmental education materials.

There are still some minor problems with this program. The logistics of sending ten trunks throughout the state and receiving them back in time for the next school can be difficult and time consuming. Scheduling problems can occur because of severe weather, school holidays, human error and UPS schedules. A precise schedule must be maintained in order to satisfy all schools.

Another problem involves teachers' lack of care for the trunk materials. Periodically, materials are left out of the trunk, broken, or misused. Also, some materials simply wear out from so much use and must be replaced.

Despite these shortcomings, we feel strongly that the advantages and success of this program far outweigh the disadvantages. The INRETT is a low-cost yet effective environmental education outreach program whose success hinges on the cooperative efforts of many resource agencies. With only minor capital investment and limited personnel costs to administer the program, the INRETT has reached tens of thousands of students in Idaho and will continue to provide environmental education in our state in the future.

Resurrection of an Old Friend–Felt Story Boards for Environmental Education

Pat Tucker, Biologist
National Wildlife Federation,
Missoula, Montana

A child's fingers move a gray wolf puppy from its den and place it with its brothers and sisters near a lake where beavers swim across the blue expanse. "Wolves eat beaver in the summer. In the winter they can't because ice protects the beaver. And puppies are never left alone because they might get hurt." She places an adult wolf near the pups. "This is one of their older sisters who's staying with them while their mom and dad and other brothers and sisters go off to work, I mean hunt." She giggles and places four other adult wolves surrounding a moose … .

Many of us remember our primary school teachers using pieces of colored felt cut into various shapes to illustrate stories. We can remember how much we liked manipulating the pieces of colorful felt and making up our own stories.

Felt story boards allow children of all ages to combine visual, tactile and auditory learning styles in creative ways. During the past few years we have been successfully using felt story boards to illustrate ecological and environmental concepts. These story boards fill many of the needs for effective environmental learning tools: they're fun, easy to make, versatile and can be used in a wide variety of situations; the materials are readily accessible, and best of all they're inexpensive.

The first thing that's needed is a decision as to what story or concept to illustrate. If the story is what happens to forest animals and plants when the forest is logged and turned into ranch land, the following felt pieces might be needed: trees, some of the animals that live in the forest, loggers, roads, trucks, bulldozers, ranchers, cattle and houses. Remember that one or two cattle will suffice. Children don't have to see a whole herd to get the picture. Sometimes it helps to write a simple script for the story to be sure that all the necessary parts are included. Give the animals and people names and a story so the students will empathize. A specific monkey, born and raised in a forest that will be logged, will catch students' attention more than an anonymous or hypothetical animal. Likewise, give

human players identities and reasons for why they're doing what they're doing. Solutions to environmental problems are complex, and your story should encourage students to recognize the points of view of all the players.

After a list of characters has been developed, it's time to take a trip to a store that sells felt (usually this is a fabric store). One large background piece in a color on which other colors will show up is needed. Grey, light green, or tan are good choices. This piece should be between two to three feet high and three to four feet wide. Next pick out colors for all the characters. The characters need to be large enough for everyone in the room to see, six inches long or high is a good choice. If the figures are much larger they tend to fall off the background piece too easily. Use the brightest colors available. Patterns for the pieces can be traced from children's books if an artist is unavailable. Silhouette designs without

a lot of detail are easier to cut out. Detail can be added with a black, felt tip pen or paint if necessary. We've found that adults are more concerned about detail and having the figures perfectly proportioned than are children.

When the pieces are cut out, pin or tape the background piece on all four corners to the wall and the story is ready to begin. Remember to help the students look for innovative solutions to problems. This may require cutting out more felt pieces, so it's a good idea to have on hand some extra felt in several colors.

We've also found that students enjoy telling their own stories in front of the class. A felt story board gives them confidence because the pieces help them remember how the story goes. This should be encouraged and is even a good assignment. Also, it may be that a story about one environmental problem (e.g., deforestation) leads students to understand its interconnection with other problems (e.g., jobs), and a new story may be inspired. Since the materials are so inexpensive, only time prevents you from following up on these opportunities. When this happens, the felt story boards are achieving their most important objective: teaching students that real solutions to environmental problems start with understanding their causes.

Powerful Slides from Simple Techniques

Gerry Snyder, Manager
Natural Resources Communication
Laboratory, College of Forestry,
Wildlife, and Range Sciences
University of Idaho, Moscow, Idaho

For me, the best part of working on a slide program is creating the graphics and images. Today people are using all kinds of highly sophisticated slide graphics to enhance the visual quality of their talks and multi-media programs, but despite all the technology at our disposal, some of the best looking and least expensive slides are the simple ones you can make yourself. Among these are the blue and black background graphic slides that are so common these days. Besides looking great on the screen, they're extremely versatile in application. They can be used as title slides, credit slides, graphics or figures.

The blue background slides have become an industry standard for slide presentations and professional talks. The royal blue background allows enough ambient light in a room for note taking, and is easy on the eyes. Similarly, the black background slides are very dramatic, and text and other details can be colored using regular ink marking pens or inexpensive dyes.

Creating both kinds of slides is easy. Be sure to prepare and organize all your materials before you start shooting. As a general rule, it's good to leave plenty of room around your originals for cropping and framing. Above all, don't be afraid to be creative. Experimenting with exposure and colors will sometimes give you surprising results.

C-41 Method For Colored (Blue) Background Slides

Use:

The "C-41 method" is used to make slides with white text and deep, royal blue backgrounds. Typically, these are used as title or credit slides and creative artwork in slide presentations. Though royal blue is the most common choice, the method can also be used to produce red, green, pink and light blue backgrounds. (An example of a blue background slide produced with the C-41 method is shown in Plate 7.)

Materials:

A. 35 mm camera with light meter (a normal lens will often do, but a

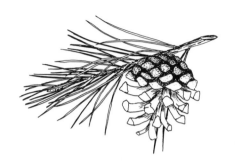 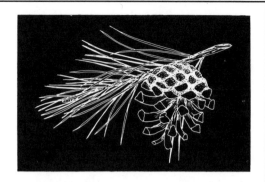

macro lens is preferred if close-ups of the artwork are needed.)

B. Ektachrome 100 slide film (it's daylight balanced and available in 24 and 36-exposure rolls)

C. Colored filters (orange, yellow, red, green, etc.)

D. Photo copystand equipped with tungsten or daylight lights. (Note: Either light source will give about the same results.)

E. If you don't have a photo copystand, a sunny day and a tripod will work fine.

Methods:

A. Set camera ISO/ASA setting to 200 (even though the film is rated at ISO 100) and attach the colored filter of your choice (orange and yellow filters give a royal blue background; no filter gives a darker navy blue background.)

B. Take your light meter reading with a "grey card" to obtain your shutter-speed and lens aperture settings. You can buy an inexpensive grey card at a photography store or you may use a piece of medium grey paper or other material.

C. Take the picture. Use a cable release if shutter speeds are 1/60 second or slower. Try "bracketing" for each shot (exposing 1/2-stop over and under your original camera settings) to safeguard and fine tune the shade and intensity of the blue background.

D. Take the film to a local professional photo lab (even 1-hour photo labs work in a pinch) for developing. Usually 24 hour turn-around is available, but don't count on it. Make these specific requests: 1) process the film using C-41 color print processing; 2) mount the negatives in slide mounts.

Additional Tips:

In general, you'll get a background that is roughly opposite to the original color and intensity of the filter you use (e.g., a light yellow filter gives a dark blue background, and a dark red filter will give a light green background). Art work or lettering done in black will photograph white and vice versa. If you don't have colored filters available, try using colored paper backgrounds. Experiment and have fun. You should try the C-41 method on outdoor scenes. The results can be surprisingly useful!

Always plan ahead. Give yourself plenty of time to retake slides if you don't like your results.

Kodalith Method For Black And White Slides

Use:

For making slides with white text and black backgrounds. You will get a solid black background with sharp white images. Art work or lettering done in black will photograph white. This film produces high impact images and best used for title/credit slides and for special effects.

Materials:

A. 35 mm camera with macro lens and light meter.

B. Kodalith (ISO/ASA 6) black and white slide film.

C. Photo copystand equipped with tungsten or daylight lights. (Note: Either light source will give about the same results.)

D. If you don't have a photo copystand, a sunny day and a tripod will work fine.

Methods:

A. Set camera ISO/ASA setting to 6. (Note: If your camera doesn't have an ISO setting of 6, set the ISO at 12 or 25. You can adjust for the difference when you take your light meter reading in step B.)

B. Take a light meter reading with a "grey card" to obtain your shutter speed and lens aperture settings. If your ISO is set at 6, no adjustments are necessary. If your ISO is set at 12, increase the aperture by opening the lens one additional f/stop. If your ISO setting is 25, open the lens two additional f/stops.

C. Take the picture. Use a cable release if shutter speeds are 1/60 second or slower. Try "bracketing" for each shot (exposing 1/2 spot over and under our original camera settings) to safeguard and fine tune the black background.

D. Take the film to a local professional photo lab for processing. Usually 24 hour turn-around is available, but don't count on it. Unless the lab routinely does Kodalith processing, you'll probably want to make these specific requests: (1) special processing using Kodak A & B developer—negatives only, (2) mount the negatives as slides. (Normally, processing labs automatically make prints when they develop black and white negative film. But since you don't need the prints, asking for only negatives will save a lot of money and waste.)

Some Additional Tips:

Your original text or art work should be solid, dark black and white (avoid materials with greys). Kodalith is a high contrast film which does not work well with most colors or grey tones.

White spots on slides can be eliminated by filling them in with a black felt tip marker. After "touching up" a spot, wait a minute or two and do it again.

For exposure, it's best to "bracket" each piece of artwork (i.e., shoot three photos) by shooting additional exposures 1/2-stop over and under the exposure the light meter gives you. Since Kodalith is a relatively inexpensive film, you might even want to bracket at four additional f/stop settings (two over and two under) the light meter reading (for a total of five exposures). Remember, the time it would take to re-shoot something that didn't turn out is almost always going to be more expensive than the extra film it takes to bracket thoroughly.

By using colored markers or photo dyes over your text, you can highlight and brighten segments on your slides. Be careful to avoid streak marks and smearing. If dyes are used, apply them with a small, fine-tipped touch-up brush for precise location. You can buy small bottles of commercial dyes in several colors at most stationery and art supply stores. "Dr. P. H. Martin's" is the most widely used brand.

References

Arévalo, Manuel. 1990. El Papelógrafo. In, Muñoz, Milton G. y Bernardo Peña. 1990. *Selección y Utilización de Ayudas Educativas.* Tegucigalpa, D.C., Honduras: Secretaria de Recursos Naturales, Departamento de Comunicación Agropecuaria, Proyecto de Comunicación para la Transferencia de Tecnología Agropecuaria, 42-49.

Bajimaya, Shyam and James R. Fazio. 1989. *Communications Manual: A Guide to Aid Park and Protected Area Managers to Communicate Effectively with Local Residents.* Kathmandu, Nepal: Department of National Parks and Wildlife Conservation/ FAO-UNDP.

Bishop, Ann. 1984. *Slides—Planning and Producing Slide Programs.* Kodak Publication S-30L. Rochester, New York, USA: Eastman Kodak Co.

Brown, James W., Richard B. Lewis, and Fred F. Harcleroad. 1989. *AV Instruction: Technology, Media and Methods.* New York, New York, USA: McGraw-Hill Book Co.

Bunch, Roland. 1982. *Two Ears of Corn: A Guide to People-Centered Agricultural Improvement.* Oklahoma City, Oklahoma, USA: World Neighbors.

Bunnell, Pille and Timothy D. Mock. 1990. *A Guide for the Preparation and Use of Overhead and Slide Visuals.* Victoria, British Columbia, Canada: Forestry Canada/B.C. Ministry of Forests, Research Branch.

Eastman Kodak. 1982. *Effective Lecture Slides.* Pamphlet No. S-22. Rochester, New York, USA: Eastman Kodak Co.

Enríquez, Jaime R. 1987. *A Proposed Methodology for Interpretive Planning in the National Parks and Similar Areas of Ecuador.* Moscow, Idaho, USA: Masters thesis, Department of Resource Recreation and Tourism, College of Forestry, Wildlife and Range Sciences, University of Idaho.

Fazio, James R. and Douglas L. Gilbert. 1986. *Public Relations and Communications for Natural Resource Managers.* Dubuque, Iowa, USA: Kendall/Hunt Publishing Co.

Freed, Mike. 1991. *Personal Communication.* Russellville, Arkansas, USA: Department of Parks and Recreation, Arkansas Tech University, March 5.

Grater, Russell K. 1976. *The Interpreter's Handbook: Methods, Skills and Techniques.* Globe, Arizona, USA: Southwest Parks and Monuments Association.

Ham, Sam H. 1990. Taller de Interpretación y Educación Ambiental, 25-27 de Abril de 1990, Valle de Angeles, F.M., Honduras. Informe final sometido a USAID/Honduras (Contrato No. 522-0292-0-00-0281-00). Tegucigalpa, D.C., Honduras: US Agency for International Development.

Ham, Sam H. and Jaime R. Enríquez. 1987. *Una Metodología Propuesta Sobre la Planificación de Interpretación Ambiental para los Parques Nacionales y Areas Equivalentes del Ecuador.* Moscow, Idaho, USA: Idaho Forest, Wildlife and Range Experiment Station Publication No. 310, College of Forestry, Wildlife and Range Sciences, University of Idaho.

Hooper, Jon K. 1987. *Effective Slide Presentations.* Chico, California, USA: Effective Slide Presentations.

Kenny, M.F. and R.F. Schmitt. 1981. *Images, Images, Images: The Book of Programmed Multi-image Production (2nd ed.).* Kodak Publication No. S-12. Rochester, New York, USA: Eastman Kodak Co.

Lewis, William J. 1980. *Interpreting for Park Visitors.* Philadelphia, Pennsylvania, USA: Eastern National Park and Monument Association, Eastern Acorn Press.

Meilach, Dona Z. 1990. *Dynamics of Presentation Graphics.* Homewood, Illinois, USA: Dow Jones-Irwin.

Moore, Alan, Bill Wendt, Louis Penna e Isabel Castillo de Ramos. 1989. *Manual para La Capacitación del Personal de Areas Protegidas (Modulo C: Interpretación y Educación Ambiental, Apunte 4a).* Washington, D.C., USA: Servicio de Parques Nacionales, Oficina de Asuntos Internacionales.

Morales, Jorge. 1987. *Manual para la Interpretación en Espacios Naturales Protegidos. Anexo 3 del Taller Internacional sobre Interpretación Ambiental en Areas Silvestres Protegidas.* Santiago, Chile: Oficina Regional de la FAO para América Latina y el Caribe, 7-12 de diciembre de 1988.

Muñoz, Milton G. y Hector R. Fonseca. 1990. *Ilustración de Materiales Escritos en el Sector Rural.* Tegucigalpa, D.C., Honduras: Secretaria de Recursos Naturales, Departamento de Comunicación Agropecuaria, Proyecto de Comunicación para la Transferencia de Tecnología Agropecuaria.

Muñoz, Milton G. y Bernardo Peña. 1990. *Selección y Utilización de Ayudas Educativas.* Tegucigalpa, D.C., Honduras: Secretaria de Recursos Naturales, Departamento de Comunicación Agropecuaria, Proyecto de Comunicación para la Transferencia de Tecnología Agropecuaria.

Pino, Georgina. 1989. *Las Artes Plásticas.* San José, Costa Rica: Editorial Universidad Estatal a Distancia.

Podracky, John R. 1983. *Creative Slide Presentations.* Englewood Cliffs, New Jersey, USA: Prentice-Hall, Inc.

Regnier, Kathleen, Michael Gross and Ron Zimmerman. 1992. *The Interpreter's Guidebook: Techniques for Programs and Presentations.* Stevens Point, Wisconsin, USA: UW-SP Foundation Press, Inc.

Risk, Paul H. 1982. The Interpretive Talk. Chapter 1 in Sharpe, G.W. (ed.), *Interpreting the Environment.* New York, New York, USA: John Wiley & Sons.

Sánchez, Enrique. 1990. La Cartelera. In, Muñoz, Milton G. y Bernardo Peña.

1990. *Selección y Utilización de Ayudas Educativas*. Tegucigalpa, D.C., Honduras: Secretaria de Recursos Naturales, Departamento de Comunicación Agropecuaria, Proyecto de Comunicación para la Transferencia de Tecnología Agropecuaria, pp. 61-68.

Stecker, Elinor. 1987. *Slide Showmanship*. New York, New York, USA: Amphoto.

Werner, David. 1986. *Donde No Hay Doctor—Una Guía para los Campesinos que Viven Lejos de los Centros Médicos*. Palo Alto, California, USA: La Fundación Hesperian.

Werner, David and Bill Bower. 1986. *Helping Health Workers Learn—A Book of Methods, Aids and Ideas for Instructors at the Village Level*. Palo Alto, California, USA: The Hesperian Foundation.

Additional Reading

In English:

Countryside Commission. 1980. *Audio-Visual Media in Countryside Interpretation*. Advisory Series No. 12. London, United Kingdom: Countryside Recreation Research Group.

Eastman Kodak. 1989. *Kodak Sourcebook: Kodak Ektagraphic Slide Projectors*. Publication No. S-74. Rochester, New York, USA: Eastman Kodak Co.

Eastman Kodak. 1982. *Effective Lecture Slides*. Pamphlet No. S-22. Rochester, New York, USA: Eastman Kodak Co.

Eastman Kodak. 1973. *Reverse-Text Slides from Black-on-White Line Artwork*. Kodak Pamphlet S-26. Rochester, New York, USA: Eastman Kodak Co.

Kuehner, Richard A. 1982. Photography and Interpretation. Chapter 20 in Sharpe, G.W. (ed.), *Interpreting the Environment*. New York, New York, USA: John Wiley & Sons.

O'Neill, Jerome P., Jr. 1979. *101 Ways to Make Copy and Title Slides—Some of Them Good! Part I. Audiovisual Notes*. Periodical No. T-91-9-1. Rochester, New York, USA: Eastman Kodak Co., p. 8-12.

O'Neill, Jerome P., Jr. 1979. *101 Ways to Make Copy and Title Slides—Some of Them Good! Part II. Audiovisual Notes*. Periodical No. T-91-9-2. Rochester, New York, USA: Eastman Kodak Co., p. 4-7.

O'Neill, Jerome P., Jr. 1980. *101 Ways to Make Copy and Title Slides—Some of Them Good! Part III. Audiovisual Notes*. Periodical No. T-91-9-3. Rochester, New York, USA: Eastman Kodak Co., p. 8-13.

Pennyfather, Keith. 1975. *Guide to Countryside Interpretation: Part II—Interpretive Media and Facilities*. Edinburgh, Scotland: Her Majesty's Stationery Office and the Countryside Commission.

Thompson, David D. Jr.. 1968. *Talks: A Public Speaking Guide for National Park Service Employees*. Washington, D.C., USA: U.S. National Park Service, Visitor Services Training Series.

In Spanish:

Asociación Norteamericana de Editores de Facultades de Agronomia. 1970. *Manual de Comunicaciones*. Buenos Aires, Argentina: Editorial Albatros.

Ham, Sam H. 1992. *Interpretación Ambiental: Una Guía Práctica para*

Gente con Grandes Ideas y Presupuestos Pequeños. Golden, Colorado, USA: North American Press/Fulcrum Publishing.

Osorio, Juan Manuel. 1990. Bases Fundamentales del Dibujo. En, Muñoz, Milton G. y Bernardo Peña.

1990. *Selección y Utilización de Ayudas Educativas.* Tegucigalpa, D.C., Honduras: Secretaria de Recursos Naturales, Departamento de Comunicación Agropecuaria, Proyecto de Comunicación para la Transferencia de Tecnología Agropecuaria, p. 18-32.

CHAPTER FIVE

HOW TO PREPARE AND PRESENT A GUIDED TOUR OR WALK

In this chapter we'll consider a special kind of presentation, tours. Although the terms "guided walk" or "hike" are often used when the tour takes place on a trail or pathway, we'll use the term "tour" here to include not only guided walks and hikes but other kinds presentations in which an interpreter leads a group of people through a preplanned sequence of narrated stops. Tours are commonly used to show people things that they'd otherwise not see or that the untrained eye probably wouldn't notice. They can be given in many kinds of settings and for several different kinds of audiences.

In some ways, tours are a lot like talks—for example, you should organize them around a theme and follow an interpretive approach in presenting them (see Chapters 1 and 2). Like talks, tours also have introductions, bodies, and conclusions, and they lend themselves to techniques such as foreshadowing, mystery,

and other communication methods that we often associate with talks. For these reasons, tours are sometimes thought of as "talks on wheels."

But despite these similarities, tours and talks differ in three important ways: (1) tours move—the presentation is mobile, going from one stop to the next; (2) tours are almost always visual, each stop serving more or less the function that a slide or series of slides might serve in an illustrated talk; and (3) tours usually require more of a commitment from their audiences, both physically and in terms of time.

Tour audiences vary greatly. Often, people who go on guided tours are willing to invest the required time and energy because they're already more than casually interested in the topic; other people might go on the tour because they think that they'll get to see things they'd otherwise miss, or because they're apprehensive about venturing into the area without a guide; and still others might be part of an organized group or special event which happens to involve a tour of your site or facility. The latter group might not have an option other than to participate in the tour, and some of the people might not even want to be there. As with any interpretive activity, you should tailor your approach as if every audience were like the last group. This will cause you to work harder at making your tour so interesting and entertaining that even people who didn't want to be with you will be glad that they are.

Types of Tours

There are many types of tours, and interpreters can present them in a number of different settings (see Figure 5-1). For example, a naturalist might lead visitors along a forest trail showing them ways that plants and animals depend on each other; a nursery manager might lead a group of college students through an experimental plot showing how seedlings grow differently in various kinds of soils; an extension specialist might guide a group of farmers around a demonstration field showing how soil conservation leads to increased yields; or a guide at a brewery or vineyard might show visitors the equipment and procedures for making a fine beer or wine. Though content and audiences differ, each presents the same challenges to the interpreter-guide.

Tours can have very specific purposes—showing the parts of an ecosystem, orienting visitors to an historic place, explaining a process, etc. Or they may have more general purposes—creating awareness, building appreciation, or suggesting a new way to think or look at

something. As with talks, your objective, and the theme you've selected to help you accomplish it, will guide your approach.

Tours can be presented on trails, in buildings and facilities, at zoos, museums, parks, forests, farms, botanical gardens, nurseries, demonstration and research sites, aboard small boats or large ships, in buses or cars, or in other settings. As Figure 5-1 shows, where a tour is presented usually has something to do with its purpose and with the kind of message you want to get across.

Qualities of a Good Tour

Good tours have the qualities that we outlined in Chapter 1. That is, they're interpretive; they're entertaining to their audiences; they present meaningful and relevant information; and they're well organized around a central theme with five or fewer main ideas. In addition, good tours usually are dynamic in the sense that there's always something going on: the interpreter is talking, or the participants are actively thinking, doing, searching, noticing or discussing something. Tours which don't hold their audience's attention very well often lack this dynamic quality. For this reason, we'll focus specifically on techniques for increasing dynamism in guided tours, as well as on how to plan and organize different kinds of tours. As experienced interpreters will tell you, the best way to recognize an effective tour is to watch the audience. If the people seem interested and involved in what they're hearing and seeing, then the tour is doing what the interpreter wanted it to do—it's capturing the audience's attention. Having accomplished this important task, communicating a theme is relatively straightforward.

Tours can be given almost anywhere there is something important to show and talk about. Following are some common examples of tours, their purposes, typical settings, and lengths.

Type of Tour	Typical Purposes	Typical Settings	Typical Length (distance/time)
Guided Walk	To orient people to a place; to show selected examples of things which illustrate a central theme	Short trails, paths, small sites	1/4 to 1 mile/ 30 minutes to 2 hours (400–1600 m)
Extended Hike	To orient people to a large or remote area; to show selected examples of things which illustrate a central theme	Long trails and large sites	> 1 mile/2 hours (> 1.6 km/2 hrs.)
Building Tour	To orient people to a building or structure; to show selected examples of things which illustrate a central theme	Visitor centers, museums, historic homes, theaters, office buildings, headquarters, and other structures	<1/4 mile/ 30 minutes to 90 minutes (< 400 m)
Facility (Process) Tour	To demonstrate a production or manufacturing process; to show selected examples of things that illustrate a theme	Factories, manufacturing plants, energy production facilities, wineries/vineyards, breweries, dairies, food processing facilities, nurseries, sawmills, research laboratories	< 1 mile/1 hour (< 1.6 km)

Type of Tour	Typical Purposes	Typical Settings	Typical Length (distance/time)
Site Tour	To orient people to a site that is specifically recognized for its natural, cultural or scientific values; to show selected examples of things which illustrate a central theme	Historic sites, cemeteries, battlefields, farms demonstration areas, research plots, plantations, sites of natural and human-caused catastrophes	1/4 mile/20 minutes (400 m)
Bus, Auto, Train, Boat, and Bicycle Tours	Any objective above which lends itself to the selected form of transportation	Highways, roads, lakes, bays, inlets	1 mile/1 hour (1.6 km)

Figure 5-1. Examples of different kinds of tours.

Of course, many factors combine to make a successful tour. Among the ones we'll consider in this chapter are careful planning, smooth transitions between stops, and a clear relationship between the stops and the theme of the tour.

Tour Guides Have Personalities

Leading a good tour starts with how you see yourself in the role of "guide." How you envision yourself in this role influences the kind of image you'll project to your audiences, and the kind of response they'll give to your tours. This is so fundamental that many interpreters give little thought to it. Unfortunately, this is often a mistake. A tour may be mechanically sound and technically correct yet fail to capture its audience. As Risk (1990) pointed out, the shortcomings of such a tour often have less to do with what was done and said during the tour, than with the kind of personality the guide projected to the audience.

Almost anyone who has taken a guided tour or walk has seen firsthand how the guide's image and demeanor can directly influence an audience's response to the activity. Most of us can probably remember one or more of four personalities types that guides sometimes project (Figure 5-2).

Cops are staunch protectors of the local environment. They're certain that without careful monitoring and continual

Figure 5-2. The four personalities of a tour guide. (Drawings by Jeff Egan)

reprimanding, their audiences will cause irreparable damage to the site. For this reason, they issue lots of reminders about rules and etiquette, frequently reminding parents to control their children and issuing periodic sermons about the fragility of the site. To these guides, every site is an "endangered species." Rather than making their audiences feel welcome, cops merely tolerate them, and sometimes only begrudgingly. It's as though they're saying that having the tour in that location is a bad idea because audiences simply can't be trusted.

Machines are human message repeaters. Once they've been turned on, they regurgitate from memory the entire tour narration, sometimes barely stopping to breathe between sentences. To the audience, it's usually obvious that the guide has given the same tour, in exactly the same way, many times before. Especially important in the machines' style is the computer-like tone which assures the audience that nothing spontaneous nor personal can possibly come out of the guide's mouth. Also clear is that communication will occur in only one direction, and that there will be no deviation from the machine's well-practiced routine. Machines don't like to be interrupted by questions nor by anything that's unplanned or outside of the "script."

Know-it-alls are the data dumpers of the tour-guide world. More than anything else, a tour represents a chance to show just how much they know about their topic. Know-it-alls are so dedicated to this task that they'll gladly extend the tour an extra half-hour or hour to make sure they get everything in. To them, saying "I don't know" is embarrassing. The theme of the know-it-all's tour is always the same: "Pay attention today and you'll see how much smarter I am than you."

Hosts are the most successful tour guides. They don't see themselves as cops (even though they're very concerned about protecting the site), as machines (even though their tours are well-planned and rehearsed), nor as know-it-alls (even though they're very knowledgeable about their topics). Hosts project the kind of personality that most people project when they invite new friends into their home. They see their audiences as guests rather than as passive listeners, insatiable learners or physical threats. And in every tour they go out of their way to make their guests feel welcome, just as they would were they at home in the guide's living room. Hosts consciously try to establish a friendly atmosphere that's conducive to two-way communication and that makes the people glad to be there. They continually show respect for their audiences—by chatting and joking, by happily taking questions whenever they arise, by making sure that everyone has a chance to speak, and by being willing to do what is of greatest interest to the audience even if it means deviating from the planned narration.

Although it's certainly possible for a guide to have traits from more than one of these "personalities," the best guides seem to be more like hosts than anything else. For many, this isn't something that comes naturally; they have to work at it. Those who work the hardest at it seem to enjoy more success with their tours, and they also seem to enjoy themselves more. Practice seeing yourself as a host, and soon you'll be acting like one in every tour.

How to Plan and Prepare a Thematic Tour

As with talks, our approach to developing guided tours will be to first consider the purposes of their main parts, and then how to design the parts to accomplish their different purposes. Since we'll emphasize the preparation of thematic tours, you should review the appropriate sections of Chapters 1 and 2 if you're not yet familiar with the development and use of themes. There are a number of good references on preparing tours and guided walks. The most useful ones in English are Lewis (1980), Grater (1976), Risk (1982), Dawson-Medina and Shank (1987), Krumbein and Leyva (1977), and Regnier et al.(1992). In Spanish, Moore et al.(1989) and Morales (1987) are recommended.

Parts of a Tour and Their Purposes

Tours usually have four parts: a **staging period**, an **introduction**, a **body** and a **conclusion**—each of which serves different purposes (Figure 5-3). The main task in designing an effective tour is to make sure that each part does what it's supposed to do.

The Staging Period

The staging period usually occurs fifteen to thirty minutes before the tour, itself, begins. It's the time you spend at the departure point greeting people as they arrive. This is an important time because it helps both you and your audience to learn about each other. It also allows the people to ask questions—about the tour or about other things they might want to know—and it serves as an "ice-breaker," allowing informal conversation, exchanging of names, hometowns, occupations, etc., that helps build rapport between you and the audience. Now is the time to make your best first impression. Smile, be open and friendly. This isn't the time to be bashful. Try to be first to introduce yourself, rather than waiting for the arrivers to make the first gesture. Offer to take group photographs and consent, if asked, to be photographed by them.

Make sure you spread your attention to as many people as possible. If your group is small enough, try to greet all persons as they arrive. Guard against being locked into conversation with a single group or individual. As Risk (1982) warned, this will not only prevent you from meeting the other people, it could actually create resentment if they feel ignored. This would be unfortunate since it's precisely the opposite of what the staging period is supposed to accomplish.

As people arrive, you'll notice certain things about them that might suggest an information need. Do they include young children or elders who should know about a steep or difficult part of a trail? Are they wearing appropriate clothing (shoes, jackets, hats, sunglasses, etc.)? If they'll need water, are they carrying a container? What about insect repellent or sunscreen? If they aren't carrying a camera or binoculars with them, might you suggest that there's still time to get them from their vehicle? Different groups, of course, will suggest different needs. The important thing in this stage of the tour is that you be anticipating them. Of utmost importance is to let people know about

the degree of physical exertion that will be required on the tour, and of any hazards that might be encountered. Unless you notice something specific (such as crutches or a leg brace), it's probably not a good idea to query each person about his or her stamina or physical condition. Save this for the introduction when you can make a general announcement to everyone, thus avoiding potential embarrassment to any individual.

In certain parks or heavily visited recreation areas, parents will sometimes ask you to take one or more of their children on the walk with you, promising to meet you back at the beginning at an agreed upon time. Typically, they claim that the youngster has expressed a deep interest in the topic of your walk, and that they don't want to disappoint him or her. Some, however, are more honest: "We really need a break from these kids. Would you mind taking them off our hands for a while?" Almost anyone who has given guided walks in a park has had to face this situation at one time or another. Although there are many ways to handle it, a good one is to say that the child is welcome to participate in the walk but that your attention will be on the whole group, and therefore you can't take responsibility for the child's safety. That is usually sufficient to avoid getting pinned into what is essentially a babysitting job.

The Introduction

At precisely the publicized beginning time (even if the assembled group is small), you should begin the introduction to your tour. A good introduction needs to do several things very well. First, it creates interest in the topic. It doesn't just make the audience willing to participate

Good Tours Have Good Parts

There are usually four parts to a good tour: a staging period, an introduction, body, and conclusion. Preparing an effective tour or guided walk is simple if you think of it as developing these four different parts and if you concentrate on designing each part to accomplish its specific purposes.

Part of the Tour	Purpose(s)
BEFORE: The Staging Period	Greet people, assure them that they have arrived at the right spot, inform them about the duration and physical requirements of the tour and about any special clothing (shoes, coat, etc.) they might need, discuss safety considerations, establish rapport, and wait for the starting time.
DURING: The Introduction	Create interest in the topic, and to make your audience want to hear more about it. Orient the audience to the theme, and to tell how your tour is going to be organized. Establish the conceptual framework by telling a little about some of the things the audience will see along the way. Set the stage for the conclusion. Repeat information about the length and duration of the tour, physical requirements, clothing, etc.
The Body (stops)	Develop the theme by showing your audience pertinent sites and objects of interest.
The Conclusion	Reinforce the theme—to show one last time the relationship between the theme and the things you showed and discussed along the way.

Figure 5-3. Purposes of different parts of a thematic tour.

in the tour—the best introductions make them want to go. This is essential for non-captive audiences, because very early in the tour they'll decide whether to continue. A lot of times, the leader of a tour starts off with a provocative statement or an interesting question that hints at the theme of the tour and stimulates interest. For example, in introducing a guided rainforest walk you might say:

> "Hi, I'm (give your name), and I'd like to invite you to join me on a short walk into one of the most unusual environments I've ever worked in. I'm referring, of course, to the rainforest behind me. A lot of you have probably been inside forests like this one before, but after today, I think you'll see them differently. We'll be seeing a lot of interesting things today. For example, you'll learn how to spot the homes of several different animals—some that are quite secretive and some that are unique to this kind of forest. You'll also be able to see for yourself what makes a 'rain' forest different from other kinds forests. Huge trees are common in an old forest like this one, and some of the ones we'll be passing today have been growing here since the time of Columbus. There'll be plenty of opportunities for photographs and questions as we get to them, and to the other things we'll be stopping to look at today."

Figure 5-4. The staging period for an archaeological site tour at Tulum, Mexico. (Photo by Sam Ham)

Capturing the audience's interest in your opening remarks is important. Although our example gives us the advantage of large old trees and secretive animals' homes, any environment offers interesting features that an imaginative interpreter will be able to capitalize on without stooping to sensationalizing or misrepresenting what's actually there. Even old familiar things can become deeply interesting when we shed new light on them or look at them in a completely new way. That's a basic premise of interpretation. What is key about this part of the introduction is that your genuine interest in the topic and enthusiasm for your job show.

At this point you probably should tell your group how much time the walk will take, perhaps looking at your watch and announcing the actual time of day you'll return. Be sure to tell exactly where the tour will end, especially if it's somewhere other than the starting point. It's also important to repeat information about physical requirements, safety precautions, protective clothing, etc., for those who might not have gotten it during the staging period.

> "Our walk today is going to cover about a mile, including our return. Although we may have to step over a couple of small limbs, the trail is smooth and mostly flat. Unless you tire very easily you'll probably have no problem. Walking slowly and stopping a lot, we'll probably be back here in about one-and-a-half hours—right around 3:30."

As Risk (1982) pointed out, giving this part of the introduction at the staging area allows time for late arrivals to join the group, more or unless unnoticed. It also provides an "easy out" for those who decide not to go any further.

At this point, many interpreters simply continue with the introduction right at the staging area. Others, however, like to move the group away from the staging area and into the tour area, itself, before going any further with the introduction. Some say that moving does two things. First, it allows those who have chosen not to go any further an opportunity to withdraw anonymously. Second, the move creates a kind of psychological transition between the distractions of the staging area and the tour, itself. This technique seems to work well in many situations, but especially when the new location will

Figure 5-5. An important purpose of the introduction is to orient visitors to the theme of the walk and to the route they'll be taking. Guayabo National Monument, Costa Rica. (Photo by Dave Sutherland)

somehow change how things sound or look to the audience (e.g., slightly inside a forest's opening, part way around a bend in a trail or road). If you choose to move the group, however, try to stay within partial view of the staging area so that last-minute arrivals can still find you.

Another thing a good introduction must do is orient the audience to the theme, and tell generally how the tour's going to be organized. This can be accomplished by stating the theme and hinting at a few of the stops you'll be making. This helps tie your tour together from the outset—as though it's a single story with many chapters, rather than several different stories. It also gives you a chance to recap some of your earlier remarks for people who might have arrived late.

> "We're about to enter a forest that people around here have known for centuries. In fact, as I was saying earlier, some of the large trees we'll see are the very same trees that people

living in this forest hundreds of years ago looked at every day. They probably used some of the boughs for making their shelters, or snacked on some of the seeds the trees produce. Almost without question, the children around here climbed some of these trees, and played hide-and-seek type games behind their trunks. Besides the trees, we'll be stopping to look at animal homes, and we'll be on the lookout for the animals, themselves—some of whom figured in the people's diet, and others in their religion. And at one of our stops, we'll be using what we see on the forest floor to piece together a picture of what this forest probably looked like to people here in the past two hundred years or so. You'll see that walking through an ancient forest like this one can really give you a sense of timelessness. Although people have changed a great deal in the past two centuries, this forest has changed very little. And using a little detective work, I think you'll see why in the next hour-and-a-half."

"Let's move now to our first stop on the trail. That's where we find our first clue about what the people here were like two centuries ago."

You should have noticed three things about this part of the introduction. First, it tells the theme of the tour—although people have changed a great deal in the past two centuries, this forest

has changed very little. Second, notice that the last two sentences are simply a transition to the next (in this case, first) stop. Third, notice the interpreter's use of **foreshadowing** to create interest in what the audience will see at the first stop. Foreshadowing (see Chapter 3) is a common technique for making strong transitions between stops on a tour. In this case, people in the audience naturally wonder what "clue" they might see at the first stop. This makes them more interested in continuing and gives them something to think about while they're walking to the next stop. **Mystery** (suspense) is also an effective transition technique. For example, the interpreter might have said, "Let's move now to our first stop on the trail. That's where we find our first clue about what the people here were like two centuries ago. When we get there, see if you can spot it."

The Body

The body of a tour consists of the narrated stops, which together try to accomplish just one purpose—to develop the theme of the tour. "To develop" means to present information that's needed to get the theme across to your audience. Therefore, you should try to select stops that will support your main idea rather than trying to tell everything you know, or comment on everything you'll see along the way. You can always answer spontaneous questions or capitalize on unexpected opportunities (or "teachable moments") when they occur. But planning to include it all in every tour only obscures your theme, and robs the tour of spontaneity.

Beginning interpreters are sometimes unsure how to plan what they'll say and do at the stops they've selected. Of course, if they've planned their stops around a central theme, the problem is easily solved: each planned, narrated stop should focus the audience's attention on something related to the theme. For example, what kinds of stops do you think the interpreter leading our rainforest walk should make? Although everyone does things a little differently, you're probably thinking that the tour should include stops which illustrate the changing of people and the permanence of the forest—since these are the two main ideas in the theme of the tour. Therefore, the guide's planned stops might include places that: (1) show evidence of human habitation, (2) display plants or signs of animals that were important to humans in the past, (3) reveal evidence of past environments (e.g., fallen "nurse-logs", fire scars, old river beds, etc.), and (4) demonstrate the natural growth and development of the forest (e.g., cones, seedlings, duff, trees with different shade tolerance, etc.). On the other hand, you might have thought of an altogether different list of stops—and that's OK. The important thing is that you arrived at those ideas by thinking first about the theme, and then about the kinds of stops that would help to develop it. If you approach your own tours this way, you're thinking thematically—and well on your way to designing effective guided tours.

In deciding what to say at each stop, it sometimes helps to think of your narration as having four steps:

1. a focusing sentence
2. a description (or explanation)
3. a thematic connector
4. a transition

Figure 5-6. A stop on a guided walk at Grand Teton National Park. The numbered post in the foreground suggests this route is also used as a self-guided trail. (Photo by Nancy Medlin)

The **focusing sentence** is a statement which focuses the group's attention on the object, scene or idea you wish to emphasize at the stop. To help, you might want to stand next to the object, point to it, or simply refer to its location in relation to one of the audience members in order to make sure that everyone knows what they should be focused on. For example, at a stop in front of one of the large trees, our rainforest interpreter might put a hand on the trunk and say, "Would anyone like to guess how big around this tree is?" With small groups, focusing the group's attention will usually require no more than one simple sentence or question.

With large groups, focusing may be more difficult. Make sure everyone can see what you're referring to before beginning your narration. This can be a problem if the group is spread out on a trail or other narrow corridor. If there are multiple exemplars of thing you want to refer to (e.g., a certain kind of plant or rock), you might want to spend a couple of minutes passing through the group and pointing them out so that everyone can look at the one nearest them while you're talking. If the group is so large that you can't be seen, try standing on a rock, a stump or other make-shift stage in order to make yourself visible to the group. (On trail walks, some interpreters position themselves off the trail near the middle of the group, and one guide reportedly went so far as to partially climb a tree!)

The **description** (or **explanation**) is the main part of the narration. Here you describe or explain the features or aspects of the scene that you want your audience to pay attention to or notice. Be selective—trying to explain too much can overwhelm the group. As always, let the theme of your tour determine your choice of information. As we discuss later, asking a few leading questions is often a good way to bring out the information you want to describe or explain. Also, think about ways you might involve some or all of the people in the group. For example, after listening to some guesses about the

circumference of the tree, our rainforest guide, might say:

> "Well those are all good guesses, but the only real way to find out is to measure it. Unfortunately, all I have with me is a meter stick and it won't bend around the tree. Does anyone have any ideas about how to measure a round tree with a straight stick?"

Someone may offer the solution—which is to connect enough people around the tree (arms stretched, hand-in-hand) until the trunk is completely surrounded. Having reached the tree's circumference, the "human chain" is then unfolded into a straight line that one of the other people can measure by moving the meter stick length-by-length down the chain. But even if nobody suggests this method of measuring the tree, the interpreter can. In either event, the simple task of

Figure 5-7. A "human measuring stick." With hands connected, visitors stretch themselves around a tree until the circumference is reached. The chain then unfolds into a straight line which is measured using a tape or meter stick. Moscow Mountain, Idaho. (Photos by Gerry Snyder)

measuring the tree's circumference is turned into a fun and instructive activity for the group. Following the measurement, the interpreter might tell how old the tree is and how its size and age compare to other trees in the forest.

The **thematic connector** does exactly what the term says: it connects the description or explanation to the tour's theme. Essentially, it reveals your reason for stopping at that particular location. A simple phrase will usually suffice. For example, after telling about the tree's size and age in relation to other trees in the forest, our guide might say, "Since this area has never been logged, an old giant like this one can tell us a lot about the way this forest looked two hundred years ago." Although the interpreter might offer additional details about the tree, issuing this statement makes part of the theme very clear: trees like the one the group has just measured were probably around then, too.

The **transition** is an important part of a narrated stop. At a minimum, it brings the current discussion to an end, and signals the group to follow the guide to the next stop. The best transitions, however, often do even more. They might foreshadow what the group will see or do at the next stop. As we've seen, there are many ways to foreshadow. For example, the guide might mention that the next stop is a good example of something the group has discussed previously: "Remember earlier when I was telling you about the importance of insects in this forest? Well, at our next stop you'll see a good example of one of these insects in action. Let's head that way now." Alternatively, a transition might refer to an exception to the norm: "So far today we've been talking about trees fighting

each other for sunlight. But the next tree we're going to stop at isn't a fighter. In fact, it's willing to wait for decades to get its day in the sun. Let's move down the trail and I'll show it to you."

Frequently, transitions not only give people something to look forward to at the next stop, they give them something to do or think about while they're traveling to it. We've been calling this technique "using mystery." As we saw in Chapter 3, using mystery is similar to foreshadowing, but instead of just hinting at what is to come, the interpreter gives the audience a question to ponder or some kind of problem to solve. For example:

> "OK, let's move to our next stop now—but while we're walking, here's a puzzle to think about: Scientists tell us that about 350 years ago a fire burned this part of the forest. But if that's so, then how could some of these trees be more than 500 years old? Be thinking about it, and at our next stop we'll find some clues to the answer and see how it compares to what you came up with."

Another variation is to give the group something to look for while it's traveling to the next stop. For example:

> "We're going move to our next stop now, but between here and there three major changes are going to take place in the forest we're walking through. See if you can notice at least two of them. Anyone who gets all three should apply for my job next year!"

Figure 5-8. A good transition suggests something for visitors to do, look for, or think about between stops. Olympic National Park. (Photo by Sam Ham)

Although experienced guides sometimes omit or combine one or more of these steps, most narrated stops include all four parts in one form or another. Although the duration of any stop depends on many factors (length of tour, size and type of group, etc.), a very rough guideline for short tours with small groups is to keep each stop under five to seven minutes unless there is something special going on that warrants additional time (Risk 1982). Of this time, you might allow about thirty to sixty seconds for focusing the group, three to five minutes for the description and explanation, thirty seconds for the thematic connector, and a few seconds for your transition to the next stop. In practice, of course, actual durations will vary widely depending on your style and the group's interest.

The Conclusion

The conclusion is usually given following the narration at the last stop of the tour. A good conclusion to a tour does what any conclusion should do—it reinforces the theme. It shows one last time the relationship between the stops that were made and the main message they were designed to get across to the audience. Sometimes the interpreter will briefly summarize what was seen and done during the tour, and then conclude by telling how it related to the theme. Good conclusions are short and specific, and they signal a clear and unambiguous ending to the activity. For example, our rainforest guide might say:

"During our walk today we've seen that a rainforest is really many forests—all growing together in one big, yet interesting ecosystem. And we found evidence that humans have been a part this forest for many centuries—first the native people and later gold miners. I'll bet you're thinking that in some ways our being here today is just one more episode in the long story of this forest. And you're right. We humans have changed a lot over the past two hundred years—not only in how we look and act—but in how we see and value a forest like this one. Fortunately, we've also seen that even though humans have had a constant presence here, the forest has managed to stay pretty much the same."

"That concludes our walk today. I hope you've enjoyed it as much as I have. Have a nice day, and thanks for coming along with me."

Often, part of your conclusion will be determined by where you are when you give it. If you've ended the walk somewhere other than at the starting point, it's a good idea to tell people the best or shortest way to return. You might also want to invite those who would like to chat more to accompany you back to the starting point.

Many trails lead to spectacular features (waterfalls, vistas, caves, unusually large trees, or other interesting places). Usually, it's not a good idea to present your conclusion at such a place unless the feature, itself, relates directly to your theme. If it doesn't, you may have a hard time competing for the group's attention because they'll be more interested in looking at the feature than in listening to your conclusion. It's often better to conclude the tour just prior to the feature, and then invite the group to go see it after you're done.

Planning the Tour Using the 2-3-1 Rule

Planning a tour starts with knowing the tour area. Whether it be a trail, a cave, a farm, a highway, a lake or some other setting, your first task is to familiarize yourself with the area so that you can: (1) decide on possible themes for your tour, (2) be able to answer questions unrelated to your theme, and (3) capitalize on the unexpected when it occurs during a tour.

Though the familiarization process really never ends, it should begin intensively—reading books, journals and other publications, and by spending as much time as you can in the area. Travel the route many times and under different conditions (mid-day, dusk, dawn, sunny days, cloudy days, and even rainy days if you can). If you work at the area year-round, get to know it during the different seasons. Know what to expect under a variety of conditions, and how things are likely to appear to your audiences. Through the course of these ventures you'll also collect personal anecdotes about your own experiences which will strengthen your narrations. When possible, invite someone who knows the area better than you do to go with you. If long-time residents live nearby, go to their homes and talk with them, and if possible, take them to the area with you so that you can see things through more experienced eyes.

As you learn more about the area, themes will come to mind. Think thematically: "After people have taken my tour here, I'd like them to know that (or appreciate that, or think that) … " As we saw in Chapters 1 and 2, completing such a sentence requires you to express a theme. Having done so, your tour will begin to come together more easily than if you start with only a vague and open-ended idea of the message you want to communicate. Thinking thematically, you'll find it relatively easy to develop several different tours in the same area. You'll discover that each theme will suggest different stops and different narrations because the story you're trying to tell will be different each time.

Once you have a theme to work with, you're ready to begin thinking about stops and narrations, and about the introduction, body and conclusion of your tour. Recall in Chapter 3 our use of the "2-3-1 Rule" to develop a thematic talk. This approach works well in planning tour narrations, too. Basically, as the "rule" says, you should think first about the body (stops) of the tour, then the conclusion, and finally, the introduction—the logic, of course, being that you can't know how to introduce something that you haven't yet developed.

In planning the stops, be sure to think about transitions. You should also be careful to keep the number of main ideas you'll treat to five or fewer. This doesn't mean that the number of stops should be limited to five—but that the kinds of information you use to develop your theme fall into five or fewer categories or main conceptual units. (See Chapter 1 for a review of the "magical number seven plus or minus two.")

Figure 5-9. The knapsack of a well-prepared interpreter. (Photo by Gerry Snyder)

Ways to Make a Tour More Dynamic

The best tours are dynamic. They don't merely consist of a series of stops in which the interpreter-guide stops the group and talks. Dynamic tours are more active, with each stop involving the audience in some exercise—intellectually, verbally or physically. Following are a few ideas of things you might do to make your tours more dynamic.

1. Carry a knapsack or day pack containing visual aids and communication helpers which you can use at planned stops or to capitalize on unexpected opportunities. Depending on your tour and audience, you might consider tools such as: field guides, binoculars, hand lens, thermometers, increment borer, hand puppets, meter stick, tape measure, string, tree cross-sections, mounted photos, drawings, a small flannel board and prepared illustrations (see Chapter 4), maps, compass, mirror, mounted animal and plants specimens, small tape player for playing bird calls or oral history excerpts, clay or "Play-Doh" for creating miniature landscapes or showing how rocks are made, a spray bottle with water for highlighting spider webs, examples of hard-to-find things such as owl pellets, old bird nests, snake skins, soil core samples, human artifacts, etc. A first-aid kit is always recommended. Lists of other useful items can be found in Freed and Shafer (1981), Krumbein (1983), Krumbein and Leyva (1977), and Regnier et al.(1992).

2. Make frequent use of foreshadowing and mystery, especially in transitions between stops.

3. Incorporate short activities into some of your stops. An example was the tree measuring exercise described earlier. Other possibilities are endless: using a bottomless soup can or paper tube as a tree-finder or "scope," guessing games, using senses (smelling, listening, touching, etc.), or simply passing around some object from your knapsack. Another example is the "scavenger hunt" tour in which people in the group are constantly searching for certain items. In 1979, an interpreter at Olympic National Park in the western U.S. conducted a guided beach walk based entirely on a "scavenger

hunt" activity. He knew what kinds of things would be carried in by the tide each day, but he didn't know exactly where they'd be found on the beach during any particular tour. So he gave everyone in the group a note card on which he'd written an interpretive vignette or short phrase about some object that he knew he'd eventually find. The objective for each person was to recognize when the interpreter's commentary was referring to the thing described on his or her card, and to say "I've got that one!" A token reward (decal or homemade ribbon) was given for a correct identification. For example:

The Phrase on the Card	The Thing in Question
•The original maker of "super glue"	A barnacle
•A delicious candy	Kelp
•A transient hobo	A hermit crab

The result was that everyone had fun and learned a lot about beach life. They paid closer attention to what the interpreter was saying—mainly because they didn't want to miss recognizing their object.

4. Ask questions to intellectually engage the people in what you're doing. Generally, questions can be closed or open-ended. **Closed questions** have a limited number of correct responses and often begin with what, where or who. For example, "What kinds of crops do you think a farmer around here would grow?" or "Where might we find these animals in this forest?" **Open-ended questions** ask your group to be creative, thinking more about possibilities than facts. Usually there are many possible responses to open-ended questions, and classifying answers as correct or incorrect is not only difficult but usually undesirable. Open-ended questions typically engage the imagination more so than closed questions. For example, "How might someone survive alone out here?" or "How do you suppose these fish find their way back to this exact spot?" As shown in Figure 5-11, questions can also be classified according to their purposes. There are a number of good sources on creative questioning techniques. In English, Boulanger and Smith (1973), and Regnier et al.(1992) are particularly good. In Spanish, Moore et al.(1989) contains an excellent discussion of interpretive questioning strategies.

5. Involve the group in your tour. Encourage everyone to keep their eyes and ears open, and to be actively searching for things that you might miss or which interest them. Establish the idea

Figure 5-10. An interpreter prepares a group of children for a "trust walk." In pairs, one child is blind-folded and guided by the other. Besides building friendships, trust walks help participants sharpen their senses of smell and hearing. Half-way through the walk the partners switch roles. Northwest Trek, Eatonville, Washington. (Photo by Sam Ham)

Asking Good Questions Can Improve A Guided Tour

Asking good questions helps you to focus people's attention and lure them into the discovery process by engaging their imaginations. Besides being "open-ended" or "closed," questions can be classified according to their purpose. Following are some examples.

Type of Question	Typical Purposes	Examples
Focusing	To focus attention on something of interest	"Can you all see this yellow line in the soil?" "What do you suppose this is?" "How many of you have seen a plow like this one before?"
Comparison	To bring out similarities and differences between things	"How would you compare these two rocks?" "In what ways are people and social insects alike?" "What does this smell like? Does it remind you of anything?"
Inference	To get the group to generalize or reason beyond the information you have given; to explore possible conclusions and implications	"If that's true, then how might we explain such and such?" "What do you think could be concluded from this?" "So how do you think this field will look in another twenty years?"
Application	To get the group to see how certain information applies in different situations	"Could you apply this knowledge at home?" "Why might it be important to know such and such?" "What do you think a tool like this could have been used for?"
Problem-solving	To get the group to think of solutions to real-world problems and issues	"What do you think is needed to stop this erosion?" "How would you make a shelter if all you had were grass and mud?" "What needs to be done to protect this species from extinction?"

Type of Question	Typical Purposes	Examples
Cause-and-effect	To get the group to think about relationships that explain the occurrence of different events and objects	"Why are there so many more frogs on this side of the river?" "Look around—what do think causes this water to be so contaminated?" "Why you suppose these beans are growing faster than those over there?"
Evaluation	To get people to express their opinions and to hear those of others; to illustrate possible choices and judgments	"What do you think would be the fairest solution?" "Who do you think was right?" "Do you believe this is good or bad?"

Figure 5-11. Examples of different kinds of questions.

that the tour is their tour and that their interests are important.

Tips on Tour Mechanics

So many factors go into leading a good tour that it's impossible to list them all. This is especially true when you consider the different forms of transportation that can be used (e.g., bus tours, boat tours, train tours, walking tours, ski tours, auto caravans, etc.). English-language readers interested in such specialized tours are referred to Lewis (1980), Risk (1982), and Grater (1976). Spanish-language readers should consult Moore, et al. (1989). Generally, however, the following guidelines pertain to most tours.

1. Stay in the lead, especially with large groups. This prevents the group from straying and makes managing the tour easier.

2. With large groups everything seems to take longer. You may need to stop fewer times than you might with a smaller group.

3. Be open to questions and casual conversation between stops, but try not to be engaged with the same people all the time. If something comes up in conversation that's important to everyone, be sure to repeat it to the whole group at the next opportunity.

4. Try to make a habit of repeating questions for the benefit of those who might not have heard them. This is especially important with large groups.

5. Capitalize on the unexpected. When possible, connect it to the theme of your tour.

6. If possible, end your tour where it began. If this isn't possible, make sure the group can easily find its way back. Remember that everyone may not want to return with you.

7. Stay on time. The people in your group believed you when you told them how much time the tour would take. At least one study (Ham and Shew 1979), found that late returns were one of the things people liked least about guided tours.

8. Be conscious of your rate of travel regardless of whether you're on foot or in a caravan. Establish a pace that's comfortable to the slowest member of the group. If someone is unable to maintain the minimum pace necessary to complete the tour on time, try to adjust the number of stops and the amount of time spent at each, before resorting to other alternatives (e.g., asking the person to speed up or informing the person that you may have to forget ahead in order to stay on time).

9. If you know you're going to be late in finishing the tour, tell the group as soon as possible. Some people may need to leave.

Figure 5-12. Even though his group is large, this interpreter makes sure everyone can see. Staying on the trail whenever possible is usually a good idea. Olympic National Park. (Photo by Sam Ham)

Figure 5-13. Staying in the lead is important, but be sure not to leave your group behind. (Photo by Sam Ham)

10. Be aware of the group's comfort. You're focused on guiding and probably excited, and you may not even be aware of a chilling breeze, a light drizzle, or the heat. Ask frequently how everyone feels, especially if there are children or elders in the group.

11. If someone is injured or becomes ill, remember that you have two responsibilities—one to that person and another to the rest of the group. Although your first concern should be for the welfare of the individual who needs attention, you should not ignore the group's need for leadership. If emergency assistance is needed, it's better for you to remain with the individual and to send a group member with instructions on who to contact for help. If this isn't possible, ask if someone in the group can care for the individual while you go for help.

Glossary terms: application questions, body, cause-and-effect questions, closed questions, comparison questions, conclusion, description/explanation, evaluation questions, focusing questions, focusing sentence, foreshadowing, guided tour, inference questions, introduction, mystery, problem-solving questions, open-ended questions, staging period, thematic connector, transition.

Guided Walks and the Protection of an Archaeological Site

Dave Sutherland, Environmental
Education Coordinator
Charles Darwin Station,
Galápagos Islands, Ecuador
Rodolfo Tenorio, Director
Guayabo National Monument, Costa Rica

Rodolfo Tenorio halts suddenly on the muddy trail through the rainforest, and points to a spiny plant lodged in the crook of a tree branch. The trailing group of fourth graders also stops, and waits in anticipation. "Anyone know what that plant is?" asks Rodolfo. After a pause, one boy raises a timid hand and offers, "A tree parasite?" Rodolfo smiles, and launches into an interactive explanation of bromeliads and their niche in tropical forests. The children are fascinated, and a few of them stay after the rest of the group has moved on, to pick up a bromeliad that has fallen to the forest floor.

Rodolfo is the chief administrator and archaeologist at Guayabo National Monument, a gem in Costa Rica's national park system, and the country's most important archaeological site. The area features pre-Columbian stone mounds, Indian burial sites, and a system of aqueducts which still deliver water to a central holding tank. A large tract of primary rainforest is preserved around the ruins, the setting for the jewel.

We walk together in front of the children. With over seventy kids and adults, this group is larger than most, which average about twenty-five people. Rodolfo explains how he came to do these walks.

Prior to 1985, he says, visitors to the national monument were allowed to enter the site alone. This concerned Rodolfo, since visitors carried away forest and archaeological resources and damaged ancient stone structures by climbing on them. The visitors also received no information about the site or its historical and educational value. "One man even suggested we bring in a gravel crusher!" Rodolfo says ruefully. "I was worried that we weren't creating a conscientious public. We needed to do something."

To address these issues, Rodolfo proposed four management objectives for the monument. These are:

1. To provide education related to the human and natural history of the site for the general public;
2. To assure the safety of visitors in the site;

3. To protect the natural and cultural resources in the site;

4. To have a uniformed, physical presence on hand to discourage destructive behavior and increase visitor contact with park personnel.

The third objective was considered the most important. "Grave robbing has been a problem in the past," explains Rodolfo. "Some visitors may come to learn about the ruins in order to rob them. We try to teach them about archaeology and the value of the site for understanding Costa Rican history, not just about the tombs."

Rodolfo decided that the best way to meet these objectives was through the development of a guided walk, while curtailing unsupervised visits to the archaeological site. He scheduled a meeting with administrators and planners in the Costa Rican National Park Service to discuss preliminary details. They agreed that a well-constructed trail leading to the ruins was a must, and that such a trail should be fairly short (1.5 km) and accessible to most visitors. "We tried to avoid steep slopes, but the topography wouldn't allow it. Eventually, we compromised, and ran a steep side trail up to the top of hill which provides a beautiful view of the main site. But people who don't want to climb the hill can continue down to the ruins on the main trail."

Once the route was established, Rodolfo and park personnel undertook an oral survey of visitors, to determine what topics were of greatest interest to the public. This information was gathered informally from several hundred visitors, and was used to plan the content of the guided walks—and to develop a provocative theme. "Of course, I had to use my common sense," he adds. "Most visitors wanted to hear about gold in the tombs. But if I found gold, I would keep it a secret from the public, so as not to encourage grave robbers."

Since the trail winds down to the ruins through thick rainforest, Rodolfo decided to devote the first half of the guided walk to the natural history of the area. The second half of the walk, which passes among the raised mounds and aqueducts of the central site, discusses the civilization that once lived there and archaeological work in progress. With a basic idea of what visitors wanted to learn, Rodolfo developed several pamphlets on the natural and human history of Guayabo for park laborers and volunteers.

Rodolfo trains his workers in basic interpretive skills—for example, how to express the 3500 mm of annual rainfall in relation to a visitor's experience. He does not concern himself much with the previous experience or background of a potential guide, but does test each one's knowledge carefully before letting them lead groups. With several trained guides to choose from, Rodolfo tries to match each guide with similar audiences. "If local people come to the ruins, I'd ask one of the day laborers to guide them, since he could explain things in their terms and have an intuitive idea of their interests. I'd send an English-speaking volunteer with a group of Canadian tourists, and I would guide groups of archaeologists myself." He adds, "The park service will not allow us to charge a fee for our guide service, but people offer—even expect—to pay for it."

At first, there was no organized format for the guided walks. Each guide received an introduction and basic knowledge about Guayabo, and was free to talk about any or all aspects of the area. But in 1988, the situation changed with the paving of much of the road leading to the monument. Visitor numbers jumped from 500 to 1500 per month. With so many tourists and school groups, Rodolfo had to divert much of his labor force from important archaeological projects to guide services—and important excavations were not getting done. To compensate, the monument was closed (except by special arrangement) on weekdays, to allow uninterrupted archaeological work. Visitors were allowed only on weekends. "But it was terrible. We would each have to do six groups a day. It was very tiring. So we had to look for an alternative."

To cope with the crowds, Rodolfo eventually decided to develop a self-guided trail along the route to the ruins, while maintaining the option of some guided walks for visitors who were willing to wait. "It was a trade-off. The self-guided trail does not meet objectives 2, 3, and 4. But it does free up some time for us. And, in developing the interpretive booklet for the stops along the trail, we were forced to review and standardize the information we gave on the guided walks. Planning the self-guided trail helped our presentations immensely." Developing the booklet for the self-guided trail also encouraged Rodolfo to standardize the information about the monument which is given to volunteers before they begin work as guides. In May of 1990, he put the finishing touches on a seventeen-page study guide in Spanish, which includes graphics, maps, historical and biological information, archaeological diagrams and, of course, some strategies for communicating with visitors and interpreting the site. "This way, I can send a copy to a volunteer before they get out to the monument, and they can be prepared to start as guides on their first day here." He adds that translating the study guide into English (and possibly German) remains one of his highest priorities, to help train foreign volunteers who come to work at Guayabo.

But are the walks effective? Do they meet his objectives? "I think so," he says. "In 1986, we did a written survey of 111 visitors, and asked about their guided walks. Most respondents were very positive, and 53% said, 'Excellent!' Most claimed to have learned a great deal from their guides. People generally prefer to wait for a scheduled walk with a guide rather than use the self-guiding booklet. And when tours or groups come back to the monument—like the groups this school sends every year—they always ask for the guide service in advance." He smiles. "I think they like the personal contact, and being able to ask questions." Damage and looting of the ruins has also dropped off considerably.

I asked Rodolfo what he would recommend to others planning a guided walk. "First," he said, "Know your area and its resources. This lets you plan a route which will touch on what people find most interesting, and visit the most appealing features. Then, decide at what level to pitch your program. If you use a lot of technical terms and statistics, be sure you interpret them for your audience. Finally, make a point to organize and standardize your information, as I did with the study guide. I also suggest that park managers learn to tap sources of volunteer labor for guides. Volunteer agencies often supply highly motivated, conscientious workers, and they're easy on my budget."

We have come full circle on the trail, and are once again at the little open-air amphitheater at the trail head. Rodolfo asks the children to sit and pay attention. "Now," he says, "Who can tell me why this national monument is so important to Costa Rica?" And twenty-two hands shoot up.

Guided Train Tours in National Forests— A New Kind of Partnership in Interpretation

Steve Sorseth, Special Projects Coordinator
Willamette National Forest, Eugene, Oregon

There aren't many programs in the Forest Service that take "non-forest" visitors on air-conditioned tours of three national forests, offer them meals, beverages, big picture windows with panoramic views, and do it all aboard an Amtrak train. That's what happens to passengers on the Amtrak Coast Starlight between Eugene and Klamath Falls, Oregon, as it passes through the Willamette, Deschutes, and Winema National Forests. In fact, about 80 percent of the 4.5-hour trip is through national forest lands. From July through Labor Day, uniformed Forest Service employees ride the train and interpret the scenery to passengers as they pass by.

The idea was spawned in 1990 by Oakridge District Ranger Bob Barstad, and Forest Supervisor Mike Kerrick (retired). They envisioned a partnership arrangement that would educate thousands of people about the philosophy and practices of the Forest Service, and would enrich passengers' travel experiences. After all, the route offers glimpses of forest management in action, as well as uncounted cultural and natural features: pioneer history, native American cultures and history, geology (the formation of the Cascade mountains), railroad history, logging history, wildlife, and notable landmarks (lakes, rivers, mountains).

So, with strong interest from Amtrak, the Willamette National Forest submitted a winning proposal to our Regional Office. The Forest Service provided interpreters and supervision, designed a brochure/map, obtained a portable public address system, and provided interpreter lodging and meals when they traveled. Amtrak provided train fare for interpreters, supervisors, and management, and printed a brochure to publicize the new program.

The train tours were a clear success in their first year. Interpreters presented programs to over 12,000 passengers, representing forty-six states and twenty-four foreign countries. Critique forms were received from over 800 passengers, virtually all of which were complimentary and supportive. As a result, the program will be continued

in the future with interpreters on-board five days per week from July 1 through Labor Day.

We're glad that our program has achieved national recognition as an innovative, high-quality interpretation partnership. It was a success because of strong support and dedication by people at all levels both in the Forest Service and at Amtrak. By the end of the summer, train riders were taking the trip specifically to hear the Forest Service programs.

If you have questions about the program or would like to know more about designing and managing such a partnership, contact me at (503) 465-6594, Willamette National Forest, P.O. Box 10607, Eugene, OR, USA 97440.

Situation Training for Tour Guides— Intensity Pays!

Christopher Whinney, President
Oxford Tourism Study Group,
Oxford, United Kingdom

Alternative Travel Group, Ltd. provides training for guides and tour managers who must work under demanding and logistically complex conditions throughout much of Europe. This includes leading hiking groups along 70-150 miles of unmarked paths in Italy, France, Spain and Portugal including some of the world's finest monuments, rare and diverse flora, and interesting wildlife. Despite the challenging nature of this work, trained personnel constantly achieve some of the most outstanding results in international tourism. The effectiveness of this training has been recognized with several awards.

The training was initiated to resolve several different problems. These ranged from endemic occupational hazards of working in the tourism industry such as stress, loneliness and strained relationships, to burnout and staff retention. There is little point in training personnel if you're going to lose this most precious asset after only a few months. Because of the sheer diversity and locations of our tours, the course had to be modular for adaptation to different programs. Most of all, we designed the training to teach our guides the most important skill they can have—the ability to think on their feet and to make good, quick decisions that have the potential to affect not only our clients' tour experience, but their well-being.

We have learned that in managing people, conscious application of a formal set of guidelines, rules, or code of practice and behavior will be neither comprehensive enough to cover all eventualities, nor immediate enough to be effective. Reactions must be spontaneous and come from inherent understanding rather than some applied formal system.

Alternative Travel Group trips had originally been led by the two directors with occasional help from friends. At that time, the company was too small to make much of a profit. Growth was essential, but not at the expense of quality. Therefore, in designing our training program, the first criterion was that trained personnel should lead and manage trips with the same enthusiasm, commitment and ethos as the two original guides.

The training begins with completion of a six-page, specially designed application form that introduces topics and concepts that are later clarified during an interview and developed during training. Using this diagnostic approach, our trainers begin learning about the special strengths and limitations of our guides from the outset. The result is that from their first contact with the organization, prospective trainees "hit the ground running" in the desired direction.

The training is intensive and effective. It involves a five-day residential course during which participants are kept in a high state of anticipation and stimulation. This not only simulates the high pressure of their future working conditions, but induces heightened experiences of enjoyment, excitement and creates an undeniably effective learning environment. The courses are immensely popular and in high demand, not only from our own prospective employees, but from other companies who send their guides to us for training.

Participants are not taught on a formal teacher-pupil basis, nor are they told what the work involves, or how to do it. They must discover this for themselves. The technique used is immediate and direct. Through participation, role playing, presentations, structured discussions and practical tasks, trainees create for themselves the knowledge base they will need to be effective guides. As they recognize optimal

solutions and actions appropriate for different situations, the nature of their job becomes clear and their confidence is progressively enhanced. In structured discussions, for example, questions are so phrased that participants discover only one answer—the right one. Here's an example:

> Question: After the first two days of a trip one person has consistently arrived late for breakfast, dinner and the beginning of each day's group activity. What do you do?
> Answer: You do nothing. The customer is always right. Clients have paid for this trip and they may not mind, perhaps even enjoy this mild eccentricity. You are being paid to facilitate their enjoyment. If they are irritated they will make their feelings clear to the person concerned or to you. You need only act if the matter develops into an issue with the rest of the group.

Through participation they discover themselves the nature of group dynamics, the ethics of tourism, effective presentation skills, and people management under harrowing conditions. In short, they learn about their job as a way of life. Involvement is so intense that realization and understanding become an integrated, spontaneous and permanent part of each trainee's thought process.

The outline of every element of the course is printed in a "manual" which each participant completes during each session—providing a permanent record (for reference) of their own creation. It also often becomes a source of entertainment, a "party game" when friends gather—"what would you do if … ?" In this way, skill refinement continues even during the guides' much-deserved leisure time.

Information specific to each particular area is provided in separate detailed notes. All our guides are required to learn these, but omniscience is not required! Sharing discovery of an area's unique characteristics with clients makes learning—e.g., the flora of the area—a continuing experience.

The effects of this training have been carefully monitored. Over a six year period, 97 percent of clients consistently rated the performance of all tour personnel as "good or excellent." Ninety-nine percent of clients rated their overall enjoyment of their trips as good or excellent. Over 90 percent of our new clients come through personal recommendation. The training not only works, it pays!

This training is transferable to any country or area and modules can easily be adapted to suit particular requirements. It is available in English, Spanish and French. Oxford Tourism Study Group, founded and sponsored by Alternative Travel Group, develops projects to resolve specific problems related to tourism and the environment. Our goal is to further environmental protection by helping tour operators bring their clients to a closer, more appreciative view of nature and culture. In our view, professional excellence in guiding is the first step.

Author's Note:
Alternative Travel Group, Ltd. organizes award-winning journeys on foot through the most beautiful and interesting parts of Europe and beyond. If you're interested in this training for your tour guides, or would like to train people to implement this training in your organization, contact Christopher Whinney at:
Oxford Tourism Study Group
69 Banbury Road
Oxford OX2 6PE, U.K.
Phone: 44-865-310377
Fax: 44-865-310299

References

Boulanger, F. David and John P. Smith. 1973. *Educational Principles and Techniques for Interpreters.* Portland, Oregon, USA: USDA Forest Service, Pacific Northwest Forest and Range Experiment Station, General Technical Report PNW-9.

Dawson-Medina, Leslie Y. and Cathy Shank. 1987. *Interpretation and Environmental Education: A Practitioner's Handbook.* Washington, D.C., USA: World Wildlife Fund.

Freed, Mike and David Shafer. 1981. The Interpreter's Knapsack: The Mini-Museum Goes Afield. *The Interpreter* 12(4):22-25.

Grater, Russell K. 1976. *The Interpreter's Handbook: Methods, Skills and Techniques.* Globe, Arizona, USA: Southwest Parks and Monuments Association.

Ham, Sam H. and Richard L. Shew. 1979. A Comparison of Visitors' and Interpreters' Assessments of Conducted Interpretive Activities. *Journal of Interpretation* 4(2):39-44.

Krumbein, William J. Jr. 1983. A Gimmicks and Gadgets Potpourri. *The Interpreter* 14(4):8-9.

Krumbein, William J. Jr. and Linda Leyva. 1977. *The Interpreter's Guide.* Sacramento, California, USA: California Dept. of Parks and Recreation.

Lewis, William J. 1980. *Interpreting for Park Visitors.* Philadelphia, Pennsylvania, USA: Eastern National Park and Monument Association, Eastern Acorn Press.

Moore, Alan, Bill Wendt, Louis Penna e Isabel Castillo de Ramos. 1989. *Manual para La Capacitación del Personal de Areas Protegidas* (Modulo C: Interpretación y Educación Ambiental, Apunte 4a). Washington, D.C., USA: Servicio de Parques Nacionales, Oficina de Asuntos Internacionales.

Morales, Jorge. 1987. *Manual para la Interpretación en Espacios Naturales Protegidos.* Anexo 3 del Taller Internacional sobre Interpretación Ambiental en Areas Silvestres Protegidas. Santiago, Chile: Oficina Regional de la FAO para América Latina y el Caribe, 7-12 de diciembre de 1988.

Regnier, Kathleen, Michael Gross and Ron Zimmerman. 1992. *The Interpreter's Guidebook: Techniques for Programs and Presentations.* Stevens Point, Wisconsin, USA: UW-SP Foundation Press, Inc.

Risk, Paul H. 1990. Using Nonverbal Cues to Meet Visitor Needs. *Legacy* 1(1):16-20.

Risk, Paul H. 1982. Conducted Activities. Chapter 8 in Sharpe, G.W. (ed.), *Interpreting the Environment.* New York, New York, USA: John Wiley & Sons.

Additional Reading

In English:

Countryside Commission. 1978. *Guided Walks.* Advisory Series No. 4. London, United Kingdom: Countryside Recreation Research Group.

Tilden, Freeman. 1977. *Interpreting Our Heritage* (2nd ed.). Chapel Hill, North Carolina, USA: University of North Carolina Press.

In Spanish:

Ham, Sam H. 1992. *Interpretación Ambiental: Una Guía Práctica para Gente con Grandes Ideas y Presupuestos Pequeños.* Golden, Colorado, USA: North American Press/Fulcrum Publishing.

Sharpe, Grant W. 1982. Selecciones de *Interpretando el Ambiente.* Turrialba, Costa Rica: Centro Agronómico Tropical de Investigación y Enseñanza (CATIE).

Tilden, Freeman. 1977. Selecciones de *Interpretando Nuestra Herencia.* Turrialba, Costa Rica: Centro Agronómico Tropical de Investigación y Enseñanza (CATIE).

CHAPTER SIX

GUIDELINES FOR OTHER CONDUCTED ACTIVITIES

In addition to talks and guided tours, there are many other kinds of conducted activities, some of which are rehearsed and presented to assembled audiences, and others which are more impromptu or extemporaneous. Among the activities we'll consider in the first group are **living history demonstrations**, **personification** and puppet shows. In the second group, we'll discuss **roving interpretation** and working at **information stations** since they're the two most common forms of extemporaneous interpretation. Though they're quite different in their settings and in the kinds of audiences they might reach (see Figure 6-1), all five of these activities are best when they follow an interpretive approach as presented in Chapter 1. In this chapter we'll consider some general guidelines for planning and carrying out these special kinds of communication activities.

Living History Demonstrations

As their name implies, living history demonstrations bring history to life. Known also as "living interpretation," "characterization," and "role playing," they are dramatic performances in which an interpreter portrays a real person such as George Washington, Thomas Edison, or Simón Bolivar, or more commonly, a hypothetical character who represents some historic period (e.g., a mid-1800s fur trapper or a 17th-century Mayan chief). Whichever approach you adopt, you should keep in mind the following general guidelines as you develop and present your living history demonstration.

1. *Strive for authenticity, both in your dress and behavior.* At least one study (Ham and Shew 1979) determined that although living history demonstrations were the most enjoyable kind of

interpretive program at a western U.S. wildlife park, they were also among the worst when authenticity was lacking. Inappropriate attire, unconvincing monologues and accents, unauthentic accoutrements such as modern-day jewelry, watches, eyeglasses and clothing can quickly undermine even the best dramatic performance. Remember that even though your audience knows you aren't really the character you are trying to portray, it will "play along" with you provided that your appearance and performance are good imitations of how they imagine the real person to have been. Conspicuous errors, however, will make your presentation less credible and your audience less likely to play along. If you lack confidence in your dramatic ability, you probably ought to consider some other form of presentation.

2. *Strive for accuracy.* Living history demonstrations must present an accurate picture of the past, undistorted by the interpreter—even in the name of dramatic impact. Remember that your job is not to create history but to re-create it. The power of living history comes from the human contact you provide. You are a living link to the past—a human connection with people and times that no longer exist. But you cannot change what occurred or how people really were in those days. To do so, even if you think it will improve your performance, goes beyond your rights and responsibilities as an interpreter.

3. *Stay in first-person.* Talk about how things are today, how we do things today, and how people think today. Avoid slipping into references to the past. For example, if you are portraying a farmer in 1825, refer to the 1820s as "nowadays" not as "back in the 1820s." Refer to people in the 1820s as "we" or "us" rather than as "they" or "them."

4. *Avoid famous personalities.* It's usually better to portray lesser-known or hypothetical figures since people already hold strong images of famous personalities. If your portrayal doesn't match their expectations of that person, you may have a hard time giving a convincing performance. For example, instead of portraying a president, consider becoming the president's personal aide or chief cook. A hypothetical character (such as a worker, a farmer, a housewife, a newspaper reporter, etc.) can give you more versatility because you can combine what you've learned about many different people from that time period into your character.

5. *Research your topic well before preparing a script of your performance.* This means learning not only about the person or craft you might be demonstrating, but also about the world, social context, customs, fashions, predominant social beliefs and values, the status of scientific knowledge, new inventions of the time, food and beverage tastes, household chores, what kind of things adults did for fun, what games kids liked to play, and generally how life, itself, was during the period you are trying to represent. The more you learn about this period, the more you'll be able to think like a person from that period, and the more convincing your presentation will be.

6. *If possible, involve your audience in dialogue.* If you're comfortable in your role and confident in your knowledge, conversing with your audience is relatively easy and, according to the study by Ham and Shew (1979), more effective in holding attention than a simple monologue. Although audience interaction requires greater versatility and can sometimes create unpredictable challenges (such as when audience members try to trick you

Five Other Conducted Activities Which Can Be Used to Reach Different Audiences		
Type of Activity	**Typical Setting**	**Typical Audiences**
Living History Demonstrations (dramatic portrayal of a real or imaginary human figure who represents the past)	Parks, forests, museums, theaters, amphitheaters, trails, any open area where an audience can sit or stand	Assembled group of people
Personification (dramatic portrayal of a nonhuman object such as an animal, rock, tree, fire, ice, etc.)	Same as above	Assembled group of people
Puppet Shows (dramatic portrayal using puppet characters)	Theaters, amphitheaters, auditoriums, street corners, in front of buildings	Assembled group of people
Roving Interpretation (impromptu communication by an interpreter as he/she walks through an area encountering different people)	Trails, beaches, campgrounds, picnic areas, areas where visitors may roam unsupervised (e.g., historic sites, demonstration areas, botanical gardens, museums, etc.)	Individuals and small family and friendship groups
Information Station/ Reception (impromptu communication with people who go to an information station or reception desk in order to ask questions or to get specific information about something of interest)	Visitor centers, museums, tourist information stations, reception desks	Individuals and small family and friendship groups

Figure 6-1. Five special kinds of conducted activities.

into present day vernacular), this can be part of the fun of a living history demonstration. As Lewis (1980) pointed out:

> "It's a game, you see, and the role played by visitors allows them the privilege of trying to trip you up."

A good example: an interpreter was portraying a 1925 logger when an audience member asked about the "war" he had recently referred to. "Which war was that?" the woman asked. "Why, it was the world war!" responded the well-prepared interpreter. Had he said "World War I" she would have caught him in an error because in 1925 nobody knew there would be a second world war which the label "World War I" would have implied.

7. *Create an appropriate setting for your performance.* Settings don't have to be elaborate. Often standing next to a conspicuous prop (such as a piece of machinery, a farm animal, a barn, a tool, etc.) or simply locating the presentation at an appropriate spot (a stream, a secluded forest opening, etc.) will be adequate. It's usually best to select a setting where reminders of the present such as cars, phones and modern-day buildings are absent.

8. *Plan the format of your presentation.* One-person and two-person formats are most common. In a one-person format, you work alone. In a two-person format, the other person sets the stage for your portrayal—giving background information and preparing the audience for your entrance and performance. This format often simplifies the logistics of a living history demonstration, and lends itself to several variations. Sometimes, for example, an ordinary talk or guided tour is "unexpectedly" interrupted by a person

Figure 6-2. A living history demonstration at an Idaho state park. (Photo by Larry Mink)

from the past who enters and performs at a carefully planned moment. Once the portrayal is over, the talk or tour continues. In addition, two people working together can orchestrate an interview in which the person from the present can ask carefully prepared questions of the one from the past.

9. *If you're working alone, plan your **entrance** carefully.* Although there are many techniques, three are commonly used:

• You're already in-role when the audience arrives.

• You enter in-role after the audience is assembled.

• You're there but not in-role as the audience arrives. Once the people are assembled, you make a brief introduction (giving background, etc.) and then assume your character's role. You may already be in costume, or you may dash behind a bush or around a corner, quickly returning in costume and in character.

10. *If you're working alone, plan your **exit** carefully.* A number of techniques have been used:

• You break role in costume and conclude your presentation as your real self.

• You remove a conspicuous part of

the costume (your hat, eyeglasses, etc.) or put down a conspicuous prop (tool, weapon, etc.), introduce your real self and conclude your presentation.

• You step out of sight (around a corner, behind a bush, etc.) and quickly return as your real self.

• You conclude your presentation in-role and then answer questions as your real self.

• You never break role, even during questions after the presentation has been concluded.

Useful English-language references on living history demonstrations include Alderson and Low (1985), Garrison (1982), Hilker (1974), Kay (1970), Lewis (1980), and Regnier et al. (1992). There are no known additional sources in Spanish.

Personification

Personification is similar to living history demonstrations in that you're giving a dramatic portrayal. The difference is that you're not portraying a human being, but rather a nonhuman object or thing. Examples include portraying a rock, tree, water drop, animal, fire, volcano, or virtually anything that an interpreter might want to focus on. Personification is a powerful technique with children, but it's also effective with adult audiences as long as it's done in fun.

In preparing costumes for personification, it's usually less important to be physically accurate than it is to exaggerate or accentuate the aspects of the object that you want to emphasize in your presentation. For example, a frog costume might include large snorkeling flippers to emphasize the webbed feet that frogs have; a tree might have a cape that can be pulled aside to reveal colored strands of fabric which represent cambium, growth rings, xylem, and phloem; a rock undergoing change might don different garments depending on whether it was being melted, twisted, smashed or eroded. One such "rock" put on a pack (telling the audience it was a parachute) because he was "about to be erupted from a volcano and had heard it was a long way down." Since almost any personification costume appears humorous to the audience, the interpreter's tone and behavior are often humorous, too.

With the exception of very young children, most audiences know that non-human animals and objects don't really talk and think like human beings. For this reason, personification is usually a tongue-in-cheek activity. Everyone knows that you're pretending to be the thing you're portraying just for the fun of it; this doesn't mean that a serious message can't be treated using personification, it simply means that a jovial or humorous approach will work best in most situations.

Figure 6-3. Interpreting bats through personification. (Photo by Larry Mink)

Puppet Shows

Puppet shows can portray human beings (as in living history demonstrations) or nonhumans (such as in personification). That puppet shows are found in cultures all over the world is evidence of their communication power. People everywhere seem to enjoy watching the semi-real world that puppets live in. Because they speak and have personalities, we can easily project ourselves into their pretend world, sometimes seeing ourselves more clearly than is ordinarily possible. Presentations with strong, serious or controversial themes often lend themselves to puppetry because the interpreter can allow the puppets to do the talking—for example, to make social criticisms or to point out conflicting interests—and therefore assume responsibility for moral content. According to Werner and Bower (1982), if a real person were to say the things a puppet might say, some people could be angry or hurt: "Puppets add a sense of pretending and humor that can make the feared parts of our daily life easier to look at."

Puppets can be used in elaborate, large-scale performances or in simple one or two-character shows. They can also be used as supplements to other activities. For example, an interpreter leading a tour for children could use a hand-puppet (stored in a bag until the appropriate moment) to explain something specific to the children; and the same interpreter could use a different puppet when the children needed to be calmed down or reminded of a rule, thus allowing the interpreter to avoid the role of disciplinarian. Puppets can include gloves, socks, or other fabric containing a face or other features, masks or giant heads on sticks, kitchen sponges,

painted balloons, cardboard boxes, paper bags, clothes pins, cardboard rolls from bathroom tissue or paper towels, and many other materials that are common and inexpensive. A saying among puppeteers is "don't throw it away, it can be a puppet someday."

Planning effective puppet shows will be easier if you pay attention to the following simple guidelines. English-language readers can find valuable discussions in Regnier et al. (1992), Forte (1985), and Werner and Bower (1982). Two superb Spanish-language sources are Ministerio Hondureño de Salud Pública (1986) and Bustillo (1990).

1. *Give puppets a face whenever possible.* Faces give puppets an identity and increase their ability to communicate. As in human communication, the eyes are especially important.

2. *Use facial expressions to establish each puppet's personality.* Facial expressions (especially the eyes) should depict something characteristic of each puppet's personality or predominant role in the presentation. For example, smiling puppets are predominantly (but not necessarily always) happy; frowning puppets are usually grumpy or mean; puppets with eyes closed are usually timid, etc.

3. *Plan the script around the amount of help you have.* Develop a story with the number of characters you actually have people for. Playing more than one part (managing more than one puppet) is usually difficult.

4. *Keep your puppets' dialogue short.* Build in a lot of action. When puppets must move or do something, make them do it quickly and conspicuously; puppets which move slowly in order to do little, or speak slowly in order to say little are boring puppets; puppets which carry out

Figure 6-4. Simple puppets are often the best. (Photo by Sam Ham)

their movements and dialogues swiftly and surely are more interesting.

5. *Create a simple but colorful backdrop for your puppets, and change it during the show if possible.* Painted fabric (even old sheets, table cloths, window shades, shawls, etc.), make good backdrops.

6. *Play records or tapes to add sound to your performances.* You can also record your own sounds and then play them during the show. Another possibility is to supplement your show with live sound effects. Beating on a drum, rubbing pieces of sandpaper together, dropping pebbles onto a piece of tin, or speaking through a paper tube are just a few ways you can create sound effects during a puppet show.

7. *Keep your performances short.* Usually ten or fifteen minutes is sufficient to get a message across. If the message is more complex, consider having two episodes. Usually it's better to leave your audience thirsting for more, rather than drowning in excess.

Roving Interpretation

"Roving" interpretation is the most extemporaneous of all conducted activities,

and is usually carried out in parks, recreation areas or other settings people visit for pleasure. As the term implies, roving interpreters move around an area, looking for people to meet and chat with. Although they've certainly thought ahead of time about important messages to communicate, roving interpreters don't present prepared talks so much as they simply greet and chat with different groups of people they encounter. The content and nature of each encounter is usually determined less by something the interpreter planned to say than by what the visitors want to know or what they're doing at the time of the encounter.

Aside from the obvious public relations value of encountering people face-to-face, the main advantage of roving interpretation is that it extends the benefit of personal contact to people who might not otherwise have it (e.g., by attending talks, tours, or other kinds of personal presentations). In addition, roving interpretation allows sudden or temporary events to be explained to people as those events occur, or before their effects disappear. In this sense, roving interpretation is opportunistic. Routes that roving interpreters travel can be changed in order take advantage of temporary events and natural phenomena. Likewise, interpreters can be stationed near potential safety hazards or to warn against ensuing dangers such as wildfire, floods, or electrical storms.

Sometimes roving interpreters are called upon to serve other management duties. Often they observe violations such as illegal tree-cutting, plant collecting, fire building, or camping outside of designated areas. Other times they observe people engaging in potentially dangerous behaviors such as swimming or climbing in unsafe places, drinking surface water, camping near dangerous plants, or unknowingly attracting dangerous animals. Because they are easily identified, uniformed roving interpreters are often the first officials to learn about accidents, crimes or other mishaps that have just occurred. Of course, in any true emergency (e.g., car accidents, injuries, flagrant poaching, theft, vandalism, etc.), your first concern must be with the well-being of the visitors and protection of the resource. But outside of crimes and serious situations, an observed rule violation frequently presents an educational opportunity for a roving interpreter. This is because visitors often act out of ignorance rather than malicious intent. In these instances, a tactful, smiling interpreter may do more to sensitize visitors to the values of an area or the rationale for a particular management policy than he/she might in a different conducted activity. Understanding the visitor's point of view and avoiding an accusatory or self-righteous tone can create good will at the same time educating the person about correct or desired behavior.

According to Wallace (1990), this can be accomplished by following a three-step process: (1) give an objective (not emotional) description of the situation you observed, focusing the people's attention on the resource without referring to your agency's policies or regulations; (2) explain the ecological or social consequences of the action or situation that you observed; and (3) tell them how you, as an expert, feel about it and what could be done to improve the situation. Wallace calls this "revealing the authority of the resource," implying that the reason certain actions are inappropriate in a protected area is not that they're illegal, but rather that they threaten the values that are being protected at the site. In his view, focusing the visitor's attention on the resource rather than on the regulation is a more convincing way to change behaviors that are based on ignorance or naiveté.

Making contact with strangers can feel awkward even for the most experienced interpreters. Following are some guidelines that might make your job as a roving interpreter not only easier, but more effective. English-language references on roving interpretation include Regnier et al. (1992), Lewis (1980), and Sharpe and Hodgson (1982). Additional Spanish-language sources include Morales (1987) and Moore et al.(1989).

1. *Smile as you introduce yourself.* Take off sunglasses so that the people can see your eyes. Offer your hand when you introduce yourself. (Oriental visitors or those from the Middle East may prefer not to shake hands; for them, a slight bow or head nod means the same thing if it's accompanied by a smile.) Above all else, appear genuinely happy to meet the people. Because a uniform is a symbol of authority, uniformed interpreters can easily and unknowingly intimidate a group. Be aware of this, and always approach groups as a friend rather than just as an official.

2. *Establish rapport immediately.* In most cases, you might start by asking questions in order to learn about the person or group. How are they? Where are they from? How long have they been in the area? Have they seen a particular feature yet? The important thing is to appear interested in them as people rather than merely as visitors. But be sensitive in what and how much you ask. Some cultural groups may consider too many questions inappropriate or even rude.

3. *Incorporate your planned messages* (e.g., about the features of the area, etc.)

into the discussion at opportune moments. When possible, give "inside" information such as "Today is an unusually good day ... "(to see flowers in bloom, observe an elk herd, etc.). Allow the conversation to take its own course. Don't worry about having to tell every group the same information unless it's related to their safety or well-being.

4. *Save regulatory messages for the end of the conversation.* Once you've made friends with the group, reminders, warnings and even reprimands will seem much more acceptable and less threatening to them.

5. *Carry a small bag or knapsack containing interpretive aids* (binoculars, field guides, specimens, etc.). See Chapter 5 for a list of other items you might carry.

6. *Try to answer every question as if it were the first time you'd answered it*—even though you may have answered it dozens of times before. Remember, in interpretation there's no such thing as a dumb question. If someone asks it, it must be important. If hundreds of people ask it, it must be extremely important. Sometimes, sharing a story about a question *you* asked when you first came to the area can put visitors at ease.

7. *Anticipate the most commonly asked questions and be prepared to answer them.* Often people will want to know how big things are, how fast they are, how powerful they are, how old they are, or other facts that help them put what they're seeing into perspective. Develop examples, analogies and comparisons that will help them do this. (See "bridging techniques" in Chapter 1.) Some roving interpreters carry a few copies of a prepared fact sheet with answers to the ten or twenty most commonly asked questions as handouts for interested visitors.

8. *Don't dominate the conversation.* Let the visitors participate fully in the discussion, asking questions, making observations, etc. They may have a lot to say and ask. Be a good listener.

9. *Don't stay too long.* If the people really want you to stay they'll let you know, but if you're overstaying your welcome it's doubtful they'll say anything. Ordinarily five or ten minutes is sufficient, and many contacts take only two or three minutes. If they would like to continue the conversation but your time is limited, invite them to talk to you later at the information station or after your next interpretive activity.

10. *When appropriate, lead the people on an impromptu tour, what Lewis (1980) calls a "mini-walk."*

Sometimes the group will be interested in something within walking distance. Don't hesitate to lead them to it, interpreting features along the way just as in a scheduled guided tour (Chapter 5). Other people may notice you, become interested, and join you—all the better. Mini-tours, of course, will require more time, possibly as much as ten to fifteen minutes or more depending on the situation and the group's interest. But be considerate—don't take any more of their time than it really takes to show them what they wanted to see. Remember, they have their own schedules and you have other people to meet. You can always invite them to participate in a scheduled tour.

Working at an Information Station

An information station or reception area can be elaborate or simple depending upon your needs and financial resources.

For example, it could be a counter in a visitor center or simply a small building at the entrance to an area; it could be a booth near a feature such as a beach or viewpoint; it could be located in an office or alongside a road; or it could consist of nothing more than a table that's set up each day and taken away at night. Sometimes giving information to visitors is a full-time job, but often it's just one part of someone's job (e.g., an entrance station attendant, office receptionist, or clerk).

Information stations serve an important, yet often underappreciated role in interpretation. Like any form of communication, they can be dynamic or they can be boring depending on the organization and skill of the people managing them. Some interpreters think that "desk duty" at the visitor center, office, or information station is less important or less exciting than other interpretive work. Quite naturally, this attitude has resulted in some unimaginative and even dysfunctional approaches to running information desks. The fact, however, is that the personal contact you have with people at an information desk is often the only contact they have with a representative of your agency or organization. Good information can be crucially important to any visitor, and if it's offered in a timely and positive way, it creates not only more enjoyable experiences but good will toward you and the organization you work for.

Following are some tips on offering more dynamic information services. Many good references on managing information desks exist. Some especially useful English-language sources are Sharpe and Hodgson (1982), Lewis (1980), Regnier et al.(1992), and Manucy (1968). Morales (1987) gives a good summary of considerations in Spanish.

Figure 6-5. Information stations serve an important, yet often underappreciated role in an interpretive program. (Photo courtesy of U.S. Army Corps of Engineers)

1. *Present a positive image both in behavior and appearance.* Be well-groomed. If you've been in the field just prior to your shift at the information desk, try to shower or wash up before going on duty. Appear like you've gone out of your way to make a good first impression. While a soiled uniform or body odor may not be offensive to you or your workmates, many visitors may form a negative impression of you based solely on your grooming.

2. *Actively greet people as they arrive.* Stop whatever else you might be doing and focus attention on the visitors. Always smile and welcome them to the area. Immediate eye contact is important. Don't begin speaking to them while you're looking at something else; it sends the message that you're doing something more important and that they've interrupted you. If you happen to be on the telephone and can't greet them immediately, look up, smile, and let them know you see them and will be with them soon.

Information Stations Serve Five Main Functions

An information station—whether it's an elaborate visitor center or simply a table in an office—should be designed and operated to serve people in five main ways.

Function	Example Applications
Welcoming visitors to the area	Make visitors feel expected and not merely tolerated. Wear a name tag, or display your name on a sign or placard that's conspicuously placed on the desk or counter. Display a welcome sign or poster saying "Hi, Can I Help You?" Let people know that they're the most important aspect of your job and that you're there to serve them. Playing soft background music may help to break the silence and encourage interaction.
Orienting visitors to the area	Let visitors know what kinds of things they can see and do in the area. Have available maps, brochures and other information not only about your area but about other areas nearby. Have on hand information about interpretive activities and other special events in the area. Display a large map of the area which shows the visitors where they are as well as the location of major features and points of interest. Include travel distances on the map if possible. Have a notebook or chart which shows travel distances and driving times between major locations. If pertinent, include biking and walking times, as well. Information on local weather is always appreciated.
Sensitizing visitors to the area's values	Give or display information which explains the reasons your area exists. Tell how the area benefits people and how visitors should conduct themselves in order to avoid damaging the site. Use positive statements: "Thanks for leaving the wildflowers for others" (not, "And remember, no flower picking!")
Responding to visitors' needs	Be prepared to answer questions on a wide range of topics including the locations of bathrooms, potable water, gas stations, restaurants, and camping and picnic areas. Have a notebook, organized by topic, which contains answers to common questions. Update the notebook regularly. When you don't know the answer to a question, say so, but find the answer as soon as possible and add it to the notebook. If it's feasible, give the answer to the person who originally asked the question.

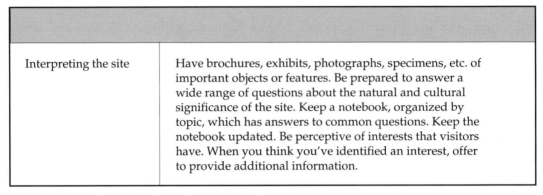

Interpreting the site	Have brochures, exhibits, photographs, specimens, etc. of important objects or features. Be prepared to answer a wide range of questions about the natural and cultural significance of the site. Keep a notebook, organized by topic, which has answers to common questions. Keep the notebook updated. Be perceptive of interests that visitors have. When you think you've identified an interest, offer to provide additional information.

Figure 6-6. Five functions of an information station.

3. *Arrange the information station in such a way that the people feel expected.* Sometimes visitors are reluctant to approach a person at an information desk because they're afraid they might be interrupting something. Besides actively greeting the people, you can counteract this feeling with a conspicuously displayed welcome sign. Many information stations even display the name of the person on duty in order to personalize the contact from the beginning. It's always a good idea to wear a name tag on your shirt. At the Mount St. Helens visitor center, U.S. Forest Service staff put a potted plant or vase of freshly cut flowers on the counter to make visitors feel at home. They always use domesticated (often home-grown) flowers to avoid giving the impression that flowers are picked from around the visitor center.

4. *Make a habit of asking if this is the visitor's first time in the area.* You'll find that your approach will be different with first time visitors than with those who already know something about the area. For example, you might have a fairly standard list of things to tell first time visitors (such as where to go, what to do, safety information, etc.), whereas the information you

give to repeat visitors might be more variable. Local residents who are very familiar with the area may bring friends and family members who are seeing the area for the first time. Often, the local residents will want to do the interpreting for the rest of their group. Be sensitive to this. Address the local residents as though they're the tour guides, and give them the option to tell the others about the area. Be sure to give them information on any changes they need to know about (a trail or road washed out, new programs, etc.).

5. *Be prepared to answer all kinds of questions*—not only about the natural or historic significance of your area, but about other nearby areas and about the locations of bathrooms, potable water, restaurants, local shopping (especially arts, crafts and souvenirs), camping and picnic areas, and other services and facilities for visitors. Compile and regularly update notebooks that contain information about these topics. A list of some possible topics is shown in Figure 6-7.

6. *When you don't know the answer to a question, say so.* But make a concerted effort to find the answer. If you can't find it, a very good idea is to tell the visitors

you'll try to get the answer before they leave that day and invite them to stop back later. Some interpreters go even further; they write down the visitor's mailing address, and when they finally get the answer they mail it either on a postcard or in a personal letter to the visitor's home. This is excellent service and excellent public relations. In either event, be sure to add the new information under the appropriate heading in one of your notebooks.

7. *Have a map of the area mounted on the counter or wall.* If it's on the counter, position it so that it's right-side-up for the visitors and oriented with north facing north. Practice reading the map upside down; with some time you'll get used to it. If a map will be given away or sold at the site, it's best that it be the same map you use to give directions. That way, the directions you've given will be more easily understood when visitors look at the carry-out map.

8. *Keep sheets of paper and a pen or pencil at the desk.* (Even scrap paper will do as long as it allows legible writing.) Use it as a visual aid when explaining something or giving directions. Encourage the visitors to take it with them for later reference.

9. *Have a collection of interpretive aids* (specimens, photos, etc.) that you can use in your discussions with visitors. These can be kept behind the desk or put on a table for visitors to see. Some interpreters create a "mystery table" containing several unlabeled specimens with a sign asking visitors to guess what the items are. Correct answers can be written on labels and attached to the bottom of the items, or they can be written on a list which is kept behind the desk.

10. *Come out from behind the desk or counter whenever possible.* This personalizes your contact with the visitors by

eliminating a physical barrier between you. Perhaps you can go to the other side of the counter to view the map alongside the visitors, to point something out in an exhibit, or to demonstrate something using a visual aid.

11. *Focus attention on the visitor.* Except in real emergencies, allowing distractions to interrupt your contact with a visitor sends a clear message: "You're not as important as the thing that interrupted us." If that "thing" was your boss, a friend or co-worker you're making a very negative statement to the visitor. Never interrupt an employee or co-worker who's speaking with a visitor unless there's an emergency. Most visitors will tolerate being interrupted by a ringing telephone, but you should inform the caller that you're in the middle of something important and that you'll be available shortly or you're willing to return the call later. If possible, locate the telephone away from the information desk where someone else can answer it.

12. *Be available to serve everyone equally.* This is especially important in busy information centers where there are a lot of people who need information. Some people may have many questions and require a lot of help, and others may simply want to chat and pass the time. If you notice that you're spending an inordinate amount of time with one person while others are having to wait, politely inform the person that even though you're enjoying the conversation, you need to attend to some of the other people. Invite the person to wait until you have a little more time to spend, or suggest something for him or her to do while you wait on the other people.

13. *Consider offering "after-hours" information for people who arrive when the*

Visitors Need All Kinds of Information

Information stations attract all kinds of people with all kinds of questions. To anticipate their need for good information you should consider compiling notebooks containing information on the topics most likely to be important in your area. Following are some ideas for main headings.

Emergency Services, Phone numbers and Street Addresses for:
- Police stations
- Fire stations
- Ambulance
- Hospitals (Have simply drawn maps available for people needing to go directly to an emergency room.)
- Veterinarians

Interpretive Opportunities
- Schedules and locations of conducted activities offered by your agency and others nearby
- Locations of self-guided interpretation (signs, exhibits, trails, etc.)
- Interpretive guidebooks available for purchase

Natural and Cultural History of the Area
- Information on important plants and animals
- Information on important historic and cultural resources

Nearby Attractions
- Natural and cultural sites
- Museums, art galleries, and theaters
- Scenic drives and viewpoints
- Unique features such as waterfalls, lakes, rock formations, etc.
- Sightseeing tours
- Recreational opportunities of the area (water and land-based)
- Potential hazards such as poisonous plants or dangerous animals (snakes, bears, etc.)

Seasonal Weather
- Typical weather for that time of year
- What visitors can do in the area even in inclement weather
- What films work best under different weather conditions

Food and Lodging (get a list from the chamber of commerce to avoid the appearance of favoritism)
- Grocery stores, restaurants, and snack bars
- Hotels, motels, and bed-and-breakfast establishments
- Camping and picnic areas
- Private resorts
- Recreational vehicle parks and campgrounds with RV hook-ups

Vehicle Services
- Gas stations, car repair shops, and towing services
- Motorcycle repair shops
- Dump stations for recreational vehicles

Tourist Transportation Services
- Distances and driving and biking times between major points
- Bus schedules
- Phone numbers for taxis, car rentals, airlines, trains, travel agencies, etc.
- Local charter flight services and bus companies offering charter tours
- Local outfitters and guides

Other Important Services
- Banks and automatic teller machines
- Camera stores that process film and repair cameras
- Souvenir shops, and arts and crafts sales
- Local churches (listed by faith and denomination)

Figure 6-7. Possible topics for information notebooks.

station is closed. A bulletin board (located either outside or inside in a window) could contain basic information such as emergency phone numbers, an area map, and information on camping, safety, major attractions and recreation opportunities. Some "after-hours" bulletin boards also have a space where people can leave personal messages for other visitors. Be sure to include information on the station's normal operating hours.

14. *Be a good listener.* Listening to the same questions again and again creates lazy listeners. Don't make assumptions about what visitors are asking or about to ask. Really concentrate on hearing questions as they are put to you.

15. *Be ready to suggest options.* If poor weather or a road closure prevents visitors from doing what they planned to do, be able to give some good alternative suggestions.

16. *Be prepared for emergencies.* At a minimum, have a fully stocked first-aid kit on hand and make sure all employees know how to use it. Knowing at least basic first-aid and CPR procedures is a must.

A Note on Handling Angry and Difficult Visitors

Roving interpreters and information personnel sometimes encounter visitors who are angry, upset or irritated. This is normal. Flat tires, engine trouble, screaming babies and other pressures can be stressful. After a particularly difficult day or irritating incident, even the nicest people can become belligerent. Unfortunately, when you encounter these people in your work, you may become the target of their frustrations. When this happens, and it will, try to stay calm. Don't get emotionally involved if you can avoid it. A particularly angry person may even call you names or launch personal attacks on your co-workers or agency. Although a normal response is to resent this treatment, a defensive reaction won't do anything to help the situation you're faced with; in fact, it could easily worsen it.

Experts seem to agree that the best strategy for handling angry visitors is to listen. Really try to understand the people's situation and why they're irritated. Don't interrupt, even if they're being verbally abusive. Let them vent their frustration. Think how you'd feel in a similar situation. Above all, show concern for the

Figure 6-8. Practice reading maps upside down. At an information desk, it's an essential skill. (Photo courtesy of U.S. Forest Service)

person's well-being. Look them in the eye and let your face and eyes demonstrate your concern and understanding. Counter abuse with charm in equal proportion. That is, the more abusive they become, the more caring you become. In most cases you'll find that once the visitors have vented their "steam" they'll respond positively to your attempts to help. And even if you can't solve their problem, they'll appreciate your trying.

Glossary terms: entrance, exit, information station, living history demonstration, personification, roving interpretation.

Puppets Are an Interpretive Resource

Larry Mink, Interpretation
Program Coordinator
Idaho Department of Parks
and Recreation, Boise, Idaho

State Park interpretive programs take on many different looks throughout the year. There are traditional slide shows, nature walks, demonstrations, and Junior Rangers, interspersed with living history, storytelling, musical programs, etc. All of these programs are well received by park visitors. But one program stands out above all the rest as an audience favorite - Puppet Shows! The reaction from children and adults is overwhelming.

Many people erroneously believe that puppetry is strictly a children's activity. Kermit and Miss Piggy would disagree. Puppetry appeals to all ages. The Muppet Show is watched by over 200 million people worldwide each week in over 100 different countries, and half of those watching are adults!

Puppetry is certainly not a new art. In fact it has been around practically as long as there have been people on earth. Puppets were used 4000 years ago in India, 2000 years ago in China, and the Greeks used puppets as early as 800 B.C. Puppet theaters have been found in ancient ruins in Greece, Italy and Egypt. Punch and Judy, two well-known classic puppets, were created in 1699 in Italy and are still used today in many puppet repertoires.

Puppetry in the United States became popular with the coming of puppeteers such as Burt Tillistrom (Kukla and Ollie), Shari Lewis (Lambchop) and the late Jim Henson, who introduced America to the Muppets. With the popularity of puppets on American television, and recognition of their educational value as demonstrated on Sesame Street, puppets seemed like a natural for park interpretive programs.

Why Puppets?

Initially, puppets were an experiment within the park interpretive program, but after just one season, puppetry became a permanent fixture. Why? It's simple—puppets work and they're versatile. Puppets can be wise, silly or obnoxious. They can tell jokes, be funny, sad or happy and still retain their credibility. Puppets provide a new, fresh, innovative piece of programming which is different from the traditional campfire program. Puppet shows provide education and entertainment,

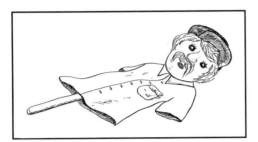

Figure 1

Figure 2

both of which are integral aspects of our state park interpretive philosophy. Whenever a puppet show is presented as an outdoor campfire program, attendance normally doubles and reactions are always favorable.

Types of Puppets

The main type of puppet we use is a hand-and-rod puppet. This puppet is simple to make and easy to use (Figure 1). As in many state park programs, our budget is very limited. Because they're so economical and at the same time effective, hand-and-rod puppets represent the ideal option. To construct a hand-and-rod puppet, the following materials are needed: one 1/4" wooden dowel about four feet in length, a 6-8" styrofoam ball, paper maché, cloth, eyes, felt, glue, pins and a wig. Simply insert the wooden dowel into the styrofoam ball and paper maché the head into a face form (i.e., cheeks, chin, forehead, nose). Be sure to use nine or ten layers of paper to form the head, and let it dry completely (this takes five to six days) before continuing work. Cloth, which becomes the puppet's skin, is tightly stretched over the paper maché head and pinned into place.

Next, the wig or other hair is pinned on, the eyes glued on, and finally a felt mouth glued into place. Your imagination can create numerous characters by adding mustaches, thick eyebrows, beards, different hair styles and even makeup. To finish, simply pin an old shirt or blouse around the neck.

Working the puppet is easy. The puppeteer places one hand through the shirt sleeve, and the other hand operates the movement of the puppet via the wooden dowel (Figure 2). Although there's not a movable mouth, these puppets are very believable in their actions.

Animal hand puppets are another easy-to-use, economical puppet. The animal puppets are purchased from Furry Folk, Inc. We often use these puppets in our regular puppet show productions, and sometimes by themselves as an attention-getting prop during campfire programs and guided walks. One popular activity is to set these realistic puppets along the trail just before a guided walk. During the walk, some visitors may observe them

Figure 3

the state. It's constructed with PVC (plumber's) pipe. Each section is no more than four feet in length. Setting it up is like playing with a big set of tinker toys. The stage pieces all fit into a cloth bag which will fit into the trunk of any car. After the frame of PVC pipe is up, we then drape it with a heavy upholstery cloth. The stage stands about 6'4" tall so that the puppeteer(s) stands while performing (Figure 3). A shelf made of two 1" x 4" boards are placed across the inside of the stage as a place to set various props that are used during the performance. Also the electrical switches and outlets are mounted on these boards. This is a simple, lightweight stage that is very durable and portable.

One of the most popular puppet shows in the state parks is a rules and regulations production starring Horrible Harvey, a menacing camper that does everything wrong. Mr. Ranger constantly tries to catch Harvey so that he can explain the rules of the park. This is a humorous, entertaining, yet very educational show. We've found it to be an excellent way to teach park visitors about rules and regulations without preaching, and it's just one of many ways we are using interpretation as a management tool in our parks.

and be shocked to see a "real" animal along the trail. This gives the interpreter a great opportunity to discuss the wildlife even though the real thing is not seen. These hand puppets can also be stuffed into an interpreter's day pack and taken out at an opportune time to interpret this particular animal.

A successful puppet show is not child's play. Puppetry may look easy, but it takes a practiced puppeteer to present a good show. Too often the production and dramatic considerations are taken lightly and the expertise of the puppeteer is neglected. A sloppy, unplanned puppet show is painfully obvious, if not outright embarrassing. Plan every detail, and practice, practice, practice.

The Stage

Puppet stages can take many shapes, forms and sizes. Some are fancy and flashy and others are plain. The stage we use in our interpretive programs is simple, lightweight and portable so it can travel to the various parks within

Why Puppet Shows Work

Puppets are a success in state park interpretive programs for many reasons:

1. They're entertaining and versatile—they can be part of large productions or used in single-person shows.

2. They create a moving and lively program.

3. They can interact with the audience.

4. Puppets are a grabber—they attract an audience.

5. Puppet shows can be very educational.

6. Puppets offer a low-cost alternative for interpretive programming.

7. Puppets are successful in reaching all age groups, not just children.

8. They can be used to interpret just about any topic, but they're especially valuable when tough or controversial topics must be dealt with.

Puppets can easily be incorporated into any interpretive program to give it some additional pizazz. Try a puppet show at your campfire programs this year. Entire families will be intrigued and entertained, and at a cost you'll like.

Interpretation on Wheels– A Mobile Information Station in Southeast Alaska

Lezlie Murray, Interpretive Specialist
Tongass National Forest
Wrangell Ranger District, Stikine Area, Alaska

The city of Wrangell is located on the north end of Wrangell Island in Alaska's panhandle. Like many other Southeast Alaskan communities, Wrangell is reachable only by boat or plane. This makes visiting Wrangell a unique experience for travelers, many of whom arrive in the summer months by ferry, plane or cruise ship.

The Wrangell Ranger District Office is not located near the main portals of entry, which are the ferry terminal, cruise ship dock and airport. This, coupled with the brevity of the visitors' stay, makes it difficult for tourists to visit the District Office.

In 1990 we surveyed visitors to learn about the recreation opportunities they'd like to experience on national forest land around Wrangell. Armed with this insight, we had to find a way to make the desired information available to our visitors. Given our remote location, I came up with an idea of putting on wheels. That was when our "Mobile Information Station" program was born. Besides the normal information we distribute, the "Station" provides an unforeseen benefit: we now

have the opportunity to answer any questions our visitors have about the local area as well as the entire national forest system. It remains today as an integral part of our visitor services program.

The Mobile Information Station has, quite literally, the ability to "get up and go" because it slips into the bed of a pick-up truck! The Station consists of a display board screwed to standards that are slid into two of the truck bed's stake pockets when the vehicle is parked. This panel sports a Forest Service flag, a brochure holder, and the important word, INFORMATION. After the first year, we added an acrylic plastic roof to the panel to help keep the brochures dry and out of the rain. The size of the display board depends on the vehicle to be used, as does the brochure holder which could be any size to match the brochures or other informational materials you wish to distribute.

The basic materials you will need to make the station include:

• a sheet of 1/4" plywood

• dimension lumber for up-right posts
• wood screws
• weatherproof paint for the board
• vinyl letters for the IN-FORMATION sign and any other messages you want to include
• two wooden wedges to slide into the stake bed pockets behind the display board uprights to steady it against the wind
• a 6" wide piece of acrylic plastic to serve as a roof

Accompanying the Station is a uniformed member of our staff who offers brochures and information, rain or shine. It's this personal touch that seems to really please people. Visitors frequently comment how glad they are to meet the Forest Service personnel, and what a great service we provide.

The Mobile Information Station has received national recognition for its originality, cost-effectiveness, and efficiency in serving the public. If you're looking for a way to provide high quality information service in remote areas, the Mobile Information Station may be just right for you!

Creative Interpretive Financing: Learning from a Cadre of World Interpreters

Jim Gale, Chief Interpreter
Mount St. Helens National Volcanic Monument,
Gifford Pinchot National Forest,
Vancouver, Washington
Lora Anderson, Regional Interpretive Specialist
Bureau of Land Management, Portland, Oregon

Do you need to increase your interpretive offerings at an existing or new location? Do you struggle with little or no funding? Are you challenged to communicate with an increasingly diverse audience? Worldwide, interpreters face the challenge of not only conveying meaningful messages, but of finding the money to do it.

A creative approach to programming can stimulate funding through use of such simple methods as conducted activities and non-profit sales. Even in public agencies, ethical and sensitive funding of interpretive programs can meet visitors' needs and provide important services without compromising our role as tax-supported servants.

In our travels, we've learned first-hand that visitors will pay for quality interpretive programs. Like most tourists, when we venture to a new environment we want to be oriented to the landscape and to learn about it. We've found that guided tours (especially if led by a local person) are excellent ways to do this. We look for posted times for guided walks, especially those that leave before first light, late afternoon or night. These times often correspond with the best time for wildlife observation and photography, allowing us to see the natural world on a cycle different from how we usually see it. On night walks we've experienced the bioluminescence of plants, the eye shine of a tarantula, and sounds we'd never have heard by day. Typically, we search through a local village or reserve to find a knowledgeable naturalist who, even though inexperienced in leading groups, is happy to act as our guide for a small fee. Our philosophy is that if we enjoy these kinds of experiences enough to pay for them, then visitors to our areas would respond the same way.

No matter how knowledgeable visitors to your area might be, most of the magic of a place is invisible when they are on their own. Successfully locating and viewing wildlife without

disturbing them can be challenging and extremely rewarding to visitors. Small creatures such as insects, many birds or tiny fungi may be hidden to the visitor without the benefit of a naturalist's eyes. Guided walks led by knowledgeable and enthusiastic naturalists give the visitor an unforgettable experience. In the tourist's mind, the fee for the walk becomes small in comparison to a lifelong memory.

Following are a few ways interpreters around the world are making interpretation pay for itself. We hope these brief vignettes will motivate you to look for ways of raising money for your own interpretive programs.

Guided Hiking—Tupee, Canaima National Park, Venezuela

We paid our naturalist guide, Tomás, to introduce us to the waterfalls, farms, and diversity of plant communities in the area. With his assistance, we stayed in the home of a local family, slept in hammocks, and ate freshly prepared chicken soup and cassava bread. Living with the family for two days also gave us new understanding of

lifestyles in rural Venezuela. A multiple-day walking tour, like the one we had, takes visitors to small family homes and provides for interpretation of a larger landscape including the natural environment as well as the culture. Foods, too, can be a part of the interpretive experience as visitors eat locally produced and prepared food, cooked according to local cuisine.

Guided Night Hikes and River Travel, Limoncocha, Ecuador

We and our naturalist-guide traveled by dugout canoe in the evening to look for the elusive caymans that live in the abandoned ox-bows of the Río Napo, in Ecuador. Traveling at dusk, we were able to observe many different birds and plants at water level. We also hiked at night to experience the sights and sounds of the forest. Because they're made of native material and put you so close to the water, dugout canoes provide the visitor a unique experience to explore a new environment and see the world through the river's eyes.

Elephant Travel—Chitwan National Park, Nepal

In Nepal, we paid park officials a fee to ride on the top of an elephant to view the park's wildlife and for a naturalist-guide to interpret the Indian Rhino. We enjoyed the safety and ease of travel on top of the elephant as we ventured through tall grass, across rivers, and through forests. The elevated viewpoint not only creates better sightseeing, it's also important if a rhino or tiger appears. The feeding, washing, training, and care of the King's elephants provide another rewarding experience as visitors come to understand the relationship between elephants and their keepers. Visitors can experience firsthand the long standing relationship between people and elephants.

The Role of Nonprofit Organizations

Private and nonprofit organizations can also contribute to financing interpretive programs. At Mount St. Helens National Volcanic Monument in the USA, concessionaires pay for interpretive staff positions as a part of the requirements for their special use permit. Private concessioners with specialty lodges who must acquire a permit to build or use the area for their facility could be required to pay for one or several interpretive positions. This is a long-term strategy which helps diversify the funding of interpretation and the shared cost benefits the concessioner, the visitor, and the resources. In addition, donation boxes located conveniently for visitors to the volcano are filling after interpretive talks. As Todd Cullings noted in his case study in Chapter 1, the donation boxes produced $11,000 in their first summer of use.

Nonprofit associations can apply for and be awarded grants which may not otherwise be available to state or federal agencies. For example, Fundación Natura (The Nature Foundation) in Ecuador works directly with granting institutions to the benefit of the Ecuadorian National Forest Service to support interpretive training, uniforms, and equipment for national park employees. All over the world, sales of common souvenirs such as T-shirts and postcards are profitable both to the organization that sells them and the natural area where they are sold.

Local communities can also benefit from the sales of handcrafted products characteristic of the area and which somehow relate to the natural resources being interpreted. Demonstrations featuring art forms such as sculpture, basketry, pottery, wood carving, and other handcrafts are common sources of revenue in many parks and forests. Simple items made of native materials, like wood or stone, are great souvenirs from the park. In this spirit, the Caribbean National Forest's Tropical Forest Visitor Center in El Yunque, Puerto Rico, is helping to form a local cooperative that will directly support interpretation at the center as well as provide income for the co-op members. They aim to accomplish this goal through sales and demonstrations of native crafts and uses of tropical woods.

Visitors who have had enjoyable, meaningful experiences are generally willing to make a contribution when they know their dollar makes a difference in supporting the program and/or the protected area. As interpreters, we need to be aware of how to create opportunities for our visitors to contribute to our programs. Then we need to concentrate on providing excellent interpretive services that are truly worth the investment.

References

Alderson, William T. and Shirley Payne Low. 1985. *Interpretation of Historic Sites*. Nashville, Tennessee, USA: American Association for State and Local History.

Bustillo, Jaime. 1990. *El Suelo Se Ha Erosionado: Modelo de Guión para una Obra Conservacionista para Títeres*. Tegucigalpa, D.C., Honduras: Ministerio de Recursos Naturales, Proyecto LUPE.

Forte, Imogene. 1985. *Puppets: Friends at Your Finger Tips*. Nashville, Tennessee, USA: Incentive Publications.

Garrison, Inger L. 1982. Living Interpretation. In, Sharpe, G.W., *Interpreting the Environment*. New York, New York, USA: John Wiley & Sons.

Ham, Sam H. and Richard L. Shew. 1979. A Comparison of Visitors' and Interpreters' Assessments of Conducted Interpretive Activities. *Journal of Interpretation* 4(2):39-44.

Hilker, G. 1974. *The Audience and You: Practical Dramatics for the Park Interpreter*. Washington, D.C.: U.S. Government Printing Office.

Kay, William K. 1970. *Keep It Alive! Tips on Living History Demonstrations*. Washington, D.C., USA: U.S. National Park Service.

Lewis, William, J. 1980. *Interpreting for Park Visitors*. Philadelphia, PA, USA: Eastern National Park and Monument Association, Eastern Acorn Press.

Manucy, Albert. 1968. *Say, Ranger: Or, How to Perform in the Information Center*. Washington, D.C., USA: U.S. National Park Service.

Ministerio Hondureño de Salud Pública. 1986. *Hagamos Títeres*. Tegucigalpa, D.C., Honduras: División de Educación para la Salud, Ministerio de Salud Pública.

Moore, Alan, Bill Wendt, Louis Penna e Isabel Castillo de Ramos. 1989. *Manual para La Capacitación del Personal de Areas Protegidas* (Modulo C: Interpretación y Educación Ambiental, Apunte 4a). Washington, D.C., USA: Servicio de Parques Nacionales, Oficina de Asuntos Internacionales.

Morales, Jorge. 1987. *Manual para la Interpretación en Espacios Naturales Protegidos*. Anexo 3 del Taller Internacional sobre Interpretación Ambiental en Areas Silvestres Protegidas. Santiago, Chile: Oficina Regional de la FAO para América Latina y el Caribe, 7-12 de diciembre de 1988.

Regnier, Kathleen, Michael Gross and Ron Zimmerman. 1992. *The Interpreter's Guidebook: Techniques for Programs and Presentations*. Stevens Point, Wisconsin, USA: UW-SP Foundation Press, Inc.

Sharpe, Grant W. and Ron W. Hodgson. 1982. Information Duty. In, Sharpe, G.W.(ed.), *Interpreting the Environment*. New York, New York, USA: John Wiley & Sons.

Wallace, George N. 1990. Law Enforcement and the Authority of the Resource. *Legacy* 1(2):4-8.

Werner, David and Bill Bower. 1982. *Helping Health Workers Learn: A Book of Methods, Aids, and Ideas for Instructors at the Village Level*. Palo Alto, California, USA: The Hesperian Foundation.

Additional Reading

In English:

Grater, Russell K. 1976. *The Interpreter's Handbook: Methods, Skills and Techniques.* Globe, Arizona, USA: Southwest Parks and Monuments Association.

MacKinnon, John, Kathy MacKinnon, Graham Child and James Thorsell (eds.). 1986. *Managing Protected Areas in the Tropics* (Chapter 7). Cambridge, United Kingdom: International Union for the Conservation of Nature & Natural Resources and the United Nations Environment Program.

Rudd, Connie. 1992. Beyond Traditional Costumed Interpretation: New Techniques for Old Stories. *Legacy* 3(3):12-14.

Tilden, Freeman. 1977. *Interpreting Our Heritage.* Chapel Hill, North Carolina, USA: University of North Carolina Press.

In Spanish:

Ham, Sam H. 1992. *Interpretación Ambiental: Una Guía Práctica para Gente con Grandes Ideas y Presupuestos Pequeños.* Golden, Colorado, USA: North American Press/Fulcrum Publishing.

MacKinnon, John, Kathy MacKinnon, Graham Child y James Thorsell (eds.). 1990. *Manejo de Areas Protegidas en los Trópicos* (Capítulo 7). Cancun, Quintana Roo, México: Amigos de Sian Ka'an A.C.

Sharpe, Grant W. 1982. Selecciones de *Interpretando el Ambiente.* Turrialba, Costa Rica: Centro Agronómico Tropical de Investigación y Enseñanza (CATIE).

Tilden, Freeman. 1977. Selecciones de *Interpretando Nuestra Herencia.* Turrialba, Costa Rica: Centro Agronómico Tropical de Investigación y Enseñanza (CATIE).

Werner, David. 1986. *Donde No Hay Doctor—Una Guía para los Campesinos que Viven Lejos de los Centros Médicos.* Palo Alto, California, USA: La Fundación Hesperian.

CHAPTER SEVEN

CASE STUDIES ON SCHOOL AND COMMUNITY PROGRAMS

Natural resource management is always easier if it's carried out in concert with an informed and supportive public. Too often, natural resource managers overlook their own communities and local schools as important audiences for interpretive programs. This is unfortunate because how local populations feel about you, and what they know about the natural resources in the local area, almost always influence how well you're able to manage them. Community interpretive programs help to win friends for conservation and support for your management activities. Well designed, they make local people feel a part of what you're doing, rather than apart from it.

School and community programs can involve any of the personal presentations and self-guided activities discussed in other chapters. These include talks, exhibits, audiovisual programs, guided

tours, puppet shows, and many other types of communication programs. Principles and techniques for developing these programs are covered elsewhere in this book. In this chapter, we'll focus on the range of programs you might offer in your community and schools, and consider some innovative approaches. We'll do this is by looking at what other interpreters are doing in their communities, and by learning from their experiences.

Toward this end, eight case studies were written especially for this chapter. The authors are people like you—people whose job it is to plan, design, and implement educational programs in the communities where they live and work. Some of the programs they describe are small; others large, some are directed at school children, others at whole communities; some are short-term educational **events**, while others are **campaigns**. But despite their diversity, they have something in common: each is an **off-site program** that takes important messages about natural resources to a critical audience—local people.

Many good references on planning and organizing school and community programs are available. In English, Fazio and Gilbert (1986), Ford (1981), Gebler (1982), MacKinnon et al. (1986), Regnier et al. (1992), Sutherland and Ham (1992), Wallin (1982) and Wood and Wood (1990) are recommended. Good references in Spanish include Ham and Castillo (1990), Moore et al. (1989), Morales (1987), Muñoz and Peña (1990), and Wood and Wood (1990).

Formal and Nonformal Community Education Programs

You can think of community education programs in two broad categories: **formal** and **nonformal**. Formal programs take place within primary, secondary, and post-secondary school systems. Their purpose is to prepare the next generation of adults to be conscientious and informed resource users and stewards. Elementary school children often are considered an important audience because their environmental knowledge and values are generally less rigid and more impressionable than those of adults. Secondary and post-secondary students are also important because they're on the verge of entering the work force at both the professional and technician levels.

School programs usually take the form of classroom presentations or field trips. Teachers are often eager to bring outside experts into the classroom, especially when doing so fits some aspect of the school curriculum. It's best to consult with teachers about the curriculum and what kinds of roles you might play. Chances are, if you gear what you're offering to the teacher's needs, you'll be welcome in his or her classroom as often as you'd like. Teachers are responsible for accomplishing a lot with their students each year, and time to do it is short. In fact, limited time (both for planning and during the school day) has been found to be one of the biggest barriers to environmental education in schools all over the world (see Ham 1992 and Ham and Sewing 1988). Offering to conduct classroom and field programs that help teachers accomplish what they're charged to do will not only be well received, it will probably endear you to them.

Recognizing this fact, many organizations have developed environmental education curricula and activity guides that are organized around the main subject areas in the typical school curriculum (science, mathematics, social sciences, language arts, etc.). Among the best and most popular of these are *Project Wild* which focuses on wildife, *Project Learning Tree* which focuses on forests, *Project Wet*, a newly released program dealing with aquatic ecosystems, and the National Wildlife Federation's *Nature Scope* which focuses on a range of global environmental topics. All of them rely heavily on games, simulations and crafts to make learning about the environment fun. (See Appendix D for addresses of the organizations who produce these and other excellent materials.)

Formal education programs focusing on children represent a long-term educational solution to environmental problems. They're an "investment" in the sense

Figure 7-1. Many excellent formal environmental education packages are available today. Among the best are *Project Wild*, *Project Learning Tree*, *Project Wet*, and *Nature Scope*.

that their goal is to nurture an informed future citizenry (Wood and Wood 1990). Since today's youth are tomorrow's resource users and caretakers, school programs are undeniably important. But unfortunately, they usually don't address the immediate, short-term need to educate adult audiences about their natural resources. Some authors (e.g., Medina 1989, Wood and Wood 1990, and Ham and Sutherland 1991), have even suggested that in some cases an over-emphasis on school children may have led to the neglect of other audiences more strategically important in the immediate protection of natural resources. Usually, these audiences are reachable only through nonformal programs.

Nonformal programs occur outside the formal school system. Typically they're aimed at local landowners, consumers of **print** and **broadcast media**, community leaders, clubs and organizations, outdoor

sports people, educators, and other people who use natural resource lands regularly or who are influential in the community. Most important is that nonformal programs are often directed at adult audiences—people whose decisions and behaviors affect the current environment, not just tomorrow's. Whole communities are often targeted by environmental education programs, but sometimes key audiences are singled out. Important among these audiences are farmers, teachers, business people, community opinion leaders, elected officials, mass media specialists, police, clergy, and in some areas, the military.

Educational Events Versus Campaigns

Although they're both valuable, educational events and educational campaigns are different. Events are short-term, often one-time, programs. They include making a presentation at a local school, giving a talk at a Rotary Club meeting, setting up an exhibit at the county fair, being interviewed by a radio station, and many other educational efforts. Campaigns, on the other hand, are long-term programs that include a coordinated series of events that you've designed to bring about awareness of some issue or need. Campaigns owe their power to repetition and constant reinforcement. They keep your message in the public eye over a long period of time. Often, campaigns include producing and giving away common, everyday items (e.g., pencils, pens, calendars, patches, decals, posters, pins, T-shirts, caps, key rings, etc.) each carrying important themes. Day after day, each time one of the items is seen, one of the campaign's

Figure 7-2. Examples of articles used in environmental education campaigns. (Photo by Gerry Snyder)

messages is also seen. You can probably persuade local business to donate some or all of the items for this kind of campaign, especially if you prepare the designs. In exchange, most businesses will either want to have their names on the items or to receive some other kind of recognition or acknowledgment during the campaign.

Mass Media

The **mass media** are powerful communicators—and they're often free—especially if what you're doing is worthy of news coverage. In addition, most newspapers will print announcements of community educational events as long as they perceive them to be in the public's interest. Small rural newspapers are especially interested in printing stories about local natural resources.

Radio can be a very strategic medium for community education programs. Radios are available to all social classes; they don't require literacy and therefore can reach young children and illiterate adults; and in some areas they're still a popular pastime. It's often easy to arrange

to be interviewed by a small, local radio station. Some natural resource agencies do weekly reports or develop an on-going series of public service announcements on environmental topics. Special reports on natural areas, how to get to them, and how to enjoy them might be popular with local audiences. In agricultural regions, early morning programs aimed at farmers are common. Make contact with the person who does the show in your area. Offer to be a regular information source on topics of interest to farmers. Such information might include ways to improve production through soil conservation or through agroforesty techniques. Convince the station to interview local farmers who are already using innovative farming practices so that they can testify about the benefits they're seeing.

Getting on a television program is harder to arrange, but stations are always looking for news. Don't be afraid to visit or call the newsroom to tell about a local event or program that you'll be offering. You'll be surprised how interested they can be in local stories. (They know who buys the products their sponsors advertise.) Try to get invited to a talk show, or cultivate the interest of a television station in doing a feature or a special report on your area.

Role Playing and Community Theater

Although dramatic role playing isn't appropriate everywhere, it's a powerful form of communication when the situation's right. If you know a group of actors, ask them about doing a play or skit related to natural resources. In the rural parts of some countries, researchers have

Figure 7-3. Exposure through the broadcast media is usually free if your message is in the public interest. An interpreter from Fort Clatsop National Memorial is interviewed at a local radio station. (Photos courtesy of National Park Service)

found role playing to be a highly acceptable and effective method of community education in natural resources, agriculture and health fields (Werner 1980, Werner and Bower 1982, Beltrán and Peña 1988, Bajimaya and Fazio 1989, Bunch 1982). Role playing, whether it involves human actors or puppets, allows people to focus on sensitive or controversial aspects of their lives without having to assume personal responsibility for its moral content. According to experts like Werner (1980) and Werner and Bower (1982), role playing is most effective when community members, themselves, do the acting.

Especially popular with schools are short plays that give some of the children or teachers simple roles to play. Two such works, *We Are One In the Forest* and *The Impact Monster*, are the focus of two of the case studies at the end of this chapter. Both plays can be modified easily to fit local circumstances, and both are relatively easy to perform.

Capitalizing on Traditional Celebrations

Almost every town has some kind of annual celebration. It may commemorate an historic event, honor a famous person, commemorate the town's founding, or simply coincide with a national holiday (such as Independence Day or Labor Day). Parades, fairs, carnivals, expositions, and many kinds of special activities are held during these celebrations, and it's important that you be involved in as many of them as possible. Try to have an exhibit or information desk at the events. If possible, arrange to present a series of talks or audiovisual programs. In addition to the obvious educational value, simply being visible at community celebrations is important. Your participation helps people to see you (and the values you represent) as part of the community rather than as an outside influence.

Many communities have celebrations that are timed with natural events or cycles. The arrival of a migrating bird species, the ripening of a fruit, or the beginning or end of a climatic season are cause for celebration in thousands of communities all over the world. These annual events represent important opportunities for community education because for a short period of time public attention is already focused on the environment. Some examples of "nature celebrations" are shown in Figure 7-5. If the town you work in doesn't have an annual celebration related to a natural event, consider starting one. Experience shows that although it may be hard to generate a lot of enthusiasm the first year or two,

Figure 7-4. An environmental education class at the University of Idaho involves local school children in a performance of *The Lorax*. Simple costumes and homespun props kept the total cost of the production extremely low. (Photo by Doug McConnell)

participation usually increases the third year, especially if the event is aggressively publicized. By nature, people like celebrations, and once one becomes a tradition its long-term educational potential is greatly magnified.

Introduction to the Case Studies and How to Use Them

The following eight case studies were selected to show just how diverse school and community programs can be. Of course, the actual range of possibilities is limited only by your imagination and local circumstances. The case studies come from four different countries in North, Central and South America, and the Caribbean. Yet despite wide variations in our cultures and environments, you'll see that the ideas presented are widely applicable.

The eight case studies are organized into four groups. The first consists of a single case study focusing on an annual nature celebration, "The Return of the Salmon Festival," held in Leavenworth, Washington. One of the most successful community programs of its type in the U.S., the "Salmon Festival" focuses public attention on the importance of anadromous fish species and the threats to their survival.

The second group of case studies highlights two innovative traveling plays. *Nobody's Ever Alone in the Forest* was developed by Wendy Walker, at the time a U.S. Forest Service interpreter in Bellingham, Washington. The cast includes her own children, some of their friends and several audience members wherever they perform. Through humor, heart-warming dialogue between the plant and animal characters, and a theme song that the spectators and cast sing together, this delightful play teaches complex forest ecology and environmental ethics to its audiences. The second play, *The Impact Monster*, is a humorous portrayal of a backpacker who unknowingly does everything wrong in the backcountry. With audience members playing the "victims," the impact monster spoils scenery, water, and wildlife habitat through careless and insensitive behaviors. In the end, a more conscientious wilderness user shows the monster the error of its ways and the audience gets a clear message about proper backcountry ethics and low impact use. Both plays lend themselves to local adaptation, and scripts are available from the authors on request.

The case studies in the third group describe mobile interpretive programs. In Bagaces, Costa Rica a group of environmental educators travels to different schools to teach children about bats and to dispel the many myths that revolve

Take Advantage of Annual Celebrations
Related to Natural Resources

Capitalize on traditional community events such as fairs, holidays, and annual festivals. Especially important are festivities that have to do with natural cycles or natural resource topics. All over the world, nature is a focal point for community and national celebrations. Following are just a few examples.

Forests and Wildlife

Jamaica: Each year, National History Week is recognized in schools and communities throughout the country. In the past few years the event has adopted a natural history focus. Citizens are reminded of their historical dependence on nature for their livelihoods and economic well-being. "Wood and Water Day" is another Jamaican celebration. It focuses on the importance of forests, clean water, and other natural resources. Although the event is beginning to lose some of its popularity, environmental educators hope to revive it. Jamaica's nick name is "the land of wood and water."

United States: Estacada, Oregon, holds its annual "Logging Festival" just as logging activities are getting underway in western Oregon forests. The festival reminds Oregonians of their forestry heritage and of the economic importance of forest industries in the western U.S.

Costa Rica, Ecuador, and other Latin American countries: An annual holiday, the "Fiesta de Los Agricultores de San Isidro Labrador" ("Festival of Farmers of Saint Isidor") occurs during the rainy season when rivers are high and erosion is at its worst. Saint Isidor is called upon to bring sun and dry weather to the rural farmers (campesinos).

United States: The only known celebration focusing on an anadromous fish is the annual "Return of the Salmon Festival" held in Leavenworth, Washington. The event draws thousands of people from five western states. Exhibitions, presentations, fish hatchery tours, children's programs, and extensive mass media coverage focus regional attention on the historical significance of salmon in the cultures, economies, and of course diets, of the Pacific states. Local businesses support the event because it brings a lot of money to the local economy at a time when business would normally be slow.

United States: In Oregon, the town of Tualatin has an annual "Crawfish Festival," a week-long event focusing on river resources and this fresh-water "lobster." In the coastal town of Yachats, "Silver Smelting Day" recognizes the importance of smelt in the community's culture and economy. Townspeople and visitors attend demonstrations that show how to catch, cook, smoke, can and pickle, and presumably, eat, smelt.

Agricultural Crops

Honduras: In the small rural town of La Esperanza (literally, "Hope"), the annual "Festival de Papas" ("Potato Festival") celebrates the central role that potatoes play in the people's lives and the community's economy.

Costa Rica: The annual "Festival de las Cebollas" ("Onion Festival") is held in the town of Santa Ana near the capital city. Community members and outsiders are reminded of the area's rich agricultural heritage.

Ecuador: Each year the long-awaited maturation of flowers and fruits is celebrated in the "Fiestas de las Flores y de las Frutas de Ambato" ("The Ambato Flowers and Fruits Festival"). The event focuses community-wide attention on the importance of nature and its economic benefits to Ambato. Each June in the small town of Cayambe, the "Fiesta de San Pedro y San Pablo" ("Festival of Saint Peter and Saint Paul") precedes the annual harvest of food crops. Interwoven into the religious significance of the celebration is an unmistakable focus on "Mother Earth" and people's responsibility to take care of her.

United States: Every winter, more than a thousand people gather at an urban nature center to celebrate the "Maple Sugarbush Weekend" in Evansville, Indiana (Dispenza 1989). Slide shows, guided tours, and syrup tasting highlight the weekend event. Interpreters use the celebration to raise awareness about the negative impacts that drought and acid rain are having on the maple trees. Money for the preserve is raised through donations and the sale of maple cookies baked by employees.

United States: Many communities organize annual celebrations around a local flower. In the state of Washington, Spokane holds its "Lilac Festival and Parade;" in Puyallup, there's the "Daffodil Parade;" in Oregon, the town of Brookings recognizes the annual blooming of wild azaleas with the "Azalea Festival" and Portland celebrates the "Rose Festival." Natural resource management agencies often coordinate community education programs with these events.

United States: The "Apple Blossom Festival" in Wenatchee, Washington, celebrates the end of winter and the beginning of the fruit-growing season. Apples are an especially important export crop. A similar event, the "Pear Blossom Festival," is held in Medford, Oregon. The ripening of wild huckleberries in Warm Springs, Oregon, is recognized each August with the "Huckleberry Festival."

Geology and Minerals

United States: "Pioneer Mining Days" in Cottage Grove, Oregon focuses on the community's mining heritage. Participants hear and read stories of early miners and the development of Cottage Grove.

United States: Nyssa, Oregon holds an annual event called "Thunderegg Days." Thundereggs are a special kind of rock considered prestigious by "rock hounds" (rock enthusiasts). The celebration focuses on the unusual geologic features of the area.

International Events

Worldwide: Every year on June 5 nations celebrate "Environment Day." In most countries, environmental problems and solutions are emphasized nationwide in print and broadcast media, as well as in celebrations and special events held in cities and towns.

Worldwide: "Earth Day" is celebrated April 22 all across the world. Global environmental issues and the global scale of environmental problems are emphasized in print and broadcast media. Schools, communities, civic organizations, and natural resource management agencies often stage special events related to nature and natural resources.

Figure 7-5. Examples of traditional "nature" celebrations.

Figure 7-6. The Fiesta of Flowers and Fruits attracts thousands of native Ecuadorians to the village of Ambato each year. (Photo by Nelly Cartagena)

around them. In Montana, a box full of wildlife educational aids and a teacher's guide was developed. Since there aren't enough employees to meet the growing demand for school programs, the box (instead of a person) can be sent to schools. The third mobile program is called "The Environmental Express," a vehicle containing environmental education materials that drives from community to community in Trinidad and Tobago. Although this particular vehicle is a bus, it could easily be someone's car or small pick-up.

The last group of case studies highlights two different environmental education campaigns. In Brazil, two components of the Fundación Vitoria Amazónica's campaign to save the endangered pied bare-faced tamarin are described. This is an expensive campaign, but the author describes how easy it was to get donations to support it. The other case study in this group describes two campaigns developed by environmental educators in Trinidad and Tobago. Even in a small country, reaching a national population is difficult. Through its high school environmental speaking competitions, Trinidad

and Tobago's Forestry Division is insuring that environmental messages reach not only secondary students all across the country, but their communities and homes. A related program, "Walk-a-thon," stresses the dangers of uncontrolled fire. Besides involving thousands of Trinidadians in a one-day noncompetitive walking event, "Walk-a-thon" receives countrywide mass media coverage.

These eight accounts are but a small glimpse of the actual range of possibilities. Hundreds of other excellent programs also could have been included. Unfortunately, there simply isn't space here for all of them. As you read each case study, pay special attention to: (1) the target audience, (2) the people doing the communicating, and (3) the materials or equipment involved. Ask yourself whether you could develop such a program, or whether it could be modified to suit your resources and needs. Most of all, let the case studies stimulate your imagination. Maybe you'll come up with an altogether different approach or one that combines ideas from two or more of the programs described here.

Figure 7-7. A storyteller weaves a tale about salmon for a group of children inside a "salmon tent." The event is part of the annual "Return of the Salmon Festival" in Leavenworth, Washington. (U.S. Forest Service photo by Don Virgovic)

Glossary terms: broadcast media, campaign, event, formal education, non-formal education, off-site program, mass media, print media.

A Community Celebrates Nature: The Wenatchee River Return-of-the-Salmon Festival

Corky Broaddus, Wenatchee River Salmon Festival Director
Wenatchee National Forest, Leavenworth, Washington

Located in North Central Washington, 470 miles upstream from the Pacific Ocean, the Wenatchee River is a last remaining treasure in the Columbia River Basin. Where else can one still find viable, natural runs of spring chinook salmon, summer chinook salmon and sockeye salmon. The recent problems surrounding the spotted owl and Snake River salmon runs highlight the growing demands upon our natural resources. Demands placed upon natural resources and land management agencies will continue to increase with the pressure of a growing human population. At the same time, with an increasingly urban population, the public's basic understanding of the natural world and environmental issues is diminishing.

The USDA Forest Service, Wenatchee National Forest and the USDI Fish and Wildlife Service, Leavenworth National Fish Hatchery recognize a responsibility to provide leadership in natural resource management. The Wenatchee River Salmon

Festival was conceived as a mechanism to educate the public about the fish and other riparian resources. This enables the public to support complex resource management decisions on an informed basis rather than an emotional one. Primary goals for this now annual festival are to increase awareness and appreciation for the unique value of the local aquatic resources, provide educational activities focusing on kids and families, and highlight the cultural significance of the salmon to the people of the Northwest. Secondary goals are to promote interest in outdoor recreation and expand visitor activities for the local tourism economy.

Guided by these goals, the first annual "Return of the Salmon, Wenatchee River Salmon Festival" was held in October, 1991. Hosted by the USDA Forest Service, Wenatchee National Forest, and the U.S. Fish and Wildlife Service, Leavenworth National Fish Hatchery, and sponsored by twenty-nine corporate, agency, and individual partners, the four-day event attracted over 8,000 people plus an additional 450 people who participated in a special organized hike. The community benefitted financially, the attendees enjoyed themselves and learned a lot, and regional and national attention to our declining anadromous fish species was greatly heightened. This case study describes how we did it.

Location

Leavenworth, Washington—approximately 25 miles west of Wenatchee and 120 miles east of Seattle—has evolved into a destination tourism center. This Bavarian theme town at the eastern edge of the Cascade Mountains attracts over one million visitors annually from all over the world but primarily the Pacific Northwest and British Columbia. The Leavenworth area and Chelan County, Washington are also rapidly growing as people seek to escape the pressures of metropolitan life and enjoy the central Washington weather. Beside being a tourism destination, Leavenworth and the adjacent Wenatchee National Forest receive a large number of weekend visitors from nearby Seattle.

The Leavenworth National Fish Hatchery, located near the national forest boundary just two miles from town, is the largest federal salmon production facility in Washington. Fish Hatchery and Wenatchee National Forest personnel have long been partners in natural resource management. Their longstanding partnership and working relationship was instrumental in the success of the salmon festival. With over 160 acres, the hatchery grounds were the obvious choice for the location of this very special event.

Planning

Early in 1991 members of the Leavenworth and Lake Wenatchee Ranger Districts and the Leavenworth Fish Hatchery met to establish a core committee to plan and implement the event. Critical to the eventual success of the project was the ability of personnel from the two agencies to work together. As Public Affairs Specialist for the Lake Wenatchee Ranger District, I was assigned the task of Festival Coordinator. In addition, very early in the planning process, the core team was joined by the Executive Director of the Leavenworth Chamber of Commerce and representatives from the Yakima Indian Nation, the Washington Department of Fisheries and a local Volkssport chapter. Eventually, the festival would involve all the hatchery employees, a wide range of Forest Service employees—from fire crews to the Forest Supervisor—and volunteers from the local community. In total, twenty-nine corporations, agencies and individual partners became involved.

To remain consistent with our overall objectives, the decision was made early that official festival activities not only needed to be educational and fun, but non-commercial. During our first few meetings several additional objectives were added, including development of a scholarship fund to assist local students pursuing higher education in natural resources, assist local schools with their environmental education programs, and to raise

interest and support for establishing an aquatic education and research center at the hatchery. A long-term goal is that both the festival and aquatic center will eventually become self-sufficient.

Prefestival Activities

One of the first tasks of the core team was to decide when the festival would take place and what activities would occur. October 10–13 were selected as the festival dates. These dates were chosen because they coincide with the peak of summer chinook salmon spawning in the Wenatchee River; they come at a time of year when the weather is generally nice; they immediately follow Autumn Leaf Festival, a major Leavenworth event that occurs the previous two weekends; and schools are in session, enabling the festival to involve the local school children. Based upon these dates, time lines were established for the timely completion of pre-festival activities such as promotion, supply purchases and facility arrangements.

Working with the Icicle Valley Chapter of Trout Unlimited, a bank account was established with the help of Central Washington Bank to which people and/or corporations could donate to a scholarship fund. The Forest Service graphics specialist designed a logo for the festival and Silk Screen Printers, a local T-shirt company, offered to print and distribute T-shirts, sweatshirts and baseball caps with the logo to local merchants. A portion of the proceeds from the sale of these items was then deposited in the bank account for the scholarship fund. A comprehensive "Spawnsorship" program was developed for interested individuals and companies to donate to a fund to support the scholarship and festival activities. Trout Unlimited's tax-exempt status allowed a tax deduction for any such donation.

Local schools were involved early in the salmon festival program. Our emphasis on environmental education was inititated with a poster contest in local schools. Forest Service interpreters developed a short, interactive program highlighting salmon and their environment and visited twelve schools to start the contest. Students were asked to design a poster along the topic "Return of the Salmon." The winning design would be used as the promotional poster for the festival. More than 230 students, ranging from first to sixth grade, participated in the contest. The winning poster created by Wenatchee fifth grader, Drew Kelly, featured a sockeye salmon and the slogan "Coming Soon to a River Near You." All the posters entries were displayed for a week at a local mall. An awards ceremony was held recognizing the work of all entrants. Five finalists were awarded a $50 savings bond and Drew was presented a $250 savings bond. The poster was taken to a graphic designer who used Drew's creation to design the promotional poster which was printed by major sponsors, Chelan County Public Utility District and Alcoa.

In addition to the poster, a broad spectrum of media opportunities were developed to make the residents throughout the northwest aware of the festival. These included: articles printed free of charge by Sunset Magazine, AAA Motorists, the Cascade Loop Tour brochure; radio advertisement by a local radio station sponsor and statewide public service announcements; a public service announcement created by a local company, Production Services, Inc. was distributed to ten television stations in Washington state as well as public television. Other promotional publications included a rack brochure printed courtesy of Luhr.Jensen, Inc., a schedule of events printed by Chelan County PUD, an article in "Pathfinder," the Northwest Volkssport newsletter, and articles published by the Everett, Washington, *Herald* and the Seattle *Post-Intelligencer*. Just prior to the event, articles highlighting the festival and the wild Wenatchee River Salmon were published in local papers. The Leavenworth Chamber of Commerce provided vital support to the promotional campaign. The executive director offered guidance in identifying and selecting media to pursue. The chamber assisted in distributing festival rack cards and other publications through their distribution network. It also included brief abstracts about the festival in its annual events handout and in the Leavenworth Directory, a glossy four-color comprehensive listing of festivals, events, information providers and business memberships.

Festival Activities

Work on the activities actually started in spring 1991 when our interpretive team, guided by the festival's goals and objectives, developed an interpretive plan for the festival. Activities included a trail at the Fish Hatchery displaying the hatchery history and the river environment, and an auto tour up Tumwater Canyon for fish viewing. Forest Service crews, with the assistance of Fish Hatchery personnel constructed the trail at the hatchery. The mile-long hatchery trail is self-guided with numbered stops keyed to a brochure. Viewing blinds were constructed so people could observe and photograph wildlife at their leisure. Ultimately, this trail will be completely accessible to persons with disabilities. Finally, brochures for the self-guided auto tour up Tumwater Canyon were printed. These trails will allow people to learn about and enjoy local wildlife resources year-round.

Environmental education and interest in outdoor recreation objectives were emphasized by displays and exhibits at the festival. Any company or group who had an environmental education or outdoor recreation message linked to aquatic resources were invited to participate as long as the display was educational and non-political; no sales were allowed. Such displays included a "conservation trail" by the Wenatchee National Forest, a Wenatchee River display from the Chelan County PUD, exhibits by Alcoa, Bonneville Power Administration, U.S. Fish and Wildlife Service, Ecological Services wetland exhibit, Washington Department of Fisheries, NOAA, the local Audubon chapter, and the Fish Hatchery sponsored a display from the Seattle Aquarium. The Chelan County Sheriff also had a display including a search and rescue boat, helicopter, and its DARE exhibit which urged children to get "Hooked on Fishing Not on Drugs." These displays, which included aquaria and hands-on activities, were enjoyed by young and old alike. Fish Hatchery tours were also conducted. Displays with more of an outdoor recreation focus included Worden Lures/Yakima Bait Co., Luhr.Jensen, Clearwater Anglers, the Wenatchee River Flyfishers, and Trout Unlimited. The Flyfishers and Yakima Bait also put on fishing clinics.

The cultural significance of salmon to the Northwest was exhibited with two activities. Thursday and Friday night, the Confederated Tribes of Colville performed cultural dances that were thoroughly enjoyed by festival attenders. The second cultural performance was presented by Susan Strauss, a well known storyteller from Bend, Oregon, who specializes in Native American stories. Her performance, specifically prepared for the festival, "Coyote Meets the Wild Salmon and Other Stories of the Columbia River" was a high point of the weekend.

Two hands-on activities were among the biggest hits of the festival. The first is Gyotaku, the Japanese art of fish printing. People painted and printed Wenatchee River sockeye and Columbia River shad, allowing them to have fun and learn about the fish at the same time. The second was the "salmon tent," a colorful inflated, salmon-shaped, nylon tent. The tent came with costumes allowing children (and some adults) to dress as bears, mushrooms, bats, mosquitoes, and the like, and parade around the tent. After the parade, they entered the salmon tent where Forest Service interpreters told local native American stories about the Columbia River, covering both the environmental education and cultural objectives of the festival.

In addition to many other activities, people enjoyed a variety of foods at booths operated by non-profit groups. Food and festival T-shirts were the only items sold at the Festival. Non-profit groups, including Trout Unlimited, Kiwanis, and others had food booths and donated 10 percent of their gross receipts to the festival account.

Outcomes and Benefits

The 1991 festival was judged a great success. Enough money was received so that two $1,500 scholarships will be awarded to students pursuing a career in natural resource management. Not only was attendance good, but comments from people at the festival and in the community at large were very positive. People especially liked the relaxed, non-commercial, educational theme, and their awareness and appreciation of the local resources also seemed to be enhanced. Especially gratifying is the fact that more people than ever before witnessed the spectacular return of the salmon from the river's edge. The regional press coverage was excellent, and there is little doubt that the Return of the Salmon Festival is creating greater public awareness about threats to our native fisheries.

It appears we were also successful in achieving our goal of assisting the local tourism economy as evidenced by the 44 percent of the out-of-area festival visitors who came specifically for this event. Of those who spent the night, 66 percent stayed in local lodging facilities and another 31 percent stayed in private campgrounds.

The first day of the festival was a local school day. Field trips brought over 1600 school children. Responses from teachers were very positive. Did the kids like it? They must have—many came back with their parents.

A positive aspect of the festival was the teamwork and cooperation exhibited by the Forest Service and Fish and Wildlife Service. Over 100 Forest Service and Fish and Wildlife Service employees worked side-by-side during the event. The cooperative relationship between the two agencies will be extremely valuable in meeting future challenges in natural resource management. In addition, thirty volunteers pitched in, making the Salmon Festival a true grass roots, community event. Amazingly, the volunteers ranged from a "senior" softball group who helped with parking, to many people from the local community, and even members of a Minnesota tour group who came back on Sunday to help with the Gyotaku activity for children.

Almost as soon as the inaugural Return of the Salmon Festival had ended, we were beginning to plan the next one. We are searching out additional "spawnsorships" and planning for even more visitors in future years. There's no feeling like success, especially when something so important is on the line.

Traveling Ecology Theater— *Nobody's Ever Alone in the Forest*

Wendy Walker, Instructor and Consultant
Huxley College of Environmental Studies
Bellingham, Washington

February 1990:

Boss: "Hey Wendy, how about putting together an interpretive program for the big Earth Day extravaganza in Seattle in April?"

Wendy: "Sure. What should it be about?"

Boss: "Anything you want. Just make sure it's fun and upbeat."

Wendy: "Is there any budget?"

Boss: "I can pay you for ten days' work. That's it."

Wendy: (Thinking) "Mmmmm, what's a gripping theme for a Forest Service interpretive program for Earth Day? What do people think of when they hear the words National Forests? Trees. That's it! An interpretive program about trees ... forests ... ecosystems. Forest ecology research is turning up astonishing processes and connections in forests. Here's a chance to tell it to the world ... or at least the 30,000

Seattle residents projected to attend Earth Day festivities. How do I get the ideas across? I've seen the glazed eyes of audiences listening to an ecology lecture, befuddled by scientific jargon and passive prose. I can't take them out into the woods. That would be my first choice. Second best: Bring the forest to them. Let's re-create the forest in the city park and bring the organisms alive before their eyes. Let's put on a play with talking trees and singing animals."

Wendy's Conscience: "But what about anthropomorphising animals and plants? Isn't that supposed to be a mistake ... sort of creating a Walt Disney artificial world?"

Wendy's Practicality: "How can we build empathy and understanding for forest organisms if people can't identify with them? Plants and animals do have some similarities to human beings. Let's build on that common ground. Then ham it up! Don't underestimate the audience. They know that trees don't talk. What they need to learn is all the other amazing things that trees can do. And why not let talking trees tell their own story?"

Wendy: "Okay, you talked me into it. So I write a play, huh. Let's see ... We're way out in the wilderness somewhere. There's a huge old Douglas fir ... say 900 years old. And growing nearby ... a little western hemlock with a droopy top ... What would a young western hemlock sound like? Whiney ... impatient ... naive. And the old tree ... grumpy and wise. What would these two say to each other, if they could talk?"

March 1990:

The play is written. *Nobody's Ever Alone in the Forest* is now a musical set to familiar old tunes, thanks to a hilarious brainstorming session with the cast. The volunteer actors are my two kids and children and parents from two other families.

We found $500 for one extravagant costume, in the mold of the big, fancy Smokey the Bear costumes. We wheedled the money out of other Forest Service departments. The costume was created by a costume designer out of an artificial Christmas tree. A Forest Service co-worker volunteered to sew an owl costume out of yards and yards of grey and beige felt. Another donated truffle puppets made of brown socks with jiggly doll eyes.

The cast made most of the rest of the costumes out of second-hand clothing and ingenuity. The vole wears a brown leotard stuffed with a pillow belly, brown leg-warmers and a brown hood with ears. The volcano wears a black skirt around his neck. A hula hoop sewn into the hem creates a mountain shape, and Christmas tinsel draped down the sides is the lava. The volcano throws handfuls of kitty litter when it erupts volcanic ash—usually into the audience.

A Forest Service graphic artist designed a backdrop scene which the cast painted onto a big piece of canvas. We painted the old tree on the backdrop and then cut holes in the "trunk" for the actress's head and hands. The artist also created coloring sheets with the backdrop scene, complete with cut-out finger puppets of the main characters.

April 1990:

The big day arrives. Our stage is a makeshift wooden affair nailed together for us by a Forest Service employee on his own time. Tens of thousands of people begin to pour into the park to see hundreds of exhibits. We perform ten times in ten hours. Audiences average around 100 people each time. The kids get better and better with each performance until, by 5:00, we're hot stuff. Two major Seattle television stations air us on the 11:00 PM news, but we're too tired to stay up and watch.

1990–1992:

Nobody's Ever Alone in the Forest won't go away! We all thought we'd retire the script and recycle the costumes into other programs. But people

began calling and writing to the Forest Service requesting performances. Teachers wanted copies of the script and asked if we had a curriculum to accompany the play. The play was published in Living With Mountains, an environmental education curriculum published by the North Cascades Institute, and presented at teacher in-service sessions. Teachers began producing the play with their classes. The Forest Service added an eight-foot-tall, old-tree costume to the props. But many of the groups used their own homemade costumes. By 1992 *Nobody's Ever Alone in the Forest* had been performed over 100 times for thousands of people.

In 1992, The Forest Service funded shooting a video of the play and writing curriculum to accompany the video. By 1993, educators nationwide will be able to purchase or borrow this forest ecology-education package.

Wendy received a grant in 1992 to produce another play, this time about subalpine ecology. "Mmmmmm … let's see … marmots, mountain goats … and a boot, a big talking boot."

Costs for *Nobody's Ever Alone in the Forest*:
Costumes: $1,000—could be made more cheaply
Backdrop: $75—paint and canvas
Stage: $100—lumber and nails
Writing/directing: $500—50 to 60 hours of employee time

Things to Ask Yourself:
If you're creative and have an appetite for hard work, consider writing and directing your own plays. The costs are low—the rewards deep. Here are a few things to consider:
1. Have you scheduled too many performances for one cast? Kids burn-out after a few months.

2. Is there enough space to set-up the play? Are the ceilings high enough for your costumes? Can you hang a backdrop from the wall?

3. Can the play be performed without high-cost costumes?

4. Does your rendition of the play present a scientifically accurate story?

5. How will you distribute the play, script and/or costumes after the initial round of performances?

6. Is the play appropriate for the ages and interests of the target audiences?

7. Can the costumes and props be transported in a single vehicle?

The Impact Monster—
A Skit for Teaching
Wilderness Use Ethics

Mary Beth Hennessy,
Outdoor Recreation Planner
San Isabel National Forest,
Leadville, Colorado

The Impact Monster skit was developed by Jim Bradley of the Eagel Cap district on the Wallowa Whitman National Forest. It has been used by wilderness rangers for years to convey the minimum impact message in an effort to improve peoples' behavior. It has since been adapted to a variety of geographic locations and management issues; as you can see the script lends itself well to versatility. We have found that ages 6 through 12 and families are the best and most appropriate audience; participation is crucial.

Preparation

Ideally, you need three people who know the skit—the narrator, the wilderness visitor, and the Impact Monster. The rest of the characters come right out of the audience. The remainder of the audience participates by the narrator asking the questions (in bold print) throughout the script.

The characters (see the list) all need some type of costume. The costume can be as simple as poster board antlers or horns, blue material for the lake, cardboard branches for the trees,

and bright colored clothing for the Impact Monster. Be creative; the more costumes, the more fun the kids will have.

We do a few activities first, teach some wilderness skills like campsite selection, using stoves for cooking, the pro's and con's of wood fires, map reading etc. This skit acts as the final act and it summarizes many of the things we have taught.

Make sure that at a minimum you get across the concept of "wilderness." We talk about all the different land management agencies—National Park Service, U.S. Forest Service, Bureau of Land Management, Fish and Wildlife Service and explain the difference and similarities of these agencies. Since we are doing this for the U.S. Forest Service, we explain our mission of multiple use—that we're managing the public lands for a variety of activities including recreation, timber, grazing, mining *and* wilderness.

"What do you think a wilderness is?" is a good question. Take the word apart, and talk about what "wild" means. So wilderness is a place that is wild,

- a tree   - some stars
- a deer   - a lake
- a bighorn sheep   - the sun
- an eagle

Note: Arrange the stage, setting the characters in their logical places. You will need to take the following characters aside and explain that they have important roles: snowshoe hare, stars, eagle and flowers. As the narrator recites his or her lines, each character (including the wilderness visitor and the impact monster) should do what comes naturally for the role.

Narrator:

We're going to take a walk. It's a summer day high in the mountains of our state. After driving to our starting point, the wilderness trailhead, our wilderness visitor begins his or her journey. After packing a backpack and then stretching, the visitor takes a good long look at the information posted at the trailhead.

[Ask why a hiker should read the information at the trailhead.]

Narrator:

The visitor begins walking quietly up the trail, looking up and around often. An eagle soaring high in the sky. The visitor watches as the eagle swoops down and just misses a snowshoe hare leaping through the meadow. The visitor starts up a hill with long, steep switchbacks.

[Ask why a person should stay on the switchbacks.]

where plants and animals are protected and allowed to exist according to natural processes. No motorized vehicles or bicycles, or hot dog stands or houses, no mining or grazing or logging. (A good quote would fit in well here.) Once they've gotten a feeling for what wilderness is, you can go into the skit.

The Impact Monster Skit

Narrator:

This skit is about walking and camping in the wilds. It's about a monster named "Impact." Do you know what "Impact" means? It means change or disturbance.

We're going to create a wilderness setting, so I need some volunteers. What kinds of things do you find in the wilderness? Let's see, I need:

- some flowers   - a snowshoe hare
- a trailhead   - a peak

The visitor stops for water at the top of the hill and notices a bighorn sheep feeding on the side of a hill in the distance. He or she takes out the binoculars and watches, content to observe from a distance.

> [Ask why it's best to watch wildlife from a distance—explain that it's important to remember that they're inhabitants and need to go about their daily business undisturbed, and that that's important to their survival as wild animals. It's also safer for the visitor.]

The visitor sees some trash on the ground and picks it up. He or she then sees a pretty flower and stops to admire it—but knows not to pick it because it will die.

The visitor finally arrives at the destination—a beautiful lake—and must decide where to camp.

> [What should the visitor think about when choosing a campsite? It should be a site that has been used before that's away from the trail, away from water, and protected from wind.]

So the visitor sets up the tent, puts on camp shoes, and goes down to fetch water from the lake. After bringing the water back up to the campsite, the visitor washes up—well away from the lake. The visitor sets up a stove to cook food, and at last relaxes in the nice protected campsite.

Then another visitor arrives on the scene. Can you guess who this is?

Yes, here it comes ...

> Impact Monster enters scene, and procedes to do the following:
>
> 1. Shortcuts trail, ignoring switchbacks and stumbling up the hill
>
> 2. Carves initials on a sign. ("I want everyone to know I was here, I.M. The Impact Monster," it proclaims)
>
> 3. Smokes cigarettes, throws butts on ground
>
> 4. Sees a flower, picks it and throws it on the ground
>
> 5. Sees rattlesnake; shoots it
>
> 6. Picks a campsite right by the lake
>
> 7. Washes right in the lake
>
> 8. Builds a big fire to cook dinner, using limbs from a live tree to build it

First Visitor (wakes up and sees the Impact Monster): "Hey what's going on?" Visitor goes down to the lake to talk to the Impact Monster. "Did you make this mess? (Very disturbed):

Oh no, the snake's dead, the flowers have been killed ... "

The Impact Monster: "Me? No, I didn't do this ..."

The visitor chases the impact monster, shakes him or her and then begins to talk about the proper way to camp and behave in the wilderness.

Narrator:

Talking with the Impact Monster, the visitor explained why a person should camp away from the lake, why using branches to build a fire damages the environment, and how being quiet helps you see more wildlife. The Impact Monster now not only knows how to be a good camper, but *wants* to be a good camper. They camp together that night ...

As they sleep through the night, nocturnal animals roam and hunt their food, the stars move across the sky, and the sun finally rises in the morning sky.

Our wilderness visitors eat breakfast, pack up, look around their campsite, and pick up some trash left behind from other campers. They walk back down the trail, arrive at their cars, and prepare to travel home.

[What new ways of thinking is the Impact Monster going to take back from this journey in the wilderness? What will the Impact Monster remember, and what can it apply to life in the city?]

It's good to wrap this up by explaining that people need to be considerate of all the other creatures in the wilderness and behave in ways that are not unlike the ways we behave in our own homes. The metaphor of "home" can be used to advantage—the wilderness is a home to many creatures, and we must take care of it.

The "Bat Show" Comes to Bagaces!

Alan Kaplan, Naturalist
Tilden Nature Area
East Bay Park District, Berkeley, California

In the winter of 1990, I went to the town of Bagaces in northwestern Costa Rica to assist in conservation education at Lomas Barbudal, a nature reserve devoted to protecting a remnant dry tropical forest. The support organization, Friends of Lomas Barbudal, has sponsored conservation education programs at the reserve and nearby town of Bagaces since 1988. Its education director, Magda Campos Barrantes, works with young people in the town and several surrounding communities to spread information about the reserve and conservation.

Lomas Barbudal Biological Reserve, a 6000-acre (2500-hectare) unit of the Costa Rican National System of Protected Areas, is a biological treasure, home to white-face and howler monkeys, coatimundis, anteaters, ocelots, bees, birds, and bats. More than half of Costa Rica's 108 bat species have been found at the reserve, or are likely to occur there.

Bats were a natural topic for environmental education programs in local schools for several reasons. They are misunderstood, and their importance in

tropical forest health is vastly underestimated by nonscientists. They are both familiar and frightening. Also simple materials could be put together easily and used to tell the bats' important story.

Sue Perin, another Friends of Lomas Barbudal volunteer, and I made "bat masks" out of poster board to represent the six feeding methods of bats. These are frugivory (fruit-eating), nectivory (nectar-eating), insectivory (insect-eating), piscivory (fish-eating), carnivory (meat-eating), and sanguinivory (blood-eating). Examples of each group can be found in Costa Rica. For each group we provided a sample food, picture, or model to illustrate the feeding method (respectively, a banana, paper flower, moth photo, fish model, frog photo, and a soda bottle filled with red colored water and a straw).

When school children were reluctant to participate at the beginning of a program, Magda would begin with a game familiar to North Americans as "Red Light, Green Light." The object was to sneak up on Magda while her back was turned, but the students had to move the way various animals do.

Magda would say, "grasshopper," and turn her back to the students. They then hopped toward her like grasshoppers, hoping to reach her before she turned around, or not get caught in motion when she did turn around. She would say, "snake," and they would crawl toward her on their bellies. Her final example was always, "bat," and the children flapped their arms and flew.

Following this activity, we would ask the students to tell us what they knew about bats. Predictably, little of what we heard was in praise of bats. With the bat masks and props, we used student volunteers to demonstrate the variety of bats' diets. Sue, Magda and I also demonstrated that bats' wings are similar to humans' hands. A class member held a triangular piece of black cloth to which we attached masking tape to form the arm, forearm, wrist and hand bones of a typical bat. We compared the demonstration bat wing to the arm of the student volunteer.

Finally, we played a game called "Bat and Moth" in which masked "bats" pursue masked "moths" by shouting, "Bat." The student moths answer "moth," revealing their location to the pursuing bat, just as real bats find their prey with sound.

When electricity was available,

Magda presented a slide show, *Bats: Myths and Realities*, with a Spanish-language narration provided by Bat Conservation International of Austin, Texas.

Before taking part in the "Bat Show," almost all the children we encountered believed that most bats drank blood, spread disease, damaged crops and generally did little or no good for people. The bat masks helped demonstrate the wide variety of foods that bats eat. The game provided a way to experience an important part of a bat's lifestyle. And the bat wing demonstration highlighted something that bats and humans actually have in common. We hope these insights will lead the children to appreciate and respect the bats around Bagaces.

Taking Wildlife to Children— Traveling Education Programs in a Box

Susan Reel, Wildlife Appreciation Specialist
Lolo National Forest, Montana

The children gathered around as the teacher slowly opened the grey plastic trunk. Anticipation was high. On top was a large laundry-sized flannel bag. The teacher reached into the bag and pulled out the huge, furry, brown hide of a grizzly bear. The children's eyes widened and their hands instinctively reached to touch the animal. The bear was so big that if you laid it over the children it would completely cover six of them. There were more surprises to come as the children unveiled the other treasures in the Threatened and Endangered Species Box.

That's what it's like having our traveling wildlife education box in a classroom. Inexpensive as it is to prepare and maintain, this box is proving to one of the most effective aspects of our environmental education program.

Why did we make a traveling box? Aside from the fact that teachers wanted it, it's an excellent way to get museum materials out to teachers across a large, rural state like Montana. For a museum or nature center, it's a cost-effective way to conduct outreach programs. JoAnn Bernofsky, one of the educational designers of the Threatened and Endangered Species Box, put it simply: "I wanted to bring the excitement of the woods into my classroom."

How do you assemble materials for such a box, and how should the use and maintenance of the box be managed? In our project, there were five steps: (1) planning, (2) collection and curriculum development, (3) packaging, (4) distribution and maintenance, and (5) evaluation.

Planning

The first step is to choose the subject matter for the box. Whatever you come up with, make it simple. Don't try to cover all the interesting aspects of an entire ecosystem in a single two by three foot box. Some example topics might include mammals, songbirds, insects, bats or predators of your area. Think about which animals, plants or biological systems you'll be working with and how you might get them into a box. Think about which teaching modes you'll use and which age groups you're trying to reach. As far as funding is concerned, you can make the box

as simple or as elaborate as you want. Most of your costs will be in labor. With some persistence on your part, people will donate a lot of materials. Look for funding and similar contributions from conservation organizations, educational groups and corporations.

Collection and Curriculum Development

Next start developing the materials you'll need. There are two different strategies you can follow depending on the kind of exercises teachers envision for using the box. The first strategy is simply to provide fact sheets on the natural history of the animal and plant materials in the box. A more time-consuming alternative is to work with local educators in developing curriculum activities associated with the topic of the box, and then to collect those materials that best illustrate the concepts you want to get across. The first way is easiest and often popular with those teachers who want to decide for themselves how to incorporate the box's contents into their curricula. However, the second strategy is probably preferred by most teachers. The curriculum activities in the box give teachers with less knowledge of the subject matter more educational opportunities, and quite possibly, improves the likelihood that key concepts will be gotten across—both to teachers and students.

If you decide to provide curriculum activities, you'll probably work on material acquisition and curriculum development simultaneously. It takes more time than you'd think to locate or put together specimen, track casts, puppets or whatever objects you plan to put into the box. When you've decided which species to include, you need to think of ways to illustrate their lives. For example, suppose you want to cover the nesting behavior of Bald Eagles? How will you get across the relationship between parents and nestlings? A video might work. So would puppets of an adult bird and nestlings. You could create a story or activity about the feeding, nesting, and incubation activities of adults and young using the puppets.

When collecting materials and background information, try to search out unusual resource people—anyone who works with children or natural resources. They may be able to provide new insights about how to approach things. Children learn in different ways, and concepts can be illustrated through a variety of media including plays, role playing, dance, puppets, and songs. Another advantage of bringing other people into the planning of the boxes is that they often carry the box's messages back to their own work. For example, a puppeteer we work with was inspired by pine martens and red squirrels and now uses these animal characters routinely in puppet shows.

Be persistent, especially if you want to get wildlife furs or stuffed specimen. If you used real animal parts (e.g., feathers, bones, furs, or even nests), be sure to check beforehand with your local fish and wildlife department. Since in the United States almost every bird and many mammals are protected by law, you'll need federal and state permits to obtain and use their parts.

Our Threatened and Endangered Species Box includes a variety of curriculum activities. Some of them are the following: traditional stories about the animals told by indigenous people; puppets (which often have an ability to get across values better than people do); animal parts; music or dramatic movement exercises; stories about people's encounters with animals told by local people; videos and color slides; tapes of animal sounds and songs about animals; felt story boards; examples of tools that wildlife scientists use in the field; color photocopies of animals or of people working with animals; natural history journal writing activities; children's books, posters, and maps.

To develop curricula, first organize your information needs into topic areas. This is fairly straightforward if you're focusing on specific animals or groups of animals. For example, our Threatened and Endangered Species Box focuses on the general concept of endangered species and specifically on the nine animals that are federally protected in Montana. Next, do some background research on the animals or plants you're featuring. Ask teachers if they use any existing activities that would fit your subject matter, or that could be adapted to fit it. State and federal fish and wildlife agencies and many conservation organizations such as the National Wildlife Federation and National Audubon Society produce booklets, classroom activities, videos, and slide shows about animals. Find out how to acquire copies of these for your box.

Packaging

Decisions about packaging are important because they affect not only the appearance of the box but its portability. As you collect materials and develop ideas for the box's contents, bear in mind that it all has to fit into a box that can be lifted and easily transported. How will your box travel to its destination—by mail, by courier (e.g., UPS or DHL), by bus, or by car? Find out if there are any size and weight restrictions.

Colorful packaging makes a box inviting to use. Teachers and students will enjoy the mystery of unpacking it if it looks like a present or a treasure box. Think lightweight and durable—you want all these wonderful things to last a long time. The life of a box, with care and periodic repairs, is seven to ten years. To soften the blows from frequent travel, put materials into cloth bags and cushion them with layers of foam or bubble-wrap. To make each box simple to repackage, you might even provide a sketch of how things are supposed to fit back into the box.

Distribution

At this stage, you're almost ready to begin sending the box. But there's one more thing to do—design an efficient and secure distribution scheme. Important decisions will be who's going to get the box, how soon in advance should they get, and how long should they be allowed to keep it. How will teachers contact you about reserving the box? It's a very good idea to set up a log to keep track of the box's whereabouts. Decide how long each school or group can use it, and how long it will need to be in transit. Remember to check for broken or missing items between each trip and the next. It's also a good idea to keep replacement parts in hands. Before a school gets our Threatened and Endangered Species Box, the teacher making the request is sent a summary of what's in it and the lock combination. The teacher must then send us a small fee and a signed contract saying that h or she will be responsible for the box and its contents.

Evaluation

Evaluating the box's success is critical to improvement. You'll need to know if the directions are easy to follow, if the background information was helpful, and which activities are most popular with teachers and students. If you hope to produce more boxes, a detailed evaluation will be invaluable. You can simply send a detailed questionnaire for the teacher each time the box is sent. In the presigned contract, make filling out the post-use questionnaire a requirement. If demand is a measure of success, our Threatened and Endangered Species box is phenomenally successful—it's booked up over a year in advance!

The Environmental Express— Trinidad and Tobago's Mobile Interpretation Center

Richard Meganck, Senior Tropical
Forestry Scientist
U.S. Environmental Protection
Agency Research Lab,
Corvallis, Oregon

During the implementation of this project, Dr. Meganck was Project Chief in Trinidad and Tobago (1981–1983) and Assistant Division Chief for the Caribbean (1983–1989) in the Department of Regional Development, Organization of American States.

Trinidad and Tobago's protected areas started through private efforts in the early 1900s and continued through the National Parks Unit established in the mid 1970s. By the early 1980s demand so far exceeded supply that the Parks Division increased the interpretive staff to six persons and began developing a comprehensive environmental education program in cooperation with the Ministry of Education. This effort involved a substantial commitment to staff development, including participation in regional and international training courses for key staff. A core of professional interpreters was a recognized necessity.

An integrated environmental awareness program including specialized curricula, permanent facilities in protected areas, and a network of environmental organizations was planned.

As a part of this project, the Conservator of Forests made a creative and farsighted decision to purchase a passenger bus for the purpose of converting it to a mobile environmental education/interpretation unit for use throughout the country.

The project was implemented in three phases, including:

Phase I (three months):
• The establishment of an interagency Program Advisory Committee to oversee the project
• The establishment of overall educational/interpretive objectives with public school curricula linkages
• The design and implementation of changes to the interior of the bus including a power (1800-watt diesel) generator, electrical outlets, exhibit spaces, small theater/lecture space, and storage space

Phase II (four months):
• The definition of specific instructional activities and support materials and teaching aids
• The design and implementation of

alterations to the exterior of the bus including entry way, awnings (for greater protection against weather), and painting of a rainforest background

• The design of the macaw parrot logo for the bus and other promotional materials, including T-shirts, posters, buttons, pencils, etc.; also, the name "The Environmental Express" was chosen and lettered on the bus

• The development of preventative maintenance procedures for the bus and instructional aids as well as a pre-trip checklist for the driver, interpreters, students, teachers, and parents

Phase III (two months):

• The development of training workshops in teaching interpretive methods to staff involved in expanding the role of interpretation nationally and the assistance to the Forestry Division in identifying funding sources

The Results

Once the Forestry Division acquired the bus and OAS technical assistance was programmed, a total of nine intensive months of work over a two-year period was required to get the program "up and running" as described above. However, even today, training and "tweaking the system" to improve the quality of the programs offered continues. It's an ongoing program.

Reading this case study might give the impression that this process went ahead, on schedule, without serious hurdles. Not true. The interior of the bus, for example, was redesigned three times, the "discussion" over the logotype and the image presented by

the bus was hotly debated for many weeks, and the inter-ministerial debate over program focus consumed many bureaucratic hours. The ups and downs of this process, while frustrating to those actively involved and anxious to "get on with the show" could have been predicted. There was no state-of-the-art example on which to model this idea. On occasion the rationale supporting a given suggestion was, frankly, based on the "best guess method."

The most obvious advantage the program had was a dedicated staff. Their willingness to adapt the design of the bus and the programs to better serve the users ensured the ultimate success of "The Environmental Express" as an interpretive and educational method. The insights gained in this process have been a function of many factors including entry level understanding of the users; the amount of time typically available for a visit, the amount of money available for the development and continued operation of the bus, and the increasing knowledge base of the staff.

Approximately US$100,000 in technical assistance (design and training), and materials and program development was expended in bringing this program to the point where it is today (exclusive of the original cost of the bus). Has it been worth this investment in time and money? Can the Trinidad and Tobago experience serve as a model for other nations? Only careful examination of the process, the resultant program and its success can answer these questions. If nothing else,

this experiment served as a highly visible means to catalyze students' (and other citizens') attention to the government's attempts to protect and manage a portion of their natural resource base for future generations. This was accomplished by building anticipation of the impending visit of "The Environmental Express," excitement through participation and finally reflection on the experience which hopefully affects behavior for the long term.

To date, the bus has made hundreds of visits throughout the country, including ferrying it to the sister isle of Tobago! Officials from other Caribbean nations have requested information on the bus and several have even experienced it firsthand. Every schoolaged child in the entire country recognized the bus and its macaw parrot symbol as something positive for their future. Using those criteria, there can be little doubt in justifying this investment.

Author's Note: But what if that kind of investment is not available? What made "The Environmental Express" effective was the creativity and mobility of the interpretive programs which allowed them to reach all areas of the country. As we hope you understand from this book, it doesn't take a lot of money to produce good interpretive materials and programs. The innovation of this project is that the interpreters found a way to reach out to rural schools and communities and developed a nationally recognized symbol—the macaw and "The Environmental Express." Any vehicle can be used to do this—even if the inside is not converted as a visitor center. The most important points are that the vehicle is recognized as part of the program so people can identify it and look forward to its visit, and that it carries interpretive materials for the education and enjoyment of other people. Even an old pick-up truck could become an "Environmental Express."

The Pied Bare-Faced Tamarin Conservation Education Campaign: How We Did It, and Cheaper

Leonardo Lacerda, Project Coordinator
Fundacao Vitoria Amazonica, Brazil

The pied bare-faced tamarin (Saguinus bicolor) has the smallest geographic range among all the Amazon primates. The species is endemic to the municipalities of Manaus and Itacoatiara—an area that has been suffering from intense human impact for the last thirty years, decimating habitat, and leading the species on the road to extinction. The pied bare-faced tamarin has now been included in both Brazil's Official List of Endangered Species and IUCN's Red Book.

The example of the pied bare-faced tamarin represents a powerful argument to destroy the myth that we can continue devastating the Amazonian forests without incurring heavy costs. The example also offers the opportunity to introduce basic concepts of ecology and conservation; to demonstrate to the general public that the forest is not merely a uniform green mass, as it is frequently seen; and, lastly, to reveal the importance of conserving the Amazon's biological diversity.

Conceiving and finding support for our Pied Bare-Faced Tamarin Conservation Education Campaign has

been somewhat like going fishing in the Amazon River. First, we put together our fishing tackle; second, we chose an appropriate bait to catch small fish; third, we are currently using the small fish we caught as bait to catch bigger ones; and, last, we hope we can cook our caldeirada (a traditional Brazilian recipe for cooking Amazon fish). Since this fishing trip metaphor can fit almost any conservation fund-raising effort, I offer it in this case study not only as a way to describe what we have been doing at my foundation, but to suggest how you could approach fund raising for your organization or agency.

Organizing Our Fishing Tackle

Before going out fishing we should already know what type and size of fish we intend to catch (let's call this ideal fish our objective). This gives a dimension to the quality and quantity of the materials needed while organizing our fishing tackle. For instance, the size of the hooks will depend on the size of the fish we want to catch. An appropriate hook for a jaraqui is just too small for a tambaqui. We should also learn from other experienced fishermen what is needed to catch the fish we want. This saves us time and money. Once we know exactly what we want, we are ready to put together our fishing tackle and begin our fishing trip.

Likewise, in organizing the Pied Bare-Faced Tamarin Conservation Education Campaign, we first identified our conservation problem, chose our target groups, spelled out our objectives and selected, within our budget constraints, the most appropriate methodology to reach our objectives. We tried to learn from similar experiences, especially the golden lion tamarin and the woolly spider-monkey projects that had preceded us. We inventoried all the bibliography and materials already produced about the pied bare-faced tamarin. By doing that, we were able to list and eventually to actually meet major contacts we would need: primatologists, key institutions, illustrators, photographers, etc. A good inventory helped us to maximize our use of resources both by avoiding duplication of efforts and by saving money. It also helped us design our project, based on what we already had or could easily obtain.

Two examples in this project are the traveling exhibit and the conservation education program for elementary school children. We only decided to include in our traveling exhibit a display with the sounds of tamarin vocalizations because all the recording had already been done. The University of Campinas donated the recordings, and the design work for the exhibit was donated by one of our board members who is an architect. The collection and production of educational materials for our school programs could also have been expensive but, again, we accepted the assistance of volunteers through which we paid minimum costs for reproduction and received donated photographs.

With these elements we wrote a convincing proposal. And, having wrapped up the proposal, we were ready to go out "fishing" for funds and help.

Choosing the Bait and Catching the Small Fish

Like fish, potential donors will only be attracted to your idea if you offer them a good "bait." We usually try to produce some exemplary interpretive material to serve as "bait." At an initial stage, we felt it would be easier to get help from people like us, individuals and other non-governmental organizations (NGOs) really committed to doing something for the environment. Reaching out to private enterprises at this stage would have been counter-productive. During our inventory phase, we had known about an excellent illustrator who had painted a beautiful illustration of the *S. bicolor* for a Dutch publication called World Primates Series. We also knew that an American artist had already designed various posters for primate conservation campaigns worldwide. We contacted both and they produced a strikingly beautiful poster. Conservation International (a U.S.-based NGO) decided to print ten thousand of these posters. And they have served us as excellent "baits."

With the posters in our hands, we were able to show to people a sample of the quality of our campaign. The poster made our contact with a local advertising company much easier, and soon its staff became really interested in the idea and helped us to conceive most layouts for our mass media campaign materials. They also became involved in fund raising activities when they perceived that the campaign would be a good chance for reaching out to new clients with a great project.

Catching the Big Fish

Once we had caught the "small fish," we were ready for the big ones. With basically all the campaign layouts in our hands and a nice info-pack, we were prepared to search for donors who would pay the heaviest costs of such a campaign: producing the materials and broadcasting. Time was ripe to contact private entrepreneurs and foreign NGOs. Our strategy was threefold:

1. Obtain most broadcasting as free service. We are now at this stage. We have found that people have generally been very receptive.

2. Get a foreign NGO to donate "seed money" to us. We are currently in negotiations, with the intention to use the money to produce a few of each campaign material.

3. Reach out to private business to ask for additional contributions to match our fund raising goals. We will be targeting private sector funds particularly for our marketing projects.

Eating the *Caldeirada*

The caldeirada is a traditional Amazon fish recipe—the final destiny of most fish caught in the region. For us, the successful implementation of the Pied Bare-Faced Tamarin Conservation Education Campaign will be our caldeirada!

Happy fishing, my friends, and good luck in your important work.

Reaching Out with Environmental Education: Two Innovations from Trinidad and Tobago

Neemedass Chandool, National Parks Specialist
Division of Forestry, Trinidad and Tobago

Mr. Chandool is currently on educational leave from his job studying interpretation and park management at the University of Idaho. His ten years of experience include two summers as an interpreter at Mount St. Helens National Volcanic Monument in the United States.

The Republic of Trinidad and Tobago is concerned about its natural resources and declining environmental quality. My government's Forestry Division (which includes a National Parks Section responsible for interpretation and environmental education programs) began in the late 1980s to attack these problems at the root through nationwide communication and education initiatives. Knowing that today's children represent tomorrow's resource users and environmental caretakers, we have been aggressively targeting schools and youth groups with environmental education. The first half of this case study reports on one of our most successful programs, an annual speaking competition on environmental topics.

The second half of this case study describes a special fire prevention campaign aimed at all age groups, "Walk-a-Thon." In terms of forest and bush fires, 1987 was considered disastrous for Trinidad and Tobago. A record high of over three thousand fires consumed 21,230 hectares of vegetative cover. Investigations indicated that humans were the main cause of these fires. The main culprits were farmers practicing "slash and burn" agriculture who disregarded adjacent forested lands and cigarette smokers who uncaringly flick their butts out car windows. These behaviors coupled with an intense dry season were responsible for the disaster of 1987. This was just cause for the Forestry Division to take action to avoid a repeat occurrence in future years.

Public Speaking Competition

In 1988, we started a public speaking competition aimed at educating teenagers about the importance of the environment and the need to prevent further degradation. All secondary schools were invited to participate in the contest; and those interested were invited to attend a briefing session at which information packages about

environmental topics were given to each school and rules of the contest were explained and discussed. Judges chosen for the competition were also given the same information package and briefed of the contest rules.

Each school was allowed two speakers, each speaking for a maximum of ten minutes. The six best speakers were chosen for the final round of the competition. All schools that took part in the contest were invited to the finals, even if they didn't have a contestant chosen to compete. The final competition was centrally and conveniently located for maximum attendance and promotion. People from different sectors of society were invited in advance, including the Prime Minister, Permanent Secretaries of Parliament, and other government dignitaries. Added to this list were businessmen,

environmentalists, and media personalities from the private sector. We found it important to invite such a wide cross section to help increase public awareness.

We accomplished this program with a minimum of human and financial resources. There is no need for a large staff if you have a few committed to the cause. We all had to work late hours, but the job was completed efficiently and on time. We also solicited the volunteer assistance of professionals to help us keep costs low. The artist at the Forestry Division's Head Office offered to make plaques and trophies out of wood. No cash prizes were given initially, but donations from the business sector allowed us to provide refreshments and make logistical arrangements for the competition. And as support grew, generous donations from companies later made it possible to give book vouchers as additional prizes for the students.

The public speaking competition started in 1988 with fifteen schools participating, and has grown to more than twenty participating schools in 1990. Not only has there been an increase in the number of schools, but also in the level of interest exhibited by the students, teachers, and parents. When we first started the program, we had little media coverage of the event, but now we are getting more attention from the radio, television, and newspapers. We have also seen an increase in the effort made by parents to take time off from their jobs to listen to the younger generation's call for environmental protection. In this way, our environmental message is reaching beyond the classroom

and into the students' homes. The business sector has also done its part and continues to show its support and contribution toward the success of the program.

Walk-a-Thon

In 1989 we extended our environmental program with a noncompetitive walking event (called "Walk-a-Thon") which we hoped would be attractive and informative to an even larger audience than the public speaking competition. Our slogan in 1989 was "A Journey Back to Nature" through which we solicited and combined the efforts of government agencies, nongovernment organizations, service groups, and individuals of the private sector toward a common goal of environmental protection. Through this combined effort, we were successful in bringing together a large group of participants to further spread national awareness about the environment.

The organization of this event was largely coordinated by a five-member committee from the Forestry Division. The eight-mile walk started with over 1000 people from the Water Authority's main office (to make the connection of forests and water supply), and ended in the Clever Woods Recreational Area with a crowd of over 3500 for the closing rally. The walkers were led by a vehicle with a PA system and promotional banner. Other promotional accessories included 500 green hats printed with the slogan, "A Journey Back to Nature," and people were encouraged to bring in T-Shirts to have the slogan "Prevent Forest Fires, Keep T and T Green Out of the Fire Scene" printed on them.

Again, we worked from a zero budget and raised the funds needed through the private sector and through volunteered services. Assistance and participation continues to grow each year, and the event is becoming more successful. In 1990 the event also included a live broadcast of an environmental question-and-answer radio program at the rally, and participants were given T-shirts. Every year, anticipation builds all over the country for the next year's Walk-a-Thon!

Between 1988 and 1990, there was a marked decrease in forest fires—more than 50 percent. This reduction may not be a direct result of our program, but I feel we are successful in educating the children and their families about environmental protection and in helping to bring a halt to degradation and deforestation. In other words, our message is gradually spreading throughout the nation, giving our citizens better information with which to do their part.

References

Bajimaya, Shyam and James R. Fazio. 1989. *Communications Manual: A Guide to Aid Park and Protected Area Managers to Communicate Effectively with Local Residents*. Kathmandu, Nepal: Department of National Parks and Wildlife Conservation/ FAO-UNDP.

Bunch, Roland. 1982. *Two Ears of Corn: A Guide to People-Centered Agricultural Improvement*. Oklahoma City, USA: World Neighbors.

Dispenza, Bob. 1989. Community Celebration: Maple Sugarbush Weekend. *Journal of Interpretation* 13(6):4.

Ford, Phyllis M. 1981. *Principles and Practices of Outdoor/Environmental Education*. New York, New York: John Wiley and Sons.

Gebler, Charles J. 1982. Off-Season, Off-Site Interpretation. Chapter 17 in Sharpe, G.W.(ed.), *Interpreting the Environment*. New York, New York, USA: John Wiley & Sons.

Ham, Sam H. 1992. Barriers to Environmental Education in Elementary Schools—Implications for Libraries. *Green Library Journal* 1(2):41-44.

Ham, Sam H. and Lizeth Castillo. 1990. Problemas Potenciales en la Introducción de Modelos de Educación Ambiental Estadounidenses—Estudio del Caso de las Escuelas Rurales de Honduras. *Biocenosis* 7(1):33-39.

Ham, Sam H. and Daphne S. Sewing. 1988. Barriers to Environmental Education. *Journal of Environmental Education* 19(2):17-24.

Ham, Sam H. and David S. Sutherland. 1992. Crossing Borders: Toward a Model of Interpretation in Developing Countries. In, Machlis, G. and D. Field (eds.). *On Interpretation—Sociology for Interpreters of Natural and Cultural History*. Corvallis, Oregon, USA: Oregon State University Press.

Ham, Sam H. and David S. Sutherland. 1991. Environmental Education and

Extension on Fragile Lands. Chapter 11 in Young, P. (ed.). *Management of Fragile Lands in Latin America and the Caribbean: A Synthesis*. Bethesda, Maryland, USA: Development Alternatives, Inc.

MacKinnon, John, Kathy MacKinnon, Graham Child and James Thorsell (eds.). 1986. *Managing Protected Areas in the Tropics* (Chapter 7). Cambridge, United Kingdom: International Union for the Conservation of Nature & Natural Resources and the United Nations Environment Program.

Moore, Alan, Bill Wendt, Louis Penna e Isabel Castillo de Ramos. 1989. *Manual para La Capacitación del Personal de Areas Protegidas* (Modulo C: Interpretación y Educación Ambiental, Apunte 4a). Washington, D.C., USA: Servicio de Parques Nacionales, Oficina de Asuntos Internacionales.

Morales, Jorge. 1987. *Manual para la Interpretación en Espacios Naturales Protegidos*. Anexo 3 del Taller Internacional sobre Interpretación Ambiental en Areas Silvestres Protegidas. Santiago, Chile: Oficina Regional de la FAO para América Latina y el Caribe, 7-12 de diciembre de 1988.

Muñoz, Milton G. y Bernardo Peña. 1990. *Selección y Utilización de Ayudas Educativas*. Tegucigalpa, D.C., Honduras: Secretaria de Recursos Naturales, Departamento de Comunicación Agropecuaria, Proyecto de Comunicación para la Transferencia de Tecnología Agropecuaria.

Regnier, Kathleen, Michael Gross and Ron Zimmerman. 1992. *The Interpreter's Guidebook: Techniques for Programs and Presentations*. Stevens Point, Wisconsin, USA: UW-SP Foundation Press, Inc.

Sutherland, David S. and Sam H. Ham. 1992. Child-to-Parent Transfer of Environmental Ideology in Costa Rican Families: An Ethnographic Case Study. *Journal of Environmental Education* 23(3):9-16.

Wallin, Harold E. 1982. Urban Interpretation. Chapter 18 in Sharpe, G.W.(ed.), *Interpreting the Environment*. New York, New York, USA: John Wiley & Sons.

Werner, David. 1980. *Donde No Hay Doctor*. Palo Alto, California, USA: Hesperian Foundation.

Werner, David and Bill Bower. 1982. *Helping Health Workers Learn*. Palo Alto, California, USA: Hesperian Foundation.

Wood, David S. and Diane Walton Wood. 1990. *Como Planificar un Programa de Educación Ambiental*. Washington, D.C., USA: World Resources Institute/U.S. Fish and Wildlife Service, Office of International Affairs.

Wood, David S. and Diane Walton Wood. 1990. *How to Plan a Conservation Education Program*. Washington, D.C., USA: World Resources Institute/U.S. Fish and Wildlife Service, Office of International Affairs.

Additional Reading

In English:

Cherif, Abour H. 1992. Barriers to Ecology Education in North American High Schools: Another Alternative Perspective. *Journal of Environmental Education* 23(3):36-46.

Cornell, Joseph. 1989. *Sharing the Joy of Nature*. Nevada City, California, USA: Dawn Publications.

Cornell, Joseph. 1979. *Sharing Nature with Children*. Nevada City, California, USA: Ananda Publications.

Ham, Sam H. and Lizeth Castillo. 1990. Elementary Schools in Rural Honduras: Problems in Exporting Environmental Education Models from the United States. *Journal of Environmental Education* 21(4):27-32.

Ham, Sam H., Mary Rellergert-Taylor and Edwin E. Krumpe. 1988. Reducing Barriers to Environmental Education. *Journal of Environmental Education* 19(2):25-33.

McNeely, Jeffrey A., Kenton R. Miller, Walter V. Reid, Russell A. Mittermeier, and Timothy B. Werner. 1990. *Conserving the World's Biological Diversity*. Gland, Switzerland: International Union for the Conservation of Nature and Natural Resources, Washington, D.C., USA: World Resources Institute, Conservation International, World Wildlife Fund-US, and the World Bank.

Samples, Bob. 1976. *The Metaphoric Mind— A Celebration of Creative Conciousness*. Reading, Massachusetts, USA: Addison-Wesley Publishing.

Van Matre, Steve. 1974. *Acclimatizing—A Personal and Reflective Approach to Natural Relationship*. Martinsville, Indiana, USA: American Camping Association.

Van Matre, Steve. 1972. *Acclimatization—A Sensory and Conceptual Approach to Ecological Involvement*. Martinsville, Indiana, USA: American Camping Association.

In Spanish:

Beltrán, Nohora y Bernardo Peña. 1988. *La Dramatización como Técnica de Comunicación para la Transferencia*. Bogotá, Colombia: Instituto Colombiano Agropecuario, Boletín Técnico 170.

FAO. 1985. *El Vivero Comunal*. Cuaderno Forestal 1, Junio de 1985. Roma, Italia: Naciones Unidas, Organización para la Alimentación y Agricultura (FAO).

García, José Manuel. 1989. Serie: Educación Ambiental. Colinas, Santa Bárbara, Honduras: Grupo Ecológico ABC ("Amigos del Bosque y del Campo").

Ham, Sam H. 1992. *Interpretación Ambiental: Una Guía Práctica para Gente con Grandes Ideas y Presupuestos Pequeños*. Golden, Colorado, USA: North American Press/Fulcrum Publishing.

Ham, Sam H. 1990. Reflexiones sobre la Educación Ambiental en Centroamérica y Algunas Sugerencias acerca de Su Desarrollo. *Biocenosis* 7(1):33-39.

MacKinnon, John, Kathy MacKinnon, Graham Child y James Thorsell (eds.). 1990. *Manejo de Areas Protegidas en los Trópicos* (Capítulo 7). Cancún, Quintana Roo, México: Amigos de Sian Ka'an A.C.

Part Three
Self-Guided Media

CHAPTER EIGHT

HOW TO PLAN AND PREPARE INEXPENSIVE EXHIBITS

In this chapter we'll consider one of the most common communication media—**exhibits**. Although the terms **exhibits** and **signs** are often used to mean different things, we'll use the word "exhibit" to include both. That's because the principles of designing effective exhibits and signs are usually the same, even though their physical appearances may differ. For example, although signs are usually placed outdoors and mounted vertically, exhibits may also be placed outdoors and mounted vertically. According to the U.S. National Park Service (1989), the difference is whether the design includes graphics along with the text. If it does, it's an exhibit; if it doesn't it's a sign. For our purposes, however, it usually won't be necessary to make this distinction. We'll treat exhibits and signs as being the same unless there's a need to distinguish between them. Appendix B includes examples of several different kinds of indoor and outdoor exhibits.

Many general references on interpretive exhibits are available in English and Spanish, and our purpose here will not be to duplicate them. Without question, the most comprehensive and best illustrated manual on outdoor signs is Trapp et al. (1991). Other good English-language sources are Brace et al. (1982), Neal (1976), Neal (1969), Sharpe (1982), McIntosh (1982) and Witteborg (1981). Two good Spanish-language sources are Moore et al. (1989), and Morales (1987). Most of these references contain useful discussions of the advantages and disadvantages of various kinds of exhibits. In addition, the books by Neal, Trapp et al., Brace et al., and Witteborg contain specific instructions for designing and constructing small exhibits. Useful Spanish-language sources on design include Muñoz and Fonseca (1990), Muñoz and Peña (1990), Pino (1989), Sánchez (1990), Gillman (1974), and Bay (1968). English-language readers who have a little more money to spend on their exhibits will find Trapp et al. (1991) especially valuable.

Do Effective Exhibits Require a Lot of Money?

Exhibits can be expensive, but they don't have to be. Yes, money is an important resource; it almost always leads to more attractive and more durable exhibits because better materials can be used and professional artists can be hired. Unfortunately, however, not all of us have the money to spend on expensive exhibits. But this doesn't mean we can't use exhibits to communicate our messages. On the contrary, some of the best exhibits are simple and inexpensive. Even though expensive exhibits are usually more attractive and more durable, they don't necessarily communicate better.

Communication is more a matter of conceptual design than it is artistic design, although both are certainly important. Indeed, some of the world's finest museums and interpretive centers contain expensive and very attractive exhibits that don't communicate very well. Studies (e.g., Schleyer 1987, Shiner and Shafer 1985) show that only a tiny fraction of viewers (often less than one percent) will read the entire text of even the most expensive exhibits, and of those who do, most are already knowledgeable in the topic being presented. Overall, viewers spend only about one-third of the time that's actually necessary to read a given exhibit. According to Neal (1976), the *maximum average attention span* is just 45 seconds, indicating that many exhibits

receive less than a momentary glance. Not surprisingly, Schleyer reported that "virtually no one grasped the entire message" from any of the exhibits evaluated in nine respected and well-funded museums and interpretive centers in the United States. The vast majority of viewers, he said, could remember "only a few facts and images."

A further point, and one that natural resource communicators everywhere should heed, is that no study has ever found a relationship between the amount of money spent on an exhibit and its communication effectiveness. As mentioned above, an exhibit's ability to communicate is probably more a result of conceptual design than anything else. Exhibits that are designed first to communicate a theme, and then to look attractive, will be more effective than those that are designed solely to look good. As we'll see in this chapter, any exhibit can have both qualities, even when financial resources are lacking.

Types of Exhibits

There are many kinds of exhibits. As Figure 8-1 shows, they can be indoors or outdoors, temporary or long-term; they can be used to educate viewers, inform them about important issues, or orient them to an area; they can quickly identify an object or site of interest, or they can raise awareness of important rules and regulations. But regardless of the kind of exhibit you're designing, you'll find that it will be more effective if you follow an interpretive approach as outlined in Chapter 1. That is, the best exhibits are those that are enjoyable, relevant, organized and thematic. We'll be applying these principles as we consider how to design inexpensive exhibits. Especially important in our approach will be thematic communication. Since the purpose of any exhibit (even regulatory signs and bulletin boards) is to present a theme, we should start with a theme and continue thinking thematically as we make decisions about organization and artistic design. For this reason, if you're not yet familiar with themes and thematic communication you should review Chapter 2 before continuing with this chapter.

Qualities of a Good Exhibit

A good exhibit is one that communicates its theme to every viewer. To do this, it must capture a person's attention long enough for the theme to be recognized and understood. Because most viewers won't spend a lot of time reading, the best exhibits communicate their themes quickly. Research shows that the best way to do this is to practice what Fazio and Gilbert (1986) called the "A,B,Cs" of exhibit design:

A = Attractive: Attractive exhibits are artistically pleasant and balanced, relying on interesting objects, visuals and appropriate colors; they call attention to themselves;

B = Brief: Brief exhibits are well organized and simple; they contain five or fewer main ideas and only enough text to develop the theme; rather than having a lot of words, they show details visually; they don't appear like they require a lot of work from the viewer;

C = Clear: Clear exhibits contain a theme that is so conspicuous it can be recognized and understood in only a second or two.

Following these simple guidelines doesn't have to be expensive. In fact, research (and common sense) shows that when expensive exhibits fail to communicate their themes, it's usually because the designers worried more about the "A" than they did about the "B" and "C." On the other hand, when even the least expensive exhibits succeed, it's usually because the designers concerned themselves with all three guidelines.

We'll be taking all the "A,B,Cs" into account as we discuss the two main phases of exhibit design: the conceptual design of the message and the artistic design of the exhibit, itself. A common mistake is to think first about the artistic considerations. This is a normal tendency because, for many interpreters, the artistic design is more fun. But as we'll see, this often leads to nice-looking exhibits that don't communicate very well. For this reason, we'll consider the conceptual design first. As always, our approach will be based on thematic communication.

Conceptual Designs Begin with Theme Titles and Levels

The first step in exhibit planning is the conceptual design of the message. Recall that in Chapter 2 we compared thematic oral presentations (such as a talk or tour) with thematic written presentations (such as an exhibit or sign). We found an important difference: in a talk, the communicator decides the sequence of the presentation; but in an exhibit, the audience determines it. Exhibit viewers, themselves, decide if and when to pay attention to different parts of the exhibit, regardless of what the designer has planned or hoped. We called talks linear because they proceed in a preplanned

There Are Many Kinds of Exhibits and Signs

Type of Exhibit or Sign	Typical Settings	Typical Primary Purposes
• Indoor exhibits (or displays) placed in cabinets, on tables or walls, or free-standing; they may be two-dimensional ("flatwork displays") or three-dimensional (dioramas and models)	Visitor centers, interpretive centers, museums, office buildings, headquarters buildings	To educate an audience by communicating a theme about a topic of interest; to orient visitors to an area, or focus their attention on particular features
• Outdoor exhibits (or "wayside" exhibits) including interpretive signs and displays mounted in weather-resistant structures; like indoor exhibits, they may be two- or three-dimensional	Roadsides, trailsides, viewpoints, in campgrounds, picnic areas, near parking lots, in front of prominent features, outside visitor centers, at entrances to an area, at stops on a self-guided trail	To educate an audience by communicating a theme about a topic of interest; to orient visitors to an area or to focus their attention on particular features
• Temporary (or portable) exhibits that will be displayed for short periods of time and then taken down or moved to a different location; they may be indoor or outdoor exhibits	Anywhere an audience is expected (both indoors and outdoors), including special events such as fairs, celebrations and school and community programs	To educate an audience by communicating a theme about a topic of interest; to orient people to an area, or to focus their attention on particular features
• Bulletin boards (and information kiosks)	Trailheads, beaches, campgrounds,picnic areas, inside or outside of buildings, near parking lots and in other areas where visitors may need or expect information	To orient visitors to an area; to provide information about safety, opportunities for enjoyment, important rules, temporary conditions such as road closures, hazards, and weather; parts or all of some bulletin boards may be thematic, essentially making them outdoor or indoor exhibits

• Markers and labels	At or in front of prominent features such as viewpoints, historic structures, geologic features, individual plants, rocks, rivers, mountains, cultural sites, and at other places of interest	To identify the feature or object, often giving a quick fact or two (e.g., size, age, distance, elevation, depth, etc.) depending upon the object or scene being identified
• Regulatory signs	At entrances, boundary crossings and at places where violation of important rules, regulations, or laws is common	To inform people about a rule, regulation or law that is frequently violated or commonly misunderstood and to explain the reason for the rule and/or the benefits of obeying it.

Figure 8-1. Six kinds of exhibits and signs. (See Appendix B for models of different exhibits.)

sequence (determined by the speaker) from a definite beginning to a definite ending. Exhibits are **nonlinear** because they don't have a definite ending. If the title or main heading is conspicuous, most viewers will probably start by reading it, but they may then continue in any order they wish—looking and reading anywhere they like, and ending at any place they like.

The drawing in Figure 8-2 shows an example of this. Two people are standing side-by-side, viewing the same exhibit. Although both start with the title, they then pay attention to different parts of the exhibit and in an order that suits each of them at that particular moment. Furthermore, they spend very different amounts of time viewing the exhibit. In this case, one person spends 30 seconds and the other only 3 seconds. Which person in Figure 8-2 do you think is most likely to recognize and understand the theme? The answer is that if the exhibit is intelligently designed, *both* of them should understand the theme. That is, a well designed exhibit should communicate its theme to all viewers, regardless of the amount of time they spend reading or looking at it. Probably the most common failure of exhibits is that they're designed as though they were linear—in such a way that the theme will be understood only if the viewer reads to the "end" in a sequence determined by the designer. This is a mistake because it assumes that everyone is going to read all of the exhibit, and in the same order. But they won't, will they? And knowing this leads us to two simple but important ideas in exhibit design: **theme titles** and **levels**.

Theme Titles

Since different people spend different amounts of time viewing an exhibit,

Figure 8-2. The exhibit designer's reality. Since only a fraction of viewers will read an entire text, exhibits must communicate their themes quickly. (Drawings by Jeff Egan)

how can you make sure they'll all understand the theme? As we saw in Chapter 2, the key is to communicate the theme at the one place most people will look first—the title. Even though especially interesting objects or illustrations may initially attract a viewer's attention, a conspicuous title is usually read almost immediately. In most cases, stating or paraphrasing the theme in the title ensures that every viewer—regardless of how much time is spent viewing the rest of your exhibit—will recognize and understand the theme. Furthermore, their understanding of the theme won't depend on the order in which they read the text, nor where they happen to finish. Obviously, those few people who spend more time viewing and reading will receive a fuller and more detailed explanation of your exhibit's main message than those who read less. But if you've selected the theme because it's an important message, then the most desirable outcome is that everyone recognize and understand it, whether or not they can explain it in detail. Building theme awareness directly into the title accomplishes this.

We'll use the term **theme title** to describe a title that makes reference to the theme of an exhibit. Generally, theme titles are preferred to titles that only describe the topic because: (1) they quickly communicate the theme of the exhibit, and (2) they're often more interesting than mere topic-titles. For example, which titles in Figure 8-3 do you think are more interesting, the ones on the left that tell only topics, or the ones on the right that give themes? Practice using theme titles in your exhibits. Besides capturing attention, they'll ensure that all viewers understand your main idea, even if they read nothing else.

An Exhibit Design Has Four Levels

Exhibits have just one purpose: to communicate a theme to the reader or viewer. As we've repeatedly stressed, this theme is the principal message you want to get across. It's the answer to the question, "So what?" For example, if we asked someone who had just read an exhibit to tell us what they learned from it, the answer we got should sound a lot like our theme. If it doesn't, we aren't doing a very good job of getting the message across. As we've already seen, putting themes right into titles makes a lot of sense because many viewers won't read beyond the title. But what's the rest of the exhibit supposed to do?

Building Themes into Titles Makes Them More Interesting

Most people read the title of a written presentation before they read anything else. In fact, many people read only the title. Therefore, the key to practicing thematic communication in a written presentation (such as an exhibit, sign, or brochure) is to build the theme into the title. Following are two lists of hypothetical exhibit titles. The first one presents titles that communicate only the topic or subject matter of the exhibit. The second list gives similar titles, but this time, with a theme built in. Notice how much clearer and more interesting the titles in the second list are. You can see that even if you read no more than just the title, you'd still know the main idea from the titles on the right. Can you say the same about the titles on the left?

Topic Titles	Theme Titles
Agriculture	Our Lives Depend on Agriculture
The Changing Forest	This Forest Is Changing
Benefits of Trees	Trees Breathe for You
The Ancient Forest	Old Forests Produce New Life
How Volcanoes Work	Volcanoes Erupt with Rock and Gas
A Landscape Covered by Lava	Lava Once Covered This Landscape
Birds of the Park	You Are Surrounded by 100,000 Beating Bird Hearts
The Danger of Pesticides	Pesticides Are Dangerous
The Great Danger of Pesticides	Pesticides Kill
The Sea	The Sea—Complex, Yet Fragile
Burning Your Field	Burning Your Field Is Unnecessary
Soil Erosion	We Are Losing Our Soil
Preventing Soil Erosion	You Can Save Your Soil
Medicinal Plants	This Forest Is Your Pharmacy
Water Contamination	We Are Polluting the Water That Dinosaurs Drank
Theme Titles vs. Topic Titles	Theme Titles Are More Interesting Than Topic Titles

Figure 8-3. A comparison of topic titles and theme titles. Note that although themes are expressed in complete sentences, some theme titles consist of two sentence fragments containing a main title and subtitle (e.g., The Sea—Complex, Yet Fragile). In such a title, the dash substitutes for the verb "to be" (i.e., The Sea [Is] Complex, Yet Fragile).

As in any interpretive device, we need to remember the "magical number 7 ± 2." That is, we should organize the information into five or fewer main parts, the fewer the better (see Chapter 1). Then we can include within each main part whatever selected details are needed to make it interesting and clear. Finally, if the exhibit has really done its job, viewers will want to act on their new knowledge by seeking more information or getting answers to questions. The four **levels** outlined in Figure 8-4 reflect these needs and purposes.

The four levels give each part of an exhibit a purpose: In level I, you use a theme-title to quickly communicate the principal idea or message of your exhibit; in level II, you quickly show viewers the organization of the five or fewer main ideas used to support the theme; in level III, you present the "color," those few selected facts, analogies and other information that help you explain each of the main ideas shown in level II; and in level IV, you quickly suggest ways for viewers to follow up on their new knowledge or interest in the topic. Realistically, the majority of viewers aren't going to read everything in your exhibit, and many will go no further than level I or II. Some simply won't have the time, and others won't be sufficiently interested. With a conceptual design based on levels you take this into account, allowing all viewers to absorb as much of the exhibit as they like, and in the order they like, but with the assurance that everyone will grasp the theme regardless of how much time they actually spend reading the text. Having developed such a conceptual design, you can then turn your attention to artistic considerations (such as layout, color schemes and illustration), with greater confidence that your communication objective will be achieved.

Using levels in the conceptual design of an exhibit is easy, and it helps set the stage for a more purposeful artistic design. Figure 8-5 shows a few examples of designs using levels. In each example, notice where the different levels are located and how they're represented artistically. Notice the variety. Levels don't constrain artistic design; on the contrary they empower the artist with a sense of purpose and a communication objective. In other words, artistic choice isn't limited; it's merely more focused. In this important respect, levels give the artistic designer a great advantage—they provide a strategy. Even though eventually the message and artwork will be integrated and refined together, it's almost always better to start with concrete ideas about titles and text before turning to artistic design.

Notice also that level I is the only level that's absolutely required in an exhibit. See if you can find in Figure 8-5: (a) a design that has no level II or III, and (b) a design that has no level IV. The levels aren't an end in themselves; they're merely a tool to focus the conceptual and artistic design of an exhibit on achieving the main objective—communication of a theme. Depending on the nature of the theme and how your presentation of it needs to be organized, you may find that any one or more of levels II, III, and IV are unnecessary. For example, notice that some of the sketches in Figure 8-6 show signs that contain only one main idea. In these designs, level II isn't needed.

In Exhibits, Think Levels—Then Think Design

The 4 Levels

I. *Theme Awareness*—In one or two seconds, the viewer should recognize and understand the theme. Display this level prominently in the theme title of the exhibit. Structure artistic design to complement and support the theme.

II. *Awareness of the Message Components*—Show no more than five parts or major divisions; the fewer, the better. Accomplish this with conspicuous headings or subheadings, colors, illustrations, or other "visual separators." If headings or subheadings are used, they should be conspicuous but appear less prominent than the title of the exhibit.

III. *Selected Details (Main Body Text and Illustrations)*—Corresponding to each message component, include only those facts, ideas and other information necessary to communicate that part of the theme. The content and tone of this information will determine whether the exhibit is interpretive or merely informational. A viewer ought to be able to read each body of text quickly—the briefer it is, the better—and immediately see its relationship to the theme of the exhibit. Designers sometimes include within this level a simple hierarchy of detail consisting of the main body text (which is intended for everyone) and secondary information that's offered primarily for people who would like even more detail. The second part of this hierarchy is usually separated in the layout from the primary body text, and typically printed in smaller and/or different type. Large, carefully designed exhibits may sometimes contain two or more of these "sublevels," but often at the expense of scaring off more casual readers. In most designs, such a quantity of detail is best saved for level IV.

IV. *How Viewers Can Act on Their New Knowledge*—This level can take many forms depending on the type of exhibit and its intended lifespan. It might be the name of a brochure, pamphlet or book that the viewer could get; it could be a box of brochures or information sheets attached to the display itself; it could be a schedule of future activities related to the topic of the display; it could be the name of an expert on the topic, his/her telephone number or office address; or it could simply be a suggestion of a place to go, a trail to hike, etc. in order to see something related to the topic or theme. Be selective—give only one or two suggestions. (In many exhibits, some of the additional information a viewer might seek is included in the second part of the level III hierarchy.)

Figure 8-4. The four conceptual levels of a thematic exhibit.

Levels Give a Purpose to Each Part of an Exhibit Design

Note: Roman numerals correspond to the four levels: I—Theme Awareness; II—Awareness of Message Components; III—Selected Details (Text); and IV—How Viewers Can Act on Their New Knowledge.

Figure 8-5. Examples of indoor exhibit designs using levels.

Levels Give a Purpose to Each Part of a Sign

Note: Roman numerals correspond to the four levels: I—Theme Awareness; II—Awareness of Message Components; III—Selected Details (Text); and IV—How Viewers Can Act on Their New Knowledge.

Figure 8-6. Examples of outdoor exhibit designs using levels.

Preparing Messages and Writing "Copy"

"Most adults read at the rate of about 250 to 300 words per minute. Readers prefer short sentences—on an 18 to 20 word average. The average viewing time for most exhibits is no more than forty-five seconds. Thus, a visitor reading at a rate of 300 words per minute will average about 5 words per second, or 225 words for the full 45-second attention span ... . The lesson should be clear. Exhibits must be concise."

Such was the advice of Arminta Neal (1976:122) to people writing the **texts**, or "**copy**" for museum exhibits. Her point was not new then, and it's not old now. It's just common sense backed up by a lot of research on how everyday people view exhibits. Most people don't like to read a lot of copy. As we saw in the levels approach to conceptual planning, we can safely assume that most people will read the title, but after that, who knows how much more, if any, a person will read—or in which order? You should approach copy writing with this in mind. The best exhibit copy is brief, clearly organized, and thematic to the core.

Two hundred and twenty-five words may not seem like a lot to you. The previous paragraph, for example, has 114 words—about half that. But re-read it, this time timing yourself. As you read, imagine you're standing in front of an exhibit,

Figure 8-7. Examples of theme-titles in exhibits. Even viewers who read only the titles will get the main idea in these exhibits. Respectively, Fort Columbia and Ginkgo Petrified Forest State Parks, Washington. (Photos by Steve Wang)

Figure 8-8. Scale models don't have to be elaborate. (Photo by Gerry Snyder)

not sitting in a comfortable chair. Imagine also that this exhibit is but one of 10 or 15 others in the same room, or of 50 to 100 others in the same building. How long did it take you to read the 114-word paragraph? It took me about 25 seconds, and I wrote the words. That's half my 45 seconds (assuming, of course that I'd actually spend that long reading the exhibit). Remember, 45 seconds is only the average. At a conference on exhibit planning in 1991, I asked a room of about 200 interpreters how many of them had read all the words of every exhibit in their own visitor centers. Not one hand went up. How can we expect visitors to make more of a commitment to reading our exhibits than even we are willing to make? The answer is that we can't. The best we can do is to communicate very quickly what's most important in the exhibit—the theme—and then to provide enough interesting information related to it that those who want a more detailed treatment can get it—either from the second rung of the hierarchy in level III or from the sources suggested in level IV (see Figure 8-4). In short, that's what the copy of an exhibit should do.

Keeping in mind the purpose of each of the four levels and remembering our focus on thematic interpretation, many of the guidelines in Figure 8-9 should sound familiar to you. English-language readers can find additional views on effective exhibit texts in Witteborg (1981), Trapp et al. (1991), McIntosh (1982), Fazio and Gilbert (1986), Neal (1976) and Tilden (1977). In Spanish, excellent summaries of important points are offered by Sandoval (1990) and Pinzón (1973). In addition, selected sections of Tilden (1977) are available in Spanish.

Artistic Considerations in Exhibit Design

Having developed an intelligent conceptual design, it's now time to think about how to present it artistically. Although training and experience as an artist are very helpful, almost anyone can produce attractive exhibits if they pay attention to a few basic concepts and principles. We're going to briefly review four of them: **unity, emphasis, balance,** and *color*. Once you've planned the artistic design of an exhibit, it's a very good idea to build a small scale model of it (from cardboard or balsa). Your model will help you see in advance how the layout and color scheme are really going to look when you construct the exhibit. It's always easier to make changes in a model than it is in the real thing. A number of excellent references on designing inexpensive exhibits are available. Some good English-language sources are Lauer (1985), Neal (1976), Neal (1969), Trapp et al. (1991) and Witteborg (1981). In Spanish, Moore et al. (1989), Sandoval (1990), Sánchez (1990), Pino (1989), Gillman (1974), Muñoz and Fonseca

Take Fifteen Steps Toward More Powerful Exhibit Texts

1. Use theme titles, not topic titles. Example: "We're Losing Our Soil," not simply "Soil Erosion."

2. When possible, build sub-themes into level II headings. These allow viewers to see at a glance the deeper meaning of the theme title. For example, if your development of the above theme were to be organized around two main ideas, the level II headings might take the form of theme statements (for example, "Wind and Rain—The Causes" might be one heading, and "You and I—The Culprits" might be the other. Notice that theme awareness, even if presented in a sentence fragment, is what's important. The same is true of theme titles in level I.

3. Limit your organization of the message in level II to five or fewer main ideas. The fewer the better.

4. Think visually. A good graphic may say the equivalent of hundreds of words. When you can't illustrate something literally, consider a visual metaphor (see Chapter 1).

5. Limit the main copy in level III to an amount that could be read by an average reader in 45 to 60 seconds maximum. Given current estimates of average reading speed, this would be about 225 to 300 words.

6. Don't include transitions from one part of the text to another. Doing so assumes that viewers will read the text in that order. There's a very good chance they won't.

7. Keep it simple and easy. Avoid having even one technical term in your text. If technical terms are absolutely necessary (and they virtually never are), be sure to explain them. Be cognizant that every word in such an explanation costs you one of the 225 to 300 words you've got to work with. Ask yourself if it's worth it. Keep texts easy to read by using as many one-syllable words as possible. This is especially important with verbs because simple verbs (other than the verb "to be") are often a language's most powerful verbs (e.g., say "kills," not "is causing the death of"). English-language readers are referred to an excellent explanation of this principle in O'Hayre (1966).

8. Limit sentence length to ten to fifteen words where possible. According to Witteborg (1981), if a sentence exceeds twenty-two words, you need two sentences.

9. Use short paragraphs. According to Witteborg (1981), two or three sentences is not too short.

10. Edit out passive tenses and substitute active verbs. Example: "Rain strips unprotected soils from our land," not "Unprotected soils are being stripped from our land by rain."

11. Put main clauses first in a sentence and subordinate clauses second. Example: say "A lot of farmers are planting trees to hold the soil in place," instead of "To hold the soil in place, a lot of farmers are planting trees."

12. Be personal. Use personal words as much as possible, and stay informal in tone. Research shows that personal words make reading easier and more interesting (see Flesch 1949 and Trapp et al. 1991). They include words such as you, me, I, we, he, she, they, mine, yours, his, hers, our(s), their(s), me, us, them, themselves, ourselves, yourself, myself, people's names (e.g., John, Jane), and words that identify people by gender (e.g., boy, woman, husband, saleswoman, spokesman). For most audiences, words like visitor or simply people

may also be personal. Build into the text self-referencing phrases (e.g., "Have you ever seen a sediment-choked river?") and labels (e.g., "The most responsible farmers are trying to stop soil erosion on their land." In some cases, you might want to use a personification vehicle in which the subject of a sign is "speaking" to the viewer in the first-person, "I." In some cases, a trail or old road may be "talking" to the viewer; in other cases, it may be an animal, a tree or a mountain that's doing the "talking." Self-referencing, labeling, and personification (among other vehicles) are discussed in Chapter 1 in the sections on enjoyable and personal communication.

13. Use bridging techniques (see Chapter 1). Brief examples, analogies, and comparisons will link your explanations to things viewers already know or care about. This is always a good idea and especially helpful when you're trying to explain the reasons for a rule or regulation. But don't get too complicated. An analogy that takes 100 words may far exceed what most people will read. Even if it's an excellent bridge, you may have wasted your time. See guideline 14.

14. Always think thematically, even when writing texts for markers and regulatory signs. Markers identify important features or objects. Usually they contain only the name of the object and one or two quick, but important facts about it. The facts you choose to include say something about the object—that is, they communicate a theme. Regulatory signs should also be thematic. They inform viewers about important rules and regulations. Done well, they give the reasons for the rules and the benefits of obeying them. These signs are thematic because they say something to viewers about the importance of the rules—that is, they communicate a theme. Simple lists of rules usually communicate nothing.

15. Proofread and spell-check the text at least three times. The last of these three times should be at least 24 hours since you've last read the copy. It's also a good idea to give the draft text to others to proofread. Never guess at the spelling of a word. In my classes at the university, even one spelling or punctuation error in a student's exhibit earns a failing grade. Be just as hard on yourself and your employees. Never tolerate spelling and punctuation errors. They reflect poorly on you and your organization, and they impede communication with those viewers who might be bothered by them.

Figure 8-9. Guidelines for writing better exhibit copy.

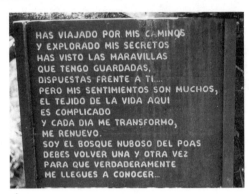

HAS VIAJADO POR MIS CAMINOS
Y EXPLORADO MIS SECRETOS
HAS VISTO LAS MARAVILLAS
QUE TENGO GUARDADAS,
DISPUESTAS FRENTE A TI....
PERO MIS SENTIMIENTOS SON MUCHOS,
EL TEJIDO DE LA VIDA AQUI
ES COMPLICADO
Y CADA DIA ME TRANSFORMO,
ME RENUEVO.
SOY EL BOSQUE NUBOSO DEL POAS
DEBES VOLVER UNA Y OTRA VEZ
PARA QUE VERDADERAMENTE
ME LLEGUES A CONOCER...

"I am an Old Time Country Lane. Now I have been officially vacated and closed. (I never liked automobiles anyway.) I invite you to walk—as folks have walked for generations—and be friendly with my trees, my flowers and my wild creatures."

a)   b)

Translation: You have walked my roads and explored my secrets. You have seen the marvels I have guarded for you here. But my thoughts are many. The web of life here is complicated and each day I transform myself—I renew myself. I am the cloud forest of Poás. You should return again and again to truly come to know me.

Figure 8-10. Examples of personified sign texts: (a) interpretive sign at Poás Volcano National Park, Costa Rica (photo by Sam Ham); (b) sign text at a Forest Preserve in Illinois (cited by Tilden 1977:62).

(1990), and Muñoz and Peña (1990) are recommended.

Unity is Consistency in a Design

Many things can go into an exhibit design—titles, subtitles, headings, text, colors, three-dimensional objects, illustrations and photographs. Artists call these things design elements because even though each is a distinct part of the exhibit, the viewer sees them all together as a whole. In other words, each is an element of the overall design. A problem in some designs is that the different elements they contain don't look like they go together; that is, they lack unity. A design with unity is easy to recognize because the elements it contains seem consistent with each other, and everything in the design appears to go together. Following are six ideas for giving exhibit designs unity:

Boundaries: Every design needs to have a defined space (or boundaries) whether physical or apparent. In most exhibits, this space is partly defined by a cabinet, panel, board, or other physical quality of the exhibit, itself. Within this physical space, however, there are some additional things you can do to unify the design. Following are three ideas. Depending upon the design you're working with, some will be more useful than others. In other words, it's not necessary (nor desirable) to do all these things in every design:

• Use conspicuous lines or bars on one or more of the margins of the design. (These can be solid or decorative, broken or continuous.)

Figure 8-11. Unity in exhibit designs. Notice the consistency in design elements in each of these exhibits. On the left, circles are complemented by curved lines and even a bowed fish silhouette; on the right, angles are complemented by other angles and diagonal patterns in the artwork; in both exhibits, the different sizes of similar type styles complement one another. Respectively, Chief Timothy and Ginkgo Petrified Forest State Parks, Washington. (Photos by Steve Wang)

• Keep a constant band of empty ("void") space around the margins of the design.

• Paint or color the outside edge of the exhibit. (Use a color that harmonizes with other colors in the design—see the section on color later in this chapter.)

Type styles: Use consistent type styles in titles, subtitles, headings, texts and captions (see the section on typefaces later in this chapter.) If you're hand-lettering, this is easy. If you're buying commercial lettering or working with a typesetter, avoid using more than two different styles. Since you can usually get most typefaces in several sizes, try to select one that comes in all the sizes you'll need.

Colors schemes: Using a predominant color throughout an exhibit can unify a design that might otherwise look disjointed. Choose colors in combinations that make sense, and avoid using too many different colors in a single design. One or two are often enough. (See the section on color later in this chapter.)

Shapes: Use consistent shapes. Shapes can be regular (such as rectangles, squares, triangle, circles, etc.), or irregular (abstract). Don't mix them unless you have a good reason. For example, a circle positioned among many boxes will stand out and seem more important. If this wasn't your intention, you'd have been better off using another box.

Lines and angles: An exhibit design contains many invisible lines and angles. Designs with unity have lines and angles that work with each other instead of against each other. Every line and angle suggests another. This is because we tend to see each design element as though every part of its contour were sending out invisible continuation lines (almost like a shadow), each one hinting at the shape or location of adjacent design elements. For example, a rectangular photograph next to a body of text usually needs the text to conform somehow to its rectangular shape. A prominent diagonal illustration in the center of a design requires that the other design elements be positioned to complement the diagonal pattern. Repeating predominant angles and lines in the design helps to give an exhibit visual identity. Continuation of a line to an adjacent design element is often pleasing to the eye because subconsciously that's what we expected.

Illustrations: Variety in illustration can be interesting, but don't mix a lot of different kinds of illustrations in the same design. For example, including combinations of pencil drawings, ink drawings, black-and-white photos, color photos, water paintings, acrylic paintings, or other kinds of illustrations in the same exhibit usually won't look very good. If you must use different kinds of illustrations, try putting a consistent border around them. With drawings, it sometimes helps to photocopy the original artwork onto a consistent type of paper and then display the copies.

Remember, these aren't hard fast rules but simply guidelines. In fact, sometimes it makes sense to make a particular part of a design different. This is called "emphasis" and it's the next topic we'll discuss.

Emphasis Tells the Eye Where to Go

Things that are emphasized draw our attention. For example, we've repeatedly made the point that exhibit viewers usually read a conspicuous title almost immediately. The key word in this sentence is *conspicuous* since if the title isn't obvious—that is, if it doesn't draw attention to itself—many viewers won't read it. Instinctively, we look for the largest and most prominent letters when we begin to read an exhibit. When we find them, we've usually found the title. Similarly, the size and boldness of different parts of

Figure 8-12. Emphasis through isolation. This outdoor exhibit interprets the life cycle of a pine beetle. Designers cut a rectangular window in the panel to draw viewers' attention to the beetle-infested forest in the background. Federation Forest State Park, Washington. (Photo by Steve Wang)

the text tells us their relative importance in the overall message. If viewers spend time reading the text, different sizes of type may even influence the order in which they do it (see, for example, Trapp et al. 1991). This is because emphasis draws the eye. Things that are emphasized in a design appear important and therefore attract our attention.

Almost any design element can be emphasized—a particular illustration, an object, headings, a key idea or a certain body of text. From a design standpoint, when we choose to emphasize something we're making a conscious decision to draw attention to it—to make it seem more important than other parts of the design. There may be many reasons to do this—for example, making the theme-title stand out from levels II and III, showing the organization of the exhibit's main ideas, highlighting an important safety message, contrasting two or more different aspects or points of view about

Figure 8-13. All emphasis is no emphasis. Can you say what's being emphasized in this exhibit? Probably not. (Photo by Costa Rican National Museum of Natural History)

something, or drawing attention to some peculiar or especially significant characteristic or feature of something. There are three basic ways to emphasize something in a design: you can make it conspicuously different from other things, you can isolate it, or you can "point" at it.

Differentiation (size, shape, or color): Conspicuous contrast in the sizes, shapes or colors of design elements creates emphasis. When size is emphasized, the viewer's eye is drawn to the biggest or the boldest; when shape is emphasized, the viewer's eye is drawn to the one that is different from the rest (for example, big, bold words stand out from those that are not big and bold, circles stand out among squares, irregular shapes stand out among regular ones, and three-dimensional objects stand out against an otherwise two-dimensional background). With color, the relationship is a little more complex (see the section on color later in this chapter). Generally, however, a color that contrasts most forcefully with the rest of the color scheme will usually draw attention. In many cultures of the Western Hemisphere, something that is colored red will almost always draw attention unless red is also used conspicuously elsewhere in the exhibit. An exhibit's title, headings, labels and captions are usually different from other design elements not only in size, but often in color. Specimen labels, for example, are usually printed on a background (such as white) that contrasts with other colors. Likewise, you can use different colors in the background of an exhibit to indicate the five or fewer parts of the message (level II).

Isolation: When you separate a design element from the rest of the design, you emphasize it. Often, an isolated element is also emphasized in size, shape or color.

Pointing: "Pointing" in a design means arranging design elements in such a way that they lead the viewer's eye to something you want to emphasize. For example, elements that radiate from a common center emphasize the element in the center; elements with a pointed shape all oriented in the same direction will lead the eye toward that direction also. Although they sometimes aren't very creative, arrows and other "pointers" also can be used to emphasize a design element.

Be selective in what you choose to emphasize. Remember, all emphasis equals no emphasis. That is, if too many things are emphasized, nothing will be emphasized. This is what happens, for example, when a display includes too many objects with labels or jars containing preserved specimens. The eye simply doesn't know where to go because they all look equally important. Most exhibits don't require a lot of emphasis. In many, in fact, the only elements emphasized are the title and main headings. The location

Figure 8-14. Fundamentals of visual balance. (Adapted from Pino 1989)

of emphasized elements also affects the "balance" of a design. This is the topic we consider next.

Balance Gives a Design Stability

Balance is a basic, yet important quality in a design. When a design has it, we think little of it, but when a design lacks it, we're disturbed—even if we can't explain why. Consider our sometimes irresistible urge to straighten a tilted picture on a wall, or our preference for symmetry in architecture. According to some designers, a sense of balance is basic to the human experience; designs that reflect this necessary quality in our lives simply make us feel good.

A balanced design is like a see-saw on which two or more people have found equilibrium. By positioning people of different sizes and weights at different places on either side of the see-saw, we can eventually bring the whole system into balance. In an exhibit, different elements in the design can be balanced by arranging their "visual weight." Visual weight is determined by how interesting or important something seems. Something that's very important might "weigh" the same as a whole group of other things that are collectively less important. As with people on a see-saw, it's possible to balance a design by moving lighter objects further from the center and heavier objects closer to it. Usually, the same things that affect emphasis (size, shape and color) also affect visual weight.

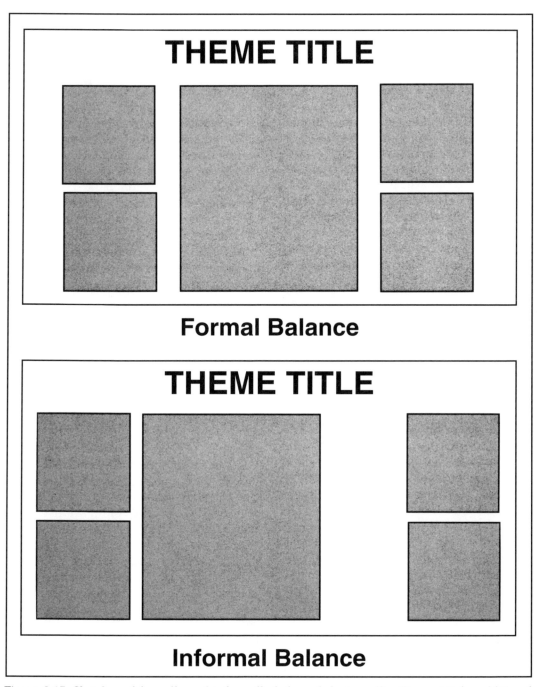

Figure 8-15. Sketches of formally and informally balanced designs. (See Figure 8-5 for additional examples.)

Generally, when we speak of balance we're almost always talking about horizontal balance—that is, the left and right sides of the design. According to some designers, vertical balance is also important, but because of our sense of gravity we're less concerned with it. There are two main kinds of horizontal balance—formal and informal.

Formal (Symmetrical) Balance: The simplest kind of balance is symmetrical or "formal." It's achieved by having identical left and right sides as when identical twins balance each other on a see-saw. In a formally balanced exhibit, each element on the left-hand side of the design is repeated on the right-hand side such that the right and left look like mirror images of each other. The first three designs in Figure 8-5 are formally balanced. Although there's nothing inherently wrong with formally balanced designs, many designers feel they lack the interest of those that are informally balanced.

Informal (Asymmetrical) Balance: Informal balance is achieved by positioning dissimilar elements so that their visual weights compensate for each other. The more an element draws our attention, the "heavier" it is. Thus it's possible for a small but interesting element (such as a label or small three-dimensional object) to weigh the same as a larger but less interesting element. The last two rows in Figure 8-5 show designs that have informal balance.

Most people can tell whether a design is balanced simply by looking at it. Sometimes, however, designers look at a design so much, and for so long, that they lose objectivity. Some designers say it helps to look at the design through squinted eyes or even to view its reflection off a mirror in order to judge its balance with greater objectivity.

How to Select a Color Scheme

A **color scheme** is a set of (usually one to four) colors that we've selected in order to make an exhibit attractive and to communicate its theme. Usually (but not necessarily always) the color scheme will consist of one "predominant" color along with one or two (rarely three) "accent" colors that harmonize with it. For instance, the predominant color might be used in the background and/or in large conspicuous areas within the exhibit design, with the accent colors being used more subtly (around edges of mounted photos, border lines, or in areas of contrast or emphasis). There aren't any firm rules for how to select a color scheme, but there are some general guidelines you can follow once you've decided on the first color.

Plan Color Schemes Around the First Color

Sometimes beginning exhibit designers are unsure how to select the first color. But once they've decided on it, decisions about the rest of the colors are usually a lot easier. Generally, there are three guidelines for selecting the first color: (1) you can select a color related to the topic of the exhibit; (2) you can select a color based on the colors in the surrounding environment; or (3) you can use a predominant color from existing materials or artwork that you've already selected for the exhibit. We'll briefly consider each of these guidelines and then turn our attention to selecting the remaining colors in the color scheme.

Topic-Related Colors

In some cases, the topic of the exhibit suggests a predominant starting color. Greens, for example, may be appropriate for exhibits on forests; browns and reds come to mind when thinking about soil; and blues may be associated with topics dealing with air, water or ice. The exhibit designer may use a topic-related color as a starting point for selecting other colors to include in the exhibit. But be careful in using this guideline. One of the most powerful effects of color is its ability to attract the eye, and one way it does this is by surprising the viewer. If every exhibit on forests had a lot of green in it, imagine how predictable and monotonous forest-related exhibits would seem to us. A common problem in forest visitor centers, for example, is that a lot of the exhibits look alike because they're all green. Generally, it's better to have variety.

Colors Based on Surroundings

Exhibits have to be placed somewhere, and the predominant colors in that environment may suggest the first color for the exhibit. In a visitor center, for example, the colors of the walls, floor or other nearby exhibits may influence our choice of color scheme. The colors we ultimately choose may have little or no relationship to the topic of the exhibit, but this usually doesn't matter. In some cases, our goal will be to select the first color to blend with a predominant surrounding color. In other cases, however, we might want to select a color that contrasts or stands out from surrounding colors.

Colors in Existing Materials

When budgets are limited, we usually have to rely on existing artwork and other materials that we can acquire at low cost. Often, posters, paintings, photographs and three-dimensional objects are available for such use. Since we usually can't change their colors, it sometimes makes sense to use one of their predominant colors as the starting point in our color scheme. This is especially true if one of the objects has a particularly strong or visible color in it. For example, a poster with strong shades of red may suggest red, or a different color that looks good with red, as the first color in our color scheme. Likewise, a tool with a bright yellow handle might lead us to select other colors that would look good with yellow, etc.

Use the "Color Wheel" to Select Remaining Colors

Once you've decided on the first color, selecting the rest of the colors is relatively easy. If you've got an eye for color, you may be able to design a pleasing color scheme without further guidelines. Most people, however, find that using the "color wheel" (Plate 1) helps them to select additional colors that look good with the first one.

The color wheel presents colors in their natural sequence, that is, based on how they appear in nature (say, for example, in a rainbow or prism). Each color is positioned such that the colors most like it are located adjacent to it, and the colors least like it are located exactly opposite to it. Generally, these are the two main relationships between colors—**analogous** (or **adjacent**) colors blend with each other, while **complementary** (or **opposite**) colors contrast. Combinations of colors that blend or contrast are usually pleasing to the eye. On the other hand, colors that are widely separated (but not opposites) on the color wheel usually don't harmonize very well. That's because they neither blend nor contrast with each other.

Blending and contrasting are the two main things that color schemes do. Using the color wheel, we're going to discuss seven different types of color schemes, any one of which could be used attractively in an exhibit. Of these seven, two are color schemes that rely on blending, four rely on contrasting, and one does both (see Plate 2).

Many helpful references on understanding and using color are available. In English, Lauer (1985), Faulkner and Ziegfeld (1969), and Zakia and Todd (1974) are especially good. In Spanish, Sánchez (1990), Pino (1989), Muñoz and Fonseca (1990), Muñoz and Peña (1990), and Bay (1968) are highly recommended.

Color Schemes that Blend

Colors that blend often give a soothing, calm, and restful effect (unless there are strong contrasts in lightness and darkness). Two kinds of color schemes rely on blending. These are monochromatic and analogous color schemes. Like all seven of the color schemes we'll discuss, both are used extensively in exhibits and signs.

Monochromatic color schemes, as the name implies, have just one color (Plate 2a). But this doesn't mean they lack color variation. Often, different shades of the color (light and dark) are used. For example, an exhibit may use three or four different shades of green. Other times, however, only one shade of a color is used. A good example is the World Wildlife Fund's red, white and black bag shown in Plate 4. Since the only "true" color it contains is red, the bag's color scheme is monochromatic. You're

probably wondering why white and black aren't considered "true" colors. It's because they fall into a special category called "neutral colors" that we'll discuss shortly. (By the way, red and black are often an appealing color combination, especially if you want the subject to somehow seem important, distinguished or formal. That's why business people and politicians often wear black suits with red ties or handkerchiefs.)

Analogous color schemes (Plate 2b) usually involve two or three adjacent colors, all of which contain one color in common. For example, a color scheme comprised of yellow-orange, yellow, and yellow-green would be an analogous color scheme because all three of its colors contain yellow.

Color Schemes that Contrast

Color schemes that contrast are usually livelier and more stimulating than either analogous or monochromatic schemes. That's because of the simultaneous emphasis that opposite colors give one another. Any color looks more vivid when it's contrasted against its opposite (or complementary) color. Four kinds of color schemes rely on contrasting.

Complementary color schemes involve two colors that are exactly opposite each other on the color wheel (Plate 2c). An example would be an exhibit containing blue and orange, or a sign containing red-violet and yellow-green.

Split-complementary color schemes contain three colors: any color plus the two colors located on each side of its opposite (Plate 2d). For example, if the first color were red, the other two colors would be yellow-green and blue-green (the two colors on each side of green, which is red's opposite).

Triad color schemes (Plate 2e) contain three colors that are located equidistant from each other on the color wheel. An example would be violet, green and orange.

Tetrad color schemes (Plate 2f) are comprised of four colors that are located equidistant from each other on the color wheel. (Obviously, these four colors will comprise two perpendicular pairs of opposite colors.) For example, a tetrad color scheme might include violet and yellow (one opposite pair) and red-orange and blue-green (the opposite pair perpendicular to violet and yellow).

A Color Scheme that Both Blends and Contrasts

Double-complementary color schemes contain four colors (Plate 2g). They consist of two adjacent colors and the two colors opposite to them. The combination of adjacent and opposite colors creates both blending and contrast in the design. For example, you could turn a simple complementary scheme (say, of blue and orange) into a double-complementary scheme by adding blue-green and red-orange.

All of these color schemes produce visually attractive results, but they're not the only possibilities. In fact, in today's world there really are very few firm rules about colors. Trained artists and designers often approach color rather freely, looking for surprising or unexpected combinations. Those of us with less experience, however, will find these color schemes a useful place to start. To simplify decision making, Figure 8-16 lists the possible combinations for schemes with two, three and four colors. Monochromatic schemes, of course, would correspond to the first column of colors only. Use the chart as a starting point, but don't be afraid to deviate from the colors listed if you have reason to believe some other combination might work better.

Using Color "Temperature" to Produce Desired Effects

An important quality of colors is their "**temperature**." Although we don't really feel heat or cold from them, we do distinguish between warm colors and cool colors. Warm colors are exciting and stimulating. They include yellows, oranges and reds because they remind of us things like fire, blood, and the sun. Cool colors are thought to be calm and soothing. They include blues and some shades of greens and violets because they remind us of things like water, ice, and cool shady environments. Pure green and violet are usually thought of as being intermediate in temperature, but may take on a warm or cool quality depending on the shade they share with adjacent colors. For example, yellow-green is a warm color but blue-green is a cool one. (Readers knowledgeable in color theory should note that we're using the term "temperature" to describe what color theorists call "hue.")

Designers distinguish between warm and cool colors because of the way humans perceive them in nature. When viewing a natural landscape, for example, warm colors look closer to us while far away objects appear to take on cooler colors. Vivid oranges, reds, and yellows seem distinct and therefore closer; by contrast, it's hard to see the colors of things in the distance and so they appear hazy and blue. Research has shown that we tend to see warm colors as being closer to us, and cool colors as being farther away—even if they are, in fact, the same distance from us. Because of this phenomenon, we say

A Guide to 84 Color Schemes

TWO-COLOR SCHEME		THREE-COLOR SCHEMES			FOUR-COLOR SCHEMES	
		Additional Colors				
First Color	Complementary	Analogous	Triad	Split Complementary	Double Complementary	Tetrad
Y	V	YO & YG	R & B	RV & BV	YG, V & RV	V, RO & BG
YG	RV	Y & G	RO & BV	R & V	G, R & RV	RV, B & O
G	R	YG & BG	O & V	RO & RV	BG, R & RO	R, BV & YO
BG	RO	G & B	YO & RV	O & R	B, O & RO	RO, V & Y
B	O	BG & BV	Y & R	YO & RO	BV, O & YO	O, RV & YG
BV	YO	B & V	YG & RO	Y & O	V, Y & YO	YO, R & G
V	Y	RV & BV	G & O	YG & YO	RV, Y & YG	Y, RO & BG
RV	YG	R & V	BG & YO	G & Y	R, G & YG	YG, O & B
R	G	RO & RV	B & Y	BG & YG	RO, G & BG	G, YO & BV
RO	BG	O & R	BV & YG	B & G	O, B & BG	BG, Y & V
O	B	YO & RO	V & G	BV & BG	YO, B & BV	B, YG & RV
YO	BV	Y & O	RV & BG	V & B	Y, V & BV	BV, G & R

Notes: For monochromatic schemes, use different values of the first color only. For two-, three-, and four-color schemes, select the first color then add the additional colors indicated in the color scheme you want to use. Be sure to look at samples of the colors together before making your final decision. Colors are abbreviated as follows:

Y = yellow
G = green
B = blue
V = violet
R = red
O = orange

Figure 8-16. A guide to color combinations for schemes with one to four colors.

that warm colors advance while cool colors recede. For example, if a large blue box and an orange box of identical size were placed exactly the same distance from you, you'd probably perceive the orange box to be closer. Generally, objects that are warm appear larger than objects that are cool. So if you want to make something in an exhibit seem bigger or closer, you might use a warm color. If, on the other hand, you want to deemphasize something or make it look farther away, you might use a cool color. You can see this effect in the circles inside the boxes in Plate 5. Although all four circles are identical in size, the two warm ones (yellow and orange) appear larger.

Notice from the color wheel that warm colors have cool opposites, and vice versa. Since the warms advance and the cools recede, putting two opposite colors into the same design causes them to contrast strongly, but in a pleasing way. This, of course, is the principle at work in Plate 5 and in the four color schemes that rely on contrasting (complementary, split-complementary, double-complementary, and tetrad).

Neutral Colors Add Variation but Not Complexity

You won't find colors such as black, white, and grey on the color wheel. They look good in any color scheme. For this reason, they're called *neutral colors*. Some designers (e.g., Machlis and Machlis 1974) include shades of brown and tan in the neutral category since they also look good with many colors.

Neutral colors like black and white are commonly used in the text and titles of exhibits. That's because they stand out yet don't clutter the design as "true" colors

certainly could. Notice that the black text in Plate 1 looks good with all the colors in the color wheel, and that both look good on the white paper. If the text and paper weren't neutral colors, the page would look "busy" and very hard to read. You can use neutral colors in any of the seven color schemes without making the design appear more complex. Titles, subtitles, headings, captions, labels, and text are often black, white, or grey. Likewise, shades of grey, whites, and tans often make good background colors because they don't compete with other colors in the design. The range of black and white neutral colors is shown in Plate 3a.

Using Color "Value" to Produce Desired Effects

Besides temperature, colors also have a quality called **value**. The "value" of a color is the amount of white it contains —in other words, how light or dark it is. Light colors have high values and dark colors have low values. Any color has shades ranging from light to dark, that is, from high value to low value. Shades of red, for example, range from very light (pink) to very dark (maroon or burgundy); blues range from light blue to dark blue; and you can think of grey as a high value black. Each of the colors in the color wheel (Plate 1) is shown at its normal value, but you can find all of them in lighter and darker shades. The bar in Plate 3b, for example, shows some different values of the color green.

Like temperature, the value of a color influences whether it will advance or recede. Generally, low values (the dark shades of colors) advance. High values (the light shades of colors) recede. Note, however, that many things can affect this relationship, especially the amount of contrast between two colors. The main thing to remember in designing an exhibit or sign is that a dark color will always stand out against a light background, and a light color will always stand out against a dark background—regardless of the colors involved.

You can use your knowledge of color value in a lot of interesting ways. A common technique in exhibits is to create color variation by using different values of a single color, rather than adding a lot of other colors that might clutter the design. This is what a lot of monochromatic color schemes do. For example, lighter shades of a color can be used as backgrounds or "frames" around darker shades of the same color in order to draw attention to particular parts of the exhibit. Of course, the reverse also could be done with the same result. In addition, contrasting the value of two different colors (e.g., one light and one dark) can sometimes make two colors harmonize that ordinarily don't look good together. For example, most people don't think that dark orange and dark violet harmonize very well. But if the violet is lightened enough to contrast with the darkness of the orange, the result is much more pleasing to the eye.

Understanding the difference between value contrasts and "temperature" contrasts can be important in choosing the background for a two-dimensional sign or exhibit (i.e., one that has colored letters or artwork directly on the background surface). Although many possibilities exist, the background must contrast to some extent with the details in the foreground. Otherwise, the words and artwork won't show up very well. Since contrast occurs when one color advances and another recedes, you'll usually want to have a background that does one, and a foreground that does the other. Beginning designers often try to achieve this contrast by superimposing opposite (cool and warm) colors. The problem is that even though some combinations of opposite colors are very legible, many are not—especially if the colors are equal in value (both dark, or both light).

Usually, you can get more attractive contrast between the foreground and background by letting value differences rather than "temperature" differences create the contrast (Plate 6). A general guideline is to use a light-colored background (or a light neutral color such as white, grey or tan) if the foreground details are going to be dark, and a dark background if they're going to be light, regardless of whether the colors you're using are cool or warm. This can be especially important in outdoor exhibits that will be exposed to the fading effects of the sun. After a few months in strong sunlight, the color in the letters and the background color will both fade, each day bringing their values closer together and reducing the contrast between them. Likewise, outdoor signs that have text on unpainted wood may eventually become unreadable because over time the contrast between the color of the letters and the natural color of the wood disappears. Unless outdoor exhibits are sheltered from the sun, periodic re-painting is almost always going to be necessary, especially in sunny climates. As Trapp et al. (1991) and others have advised, signs located in open sunlight are more readable if light-colored letters are used on a dark background. However, if the sign is shaded (whether by a roof, natural vegetation, or other means), dark letters on a light field is preferred.

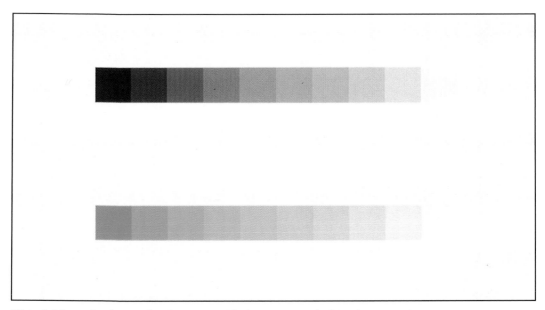

Plate 3. Neutral colors and value vary with the amount of white they contain.

Plate 4. Example of a monochromatic color scheme. (Photo by Gerry Snyder)

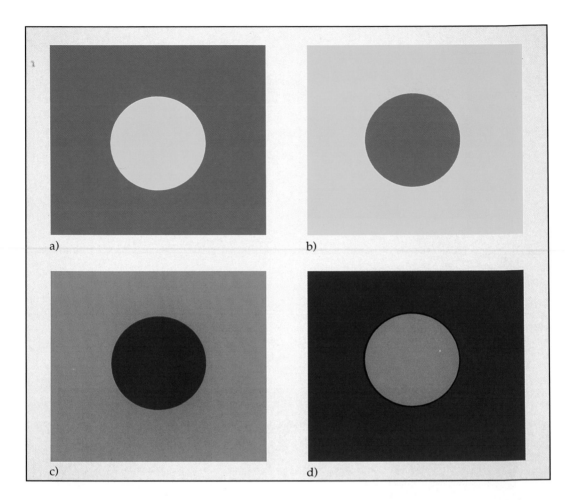

Plate 5. Examples of complementary color schemes: *a)* yellow on violet, *b)* violet on yellow, *c)* blue on orange, and *d)* orange on blue. The four circles are identical in size. Since warm colors advance, the yellow circle in *a* and the orange one in *d* appear bigger than the other two.

Plate 6. Contrasts in light and dark (rather than color contrasts) create exhibits that are easy to read. Notice that black letters are used against the light backgrounds on the left and center, whereas white letters are used against the dark background on the right. (Photo by Steve Wang)

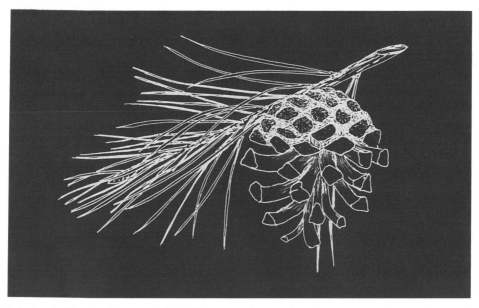

Plate 7. A simple blue-background slide. The original artwork and instructions for producing this type of slide are included in Chapter 4. (Photo by Gerry Snyder)

A Word About Indoor Lighting and Color Schemes

The kind of light that illuminates an exhibit has a definite effect on the way colors look. Unfortunately, we often have little control over the kind of lighting that's going to be used. In a visitor center, for example, unless you have the money to change the lighting system (e.g., to buy new bulbs or change the fixtures), you're probably going to have to live with the system that's already installed. In most cases, this will be fluorescent or regular incandescent lighting. If you've ever taken a photograph using daylight film in a room with either of these kinds of lights, you already know how they affect color. If the lighting was fluorescent, your photographs came out green. If the lighting was incandescent, they came out red (or orange). That's because fluorescent light *is* green, and incandescent light *is* red. Even if our eyes don't see them this way, the proof is in the photographs. Casting a green or red "shadow" on any color scheme will distort it. The best lighting comes from sources that don't have any color in them, but rather (like the sun), send out all wave lengths of pure, white light. Sunlight is an example of "full-spectrum" lighting.

There are three ways to overcome this problem. First, if there are windows in the room, keep the curtains open to allow sunlight to at least mix with the overhead lighting. Be careful, though, because strong sunlight causes colors to fade quickly. Second, if you have the money, replace the existing light bulbs with full-spectrum bulbs of the same type. You can purchase full-spectrum replacement bulbs for both fluorescent and incandescent fixtures at stores that specialize in lights and lighting systems. Third, you can minimize the distortion by viewing and selecting colors for the exhibit in the same room or under the same type of lighting in which the exhibit will ultimately be located. This is always a good idea since you'll at least be able to predict ahead of time how your color scheme is going to work once the exhibit is in place. If you go to an art supply store to buy materials for an exhibit, be sure to check their color near a window if possible. They may not look the same as you thought once you see them in full-spectrum sunlight.

Texts and Type Styles

An exhibit's text (or "copy") includes all its words—titles, subtitles, headings, subheads, photo captions, specimen labels, and bodies of text. Together, these words focus attention, first, on the theme of an exhibit and then on its conceptual organization and content. To do these things, words must be readable. Several things affect the readability of letters in an exhibit. As we saw in the section on color value, strong contrast between the letters and the background is especially important. In most indoor exhibits, black letters on a white or light neutral background is best, but this isn't necessarily always the case. In addition, three other factors influence the readability of letters: their size and spacing (the amount of space between letters, words, and individual lines of text), and whether they're in upper or lower case.

Why Using All Capital Letters Is a Bad Idea

As we saw in Chapter 4, words in all capital letters are fine for titles of four or five words, but that's only because it doesn't take the reader a lot of time to read them. The fact, however, is that all texts are more readable if both capital and lowercase letters are used. There are many reasons for this, but the main one is that capital letters seem crowded together and their uniform rectangular shape makes it harder for us to distinguish between them. This isn't an issue of cultural preference (as a colleague once tried to argue); it's a physical reality that the human eye likes variation in the heights and widths of letters. Psychologists have shown that the pattern of "ups and downs" in the letters that comprise words, and in the words that comprise sentences, is the key to our being able to recognize and remember words in text form. Using these recognizable patterns, we're able to read word *groups* (usually of three or four), rather than only one word at a time. Capitalizing all the letters in a body of text gives them the same height, and a uniform rectangular outline, effectively robbing them of their distinctive patterns. Therefore, when we have to read text in "all caps" we have to read it one word at a time, greatly increasing the amount of work we have to do. According to studies, this not only slows us down, it reduces our comprehension of the material by 10 to 25 percent. Expert typographers (people who design and make type styles) insist that all "caps" is bad typography, often even in titles. According to Haley (1991:14):

> "If there were a ten commandments of typography, "Thou shalt not set in all caps" would be the first. And if there were a typographic heaven and hell, some of us would be in a good deal of trouble …"

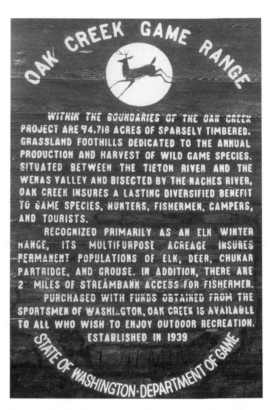

Figure 8-17. Texts in "all caps" are harder to read than those that use both upper and lower case letters. (Photo by Sam Ham)

Haley makes an important point. In order to see why it's true, let's look at his statement again, this time in all caps:

> "IF THERE WERE A TEN COMMANDMENTS OF TYPOGRAPHY, "THOU SHALT NOT SET IN ALL CAPS" WOULD BE THE FIRST. AND IF THERE WERE A TYPOGRAPHIC HEAVEN AND HELL, SOME OF US WOULD BE IN A GOOD DEAL OF TROUBLE …"

Comparing the two versions, you'll see that lower case type is not only easier to read, it also saves space—up to 35 or even 50 percent more space—than all caps. Reading the lower case version of Haley's words takes less work because we have to move our eyes fewer times from the end of one sentence to the beginning of the next. Even more important, though, is that the lower case version *looks* like less work. As we saw in Chapter 1, most non-captive audiences won't pay attention to a message that appears to require a lot of effort. Imagine how laborious an exhibit text of 225 to 300 words would seem if all the words were capitalized. Except for short titles or headings, don't use all caps. Even in titles, a combination of upper and lower case letters often looks better.

How Big Should Letters Be?

Even people with perfect vision can't read letters that are too small. What constitutes "too small," of course, depends not only on the size of the letters but on their viewing distance. A typographer measures the height of letters in "point size" or simply "points." The point size of a type style is measured from the bottom of the lowest letter (usually the tail of the letter "y") to the top of the tallest capital letter (usually "T"). A type style that's 1 inch (2.5 cm) high measures 72 points from the bottom of the "y" to the top of the "T." Ignoring the rare "tail," however (only "y" and "g" have them), the actual appearance of 72-point letters in most type styles is about 3/4 of an inch (2 cm). A 1-inch (2.5 cm) letter is ordinarily 96-point. This book is printed in 10-point type. Texts intended for close-up reading (e.g., books, newspapers, Bibles, etc.) usually have letters that are 12-point or less. Since

people normally read exhibits from a distance of at least two feet and often further away, it stands to reason that no part of an exhibit text should ever be printed this small. As Figure 8-18 shows, the smallest letter size recommended by exhibit experts is 18 to 24 points (about 1/4-inch or 0.6 cm), and this size should be reserved only for the least important part of a text (specialty information, captions, specimen labels, etc.). Exhibits with texts at least as large as those recommended in the guide usually will be readable even to people who have less than perfect vision.

Spacing Between Letters

One way to save money on an exhibit is to create your own titles, headings, and body text. If you do this, the amount of space you put between letters is important. If you put them too close together they'll be hard to read, and if you position them too far apart viewers will have a hard time following the flow of ideas. The best way to determine if letters are properly spaced is to look at them. You'll probably find that wide capitals like "A," "M," "W," and "Y" will need closer spacing than straight characters such as "I" and "l." Likewise, letters with curves (such as a, b, c, d, g, o, p, q, etc. and all their capitals) may need to fit a little snugger than other letters in order to look right. As a very rough guideline, Neal (1976) suggested using one and a half times the thickness of the letter "I." But as she warned, visually correct spacing will vary depending upon the size and style of the letters you're using. In lettering, it's always better to trust your eye.

Spacing Between Words

Spacing between words is also important because readers need to be able

Readability Depends on Viewing Distances

Viewing Distances and Minimum Heights of Letters

Type of Text	1 to 4 ft 0 to 1.5 m	4 to 6 ft (1.5 to 2 m)	30 ft (9 m)	60 ft (18 m)
Titles	2 cm (3/4″) > 72 pt.	2.5 cm (1″) > 96 pt.	10 cm (4″) > 384 pt.	15 cm (6″) > 576 pt.
Headings	1.3 cm (1/2″) > 48 pt.	2 cm (3/4″) > 72 pt.	8 cm (3″) > 288 pt.	13 cm (5″) > 480 pt.
Body text	0.6 cm (1/4″) > 24 pt.	1.3 cm (1/2″) > 48 pt.	6 cm (2″) > 192 pt.	10 cm (4″) > 384 pt.
Captions and specimen labels	0.5 cm (3/16″) > 18 pt.	.6 cm (1/4″) > 24 pt.	N/A	N/A

Notes: Sizes given are the minimum for each viewing distance. N/A = not applicable—exhibits intended to be viewed from this distance normally shouldn't include items requiring captions or labels. You may notice that the sizes shown here are much bigger than those shown in Figure 4-2 (which pertains to visual aids for use in an illustrated talk). The difference, of course, is that an exhibit must communicate its message by itself, without the assistance of a speaker. In a talk, the speaker's commentary makes reading the words on a visual aid easier for an audience. (Sources: Sánchez 1990, Pinzón 1973, Witteborg 1981, Neal 1976, U.S. National Library Service 1979, and Trapp et al. 1991).

Figure 8-18. A guide to selecting type sizes for different viewing distances.

to see where one ends and the next one begins. Sometimes beginning designers try to crowd words together in order to "cram" a little more copy into an available space. But this is never a good idea. Faced with such a dilemma, it's almost always better to find ways to reduce the number of words rather than the amount of space between them. On the other hand, too much space also can be a problem. Unfortunately, there aren't any formulae or firm rules that tell us how much space is best. That's because our tastes about such things change over time. In the 1970s, for example, a widely used rule in exhibit design was to allow about the width of the capital letter "M" between words in a sentence. In the 1990s, however, we seem to prefer our words a little closer together than "M-spacing" puts them, often as close as the width of a lower case "t." Depending on the size and style of the letters you're using, both M-spacing and t-spacing will probably look fine but the effect will be different. When texts are intended to be viewed from a close distance, tighter spacing tends to look better. Conversely, when the viewing distance is greater, wider spacing is necessary for distinct words to appear. Judge for yourself which looks best in your exhibit.

Obviously, since a "t" is narrower than an "M," t-spacing allows more words per line of text than M-spacing. Be careful, though, not to have too many words on a line. According to experts, a single line of text should rarely exceed about 50 characters (including letters and all the spaces between words). According to Neal (1976), the upper limit is 65.

Many exhibit experts claim that the amount of space between words should be uniform. That is, all words should have the same amount of space between them. If you "justify" the text (vary the spacing between words in order to produce a right-hand margin that's straight), the words on each line won't be evenly spaced. Although there's no firm evidence that either is better in terms of readability, most experts agree that an unjustified or "ragged right" look is more inviting and more informal than justified type. This may be because we usually associate justified text with formal publications such as newspapers and books. This book, for example, has justified text. Notice the irregular spacing between words in some sentences. So that you can see the difference, compare the justified sign text shown in Figure 8-17 with the "ragged right" text shown in Figure 8-19.

Spacing Between Lines of Text

Spacing between lines of text (or "leading," as graphic artists call it) is one of the most important yet ignored factors in exhibit design. Lines of text that have too much space between them are often hard to read because the eye loses track of which line it's on. Lines that are too close together are even harder to read, and they *look* that way—effectively scaring off potential readers unwilling to wade

Figure 8-19. An example of "M-spacing" between words. Because this sign is intended to be read from several feet away (and in part because of the upper case text), wider spacing between words was necessary to make the sign readable. Notice also the "ragged right" look and the amount of space between lines of text—about half the height of a capital letter. (Photo by Sam Ham)

through them. Both beginning and expert designers are guilty of crowding lines of text in their exhibits. There probably are a lot of reasons for this, but often it's because they're trying to squeeze a little extra information into a particular part of an exhibit. The result, of course, is a text that few people (probably only the connoisseur) will read.

Adequate space between lines of text gives an exhibit a more informal look than tightly crammed blocks of sentences. Trapp et al. (1991) called it "breathing room," an apt metaphor because the words in crowded text do indeed have the appearance of suffocating under their own weight. Opinions abound about the best or optimal spacing, but the fact is that no firm guidelines exist because of the sheer number of variables that can affect readability (especially type styles, type sizes, line lengths and intended viewing distances). According to typographer, Richard Dahn (see the case study at the end of this chapter), the best approach is to arrange the text early in the design process, view it from the distance and under the same circumstances the audience will read it, and continue changing it until it has the look you want. He advises organizing the textual material first since the typography in a design has such an impact on how everything else will look.

Placement of Text in an Upright Exhibit

Where you put words in an upright exhibit influences whether they'll be read. Because of our limited range of comfortable head movement and the number of viewers who wear bifocals, you should try to keep all text as close as possible to a right angle with the viewer's line of sight. Unless there's a very good reason, no text and no small objects should be located any lower than 2 feet (60 cm) from the floor. To achieve this you may have to elevate the exhibit by mounting it on a stand or support of some kind. Another option is to hang the exhibit on a wall at the optimal height. Some experts suggest 7 feet (2.15 m) as the maximum height for the top of the display case, itself. Use the following guidelines (adapted from Neal 1976 and Witteborg 1981) to determine the optimal heights of different parts of an upright exhibit:

1. Titles/subtitles (Level I): Place them about 1 ft (30 cm) above eye level. Assuming an average adult height of about 5 feet, 9 inches (1.75 m), the normal maximum height of a title would be around 6 feet, 9 inches (2.05 m).

2. Headings and body text (Levels II and III): Place them somewhere between eye level and about 1 ft (30 cm) below it. Again assuming an average adult height

of 5 feet, 9 inches, headings and body text would normally be placed within 4 feet, 6 inches (1.4 m) to 5 feet, 6 inches (1.7 m) above the floor or ground level.

3. If you must mount a body of text or label much lower than this, prop it up toward the viewer at about a 45-degree angle. If you have to locate headings or texts above the recommended level, tilt the text downward from the top edge at about a 45-degree angle.

4. If you need to mount blocks of text on the inner sides of a case, angle them in toward the viewer.

Type Styles

Words in an exhibit text are meant to be read. They aren't to be used to "decorate" an exhibit, and they aren't to be decorated themselves. They're meant to be read and nothing more. This advice, more than any other, should guide your choice and use of **type styles** in an exhibit text (level III). While it's certainly true that different styles of lettering (typefaces) communicate different moods or, as Trapp et al. (1991) called them, "personalities," it's best to avoid strong ones in an exhibit text. That is, keep the lettering style conservative and readable. In this context, conservative means not frilly or fancy, and readable means just what it says. The two are often related. Although fancier typefaces are sometimes selected for titles and main headings, embellished body text in whole paragraphs is difficult to read even though the type style may complement the rest of the design nicely.

Beginning designers sometimes "get carried away," trying to make a visual statement in every design element, including type styles. A few years ago, an introductory student produced an exhibit

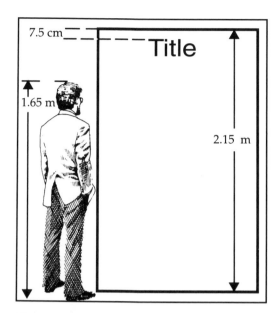

Figure 8-20. Optimal height for an upright exhibit title. Experts say that the top of the exhibit panel or case should be about 7 feet above the ground and the title no lower than about 6 feet, 9 inches.

entitled "Fall Colors—They Fall Every Year," in which each letter of the title was a different shade of orange, red, yellow, green, or brown (colors typical of autumn leaves in deciduous forests). In addition, behind each letter was the silhouetted shape of a leaf from one of the tree species he discussed in the text of the exhibit. Although his exhibit was otherwise very well designed, he noticed that few people stopped to view it—probably because they couldn't read the title. After some persuasion, the student conducted an experiment. He substituted large black letters for the decorative title. A day later he notice that people were stopping to view his exhibit. Through his experiment, the student demonstrated a simple but important principle: titles and texts that are readable command more attention than

those that aren't. Always use letters that are easy to read.

Commercial Lettering

All letters, whether they're titles, subtitles, headings, subheads or text, need to be readable. Commercially produced letters are best if you can afford them. Literally thousands of type styles are available today, and the beginning designer can easily be overwhelmed by the sheer number of choices. Fortunately, the situation really is far less complicated. The basic choice is between "serif" and "sans serif" type styles. Serif type styles have a serif, a bar or "tail" connected to the ends of each letter. Sans serif type styles don't have tails. Witteborg (1981) and Trapp et al. (1991) recommended two basic type styles (one serif and one sans serif) that can be used in almost any kind of exhibit, indoor or outdoor (see Figure 8-21). These are Times Roman (a legible serif type style) and Helvetica (a block style, very readable sans serif type). Both are used extensively in exhibits and signs all over the world, and they're two of the most common type styles found in computer word processing programs. Their popularity is due to their appearance: they have "personality," but not too much, they're pleasant to view, and most important, they're readable. Since these and other "conservative" type styles are available in bold, italics, and in many different sizes, they're extremely versatile. Some common serif and sans serif characters are included in Appendix C. You can use them as tracing templates if you have to make your own letters.

You can get these and other typefaces at art supply stores in either transfer letters ("press type") or vinyl stick-on

Two Old Favorites—Times Roman and Helvetica

A a *A a*   **A a** ***A a***

Normal   Italic   Normal   Italic
Times Roman (a serif type style)   Helvetica (a sans serif type style)

Figure 8-21. Popular serif and sans serif type styles. (Templates of similar characters are included in Appendix C.)

letters. In indoor exhibits you may be able to use the letters directly in the exhibit. If you're producing an outdoor exhibit, however, you'll probably want to transfer the letter shapes to the actual surface and then paint them. We'll discuss ways to transfer type later.

Some graphic art businesses have computerized machines that can cut out vinyl letters in a wide range of colors, type styles, and sizes. When applied to a smooth background surface, these letters appear painted or silk-screened. The effect is professional, and it's often available at much less cost than a professional sign maker would charge, especially when long term costs are considered.

You can purchase letters for large titles and subtitles at most art supply stores. Three-dimensional letters add emphasis to the title. You can get them in many different sizes and materials including wood, cork, cardboard, plastic, plaster, and even metal. Some people save money by buying one set of commercial letters, and using them as templates for making their own letters. For example, they can trace the outline of needed characters onto a desired type of material (for example, colored paper, cardboard, wood, cork, Styrofoam, etc.), cut them out with a tool

appropriate for the material (a sharp knife, coping saw, jig saw, or hack saw), and then apply them with glue to the exhibit.

If you're near a city, you ought to see about having your text typeset. Typesetting is done by machine (mostly by computer, today) which produces any number of different typefaces in a range of sizes and in light, medium, bold and italic versions. Most universities, printers, newspapers and magazine publishers have typesetting machines. In large cities you may be able to find "type houses," businesses that specialize in producing typefaces. In some cases you may be able to get a small amount of copy typeset free of charge. In most cases, however, you'll have to pay. Prices can vary a lot, so "shop around" a little.

Some Ways to Produce Your Own Lettering

Since our focus is on exhibits that don't cost a lot of money, there's a chance you'll be making some or all of your own letters. We'll discuss several ways to do this. You should note that many of these methods are time-consuming, and that they produce results that may be acceptable for a given situation, but certainly not professional quality. If you can afford more sophisticated techniques you should consult a professional exhibit fabricator (Trapp et al. 1991, Witteborg 1981, Neal 1976, and Neal 1969 are good sources of additional information for English-language readers). Nevertheless, the methods do work, and if you're financially constrained but willing to invest the necessary time, you'll be able to produce titles and texts superior to hand lettering.

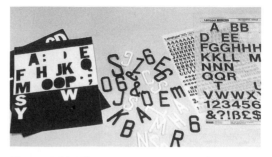

Figure 8-22. Three common types of commercial letters: transfer letters, vinyl adhesive, and three-dimensional letters. (Photo by Gerry Snyder)

Computer-Generated Type

Computers are increasingly common, even in very remote locations, and by far, the preferred method of creating text for a homemade exhibit. Most commercial word processing programs support a number of typefaces and accept supplementary fonts that can be added to them. The limiting factor in generating type with a computer usually isn't the computer or software, but rather the printer. High resolution laser printers are the best, but others printers may give acceptable results, too, especially if the required type size isn't large. You can use the printed results directly in an exhibit or photocopy them to other paper.

Word processors make arranging the text of an exhibit easy. Their main advantage is that they allow you to try out different ideas and get immediate feedback. With just a key stroke or two you can change typefaces, letter sizes, line lengths, spacing between lines, and justification. If you don't like how the text looks, you can make a change and see the results almost instantaneously. If you have access to a word processor and a good printer, there really is no reason to consider any of the other five lettering methods described here.

Manual Lettering Machines

Some offices have machines for making letters. Probably most common is the Kroy Lettering Machine, an easy-to-use lettering device that's operated simply by turning a dial to the letter desired and pushing a button. Each character is transferred in a desired color to transparent tape which can later be adhered to paper or some other surface. Since letters and sentences can be created in sequence and with proper spacing, you can avoid the time consuming task of positioning each character individually as you must with other methods. Results can be used directly, but because the tape glares, and with time will yellow, it's usually better to transfer the final layout before using it in an exhibit.

Although they're getting harder to find, a good typewriter can produce acceptable results if nothing else is available. A fresh ribbon and clean paper are an essential combination. Typed copy can be used directly or transferred onto different paper.

Leroy Lettering Guide

With some practice, you can produce very neat and legible copy using a "Leroy" lettering guide. With the advent of computers and cheap available typesetting services, Leroy lettering is falling out of use in many cities. But if you work in a remote area, a Leroy lettering guide may be an extremely useful piece of equipment. If you work for an agency, ask the artists at your central office about Leroy lettering sets. There's a chance one is tucked away in a closet somewhere waiting to be rediscovered by you.

Tracing from a Stencil or Template

Probably the easiest and fastest way to trace letters is to use a stencil. Stencils are commercially-made cardboard or plastic lettering guides that are available in art supply and stationery stores. You can use them to make acceptable looking letters for both indoor and outdoor exhibits. Their main advantage over other tracing methods is that you can trace directly onto the exhibit surface, avoiding the time-consuming task of making a "master" and then transferring the words to a desired surface. Another advantage is that you can easily make consistent-looking letters in most or all the sizes you'll need. Some of the other tracing methods can't be used as easily to make small letters. To use a stencil, you simply position it so that the letter you want to trace is in the right place, then fill in the stencil using a marker —black is usually best. Stencils are also useful in making wood signs. Once the outlines of the titles and text have been traced onto a piece of wood, they can be routed (or carved out with a gouging tool) and then painted. (See "Making

Figure 8-23. An example of unacceptable lettering. Besides the hard-to-read letters, the word "common" is misspelled. (Photo by Sam Ham)

Inexpensive Outdoor Wooden Signs" later in this chapter.)

We've already seen how to use commercially produced three-dimensional letters as templates for tracing. But what if you can't afford to buy them? Fortunately, if you have the time and a steady hand, tracing can be accomplished in two additional ways. With some light and a piece of white paper, you can use the lettering grid in Appendix C to trace block-style capital letters for titles and main headings. If you need letters that are larger than the ones this guide will produce, make an enlarged photocopy of the page or use the "projection method" discussed later in this chapter. Although lower case letters aren't as easy to make with this guide, with some practice and experimentation you'll be able to master that, too. You can make two or three-dimensional letters by tracing the letters onto a piece of white paper, superimposing the paper over a sheet of colored paper, cardboard or other desired material, and cutting out the letters with a sharp knife or other tool (see the "cut-paste" transfer method). The "circular form" in the upper left hand corner of the guide provides circles of the proper diameter for making the letters B, C, D, G, R, S, and U. This method works best if you're making large letters. Small letters are hard to cut out smoothly.

A third tracing method works exactly the same way as the second except that it involves tracing letters directly from the serif and sans serif type style templates shown in Appendix C. It's usually best to select one of these type styles, not both, for the body text of an exhibit. (Often, however, a serif type style is used in the title and sans serif type in the body text of the same exhibit.) Since both upper and lower case letters are provided, you can use the templates to produce both titles and text (as long as it's not too small). Be warned, however, that this is a time-consuming task because of the care you'll have to take in getting everything lined up and spaced properly. Give yourself plenty of time. Do the tracing on a light table if you have one. As with the previous tracing method, if the letters in the templates are too small for your needs, use a photocopier to enlarge the templates before tracing, or enlarge the traced text using the "projection method" discussed in the next section. This tracing method works best if you're making large letters. Small letters are hard to cut out smoothly. (If you prefer a type style other than those provided in Appendix C, you could buy a sheet of transfer letters in the desired style and use it as the template.)

Hand Lettering

As a last resort, you may need to hand letter parts or all of the exhibit. This can be acceptable if you're a neat printer and take great care in making each letter. Guides on printing technique are abundant. Good ones in English are Neal (1964) and Meyer (1984). In Spanish, Muñoz and Peña (1990) present several useful tips on painting letters and writing with felt markers.

Three Inexpensive Ways to Transfer Titles and Text

Although it's sometimes possible to do your lettering work in one step, it's often better to prepare a master and then transfer it to the material or surface that will go into the exhibit. If your budget won't allow you to pay for a professional to transfer your titles and text, you can do it yourself in one or more of three ways. The first two (photocopying and the cut-paste method), apply to indoor exhibits only. The third (the projection method) can be used with any kind of exhibit. Although we're talking specifically about titles, copy, and textual material here, these methods also could be used for transferring other design elements such as drawings and illustrations. (Additional ways to produce inexpensive illustrations are presented in Chapter 4.) Good descriptions of more expensive transfer methods (such as silk-screening, sand-blasting, fiberglass embedments, and metal-imaging processes) can be found in Witteborg (1981), Trapp et al. (1991), and Fazio and Gilbert (1986).

Photocopying

As described in Chapter 4, once each title or block of text has been prepared on white paper, you can photocopy it onto any kind of paper you wish (including colored or textured paper). The photocopies, in turn, can be mounted on cardboard, foam core, plastic or other sturdy backing for mounting in an indoor exhibit. This method wouldn't be good for most outdoor exhibits because it's so hard to

1. Word processor and printer

2. Manual lettering machine

3. Lettering template

4. Tracing grid (see Appendix C)

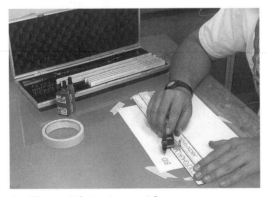

5. "Leroy" lettering guide

6. Tracing on a light table

Figure 8-24. Six ways to produce inexpensive lettering. (Photos by Gerry Snyder)

protect paper from moisture. Before beginning, wash your hands in order to avoid unsightly finger prints and smudges on the photocopy. It's best to use rubber (contact) cement or spray-on adhesive (photo-mount) to attach the photocopy to the backing. Be careful not to use too much adhesive (see "Making Exhibits Visual" in the next section of this chapter). Attach the mounted piece to the exhibit with a good glue or rubber cement, if possible. Scotch brand adhesive "squares" are even better if you can get them. If you have to use nails, clip off their heads afterwards, and if possible, "touch up" the exposed ends with a little paint or dye that matches the color of the photocopy. Staples can also be disguised with matching paint. Generally, mounting the backing with thumb tacks and "push pins" is not a good idea.

Cut-Paste Method

The cut-paste transfer method has already been described somewhat. It involves cutting out a traced letter and gluing it in place in an exhibit. You do this by placing an individually traced letter onto the desired material and cutting it out. This procedure requires some care and patience to achieve a smooth and uniform appearance. For three-dimensional materials such as wood or plastic, it's a good idea to adhere the paper containing the traced letter onto the material before cutting. Rubber cement works fine. For best results (see Figure 8-25), glue the traced image *backward* onto the *back* of the material you're transferring it to. That way, you can glue the whole image firmly to the backing. This makes cutting easier because you don't have to worry about marring the front side of the letter. When

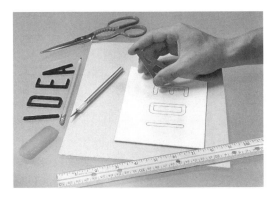

Figure 8-25. Using the "cut-paste" transfer method. Notice that the letter is traced and cut out backward on the back of the mounting surface. This is done to minimize the chance of marring the visible surface of the letter. (Photo by Gerry Snyder)

tracing, you'll need to use a dark pencil or felt-tipped pen to be able to see the reversed tracing lines through the back of the paper. Be sure to use a sharp cutting tool. A cardboard pad placed under the backing will help you make smoother cuts and protect the table you're working on. If the backing is made of wood or plastic, you'll need a saw (such as a coping saw or jig saw). Once each letter is cut out, you can paint it or mount it as it is.

Projection Method

The projection method was described in detail in Chapter 4. It involves projecting the image of a letter, a title or even a whole body of text onto a desired surface and tracing the outlines. Once the outlines have been traced, they can be painted or colored. If you're making a wood sign, you could route the traced letters before painting them. (See "Making Inexpensive Outdoor Wooden Signs" later in this chapter.) Remember to select colors

Figure 8-26. Using the projection method to transfer letters. In this case, the person is using an opaque projector. (Photo by Gerry Snyder)

that contrast in value (i.e., dark letters on a lighter background or vice versa).

Thinking you'll save time, you may be tempted to try projecting the text, letter-by-letter, directly from a lettering guide or template onto the exhibit surface. In theory, this seems a reasonable idea, but in practice you'll probably find that it ends up taking more time and that the results will be inferior. That's because you'll have to reposition the projector for each letter. If the projector isn't oriented to the tracing surface at precisely the same angle each time, your letters won't appear very uniform, and in fact, will probably look distorted. This creates a serious challenge for even a ten- or fifteen-letter title. Imagine how difficult it would be for 200 words of copy! For best results, try the following:

(1) Using a chosen method of making letters (one of those we earlier discussed, or some other method), prepare the text you want to project (a title, a block of copy, etc.) on a piece of white paper. As you make each letter and word, make sure to space them the way you want them to look in the exhibit. This is your camera-ready master. (See "Spacing Between Letters," "Spacing Between Words," and "Spacing Between Lines" earlier in this chapter.)

(2) Prepare the master for projection. As we discussed in Chapter 4, if you're going to use a slide projector you'll need to take a picture of the master using slide film. Be sure to position the camera at a 90° degree angle (perpendicular) to the paper so that the shapes of the letters won't be distorted. If you're going to use an overhead projector, have an acetate transparency made. If you'll be using an opaque projector, you needn't do anything else because you can project the image directly off the paper master.

(3) Attach the surface you want to transfer the words to on a wall. (If it's a piece of wood you may want to put it on a table and prop it straight up against the wall.) Turn on the projector and align it at a 90° degree angle to the surface. If the projector doesn't have a zoom lens, move it forward or backward until the letters are the size you want them. Be sure to readjust the projector's focus each time you move it.

(4) Once you've found the right image size, begin carefully tracing the lines of each letter. To minimize the annoying shadow that your hands will cast on your work, keep the room partially lighted. (Refer to the instructions in Chapter 4 for additional tips on tracing.)

(5) Depending on what you've planned, when the tracing is completed

you can use it as it is, or utilize either the photocopying or cut-paste methods to further prepare it for the exhibit. This method is especially useful for producing large letters and banner-size words. Unless you have a very steady hand, it wouldn't be very useful for creating type smaller than, say, 72-point (2 cm or 3/4-inch).

Adding Interest to Exhibits

Because exhibits are usually a one-way communication medium, making them interesting can be challenging. Adding interest is particularly important when you're designing an exhibit for a museum or interpretive center that already contains a lot of other exhibits. Viewers tire quickly when they're doing a lot of reading (a condition called "museum fatigue"), especially when they've been standing on their feet the entire time viewing exhibit after exhibit. One way to reduce museum fatigue is to provide benches, rails, foot rests and other resting devices for visitors (see Neal 1976 for detailed descriptions of these methods). Another way to reduce fatigue is simply to make your exhibits as interesting and as stimulating as possible. Studies have shown that there are at least three inexpensive ways to do this: (1) you can make exhibits visual, (2) you can make them three-dimensional, and (3) you can make them interactive or "participatory." Following are some ideas for how to give exhibits each of these qualities. Remember, however, that these are simply ideas to consider, not hard and fast rules, and they may not all apply to every exhibit.

Making Exhibits Visual

Most exhibits contain words, even if only a title, but that doesn't mean that the words have to convey all or even most of the message. As we've seen repeatedly in this chapter and in Chapter 4, visuals are powerful communicators. Don't forget this when you're planning an exhibit. For every word you consider, consider also whether a visual might serve you better. This won't always be the case, but if you let this become your guiding philosophy of exhibit design, you'll find that your exhibits will soon be saying more with less (words, that is).

Take advantage of existing visual materials such as maps, magazine photographs, pictorial calendars, and artwork, if you have access to them. Be sure to request permission to use copyrighted materials. But if you describe your need and financial situation, and if you work for a government or nonprofit organization, you'll usually be granted permission and asked simply to credit the source. (If you're denied permission, however, you'll need to search for a different illustration to use in your exhibit.) Materials printed on paper can be mounted on a sturdy backing (such as cardboard, construction board, foam core, masonite, or particle board) for use in the exhibit. To avoid "bleeding," it's best to use rubber cement

Figure 8-27. A highly visual exhibit with minimum text. Although the theme is unclear without further reading, the appearance is visually inviting. Columbia River Gorge, Mt. Hood National Forest. (Photo by Sam Ham)

or a spray adhesive to mount artwork that's printed on thin paper (this includes most magazine photographs). Water-based glues will moisten the paper allowing the material printed on the other side of the photograph to "bleed" through, effectively destroying your visual aid. Be sure to apply adhesive to both surfaces before attaching the illustration to the backing. Many visual aids are three-dimensional or can be made to be three-dimensional. These are discussed next.

Making Exhibits Three-Dimensional

Studies have shown that three-dimensional exhibits are more interesting to viewers than flat ones. Although some exhibits are, by nature, three-dimensional (e.g., dioramas and models), adding a third dimension to almost any indoor exhibit is easy. Following are eight inexpensive ways to do this. Although you might be able to apply a few of these methods to certain kinds of outdoor exhibits, you should carefully consider the climatic conditions and the potential for vandalism and theft before doing so. (Several of the examples in Appendix B are especially suited to three-dimensional exhibits.)

1. You can use three-dimensional letters in the title. If you have the money, you can purchase three-dimensional letters made from any of several different materials (see "Commercial Lettering"), or you can use one of the tracing methods to make your own (see "Cut and Paste Method"). If you make your own letters, be sure to use a sharp cutting tool so that your cuts will be smooth and uniform. You might want to use paint or a felt-tipped marker to color the exposed edges of each letter. Black is often best.

2. You can hide "spacers" behind mounted photographs or blocks of text in order to bring them out from the wall. You can use almost any three-dimensional material as a "spacer." Small pieces of wood or even sturdy cardboard work fine. The thickness of the spacers depends on the distance you want between the mounted material and the wall. Generally, you shouldn't make them so thick that they'll be visible. Commonly they're between about 1/4 to 1 inch (6 to 25 mm).

3. You can put a real object or prop in the foreground of an exhibit case. Even if the rest of the exhibit is only two-dimensional, such an object can give the whole design a three-dimensional quality. If the object is large, you'll probably need to place it low in the design, if not on the floor. Smaller items may look better higher in the exhibit. As with many of the techniques that follow, adding a small label that identifies the object is often a good idea, but it's not always necessary.

4. You can make three-dimensional supports for displaying objects and specimens. Boxes and shelves are especially easy to make if you have the wood or other material. Boxes (usually called "pedestals") can be made different heights and widths so that objects of different sizes can be placed on top of them and extend to different heights in the design. Painting the boxes, varnishing them, or covering them with a fabric (such as velvet, flannel, or cotton) adds to the three-dimensional appearance. Shelves can be the simple "L" kind (back and bottom only). You can mount them on the background surface with screws and put objects or specimens on top of them.

5. You can make a small plastic or plexiglass box (using glue) and put small objects or specimens (such as artifacts,

mounted birds or small mammals, insects, etc.) inside of them. You can mount the boxes directly to the background surface or place them on a shelf. Besides adding a third dimension, plastic boxes make the items they contain seem important. If you're not experienced working with plastic and glue you might want to ask the advice of a plastics specialist before attempting your own boxes. Commercially-made plexiglass boxes are surprisingly expensive. But if you're good with your hands, you can make nice-looking boxes of your own.

6. You can mount three-dimensional objects on the background surface of the exhibit or on a wall adjacent to your exhibit. Using thick wire or bent nails (be sure to clip the heads off after bending), you can hang things like tools, implements, tree limbs, and other relatively heavy objects on a vertical surface without having to mar them with a screw or nail.

7. You can suspend especially large objects from the ceiling above an exhibit if the building is well constructed and there's enough clearance. Examples of suspendable items include plows, carts, tools, large mounted birds with wings extended, and large animal skeletons or parts thereof, among other things. Depending on the size of the item you want to hang, ceilings usually must be at least 12 feet (4 m) high to avoid injury to viewers or damage to the object. If the object you want to hang isn't too heavy, you might be able to safely attach it directly to the ceiling using toggle bolts or "molly" ("butterfly") bolts. For heavy items, however, it may be safer to drill one or more holes through the ceiling and firmly attach the wire(s) to a piece of framing in the attic. Be sure to plaster and paint over the holes afterwards. A sturdy, well-built

ceiling or building frame is absolutely necessary. Use only strong thick wire for hanging heavy objects.

8. You can glue small replaceable or perishable items such as plant specimens, nuts or cones directly to an exhibit surface. To hang heavier objects like small rocks and dense pieces of wood, use "super-glue." Don't directly glue any object that's valuable or irreplaceable. Once it's glued to a wall, it's essentially destroyed.

Making Exhibits Interactive

Interactive exhibits invite viewers to participate physically in the learning process. That is, they give them something to do. Besides being more enjoyable, interactive exhibits are better "teachers" than static ones. Four popular types of interactive exhibits are **quiz boards, arrow-window boards, mechanical exhibits** and **tactile exhibits**. All four types can be used outdoors as well as indoors, but be sure to consider climatic conditions and the potential for vandalism and theft if you're planning to use them outdoors. Use interactive techniques to create variety in your exhibits, but don't try to make every exhibit interactive. Doing so would make all your exhibits seem the same. Occasionally, large urban science centers have this problem. They may have dozens of nice looking (and expensive) interactive exhibits, each one very well designed. But after an hour of pushing buttons, pulling knobs, and playing games they all start to seem alike to their viewers, even though each exhibit is somehow novel. Remember, all emphasis is equivalent to no emphasis.

An exhibit becomes a *quiz board* simply by giving viewers a chance to test their

a) Using "spacers" behind two-dimensional objects, Salango Museum, Manabí, Ecuador. (Photo by Sam Ham)

b) Placing three-dimensional objects on pedestals, Salango Museum, Manabí, Ecuador. (Photo by Sam Ham)

c) Placing artifacts on the bottom and back wall of a display case, Ft. Columbia State Park, Ilwaco, Washington. (Photo by Steve Wang)

d) Mounting objects on shelves, Ginkgo Petrified Forest State Park, Vantage, Washington. (Photo by Steve Wang)

e) Hanging large objects on the wall, Old Mission State Park, Idaho. (Photo by Bill Scudder)

f) Placing artifacts in a plastic box, Old Mission State Park, Idaho. (Photo by Bill Scudder)

Figure 8-28. Some ways to add a third dimension to exhibits.

knowledge. Providing feedback to viewers is the key feature of a quiz board. The two most common formats are question-and-answer boards and matching games. Question-and-answer boards pose one or more questions to the viewer. Correct answers (the feedback) are usually provided under a hinged flap or cover of some kind. (In some cases, viewers are instructed to cover up correct answers with their hands.)

Matching games are often a little more elaborate. Typically, they present the viewer some set of objects (e.g., several different bird nests) and another set of related items (e.g., photographs or drawings of different birds) and ask the viewer to test his or her knowledge by matching each item in the first group to one of the objects in the second group. In our example, for instance, we'd ask viewers to match each bird nest to the kind of bird that built it. Matching may be mental (using labels like A,B,C, etc., in one group and 1,2,3, etc., in the other group) or it may be electronic (e.g., each correct match causes an electrical circuit to be completed which in turn illuminates a light or rings a buzzer, etc.). If you use mental matching, be sure to provide a list of the correct answers so that viewers can find out how well they did. You could build this list directly into the exhibit (be sure to cover it), or it could be kept nearby (at the information desk or in a notebook). Generally, it's best to provide the answers in the exhibit, itself, but if this isn't practical be sure the exhibit informs viewers where they can get the correct answers.

Arrow-window exhibits are just what the name says. They have an arrow (usually painted or drawn on a large wheel of some kind). On the background of the exhibit are different headings or illustrations corresponding to different topics. Viewers can rotate the wheel to make the arrow point at any topic of interest. As this is done, information related to the topic (usually some interesting, important or surprising fact) is exposed in a window on the opposite side of the wheel. Instructions for a simple window-arrow exhibit are included in Brace et al. (1982).

Mechanical exhibits include some type of device that viewers can operate. This device doesn't necessarily have to demonstrate or teach anything (for example, visitors may simply push a button to start a tape player, or pull a handle to expose a picture or some kind of information). Often, however, mechanical exhibits involve viewers in an activity that is, itself, instructive (e.g., turning a crank or pushing a plunger to see how a cider press or butter churn works, inverting a jar containing sediment and water to see how soil erosion affects domestic water supplies, etc.).

Tactile exhibits invite viewers to touch objects that are being displayed. The objects are usually labeled and either mounted (on a wall or large board) or simply placed on a table. Good touchable objects include things like rocks, soil samples, animal bones, antlers and horns, pieces of animal skins, fur and hair, shells, aromatic plants, nuts, fossils, and common (easily replaceable) artifacts. Since exhibit viewers so often are asked not to touch things, it's usually a good idea to include a sign or placard that invites them to handle the objects (e.g., "Please Touch!"). Be sure not to include sharp objects or anything that might be dangerous to viewers. Also, don't put artifacts or stuffed/mounted animals into a tactile display if they're valuable, irreplaceable, fragile, or especially significant. There's a good

a

b

c

d

Figure 8-29. Examples of low-cost interactive exhibits: (a) arrow-window board, La Tigra National Park, Honduras (photo by Sam Ham); (b) quiz board, Dean Creek Elk Viewing Area, Reedsport, Oregon (photo by Jim Gale); (c) tactile exhibit, Pacific Science Center, Seattle, Washington (photo by Sam Ham); and (d) mechanical exhibit, Fort Canby State Park, Ilwaco, Washington (photo by Sam Ham).

chance they'll deteriorate, get broken, or even worse, be stolen. It's easy to turn a tactile display into a quiz board. All you have to do is include a sign that asks viewers if they can identify the objects on display. Label each object with a number or letter and provide a list that tells which is which.

Making Inexpensive Outdoor Wooden Signs

Probably the most common type of outdoor exhibit is the wooden sign. Although commercially-produced wooden signs can be expensive, you can make attractive ones yourself even if you have only enough money for the wood, posts, and paint. This is accomplished by routing or carving out letters and/or simple drawings that have been transferred to the wood, and then painting them a desired color scheme. Following are instructions for making a simple wood-routed sign. (See Appendix B for examples of sign shapes and installations.)

Step 1: Select the sign posts and decide how you'll mount the sign to them. Although you won't actually attach the sign to the posts until later, you need to plan how to do it before making the sign. If you don't, you may end up having to drill a hole through a word or illustration, effectively ruining it, in order to mount the sign on the post(s). Pick sign posts that are long enough to support the sign at the desired level once they've been put in the ground. Plan to submerge the posts at least 3 feet (1 m) into the ground. The thicker and heavier the posts, the more resistant they'll be to weather and vandals. Although one post may be sufficient for some signs, two are almost always better.

Step 2: Cut and sand the wood you're going to use as the sign face. Carefully clean all the dust from the wood when you're done sanding. If you don't have a router or electric carving tool to use in step 3, choose a softer wood. Consult a lumber store to find out what species of wood are best for outdoor signs in your area. The thickness of the wood is also important. The minimum recommended thickness is .5 inch (1 cm). Larger signs, of course, require thicker wood. If the sign is going to be very large, you should make the sign face by laminating smaller pieces of wood together (using a good outdoor glue). Trapp et al. (1991) recommended inserting threaded rods (long screws) in order to hold the pieces of wood firmly

together. If at all possible, it's a good idea to drill the mounting holes in the sign face and post(s) now.

Step 3: Using a pencil, trace or transfer the desired words and illustrations onto the wood. If you didn't actually drill the mounting holes as recommended in step 1, at least make sure you know exactly where they're going to be drilled. Don't put words or illustrations in those spots. To avoid a cluttered look, it's best to leave a left and right margin for the mounting holes and confine the design to the part of the sign face inside the margins. Avoid small letters and highly detailed artwork. Letters smaller than about .75 inch (2 cm) may cause problems in step 3 unless you have a gouging tool or router bit small enough to follow them. For the same reason, illustrations such as simple maps, trail routes, and outline drawings of trees, leaves, or animal shapes are usually easier to make than complex drawings.

Step 4: With a router or gouging tool, carefully cut out (or carve) the letters and drawings. Be careful to stay within the pencil marks of the outlines. If you're using a gouging tool, be careful to cut the grooves the same depth throughout the sign. Use a ruler to check the depth of each cut. A good depth for most signs is 1/8 in (3 mm). Be conservative in cutting. You can always deepen a groove that's too shallow, but you can't do the reverse.

Step 5: Choose a simple color scheme using the following guidelines:

a. If the sign will be located in bright sunlight, consider painting the background a dark color (such as brown, reddish-brown or a dark shade of some other color) and the letters and artwork lighter colors (such as white, yellow, or high value shades of other colors). See "Using

Color Value to Produce Desired Effects" earlier in this chapter.

b. If the sign will be located in strong shade (such as in a forest or under a protective cover), consider painting the background a light color and the letters and artwork darker colors.

c. If desirable, you can add accent colors to embellish the artwork. (See "How to Select a Color Scheme" earlier in this chapter.)

Step 6: Paint the sign. It's usually easier to paint the background surface first and then to paint the letters and artwork. Some sign makers recommend using a squeeze bottle to apply paint to letters and artwork, and then to use a very small brush to spread the paint evenly in each groove. Exterior paints are best. The better the paint, the longer it will last. If you plan to cover the painted sign with a varnish or sealer, be sure to select a paint that won't react with the type of coating you're going to use. It's best to ask the advice of someone who sells paint. Make sure the paint is completely dry before coating it.

Step 7: Unless you want a rustic look, it's a good idea to protect the sign face with two or more coats of varnish or wood sealer before installing it outdoors. Before coating your painted sign, test the coating on a scrap piece of wood that has been painted with the same paints you used on the sign.

Step 8: Treat the posts. If you can afford pressure-treated posts, buy them. They'll save money in the long run. If you can't afford them, you can treat each post by soaking it (or the part of it that will be underground) in a wood preservative for at least two days. There are many kinds of wood preservatives. One commercial preservative, called "Wood Pressure," is reportedly safe and can be painted over once it's dry. Another commercial water repellent is pentachlorophenol (or simply "penta"). Although it's an excellent water repellent, penta has been outlawed in many countries as a health hazard. If it's available where you work, be extremely careful with it. Wear protective rubber gloves at all times when using it, and dispose of it properly. Observing these precautions, you can soak the post ends in a solution of 100 percent penta or in a mixture containing 10 percent penta and 90 percent used motor oil. According to Brace et al. (1982), used motor oil (old crankcase oil) can also be used by itself. They point out, however, that the oil may contain chemicals harmful to some cattle (and presumably to local wildlife). As a substitute, pure creosote or creosote mixed in even proportions with used motor oil will also work. If you plan to paint the posts, treat only the part that will be put underground.

Step 9: Mount the sign to the post(s). Use bolts and nuts (not nails). Optional: If

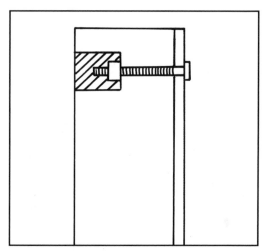

Figure 8-30. Counter-sinking the bolt holes on a mounted sign.

a)

b)

c)

Figure 8-31. Examples of sign installations: (a) poor installation—the sign is merely propped up using rocks; (b) good installation—the sign post is packed firmly into a deep hole; (c) good installation—the sign is suspended securely from massive posts deeply imbedded in the ground. (Photos by Sam Ham)

you have a ratchet and a deep-well socket, you can "counter-sink" the bolt holes to prevent theft of the signs. On the back of each post, drill a shallow but slightly wider hole over the top of the original bolt hole. The second hole should be only wide enough for your socket to fit over the nut for tightening. You'll know how deep to make the hole by looking at how far the bolt will extend into the post from the front side (be sure to take into account the thickness of the sign face and a washer). When you're done, only the last centimeter or so of the bolt's threads should extend past the end of the original bolt hole. Put the nut on the bolt and tighten it with the socket. You can then fill in each hole with plastic wood or other hardening filler and paint over it to hide the nuts. In areas where signs and sign posts frequently become firewood, counter-sinking can be especially important. Another way to make bolts vandal-resistant is to file the corners off the heads so that a wrench or socket can't grab hold for turning. To keep vandals from sawing the support posts, park managers in Ecuador have even "spiked" the posts. That is, they've driven long nails deep into the post in random patterns (punched to embed the heads) so that a saw can't easily be used to cut through them.

Step 10: Install the finished sign. Don't try to support the sign posts with a pile of rocks. Put the sign posts in holes that are at least 3 feet (1 m) deep. A sign that is intended to be viewed 1 foot (.3 m) above the ground will require a 4 feet (1.2 m) post. A very rough rule is that at least one third of the total length of the post should be underground. For example, a 8 feet (2.5 m) post would have at least 2.5 feet (80 cm) underground, and a 12 feet (4 m) post would have 4 feet (1.3 m)

underground. If you're using more than one post, their holes must be the same depth or the sign won't be level. Although it's possible to firmly install a post in soil (perhaps using an occasional rock to help compact the soil), the only truly effective way to prevent your sign from being stolen is to use cement. A gravel bed and a piece of "rebar" (scrap iron rods or even just long nails or spikes driven partially through the post bottom on all sides) will help hold the post securely in the cement. Even if you don't use cement, putting rebar into the post is a good idea because it makes pulling the post out of the ground much more difficult.

A Word About Regulatory Signs

Signs that simply list all of an area's rules are usually a waste of time and money. That's because few, if any, people will read them. As emphasized earlier, all exhibits—even regulatory signs—should be thematic. In other words, they should communicate a message about the rules, not merely list them. Thinking thematically, you would ask yourself: "What rules are most important, and what do I need to say to get them across to people?" Studies show that giving the reason for a rule is almost always going to be more effective than just giving the rule, itself. Research also shows that when observing the rule will benefit the viewer as well as the site, it's best to tell how. For example, if a road is closed to motor vehicles because of soil erosion problems, the closure sign might show a car or truck hopelessly stuck in the mud. Signs asking park visitors not to feed wild animals have been shown to be more successful when they stress the danger to *visitors* rather than just the impact

Figure 8-32. Examples of thematic regulatory signs. In each case, the theme is the regulation and the reason behind it: (a) management message, Newberry Crater National Monument, Bend, Oregon (photo by Jim Gale); (b) safety message, Mount St. Helens National Volcanic Monument (photo by Jim Gale); (c) bilingual warning sign, Manuel Antonio National Park, Costa Rica (photo by Sam Ham).

on the animals. Similarly, signs in natural areas that ask people to keep their pets on a leash are more effective when they stress the safety of the pet rather than the danger to the wild animals that live there. And signs asking people to stay on trails may be more effective when they stress the benefits to the hiker (e.g., avoiding contact with poisonous plants or the danger of loose rocks). A moment's reflection will remind you that this is precisely the principle we discussed in Chapter 1: information

that's connected to something people care about (in this case, their well-being and that of their pets) will almost always attract attention.

Of course, not all rules are intended to benefit people directly. For example, sometimes people need to be kept on trails simply because the site is being degraded. Staying on the trail doesn't really benefit them, and it would be dishonest to tell them that it would. But research shows that even in a situation like this, giving the reason for the rule will more likely lead to compliance than a sign that simply gives the rule. For example, an area that's closed for regeneration might have a sign that says: "Area Temporarily Closed for Recuperation," or "Newly Seeded Area— Temporarily Closed." Signs such as "Keep Out," "Stay on Trail," or simply "Closed" wouldn't have the same effect. That's because they don't say anything; they're not thematic. Too many regulatory signs lack themes.

A final point has to do with the tone of regulatory signs. They should be firm, but not necessarily negative. When an adult tells a child "Don't," it usually achieves its purpose (depending, of course, on the child). But as adults, we respond to the "don't" word differently. There are probably a lot of reasons for this, but one may be that we're simply not awed by the assumed authority of the "don't" sayer quite the way we were as children. As a child, we paid notice when almost any adult said "no" or "don't." As adults, we sometimes ignore or even question authority, and particularly problematic adults may even openly defy it. Obviously, signs that simply say "No" or "Don't" to adult viewers aren't going to be very effective.

Signs that politely ask for compliance seem to be more accepted by adults than those which merely demand it. An example is littering. There have been many studies on ways to convince people to use trash barrels instead of throwing their garbage on the ground. Decorated garbage cans, trash barrels made to look like hungry animals, and pleasant little reminders about the benefits of a clean environment are but a few of the communication strategies that have been found to work best (Geller et al. 1982). But no study has ever found a sign that says "No Littering" or "Don't Litter" to be effective. This being the case, one really must wonder why so many signs still have these awful words on them. Phrases such as "Keep Your Forest Clean" or "A Clean Environment is a Healthy Environment" would probably be at least as effective— and they would certainly be better from a public relations standpoint.

Glossary terms: analogous colors, arrow-window exhibit, balance, color scheme, color temperature, color value, complementary colors, copy, emphasis, exhibit, levels, mechanical exhibit, quiz board, sign, tactile exhibit, text, theme-title, type style, unity.

Planning Exhibits– Creative Teamwork Puts Magic in the Message

Jim Gale, Chief Interpreter
Ralph Naess, Interpretive Specialist
Mount St. Helens National
Volcanic Monument
Gifford Pinchot National Forest,
Vancouver, Washington

In planning dozens of exhibits, we've found that the magic in the message usually comes from a creative team process. It's said that "when one bamboo blossoms, all the bamboo blossom at the same time." This could well have been said to describe our team approach to creative exhibit planning.

Each time an exhibit increases a visitor's heartbeat, it represents the success of the team process. This is a fragile process that requires nurturing so that the "wild ideas" (the ones that make an exhibit truly provocative) can take hold.

We've found that only the rare interpreter can create an exciting, interpretive exhibit alone, whereas the support and creative input from a team process almost always brings an exhibit to life. This case study briefly describes how we do it.

Creating the Team

Creating the team nurtures the roots of success. The principle of synergy posits that the whole is greater than the sum of the parts: The interpretive specialist should take the lead in gathering the team and guiding the process. The team should always start with someone who: (a) understands thematic interpretation and (b) is familiar with the subject, the land and the audience. Other team members could include interpreters, graphic artists, illustrators, designers, public information staff, and other specialist (scientists, historians, passionate people who are knowledgeable about the topic). In addition, some people may be politically necessary to include as team members (e.g., bosses or those whose approval on written material is required, etc.). If you don't try to involve these people at the start, you might run into serious obstacles later on. If they don't want to be involved, make sure they understand your process and agree to accept the product that comes out of the process.

It may happen that you have more team members than you can

handle. If so, you may have to select a few players that will stay with the process all the way through, and let other players play a supportive role. For instance, a manager may be very important in the initial stages when the characteristics of an ideal exhibit are being formulated. The manager's early acceptance of the process and realization of its potential empower the team to create a superb exhibit; yet he/she may only want to see the final product at the end.

If you don't have a team of people to work with, involve your friends, neighbors, and family. This can be an eye opener, as these people are likely to be your "audience" at some point. If you can, get them out to the site, and ask, "What do you want to learn about here?" Listen very carefully to what they say, watch how they move and note what they're attracted to. This will be your best indication as to what is interesting to your future audience. Once you've developed the first draft of the exhibit text and graphics, ask them, "What do you think the message is in this exhibit?" If they respond with something close to the theme of the exhibit, you know you're on the right track.

Developing a Common Vision

All members of the team should have an idea of what the elements of a good interpretive exhibit are. In general, it's one that incorporates the principles of interpretation in a provocative, creative format (see "interpretive approach to communication" in Chapter 1). At this point, the interpreter in charge of the exhibit must challenge all

involved to verbalize and visualize the characteristics of their ideal exhibit. Here are some examples of what our teams have come up with:

- Visitors will be attracted to the sign.
- Visitors will read the entire sign.
- Visitors will understand the message of the exhibit in the first 5 seconds.
- The exhibit will be easy on the eyes.
- The exhibit will look professional.
- The exhibit will look like "a work of art."
- The text will be interpretive, fun, relevant, and take the content beyond the obvious.
- The exhibit will contain more than one color.
- Etc.

The important thing is that your group find a common vision, as this forms the basis for your evaluation and development of the exhibit. Having an ideal to shoot for allows the team to use it as a measuring stick, evaluating progress and ideas against it at every step of the way. Starting with a vision of the ideal exhibit also creates an atmosphere wherein ideas for the text and illustrations become the focus of refinement, rather than the people who suggested them. In this process, critiquing ideas, not people, becomes the norm.

Clearly establishing responsibilities and expectations at the start can alleviate misunderstandings in the future. It should be clear from the start what everyone's role is. The interpretive writer is responsible for writing accurate, interpretive text. The scientific advisory person is responsible for ensuring the technical accuracy of the text, and can be invited to make editorial changes. The rest of the team is responsible for making sure the exhibit is meeting the goals, objectives and vision established at the beginning.

The Site Visit

After creating a group vision of the ideal exhibit, going to the site with the whole team is the next most important step. The on-site experience creates a common understanding of features, and what can and will be interpreted. It sets the framework for the rest of the process. Before visiting the site, make sure that all guiding documents (interpretive plan, management plan, etc.) and related information are available to the team. This may put some constraints on what is to be interpreted at this site, but don't be afraid to question it. During the field visit, the land will speak, and you all must listen. What it "says" may not be in the official plan.

Bring a chalkboard, flip chart, or other large note-taking object. Record all ideas, no matter how wild. This can be facilitated by using non-linear techniques such as clustering or mind mapping (see *Using Both Sides of Your Brain* by Tony Buzon and *Writing the Natural Way* by Gabriel Rico). Nonjudgmental response encourages creativity and sharing: All (including "good" and "bad") ideas are neutral, responded to with "uh-huh" and recorded for later reference. It's important for the interpretive writer to set the stage for this and to model it constantly throughout session. Very few people have had experience with this form of response, so it may take a conscious effort. But stay with it—it will allow all ideas, no matter how unusual, to be captured. It's always easier to tame a wild metaphor than breathe life into a dead one.

It's during the on-site experience that the land speaks to the team, just as it will speak to the visitors who come to view the exhibit. Listen carefully, because you may have arrived with a preconceived notion of what "should" be interpreted at that site, oblivious to the land and features crying out to be heard. The topic that you're interpreting has probably been interpreted before. The challenge here is to find the special (relevant, meaningful) part of the topic that fits best with the site. The brainstorming ensures that you can get from an obvious theme (e.g., bacteria cleaned the lake) to the sublime (a feeding frenzy clears the lake). Experts (biologists, ecologists, geologists, archaeologists, etc.) can provide the hidden depth of understanding. Once hundreds of ideas have been collected, the group then sits and writes themes for each exhibit. Each team member should produce three to five themes. It's hard to write themes, and people who have never written themes before need to have practice before embarking on this journey (see Chapter 2 of this book).

Before leaving the site, try to gain consensus on what the topic and theme are for each exhibit. On an interpretive trail, agree on a message for each sign.

Graphics Tell the Story

At the site, take a lot of photographs and make preliminary sketches to assist in developing the graphic elements in the exhibits. Think of how images might be created to convey the central message of each exhibit, treating text as a supporting element.

Nurturing the Process

The interpretive writer takes notes during the site visit and synthesizes them. Then, using "expert" information and the ideas from the field, he/she writes as much as possible without input from the team. This output is presented to the team along with the conceptual graphics and layout so that the team can respond to the whole concept. The process, each time with the text and graphics presented as a whole, repeats itself until the team arrives at a final concept. The team provides supportive critique by evaluating the preliminary design against the vision, goals, and objectives of the exhibit. All comments are given and accepted in the spirit of trying to achieve the ideal interpretive exhibit. How is it relevant, meaningful, personal? Does it meet the goals and objectives? How does it compare to the ideal interpretive exhibit? Carrying out this process takes time, sensitivity, and patience. Comments should not be taken as a personal attack. Comments that relate to style should be separated from comments about content. Does the theme convey the message? Does the metaphor overpower the message? Read it from the minds and hearts of the visitor. Is it at a reading level that allows all to access it? If the text is too complex, find a graphic solution. Remember what Mark Twain said, "If I'd had more time, I'd have written a shorter letter." Every word removed makes every remaining word more powerful. Once this level of critiquing has been achieved, continue it until the final, magic message is achieved.

Trust in the process. If you have a good one, you'll get a good product. We've found our creative team process can be not only fun, but it can produce the magic in the message. Contact us if you'd like to learn more about it.

Type Matters–Some Typographical Guidelines for Interpretive Texts

Richard Dahn, Co-Owner of Dahn Design
and Professor of Graphic Design,
University of Washington, Seattle, Washington

Your choice of typefaces for an interpretive sign can have a powerful effect on its appearance and audience response. In approaching typographic choices, it's helpful to keep in mind that typography has a "visual voice" that is dependent on the typeface chosen, its sizes and organization within the sign format, and the nature of the message. Emphatic messages such as EXTREME DANGER, KEEP OUT would demand the use of a heavy bold sans serif type, while a quote by Aldo Leopold would look better in a Roman serif set with generous line spacing. The visual impact of type on a sign can welcome the viewer to read and reinforce the meaning and sense of the message, or it can speak in such a dull or confused voice that the viewer will totally ignore the sign, or worse, misinterpret what is being said.

Reading Hierarchy and Typographical Choice

At Dahn Design, we start with typography in the artistic design of each interpretive sign. Once goals and a preliminary text for the sign have

been developed, we begin by making a typographical grid and selecting the type within the sign rectangle. This beginning typographic structure provides a framework to build on while developing the illustrations, diagrams, symbols, maps, or other elements that are being considered for the content of the sign.

At this point, decisions about typefaces, sizes, and weight of type (light, medium, bold, etc.) should be made. Making these choices should be guided by one overriding principle: hierarchy. The effective use of hierarchy can give a sign a compelling quality—inviting reading, engaging the viewer's attention and quickly presenting the core idea, or theme. Typographical hierarchy, simply stated, means that some headings or bodies of text are somehow emphasized and clearly more visible (e.g., larger, a different typeface, a different color, or reversed out) and therefore invite a first reading by the viewer. This is the principle that Ham described in the "levels" approach to conceptual design earlier in this chapter. The importance of this principle cannot be overstated because you have to remember that an interpretive sign is not a favorite book that someone has pulled off the shelf to read. For a noncaptive audience, the main message must be quickly recognizable, strong, and clear enough to attract immediate attention.

The number of typographical levels in the hierarchy can vary, but there are usually at least three: the title or main heading type, the main text type, and the subordinate detail type. Occasionally, large and complex signs may have as many as six or seven typographical levels. But again (particularly with a large, complex sign), there must be a clear visual difference in the reading at these various levels. Making everything large does not make it more readable; in fact it tends to repel the viewer. As this book has repeatedly stressed, "all emphasis is no emphasis." Everything is not as important as everything else in a sign text, and research shows that only the rare viewer reads it all. In deciding the hierarchy, ask yourself what is most important for everyone to read, and let this be your largest, most conspicuous type.

Hierarchy of reading can also be affected by positioning left to right and top to bottom. Because the English-language tradition has a top-to-bottom and left-to-right reading bias, positioning of text can affect reading—particularly that all-important first glance. If everyone involved in the decision making about an interpretive sign understood this important principle, many boring and unread signs could be avoided.

Selecting Typefaces

Once you've made some basic choices of typographical hierarchy and developed a grid or framework for positioning, you can turn your attention to selecting typefaces for the sign. There is an overwhelming number of typefaces instantly available to you, yet the majority of them are not appropriate for interpretive signs—either for stylistic or functional reasons. Many new typefaces (and old typefaces) were designed primarily to have a certain style or "newness" contemporary for the time in which they were created. Yet typographical "fashion" changes quickly, and most of these typefaces become outmoded and therefore inappropriate for an interpretive sign that must last for many years and be read by a large, diverse audience consisting of varying ages and backgrounds.

The choice of type should begin with its most fundamental character. As pointed out earlier in this book, the basic choice is between serif type (letters that have finishing strokes or "tails") and sans serif type (letters that lack the ending strokes). Generally, I feel that serif type is most appropriate for the text or main body of an exhibit or sign. Sans serif type works well for captions and smaller informational parts where fitting and functional readability are more critical.

The main heading or title of the sign is where a maximum of possibilities of type styles and treatments can be most readily applied. The expressiveness of a particular type, its boldness or general character, and the way it is positioned and spaced (all caps or caps and lower case) can add to the effectiveness and attention-getting quality of the heading. Two personal favorites that I recommend for signs are Times Roman (serif type) and Helvetica (sans serif type). They come in a variety of weights and have a great, time-tested functional character. A recent computer typeface that I recommend because of its versatility and readability is Stone. Stone comes in various weights of a serif and sans serif, and in an "informal medium" which is half way between a serif and sans serif. There is a great and long tradition of type design that extends back more than 2000 years to Roman letters carved into triumphant arches. The subtle but powerful effect of letter forms has been the life work of countless designers over many centuries. Anyone interested or involved in the use of type might well enjoy looking further into this aspect of history.

Spacing Considerations

The interrelatedness of type is always an important consideration when organizing the various typographic parts of a sign. The type designer gives a great deal of thought to how the various forms of the alphabet being designed fit together. The sign designer, in turn, has decisions to make about the letter, word, and line spacing of text as it is grouped within the sign. There are no absolute rules for spacing, but some common-sense guidelines should always be considered:

1. Spacing between letters should take into account how the letters fit together visually. Generally, one should try to achieve an even letter

An 8 ft. by 8 ft. porcelain enamel panel, one of 11 interpretive signs for the Bureau of Land Management's Dean Creek Elk Viewing Outdoor Interpretive Center. Note that the size of the words ROOSEVELT ELK allows them to serve as a title, not only for the panel but for the entire series of panels. Informational facts listed on the left are aligned in a list format and spaced more tightly to contrast with the Indian story on the right. (Design and illustration by Dahn Design)

spacing so that no one space or letter has a gap around it or is "crushing" (overlapping) another.

2. Word spacing should always strive for an evenness so that there are no gaping holes and no words running together.

3. Line spacing has a greater range of possibilities. Paragraphs or blocks of type can sometimes be set tight with very little line space if compactness and space are needed in the design. Sometimes tight spacing can give an urgency to a block of text, particularly

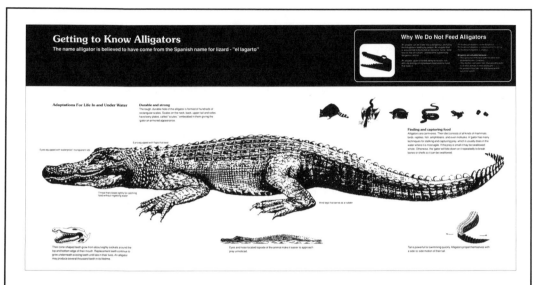

One of seven interpretive panels along an auto tour at Ding Darling National Wildlife Refuge. There are two main ideas here. In the more interpretive, "Getting to Know the Alligators," the message is given the preferred left position set in a serif type that contrasts with the Helvetica used for the management message, "Why We Do Not Feed Alligators." Notice that this message is fitted and packed with less line space to give a more authoritative appearance. The interpretive lines are strung out to relate to the lineal alligator drawing. Notice also the alignment left to right and top to bottom to give a related reading to elements and to add structure to the total design. On both panels, notice the clear hierarchy of reading created by size, placement and sizes of type used. (Design and illustration by Dahn Design)

if it is set in contrast to another block of text that has more line spacing.

Often, however, tight line spacing in large blocks of text or headings slows down reading. Tightly spaced copy usually conveys an unpleasant "read-me-only-if-you-must" quality that is seen in its most extreme form in legal contracts where reading is intended to be obscured. Conversely, lines of type can be spaced out so far that they lose their continuity, line for line. Yet, a slower or more poetic reading can be very effective in some situations. As always, visual common sense should prevail.

All of these spacing considerations become even more important when working with headings and titles, and they should all be considered to get the most expressive and effective reading. Spacing and size of type are to some degree a matter of opinion, but they will most definitely impact how the type will look in the final design. The ready availability of computer output today greatly facilitates decision making. The best visual judgment can be made by printing the words several ways and then looking at them, thinking about their visual effect, and then making your selection.

Two additional spacing considerations that impact the readability of a sign are blank space (sometimes called air or white space) and alignment. Alignment is the positioning of type either horizontally or vertically so that it aligns. This alignment can give a relatedness to different parts of the design (see "unity" earlier in this chapter), and it also helps the structural framework quality of the type. Blank space gives a sort of visual pause between elements with a sign. White space around text or a heading can also give it more importance or visual presence in the design (see "emphasis" earlier in this chapter).

People today make thousands of visual judgments in their daily lives. We read countless messages—some without thinking, some with care, and some for simple enjoyment. Bombarded as we are by information, our visual judgments concerning messages is becoming more and more discerning and critical. Making appropriate and visually sensitive decisions in designing with type for an interpretive sign can have an important outcome on the effectiveness of that sign.

Just Say No to Litter— Untraditional Signing Supported by Enlightened Regulation in a Costa Rican National Park

Sergio León, Director
Manuel Antonio National Park, Costa Rica

Manuel Antonio National Park is one of the most popular and heavily used parks in Costa Rica, mainly because of its beaches. A problem in areas with high levels of visitation is that the majority of the visitors don't follow the rules established for the park and litter is a constant problem. We noticed long ago that our traditional methods of asking people not to litter were not effective; they were obviously being ignored. We needed to find more creative ways to capture the visitors' attention and communicate the problem to them. For this reason we decided to try some non-traditional interpretive approaches. We decided on a sculpture, a giant-sized sign, and stricter regulations for visitors entering the park.

Our most creative approach to the litter problem is a sculpture resembling a spider web with a message from the spider himself. We chose the spider because it is a widely recognized part of the ecosystem that people could relate to. And it didn't cost much to produce. The materials included a type of cord that would not deteriorate in

high humidity, wooden stakes, a small wooden sign about 1.5 m x 50 cm, and litter from the park. An artist with experience in these kind of sculptures volunteered his work, and the park

DONADO POR CARDISO

TRADUCCIONES E INTERPRETACION SAN JOSE

volunteers also assisted in getting the materials together. We began by weaving the spider web with the cord and attaching selected litter from the beach in different sizes, colors, and shapes. When the web was completed, the pieces of litter appeared to have been "caught" in the web. We decided on a place for the web where it would blend with the surroundings, but also draw people's attention. As the finishing touch, we attached a sign to it which said, "Don't dirty my home - The Spider."

The spider web is a message with a visual impact; visitors who see the sculpture are immediately aware of the litter problem and of the need to protect the resources of the park. The design and implementation of the sculpture was an excellent project in that it integrated the knowledge and talents of various people who worked together on the project. It conveys a simple message that doesn't demand much time from the visitor, and it was very economical to produce.

Another interpretive approach we took was the creation of a giant-sized sign with bold lettering and a single word of text: "CONTAMINATION." To do this, we used administrative and logistical support of graphic arts students from the University of Costa Rica. The students donated their work and, in turn, received credits toward their degrees. We bought second-hand pieces of plywood and exterior paint (in the colors sky blue, ocean blue, white—to go along with our theme— and black for the lettering). The total cost of these materials was less than $20. Then we selected a site where the sign would blend nicely with the environment, but would also be highly visible to visitors.

Within six months the sign was ready and installed. Combined with the spider web sculpture, it has made an impact on how our visitors think about littering the beach. The visitors can understand the conservation theme in one or two seconds. Although this sign cost us next to nothing, it has proven to be very valuable.

One management strategy we used to combat litter was to charge a refundable deposit on items which visitors brought into the park and that would ordinarily end up as trash. Very few visitors see the cause-and-effect relationship between the objects they bring into the park and the trash they see in the park. Our deposit strategy helped them to become more aware of what they were bringing in and taking out. All of our staff were trained to impart the new regulation to the visitors in a practical and friendly manner; our philosophy was that the visitors would react more favorably to the regulation if it was described to them in a positive manner.

Today, most groups of visitors carry out their own trash. We see that most people accept the rule and it has become rare to see litter in the park. People have been able to compare the amount of trash inside and outside of the park, and seeing that our strategy works, we receive very few complaints. In fact, we have begun to receive compliments!

Our approach to the litter problem is a combination of interpretation and supporting regulation. One very important point to this is that we have had to train our staff to see themselves more as interpreters and educators rather than as police officers. The formula is simple: if visitors understand the reasons behind a regulation, they are more likely to follow it.

Sign for the Times— Some Design Considerations for Today's Visitor

Gary L. Bartlett, Forest Landscape Architect
Rogue River National Forest, Medford, Oregon

Interpretive signs are far more than "objects in the landscape" displaying fun facts and appealing graphics. They're strategic communication media that convey important messages to important people—our visitors. Today's visitors come in all shapes and sizes and with a variety of physical abilities. Their sheer diversity and special needs require designers to be more sensitive than we have sometimes been in the past. Skillfully designed in harmony with the setting, attractive signs can turn an entire site into an interpretive opportunity for all kinds of visitors. With this concept in mind, two sites on the Rogue River National Forest—the Natural Bridge and the Rogue Gorge—were recently developed using static displays as the primary interpretive media.

In order to serve the greatest cross-section of visitors, we knew our signs had to be:

• usable by all persons including the elderly and physically disabled (including being able to be read from a wheelchair)

• readable by vision-impaired people (but not to the totally blind)
• designed for low maintenance and able to withstand harsh weather and vandalism
• designed so that the sign structure is complementary to the message and not distractive
• designed and located so as not to detract from the natural forest character and the object of interpretation.

For the first set of signs the visitor encounters, we designed a wooden kiosk with orientation and general interpretation messages. The signs are

SKETCH A.

SKETCH B.

mounted vertically with the viewing space between 2' 6" and 6'0" above the finish grade (see sketch A). Individual signs on slanted standards along the trail provide site specific information. These standards are fabricated from steel with a 1/4" thick steel plate supporting the sign board. The sign board is 2'6" above the finish grade and sloped 40 degrees from horizontal for ease of reading whether standing or reading from a wheelchair (see sketch B). Vandal-resistant screws were used to attach the frame to the sign standard. Each steel standard was painted black to reduce the visual impact of the signs on the forest setting. Experience has taught us that black, more than any other color, "fits" the forest scene while not drawing attention to themselves. In some environments, however, other colors may work better.

The sign texts were silk-screened graphics embedded in fiberglass which allows for a full range of colors along with high resistance to adverse weather conditions. A minimum 36-point text size was used on high contrast backgrounds to accommodate those with poor eyesight. The larger print allows readers to view the signs at a comfortable distance while at the same time being able to view the object of interpretation. Three signs were fabricated for each location to provide replacements for those damaged by vandalism or other means. Since the major cost is usually associated with the initial set-up for silk-screening, additional copies should be purchased during the original fabrication of any sign.

Each sign was carefully located on-site so as not to interfere with the specific view or object being interpreted. The site planner and interpretive specialist need to work together to assure the visitor has the best interpretive experience possible. Making the signs accessible to physically impaired people did not cost any extra. It was simply a matter of careful and sensitive design.

Both of these interpretive sites have been open to the public for several years. On-site monitoring indicates the site and signs are performing as intended and have generated many positive comments from visitors.

From Bulletin Boards to Information Boards— User-Friendly Communication Is the Key

Celese Brune, Interpretive Specialist
Mount St. Helens National Volcanic Monument
Gifford Pinchot National Forest,
Amboy, Washington

"Bulletin boards!"—The sheer words conjure up images of boring, unimaginative designs and meaningless lists of rules and regulations that are aimed more at legal backstopping than at real communication. Visitors have learned not to expect much from bulletin boards, and most bulletin boards give them exactly what they expect.

The sad thing is that bulletin boards are an important communication medium in recreation areas. Attractive and designed with the visitor's needs in mind, they guide recreationists to safe and enjoyable experiences that have minimum impacts on the setting. Moreover, they have the potential to be key components of an interpretive program by delivering essential, even critical, messages about natural resources and management. To revive this potential, the interpretive staff at Mount St. Helens National Volcanic Monument has adopted a new view of bulletin boards, one that recognizes their interpretive potential and capitalizes on their

ability to communicate important information quickly and efficiently to pleasure seekers. This new perspective has given rise to a new term, "information board."

Our information boards differ from the old bulletin boards in how they approach the task of communicating with visitors. What follows is a description of how we made the conversion.

The Site Visit

Thirty-five information board sites were selected. Once we identified where the information boards would be located, we formed a writing team and inventoried each site. The writing team consisted of writers, artists, resource managers, and others with special technical expertise. At each site we brainstormed communication goals and objectives that would be pertinent to that location. A special focus at each site was visitor safety. Once the site evaluations were completed, we were able to see each location's unique

opportunities as well as the objectives they shared with one another.

The Map

The map is the centerpiece of all the information boards, and it takes the most time to prepare. Viewers need to know where they are in relation to where they want to go. The map should be easy to read and include only what the visitor needs at that particular location. After five separate reviews (each involving rewrites and redesign), we were able to agree on two kinds of maps that met our objectives at different sites. Road maps would be placed at entry sites and major viewpoints; trail maps would be included on trail-head information boards.

We had to be very selective in what we chose to include on the maps. To do this, we analyzed existing maps and drew boundaries around the portions that would be important to include at each of the sites. Not surprisingly, the result in each case was an irregularly shaped area. Noting this, we decided to design the map on each information board as an irregular trapezoid printed in vibrant color. To our delight, this shape (unlike the more conventional rectangles found on traditional bulletin boards), seemed to attract viewer attention immediately. People approached the boards from a distance, curious to find out what they contained.

Since each map needs a "you are here" notation, we developed a simple sticker that could be adhered to the appropriate location on each map, rather than having to redesign and reprint each one. The adhesive is the type used on license plate tabs. Once in place, the stickers are almost impossible to remove.

The Messages

Each objective described a communication outcome (such as quickly orienting visitors to certain locations, or reducing some management problem such as pumice removal). These objectives guided the preparation of messages at each site. Text and designs were created, reviewed, and revised— some several times—before they were ready. Some of the messages are site-specific and were included on only one information board. Others were more generic and used on all the boards. Some of these are even being used on other districts and on other national forests.

Preparing the messages was challenging. It was a task of balancing the type and quantity of information we felt was needed against the visitor's attention span. Besides being readable and attractive, the messages had to be accurate. Here's where we were extra careful to involve the technical experts on each writing team. Creating an information board for mountain climbers, we enlisted the aid of our climbing rangers; when the information dealt with ongoing research in the monument, we called upon the scientists who were conducting the studies; and when the information pertained to the biology of the area, biologists were consulted.

Creative ways to tell old stories were explored. For example, all of our information boards need to let visitors know that they are required to take their garbage out with them (there are no garbage receptacles in the core area). Our old approach of telling them that the money saved from garbage pick-up helped to fund other visitor services didn't work well. Our new approach, and one that has had better success, is a song about taking your garbage home printed on a small panel with a notation to sing it to the tune of "Row, Row, Row Your Boat." Now visitors sing the song and get the message—"Leave your forest clean!"

When regulatory messages are necessary, try to keep them simple and fun, but clear in meaning. Using cartoons or jingles can be effective. Be sure to use strong, active verbs wherever possible. And by all means, don't be afraid to say, "Don't." But if you say it, say it creatively. For years we've had the problem of visitors carting souvenir pumice from the volcanic area. We've tried to deter it by asking them not to

take the pumice and to "Leave Natural Features for Everyone." But our new information boards seem to be having more effect by using a negative label (see Chapter 1) and the word "don't." Each one says: "Don't Be a Pumice Picker."

All the messages on the information boards are of the same size. Some are illustrated, some are not, but all have a bright blue component which matches the border of the map and creates a cohesive information board with visual unity.

Layout

Each information board has one map and six messages (some site-specific and some generic). Early in the process, the team decided to keep the information boards modular by using individual message panels that could be replaced easily as site objectives and visitor interests changed. Exact layouts were drawn for each of the thirty-five sites and included in an information board plan. In each layout, the most important message (such as "Don't Be a Pumice Picker") was placed prominently in the middle left of the board. Since most people read from left to right, they read this message first. That way, even if they read nothing else, they get the main idea.

Fabrication

Different fabrication processes were used for the maps and messages. Since the maps would not change as often as the messages, fiberglass embedments were used. The embedments are durable and very attractive. The messages were back-screened onto plexiglass and mounted directly on the information boards. This process is a lot less expensive than fiberglass embedments, but the results are less durable. In the first two years we found that heat from the sun swells the plexiglass and distorts the printed letters. Since then, we've been covering the back of each piece of Plexiglass with a sheet of contact paper. This seems to have solved the swelling problem.

Maintenance

Maintenance of the information boards is vital both to their longevity and usefulness. Why spend time and energy creating them if there's no plan to maintain them? Physical mainte-nance and subject-matter changes are necessary to keep the information boards in good condition and to ensure that the information they contain is cur-rent and appropriate for our ever-changing audiences. To facilitate these changes, we included in our plan the details of the creative process and fabri-cation specifications, along with proto-types of each board's layout and messages. Included also are monitoring and evaluation forms to guide our ongoing critical analysis of the condi-tion and effectiveness of each informa-tion board.

Evaluation

Our ongoing evaluation is based on the recorded observations of our field interpreters. They watch visitors and determine whether they're getting the information they're seeking, and whether they're understanding and behaving consistently with the regula-tory appeals included in the boards. Do they put a piece of pumice in their pocket? Do they know where to go? If the board isn't working, or if it can be improved somehow, we plan to fix it.

References

Bay, J. 1968. *Cómo Se Armonizan los Colores.* Barcelona, España: Editorial LEDA.

Brace, Judith, Ralph R. White and Stephen C. Bass. 1982. *Teaching Conservation in Developing Nations.* Washington, D.C., USA: U.S. Peace Corps, Information Collection and Ex-change, Manual M-7.

Faulkner, R. and E. Ziegfeld. 1969. *Art Today.* New York, New York, USA: Holt, Rinehart and Winston.

Fazio, James R. and Douglas L. Gilbert. 1986. *Public Relations and Commu-nications for Natural Resource Managers.* Dubuque, Iowa, USA: Kendall/Hunt Publishing Co.

Flesch, Rudolf. 1949. *The Art of Readable Writing.* New York, New York, USA: Harper and Row.

Geller, E. Scott, Richard A. Winett and Peter B. Everett. 1982. *Preserving the Environment: New Strategies for Behavior Change.* New York, New York, USA: Pergamon Press.

Gillman, Scott R. 1974. *Fundamentos del Diseño.* Buenos Aires, Argentina: Editorial Victor Leru.

Haley, Allan. 1991. All Caps: A Typographic Oxymoron. *Upper and Lower Case* 18(3):14-15.

Lauer, David A. 1985. *Design Basics.* New York, New York, USA: Holt, Rinehart and Winston.

Machlis, Gary E. and Sally G. Machlis. 1974. *Creative Designs for Bulletin Boards.* Seattle, Washington, USA: Cooperative Park Studies Unit, College of Forest Resources, University of Washington.

McIntosh, Paul A. 1982. Signs and Labels. Chapter 12 in Sharpe, G.W.(ed.), *Interpreting the Environment.* New York, New York, USA: John Wiley & Sons.

Meyer, Hans Ed. 1984. *The Development of Writing.* Natick, New York, USA: Alphabet Press.

Moore, Alan, Bill Wendt, Louis Penna e Isabel Castillo de Ramos. 1989. *Manual para La Capacitación del Personal de Areas Protegidas* (Modulo C: Interpretación y Educación Ambiental, Apunte 4a). Washington, D.C., USA: Servicio de Parques Nacionales, Oficina de Asuntos Internacionales.

Morales, Jorge. 1987. *Manual para la Interpretación en Espacios Naturales Protegidos.* Anexo 3 del Taller Internacional sobre Interpretación Ambiental en Areas Silvestres Protegidas. Santiago, Chile: Oficina Regional de la FAO para América Latina y el Caribe, 1988.

Muñoz, Milton G. y Hector R. Fonseca. 1990. *Ilustración de Materiales Escritos en el Sector Rural.* Tegucigalpa, D.C., Honduras: Secretaria de Recursos Naturales, Departamento de Comunicación Agropecuaria, Proyecto de Comunicación para la Transferencia de Tecnología Agropecuaria.

Muñoz, Milton G. y Bernardo Peña. 1990. *Selección y Utilización de Ayudas Educativas.* Tegucigalpa, D.C., Honduras: Secretaria de Recursos Naturales, Departamento de Comunicación Agropecuaria, Proyecto de Comunicación para la Transferencia de Tecnología Agropecuaria.

Neal, Arminta. 1976. *Exhibits for the Small Museum.* Nashville, Tennessee, USA: American Association for State and Local History.

Neal, Arminta. 1969. *Help! For the Small Museum.* Boulder, Colorado, USA: Pruett Press.

Neal, Arminta. 1964. Legible Labels: Hand Lettering. *History News,* Technical Leaflet 22. Nashville, Tennessee, USA: American Association for State and Local History.

O'Hayre, John. 1966. *Gobbledygook Has Gotta Go.* Washington, D.C., USA: U.S. Interior Department, Bureau of Land Management.

Pino, Georgina. 1989. *Las Artes Plásticas.* San José, Costa Rica: Editorial Universidad Estatal a Distancia.

Pinzón, Isabel. 1973. *Ayudas Visuales de Exhibición.* In, Institución Internacional de Capacitación Agropecuaria, Curso sobre Comunicación Escrita, Marzo 20-30, Bogotá, Colombia, pp. 11-14.

Sánchez, Enrique. 1990. La Cartelera. In, Muñoz, Milton G. y Bernardo Peña. 1990. *Selección y Utilización de Ayudas Educativas*. Tegucigalpa, D.C., Honduras: Secretaria de Recursos Naturales, Departamento de Comunicación Agropecuaria, Proyecto de Comunicación para la Transferencia de Tecnología Agropecuaria, pp. 61-68.

Sandoval, José Eladio. 1990. Los Carteles. In, Muñoz, Milton G. y Bernardo Peña, *Selección y Utilización de Ayudas Educativas*. Tegucigalpa, D.C., Honduras: Secretaria de Recursos Naturales, Departamento de Comunicación Agropecuaria, Proyecto de Comunicación para la Transferencia de Tecnología Agropecuaria, pp. 54-60.

Sharpe, Grant W. 1982. Exhibits. Chapter 16 in Sharpe, G.W.(ed.), *Interpreting the Environment*. New York, New York, USA: John Wiley & Sons.

Schleyer, James. W. 1987. *Exhibit Survey Results—Fall 1987*. Washington, D.C., USA: U.S. Department of Agriculture, Office of Governmental and Public Affairs, Design Division.

Shiner, J.W. and Elwood L. Shafer, Jr. 1975. *How Long Do People Look At and Listen to Forest-Oriented Exhibits?* U.S. Department of Agriculture, Forest Service Research Paper NE-325. Upper Darby, PA, USA: Northeastern Forest Experiment Station.

Tilden, Freeman. 1977. *Interpreting Our Heritage*. Chapel Hill, North Carolina, USA: University of North Carolina Press.

Trapp, Suzanne, Michael Gross and Ron Zimmerman. 1991. *Signs, Trails, and Wayside Exhibits—Connecting People and Places*. Stevens Point, Wisconsin, USA: UW-SP Foundation Press, Inc.

U.S. National Library Service. 1979. *Reading Materials in Large Type*. Circular No. 79-3 of the U.S. National Library Service for the Blind and Physically Handicapped. Washington, D.C., USA: Library of Congress.

U.S. National Park Service. 1989. *National Park Service Wayside Exhibits—Selected Information Sheets*. Prepared by Harpers Ferry Center, Division of Wayside Exhibits. Washington, D.C., USA: National Park Service.

Witteborg, Lothar P. 1981. *Good Show! A Practical Guide for Temporary Exhibitions*. Washington, D.C., USA: The Smithsonian Institution.

Zakia, Richard D. and Hollis N. Todd. 1974. *Color Primer I & II*. Dobbs Ferry, New York, USA: Morgan & Morgan, Inc.

Additional Reading

In English:

Alderson, William T. and Shirley Payne Low. 1985. *Interpretation of Historic Sites*. Nashville, Tennessee, USA: American Association for State and Local History.

Bajimaya, Shyam and James R. Fazio. 1989. *Communications Manual: A Guide to Aid Park and Protected Area Managers to Communicate Effectively with Local Residents*. Kathmandu, Nepal: Department of National Parks and Wildlife Conservation/FAO-UNDP.

Berkmüller, Klaus. 1981. *Guidelines and Techniques for Environmental Interpretation*. Ann Arbor, Michigan, USA: School of Natural Resources, University of Michigan.

Berryman, Gregg. 1990. *Notes On Graphic Design and Visual Communication.* Los Altos, California: Crisp Publications, Inc.

Harrison, Anne. 1982. Problems: Vandalism and Depreciative Behavior. Chapter 25 in Sharpe, G.W.(ed.), *Interpreting the Environment.* New York, New York, USA: John Wiley & Sons.

MacKinnon, John, Kathy MacKinnon, Graham Child and James Thorsell (eds.). 1986. *Managing Protected Areas in the Tropics* (Chapter 7). Cambridge, United Kingdom: International Union for the Conservation of Nature & Natural Resources and the United Nations Environment Program.

Tyler, Barbara and Victoria Dickenson. 1977. *A Handbook for the Travelling Exhibitionist.* Ottawa, Ontario, Canada: Ottawa Canadian Museums Association.

U.S. Forest Service. 1990. *Exhibits Guide— How to Plan, Design, Build and Show Your Own Exhibits.* Washington, D.C., USA: U.S. Forest Service.

U.S. Forest Service. 1966. Sign Handbook. Chapter 90 (Outdoor Interpretive Signs) in *Forest Service Handbook.* Washington, D.C., USA: U.S. Forest Service.

In Spanish:

Berkmüller, Klaus. 1985. *Educación Ambiental sobre el Bosque Lluvioso.* Gland, Suiza: Unión Internacional para la Conservación de la Naturaleza y los Recursos Naturales.

Ham, Sam H. 1992. *Interpretación Ambiental: Una Guía Práctica para Gente con Grandes Ideas y Presupuestos Pequeños.* Golden, Colorado, USA: North American Press/Fulcrum Publishing.

Kandinski, Wassilly. 1974. *Punto y Linea Sobre el Plano.* Barcelona, España: Barral Editores.

MacKinnon, John, Kathy MacKinnon, Graham Child y James Thorsell (eds.). 1990. *Manejo de Areas Protegidas en los Trópicos* (Capítulo 7). Cancún, Quintana Roo, México: Amigos de Sian Ka'an A.C.

CHAPTER NINE

HOW TO DEVELOP INEXPENSIVE SELF-GUIDED TOURS

In this chapter we'll consider a popular interpretive method, **self-guided tours**. Although the term "self-guided trail" is used when the tour takes place on a trail or pathway, self-guided tours also can be offered in many other places. Like guided tours, they usually lead people through a pre-planned sequence of **stops**, each one presenting a part of a theme. Self-guided tours are commonly used to show people things that they'd otherwise not see, or which the untrained eye probably wouldn't notice. Yet because they do it unaided by an interpreter, they're much less expensive than guided tours. Another advantage is that they're often available to people everyday and at all hours. Although most self-guided tours can't achieve the dynamic quality of a good guided tour, if they're imaginatively designed, they can approximate it.

Three different media are commonly used on self-guided tours. Two of them (signs and brochures keyed to numbered posts) require users to read. The third (audio devices) requires them to listen. Each of these media has several advantages and disadvantages. But judged against the single criterion of long-term cost, audio devices probably wouldn't be a good choice for anyone working on a shoe-string budget. This is true even for basic cassette tape systems, much less for more advanced audio technologies such as FM transmitters and infrared and digital sound playback units. Besides the initial expense of producing the audio messages and duplicating them, the costs of tape players, batteries, periodic repair and maintenance, and the salary of the person who must check the units out and in, make even the most economical audio tour expensive. For this reason, we'll be focusing on self-guided tours that rely on signs and brochures to tell their stories. As always, our approach will be thematic. If you're not yet familiar with themes and thematic communication, you should review Chapter 2 before going any further with this chapter.

Several good references on self-guided tours are available. Some recommended sources in English are Brace et al. (1982), Grater (1976), Sharpe (1982), Trapp et al. (1991), U.S. Forest Service (1964), and Wetterberg (1982). In Spanish, Berkmüller (1981), Moore et al. (1989), and Morales (1987) are recommended.

Types of Self-Guided Tours

Self-guided tours can take many forms. For example, members of a family might walk a forest trail reading signs that tell them about the environment they're passing through; a group of junior high school students might walk through a forest nursery reading a brochure that explains what different parts of the nursery do; passengers on an airplane might read a booklet that explains what they're seeing beneath them; or a group of friends in a car might listen to a cassette tape explaining important roadside features. Although the setting, subject matter and audience are very different in each of these examples, each one is a self-guided tour.

Just like guided tours, self-guided tours can have very specific purposes (such as showing how plants and animals are interdependent, explaining the significant features of an historic site or building, or demonstrating how something is made). Or they may have more general purposes—creating awareness, building

appreciation, or suggesting a new way of thinking or looking at something.

You can develop self-guided tours almost anywhere there is something important to show and talk about. Figure 9-1 shows some common examples of self-guided tours, their purposes, typical settings and common lengths.

You can develop self-guided tours for forests, parks, buildings and facilities, at zoos, museums, farms, historic sites, botanical gardens, nurseries, demonstration and research sites, aboard small boats or large ships, or in other settings. As Figure 9-1 shows, where a tour is presented usually has something to do with its purpose and with the kind of message you want to get across.

Self-Guided Tours are Sequential

Most self-guided tours are sequential—they lead people through a series of interpretive stops in a pre-planned order just as a tour guide would. Like guided tours, they have a definite beginning and a definite ending that are determined by the interpreter. Knowing the order in which people will move through the tour area allows the use of communication techniques such as foreshadowing, mystery and transitions. As we saw in Chapter 5, these make tours more interesting and easier to follow.

Brochures, Signs, or Audio— Which Is Best?

The "jury is still out" when it comes to the effectiveness of different self-guided tour media. Some authors claim that signs are "better" than brochures, or that audio tapes are "better" than signs, but "better"

There Are Many Kinds of Self-Guided Tours

Type of Self-Guided Tour	Typical Purposes	Typical Settings	Typical Length (distance/time)
Self-Guided Trail	To orient people to a trail environment; to show and explain things that illustrate a theme	Short trails, paths, small segments of longer trails, bike ways, horse trails	1/4 - 1 mi./ 30-45 min. (400 - 1600 m)
Self-Guided Underwater Tours	To orient people to an underwater environment; to show and explain things that illustrate a theme	Bays, inlets, lagoons, lakes, coral reefs, marine coves	< 1/4 mi./ 20-30 min. [< 400 m]
Self-Guided Building Tour	To orient people to a building or structure; show and explain things that illustrate a theme	Visitor centers, museums, historic buildings, theaters, libraries, capitols, offices, and other structures	< 1/4 mi./ 20-30 min. [< 400 m]
Self-Guided Facility Tour	To demonstrate a production or manufacturing process; to show and explain things that illustrate a theme	Factories, manufacturing plants, energy production facilities, wineries/vineyards, breweries, dairies, food processing facilities, nurseries, sawmills, research laboratories	< 1/2 mi./ 30-40 min. [< 800 m]
Self-Guided Site Tour	To orient people to a site that is recognized for its cultural or scientific values; to show and explain things that illustrate a theme	Historic sites, cemeteries, battlefields, frams, demonstration areas, research plots, plantations, sites of natural and human-caused catastrophes	< 1/2 mi./ 20-30 min. [< 800 m]
Self-Guided Auto, Motorcycle, Bicycle, Bus, and Train Tours	Any objective above that lends itself to the selected form of transportation	Highways, roads, off-road vehicle areas; railroads, scenic routes, and historic corridors	> 10 mi./ > 1/2 hour [> 16 km]
Self-Guided Boat and Airplane Tours	Any objective above that lends itself to the selected form of transportation	Lakes, bays, inlets, rivers, open sea, over land or water	Highly variable

Figure 9-1. Seven different kinds of self-guided tours

is a complex idea. *No known study* (and there have been many) has demonstrated conclusively that any of them is inherently better or worse than the rest. As with most interpretive media, each one has strengths and weaknesses. In deciding which one would be best for *your* self-guided tour, you should take into account your biggest constraints (probably money and time) and select the medium that makes the most sense for your situation. As earlier suggested, audio devices probably won't be a logical choice because of their cost. Both signs and brochures, however, *can be* cost-effective and enjoyable media for self-guided tours. In fact, one study (Tai 1981) found that they were *equally* enjoyable to users of a self-guided trail in Yellowstone National Park. Interestingly, Tai also found that although signs produced better *short-term* retention of factual information, brochures led to better *long-term* retention—presumably because people can take brochures with them for later reading, reference, or sharing with others.

Brochures and signs have other advantages and disadvantages. Since signs are bigger, they're more conspicuous than the small numbered posts that brochure trails typically utilize. Unless they're designed to harmonize with the site, signs can intrude on a visitor's esthetic experience. Another advantage of brochures is that they can be offered in several languages. Signs often appear cluttered when more than one language is included. A disadvantage of brochures is that they can present daily maintenance problems. Since visitors may take them when they leave, brochures have to be replenished periodically. In addition, careless or uncaring visitors may drop them on the ground creating a litter

problem. In terms of cost, brochure trails are less expensive initially but may be more expensive in the long run, especially if the brochure needs to be reprinted or recopied frequently. However, you can reduce this cost by asking for payment or a refundable deposit from people who want to use a brochure. Finally, signs have another advantage over brochures in that they allow everyone in a group to do their own reading rather than passively listening to someone else do it for them. This allows them to go at their own pace and to reread parts of the text that are especially interesting or confusing.

Qualities of a Good Self-Guided Tour

Good self-guided tours have the qualities that we outlined in Chapter 1. They're interpretive; they're entertaining to their audiences; they present meaningful and relevant information; and they're well-organized around a central theme with five or fewer main ideas. The best way to recognize an effective self-guided tour is to watch the audience. If people who take the tour seem interested and involved in what they're doing and seeing, then the tour is doing what the interpreter wanted it to do—it's capturing the audience's attention. Having accomplished this important task, communicating a theme is much easier.

Guided tours and self-guided tours are similar in many ways. As mentioned, they're both sequential and they both have introductions, bodies, and conclusions. Like guided tours, self-guided tours must engage visitors' minds and imaginations, focusing their attention on the environment in front of them. The difference, of course, is that self-guided tours must

Figure 9-2. Three common self-guided trail media. Left to right: brochure and numbered posts (photo by Jim Fazio), signs-in-place (photo courtesy of National Park Service), and audio stations (photo by Sam Ham).

accomplish these things without the aid of an interpretive guide. Still, the two media are so similar in structure and format that you'll find many of the techniques discussed in Chapter 5 equally pertinent to this chapter.

Of course, many factors combine to make a successful self-guided tour. Among the ones we'll consider in this chapter are careful planning and providing clear relationships between the stops on tour and its theme. These factors, more than any other, distinguish thematic self-guided tours from those that merely identify things. Thematic tours consist of stops that together tell a story or make a point. Identification alone doesn't say much, and to the nonscientist, doesn't mean much.

Although there may be rare situations when simple identification is appropriate (for example, when communicating with scientists is the main goal), it's almost always better to think thematically when developing a self-guided tour. Even for scientists, thematic tours will probably be more interesting and easier to understand.

The Self-Guided Walking Tour

In the remainder of this chapter, we're going to focus on self-guided walking tours because they're the most common type of self-guided tour in natural resource settings. Although automobile cassette tape tours are becoming common in some areas, their expense makes them cost-prohibitive in programs where money is severely limited. English-language readers interested in this specialized form of self-guided interpretation should consult Wetterberg (1982) and Grater (1976).

Where Should Walking Tours Be Located?

Often you won't have to worry about where to locate a self-guided tour because the tour route is already in place. This is especially true of trails. Although the ideal case is to be able to design and build your own trail, this often isn't practical because of the costs involved. Usually, your task will be to adapt or convert an existing trail into a self-guided interpretive trail. Whether you're deciding the route of a new trail or deciding whether an existing trail or trail segment should be used as a self-guided tour, you should consider a number of factors including the site's interpretive potential, accessibility, user safety, and environmental impacts.

What Is Interpretive Potential?

A trail has interpretive potential when it brings important features and environments into the view of people walking the trail. The features could relate to plants, animals, geologic formations or cultural history. Variety along the trail is important. As we'll see later, a trail that doesn't change is often a boring trail. In addition, trails which take people to some special or outstanding feature have even more interpretive potential (see Figure 9-3). Often such a feature will inspire a name for the trail (e.g., "Mystery of the Solitary Tree," or "Trail of Two Caves.") As Sharpe (1982) pointed out, an interesting feature can be used to lure people onto the trail thereby increasing the number of

people it can reach. But a trail that doesn't have a conspicuous feature doesn't necessarily lack interpretive potential. You'll simply have to attract people's interest in other ways.

When Is a Trail Accessible?

In interpretation, the term "accessibility" has two different meanings. In the conventional sense of the word, a self-guided trail is "accessible" when it's located conveniently for intended users, when there's room for people to park their vehicles or bicycles, and when the trail surface is comfortable and safe for users. Additionally, however, the term has come to mean **barrier-free** for people with certain types of physical disabilities. Both meanings are considered in the following discussion.

In a forest or park, self-guided trails are typically located near areas where relatively large numbers of people go. Such areas include visitor centers, picnic areas, campgrounds, scenic viewpoints, information offices, historic sites, and other places that attract people (such as those listed in Figure 9-3). Since routine maintenance is required on almost any self-guided trail, the closer it can be located to an official building, the more convenient it will be to check the trail periodically for obstacles, to replenish brochures, or to check for vandalism to numbered posts, signs, or auxiliary facilities such as brochure boxes, garbage cans and latrines.

Parking is an important consideration both to protect the environment and people's safety. Self-guided trails which begin at a visitor center or main office usually are able to capitalize on an existing parking lot. If a parking lot doesn't already exist, you should plan to create

Choose Trails That Have Interpretive Potential

The best self-guided trails have interpretive potential. They pass through a diversity of environments and habitats, and they take people near significant features that enhance the trail experience. Although not all self-guided trails can (or should necessarily) have a truly outstanding feature, any trail that puts people in viewing distance of the following kinds of features probably has interpretive potential.

- a lake
- a river
- a cave
- a hot springs
- a scenic viewpoint
- a cultural site
- a particularly large or very old tree
- a waterfall
- a place where a certain species of animal is likely to be seen

- a site impacted by a natural disaster such as a flood, earthquake, fire, volcanic eruption
- a place where fossils are exposed
- a place where a famous event took place
- an unusual example of something such as a crystal blue lake, a species of tree that grows nowhere else in the area, or a type of habitat that's unusual in the region

Figure 9-3. Examples of significant features on a self-guided trail.

one before opening the trail for use. Frequently, this is as simple as moving (and partially burying) some large rocks to define the parking area. Logs can work well, too, but rocks or other nonburnable material would be better if fires are allowed and wood is in short supply. If tour busses or large recreational vehicles are expected, be sure to provide parking and turning spaces large enough for them.

As noted previously, "accessibility" has also come to mean "barrier-free" for people with physical disabilities. These people may be blind or visually impaired, deaf, confined to wheelchairs or unable to walk without special apparatus. Clearly, not all trails can be made completely accessible to people with such a wide range of disabilities, but as Brian O'Callaghan and Susan Jurasz note in their case study (at the end of this chapter), taking their needs into account

in the earliest stages of planning and design leads to more sensitive decision making and often prevents thoughtless and unnecessary barriers from occurring—barriers that may cost a lot to remove later. Often, the necessary design specifications are relatively easy and inexpensive to meet. For example, people in wheelchairs simply require a gentle **grade** (rarely exceeding 5 percent and never more than 8 percent). For safe movement, they also need trail-side curbs and a hard smooth surface. Overhead clearance should be a minimum of 8 feet (2.5m), and a horizontal clearance of at least 6.5 feet (2 m) is needed to accommodate two wheelchairs passing each other on a two-way trail. Once the trail is constructed, adding or "retrofitting" such features would be more difficult and much more expensive —as much as 40 percent more expensive, according to O'Callaghan and Jurasz.

With such a range of disabilities to consider, it's not surprising that there are many other specifications regarding the size of print in signs and brochures, the use of braille and three-dimensional letters, bridges, boardwalks and **switchbacks**, among others, that are too detailed to include here. Interested readers should consult Beechel (1975) and U.S. Architectural and Transportation Barriers Compliance Board (1985 and 1991). In the United States, there are two federal laws (Section 504 of the 1973 Rehabilitation Act and the 1990 Americans with Disabilities Act) that give physically disabled citizens the right of access to most kinds of public (and some private sector) facilities and programs. Make sure your design conforms to the standards required by these laws and any similar state and local laws. Comprehensive lists of the required architectural standards for public facilities, including trails, are contained in the two previously cited publications by the U.S. Architectural and Transportation Barriers Compliance Board. For quick information or to obtain a list of publications on barrier-free design, call the Architectural and Transportation Barriers Compliance Board (ATBCB) toll free at 1-800-USA-ABLE. In addition, Majewski (1987) provides a book and videotape discussing the range of disabilities and their implications for barrier-free designs.

What Kinds of Areas Should Be Avoided?

Be careful not to lure people into potentially dangerous or ecologically fragile sites. Avoid locating self-guided trails near power lines or next to highways and roads, unprotected cliffs, areas where there are abundant poisonous plants or aggressive animals, the edges of swift rivers and white water (unless a sturdy railing low enough to protect children and high enough for adults is provided). Long steep grades should be avoided. Besides turning an educational event into a physical fitness test, trails on steep grades create erosion and run-off problems. Be sure to install **water bars** to channel run-off down the side of the hill rather than down the middle of the trail. Also, don't design a trail to cross wet or fragile areas unless a boardwalk or bridge is planned. High altitude sites have short growing seasons and a foot's impact on alpine or subalpine plants may remain for years.

As previously suggested, locating self-guided trails near areas of visitor concentration is usually a good idea. Sometimes, however, you might want to attract users to a different area by locating a self-guided trail there. This strategy makes sense if the idea is to lure visitors to important features or a significant story opportunity. But it is not recommended if the purpose is to disperse physical site impacts by diverting a portion of an area's use to previously unused or under-used sites. Research [see Cole and Krumpe (1992) and Hammitt and Cole (1987)] has shown that a small percentage of the total use of an area causes the majority of the impact. Attracting visitors to new areas is not likely to reduce impacts elsewhere, and may well have the net effect of simply spreading new impacts.

Designing a Self-Guided Trail

Self-guided trails are usually less than one mile (1.6 km) in length. Although lengths vary, an *average* recommended by most experts is about half a mile (800 m). Remember that the main purpose of the trail is to stimulate interest in the local

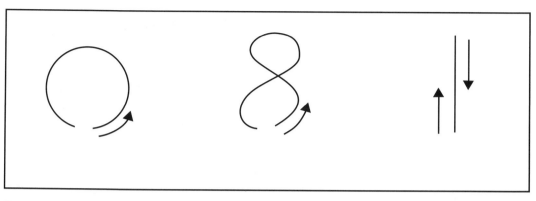

Figure 9-4. Three common layouts for self-guided trails. From left to right: a circular trail, a figure-eight trail, and a linear trail.

environment. The idea is to keep interest so high and fatigue so low that even people who don't like to hike would be very happy to be on the trail. Half an hour is often time enough for a person walking at a leisurely pace to complete a self-guided trail. A trail that takes forty-five minutes is usually considered a long trail.

How Many Stops?

There's a lot of disagreement about how many stops are best for a self-guided trail. That's probably because a great many things can influence the number of stops. Some authors have recommended fifteen to eighteen stops on a half-mile (800 m) trail. Another author puts the range at twenty to thirty stops, and another says that twelve is optimal. Although few studies have been conducted that could tell us which range is best, it's probably better to err on the lower side. More than twenty stops would put one stop at least every 130 feet (40 m). Since it's generally considered bad technique to have stations in view of one another, spacing them so closely together could present a problem. Fifteen stops, on the other hand, would

allow 175 feet (53 m) between stations, giving you more flexibility in locating each stop. But even only fifteen stops may be asking *a lot* of a noncaptive audience. As a very rough guideline, try not to exceed fifteen stops (fewer is often better), and include only those stations that relate (or can be made to relate) to your theme. If you do this, and if you keep each one simple, clear and short, you'll be practicing the best advice regardless of the actual number of stops the trail has.

Most experts recommend that the majority of stops be located on the first half of the trail, and that the first stop be visible from the introductory sign. Again, there's not much research evidence to support this recommendation, but if signs are being used to interpret the trail it does make sense that if visitors see the first one they might be curious to find out what it says. On a brochure trail, of course, they'd have the text in front of them whether or not they could see the numbered post.

Placing most of the stops in the first half of the trail also makes sense. Since at the beginning people are likely to be eager to see what the trail is about, their curiosity may be higher and their attention

Figure 9-5. A planning team designs the stops for a linear self-guided trail in Ecuador's Cotopaxi National Park. (Photo by Sam Ham)

Figure 9-6. Example of a trail with mystery. The path continues to the left but the curve and dense forest block the visitor's view, creating a sense of curiosity about what lays ahead. (Photo by Sam Ham)

spans longer. You should capitalize on this—later in the trail they may not be so interested in reading.

Three Self-Guided Trail Layouts

The most common type of self-guided trail is the **loop trail.** Loop trails are *circular*—that is, they start and finish at the same point (see Figure 9-4). Because of their circular form, loop trails are normally designed for one-way travel. One-way traffic is advantageous because it allows visitors to follow the sequence of interpretive stops without encountering other people walking in the opposite direction. Because of this, one-way trails often seem less crowded than two-way trails. Often, loop trails are designed so that people on one side of the loop can't see those on the other side. Besides adding to the sensation of remoteness, such designs reduce the occurrence of short-cutting, thereby helping to protect the site.

Sometimes a loop trail is connected to another loop trail, forming a "figure eight." **Figure-eight trails** give people the option of returning when they've completed the first loop, or continuing on to the second loop. The topic of the second loop could be related to the topic of the first loop (but with a different theme) or it could focus on an entirely different set of ideas.

The least common design is linear. **Linear trails** aren't circular. They require people to go and return on the same trail, creating a two-way traffic pattern. Although linear trails aren't usually preferred, sometimes they're necessary. For example, you might have to convert an existing linear trail into a self-guided trail, or physical obstacles like rocks, hillsides and bodies of water might make a loop or figure-eight design impossible. Often, using a linear design is the only way to keep the trail from becoming too long for interpretive purposes. For example, a linear self-guided trail was developed on one side of a high-altitude lake in Ecuador's Cotopaxi National Park. Although an existing circular trail continues all the way

A footbridge (photo by Jim Pollock)

A brick trail (photo by Sam Ham)

A simple railing (photo by Sam Ham)

A tree-limb route marker (photo by Sam Ham)

Figure 9-7. Some ways to define and protect a trail corridor.

around the lake, it's about 1.6 miles (2.5 km) in length. The trail planners correctly decided to discontinue the interpretive part of the trail at the half-mile (0.75 km) point, and to give visitors the option of continuing around the lake or returning on the same trail they'd just walked.

Add "Mystery" into the Trail Layout

Studies have shown that people prefer trails with curves to trails that are straight. Since curves prevent us from seeing what is ahead on the trail, they create a sense of curiosity or "mystery" about what lies around the corner. Curves (and other visual obstacles such as landforms, trees and rocks) make trails more interesting because they entice us to keep going. Straight trails give us too much information. There's no mystery about what we might see because we can already see it.

Keep Curves Gradual

Be careful not to make curves so sharp that people will want to "cut across" them to the other side rather than following the trail. This is especially important on trails that meander up an incline using a series of "switchbacks." If the curves are too sharp, some users will ignore them and walk straight up or down the hill. Make switchbacks smooth and gradual. On particularly steep hills, be sure to install a water bar between switchbacks in order to channel rain water off the trail. You can make a simple water bar by digging a shallow (2 in or 5 cm) downward sloping trench across the trail and lining it with pebbles or wood.

Make the Trail Conspicuous

It's important that the trail corridor be conspicuous. Most people walking the trail won't know the area as well as you do. If they can't easily see where they're supposed to go at any given moment they may feel lost. Not only would this interrupt their educational experience, it could cause them to venture into dangerous or fragile areas looking for the trail. Often a simple cleared path is sufficient. However, trails in rocky, sandy and wide open areas are sometimes harder to see unless they're marked somehow. You could erect a small sign with an arrow to point people in the right direction, or you can install more elaborate markers such as tile, flat rocks, gravel, sawdust, wood chips, or even a railing. Boulders, sticks, or posts driven into the ground at regular intervals also make useful trail markers. If you work in a heavy-rain area, it's not a good idea to line the trail with logs or large rocks because they can impede drainage, in time creating a muddy trail.

Protect the Environment and Visitors' Safety

Depending on the area, you may need to build additional structures in order to protect the trail environment and people's safety. Trails that cross fragile sites (such high elevation meadows and marshy areas) or that present obstacles to safe travel (such as streams and areas where there are loose rocks) may need footbridges, boardwalks or a hard, erosion-resistant surface such as bricks, rocks, gravel or even pavement. If your budget is too small to pay for these types of improvements, you shouldn't locate an interpretive trail anywhere they would be needed.

Take Care of People's Wants and Needs

An interpretive trail encourages people to use a site. When they arrive, they bring with them certain needs. As earlier discussed, providing a place for visitors to park is essential. And depending on the site, latrines and garbage cans can be just as important. Unless latrines or bathroom facilities are located nearby, sanitation problems can occur. At a heavily used site, human waste also can create serious ecological problems, especially if the trail borders a lake or stream. Litter is a potential problem at any site, but it accumulates especially fast if garbage cans aren't provided (and a pack-it-in, pack-it-out ethic isn't aggressively interpreted).

Developing a self-guided trail implies a commitment on your part to maintain the entire trail environment so that it's safe and enjoyable for human use. In the case of a brochure trail, this means keeping brochures printed and available. It also means periodically checking the trail for obstacles such as blown down

Good Self-Guided Tours Have Good Parts

There are usually three parts to a good self-guided tour: an *introduction* (usually a sign at the beginning of the tour), *a body* (the stops on the tour) and a *conclusion* (either a sign or a concluding paragraph in a brochure). Preparing an effective self-guided tour is easier if you think of it as developing these three different parts, and if you concentrate on designing each part to accomplish its specific purposes.

Part of the Tour	Purpose(s)
The Introductory Sign	• To stimulate interest in the topic and to make the audience want to take the tour • To orient the audience to the theme, and to tell briefly what it will see during the tour • To inform the audience about the length of the tour-route, and the degree of physical exertion required
The Body (thematic stops)	• To develop the theme by leading the audience to interesting sites and features that collectively support the theme
The Conclusion (the final stop; it could be a special sign or take the same form as the other stops)	• To reinforce the theme—to show one last time the relationship between the theme and the things that were shown and discussed along the way; if necessary, to direct people back to where they started.

Figure 9-8. Purposes of different parts of a thematic self-guided tour.

trees and for litter and vandalism. If garbage cans are provided, you should take the trash away frequently enough that they never are filled. Besides attracting animals, overflowing garbage cans create an eyesore and actually *encourage* littering. Studies show that people are more apt to litter an area that's already littered than they are an area that's clean. Likewise, latrines should be kept clean and well maintained at all times. If the trail is located in a remote area and vandalism is a significant problem, consider using bricks or rock and mortar for the latrine walls.

A trail environment can be enhanced in other ways without a lot of expense. For example, you might consider providing simple benches for resting, blinds for wildlife viewing, or even a rustic scenic overlook with a railing and logs for sitting. Little touches like these tell visitors that you care about them and that you want them to enjoy themselves. Examples of simple trail structures are included in Appendix B.

Anatomy of a Good Self-Guided Trail

Many of the best self-guided trails have three parts: an ***introductory sign,*** a body consisting of the ***stops*** on the trail,

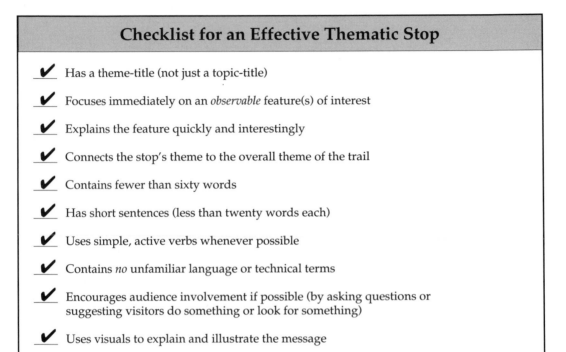

Checklist for an Effective Thematic Stop

✔ Has a theme-title (not just a topic-title)

✔ Focuses immediately on an *observable* feature(s) of interest

✔ Explains the feature quickly and interestingly

✔ Connects the stop's theme to the overall theme of the trail

✔ Contains fewer than sixty words

✔ Has short sentences (less than twenty words each)

✔ Uses simple, active verbs whenever possible

✔ Contains *no* unfamiliar language or technical terms

✔ Encourages audience involvement if possible (by asking questions or suggesting visitors do something or look for something)

✔ Uses visuals to explain and illustrate the message

Figure 9-9. Ten considerations in writing the text for a self-guided trail stop. (Note: More tips on text writing were included in Figure 8-9.)

and a *conclusion*—each of which serves different purposes (Figure 9-8). The main task in designing effective interpretation for a self-guided trail is to make sure each part does its job well. As with the two other sequential media we've discussed (talks and guided tours), it's best to develop these parts in the 2-3-1 order (first the stops, then the conclusion and finally the introductory sign). If you're not yet familiar with the "2-3-1 Rule," see Chapters 3 and 5.

What Goes Into a Stop?

Every stop on a self-guided trail needs a *theme-title*. As we saw in the last chapter (exhibits), titles that communicate the theme of a body of text are better than

titles that give only a topic. This is because all people won't read the entire text. Theme-titles make sure that everyone who reads *at least* the title will know the theme of the stop even if they read nothing else. (Examples of theme-titles were presented in Figure 8-3.) Use the checklist in Figure 9-9 to make the stops on your self-guided trails thematic and interesting.

Each stop is a thematic part of the whole tour. As we saw in Chapter 1, little meanings add up to bigger meanings. Nowhere in interpretation is this more obvious than in a self-guided trail. It's easy to see each stop's connection to the overall theme since we selected each one precisely *because* of this relationship. It's the recognition of this relationship that we want to leave with the audience at each stop.

Achieving this outcome is relatively easy if you make sure that *each stop* has a clear theme, and that each of these relates to the overall theme of the tour.

Just as in guided tours, most stops on a self-guided tour:

1. *focus* the audience's attention on the feature being interpreted,

2. *explain* what's significant or important to notice about the feature, and

3. *connect* the explanation to the theme of the tour.

At some stops, the final part of the text may also provide a transition to the next stop, but this isn't always necessary as it is in a guided tour. The reason has mostly to do with social etiquette. A good tour guide would never turn his or her back and just start walking toward the next stop without first informing the audience. The same would be true of a narrated audio tour. People *expect* a human voice—whether it's live or recorded—to let them know when it's time to move. But people on a self-guided tour don't expect this treatment. Nevertheless, transitions are a good idea if adding them doesn't make the text too long. As we'll see shortly, a text is too long when it has more than fifty or sixty words. Some texts, however, are very short (sometimes as little as one twenty-word sentence). With these, adding a transition that makes use of foreshadowing or mystery (see Chapter 5) is an excellent idea. You might even consider planning one or two "transition stops" that are intended solely to prepare visitors for subsequent stops. (See "Ways to Make Self-Guided Tours More Dynamic" at the end of this chapter.)

From a physical design standpoint, each stop should be located in a clearing large enough for a small group (e.g., four or five people) to congregate. Ideally, other stops would not be visible from that location, thereby creating a sense of anticipation.

Focusing

Whether the interpretation is offered by a sign or brochure, the feature of interest must be clearly visible to visitors. If it's a plant, they need to be able to see in a glance which plant is being called to their attention. If it's a fire scar on a tree, how are they going to know what a fire scar is or what one looks like unless the brochure or sign tells them? If the label says "This pine tree ...", are they expected to know what a pine tree looks like? If one is growing next to a hemlock, will they know which is which? Obviously, one way to make sure is to locate the sign or numbered post *directly* in front of the feature in such a way that *no other* feature could be confused with it. Including a drawing or photograph of the feature is one way to visually orient the visitor to the focal point of the sign or brochure text. When possible, try to find features that aren't grouped closely with other features. This will make focusing on it that much easier.

Explaining

In as few words as possible, describe what the visitor is seeing and tell what aspects of it are most important to observe. Frequently, the explanation goes beyond the observable aspects of the feature to the story or significance behind it. The theme title and this explanation should correspond very closely. If you find yourself explaining things that aren't directly related to the theme title, you probably need to change your approach or develop a new theme title that more closely relates to the explanation you've written.

Most Stops Have Three Purposes

Each stop on a self-guided tour (whether it's a trail, road, building or other site) usually has three purposes: (1) *to focus* the audience's attention on an object of interest, (2) *to explain* the importance or significance of the feature, and (3) *to connect* the explanation to the overall theme of the tour. The theme-title and the information that follows it must accomplish these purposes quickly, yet interestingly. Below are the theme-title and text for a stop on a hypothetical self-guided trail. See if you can find the words that accomplish each of the three purposes. The overall theme of the trail is: "Small, unnoticed creatures are an important part of the forest environment."

Small Creatures Do Big Work

Carpenter ants are hollowing out this old tree—converting dead wood into soil for tomorrow's forest. Ants are tough. Day after day they excavate underground tunnels lugging heavy loads up and down steep hills. Watch an ant. It never rests.

Thousands of ants are at work around you. Like many small creatures, their important role in nature often goes unrecognized.

Figure 9-10. Example of a stop on a thematic self-guided trail.

Connecting

Each stop's *theme title* tells the audience what's important about the feature being interpreted, but it doesn't necessarily tell how it relates to the trail's bigger story. Often only one sentence is needed to do this. Be specific and clear. Sometimes, separating the thematic connector from the rest of the text gives it added emphasis.

Focusing, Explaining, and Connecting— An Example

Figure 9-10 shows an example text for a self-guided trail stop. Notice the theme title—it presents the main idea of the stop. Notice also that the rest of the text is written to cover the three main things a stop should do—focusing, explaining and connecting. Can you tell which part does each? The first half-sentence *focuses* attention on the tree that's being excavated by ants. This is the subject matter and focal point of the stop. The rest of the first paragraph *explains* what the viewer should notice about the tree and what's important about the ants. The second paragraph is the thematic connector—it *connects* this stop to the overall theme of the trail. In this case, the theme

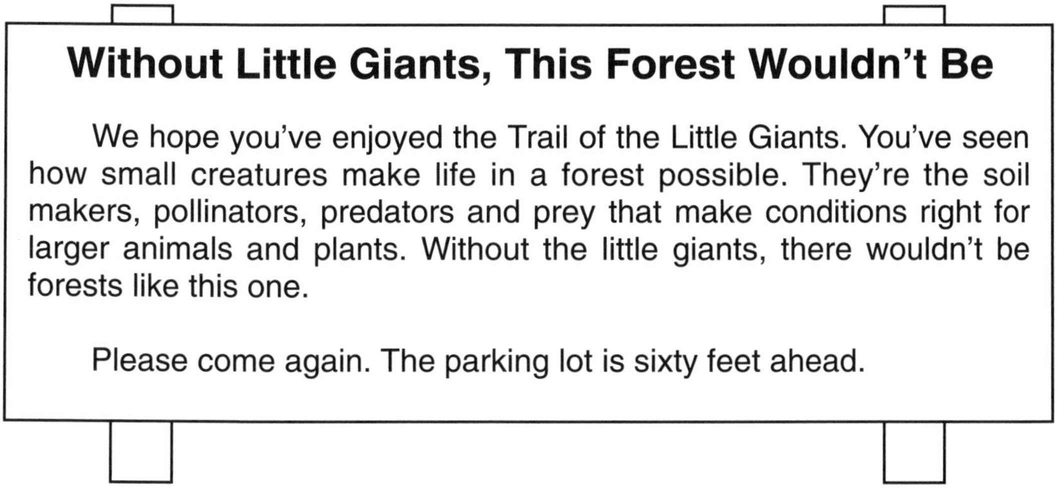

Without Little Giants, This Forest Wouldn't Be

We hope you've enjoyed the Trail of the Little Giants. You've seen how small creatures make life in a forest possible. They're the soil makers, pollinators, predators and prey that make conditions right for larger animals and plants. Without the little giants, there wouldn't be forests like this one.

Please come again. The parking lot is sixty feet ahead.

Figure 9-11. Example of a conclusion to a thematic self-guided trail.

is that small, unnoticed creatures are an important part of the forest environment. Notice how the words in the second paragraph connect what the audience has learned about ants to the trail's theme.

The text in Figure 9-10 is only one example, and you shouldn't think that *every* stop has to be organized this way. In other words, it's not a template. The important thing is simply to remember the three purposes, and to look for ways to accomplish them in a brief message. Doing so will focus your attention on carrying out a *communication strategy* rather than on simply giving information. You'll find that approaching text writing this way simplifies your task because it gives you direction and a sense of purpose in preparing each stop.

The entire text in our example comprises exactly sixty words. Look at it again. You should consider this a *long* text—the maximum length you could expect the average visitor to read. You wouldn't want every stop on a self-guided trail to contain this many words. Fifty

words would be a reasonable average, but even fewer is better. Some authors (e.g., Sharpe 1982 and U.S. Forest Service 1964) say that forty to fifty words is the optimal length. Rarely, if ever, should a text at any given stop exceed sixty-five words—that is, if you want someone to *read* it.

No known research has been done on the optimal length of stops for a walking audio tour. To be on the safe side, however, you might try to limit them to twenty to thirty seconds—roughly the amount of time it takes most people to read sixty words. (Since automobile tours usually ask visitors to listen while they're *moving*, not while they're stopped, this guideline wouldn't apply to them.)

The Conclusion

The conclusion is always the final stop on a self-guided trail. It could be a special sign—perhaps similar in size and design to the introductory sign—or it could take the same form as the other

Figure 9-12. Example of a good introductory sign. The design is simple and attractive, and the brief text quickly orients users to the theme and route of the trail. Mount St. Helens National Volcanic Monument. (Photo by Jim Pollock)

stops on the trail. A good conclusion to a self-guided tour does what any conclusion should do—it reinforces the theme. It shows one last time the relationship between the stops that were made and the main message they were designed to get across to the audience. Some conclusions briefly summarize what was seen and done during the tour, and then conclude by telling how it related to the theme. Good conclusions are short and specific. At the end, be sure to thank visitors for coming, and give simple, clear directions to guide them back to the starting point—even if the route seems *obvious* to you. Often, an invitation to return is included.

The Introductory Sign

Ordinarily, a self-guided trail begins with an introductory *sign*—even if the rest of the trail utilizes a brochure and numbered post system. The sign should call attention to the trail and make people *want* to explore the trail environment. Attractive, well organized and artistically pleasing signs do this. An imaginative title—inspired by an outstanding feature or the theme of the trail—should be prominently displayed and should stand out from the rest of the text. (Note that the title doesn't necessarily have to be a themetitle, as is so important in the individual stops.) One of the introductory sign's most important tasks is to capture the attention of the visitor and to spark an interest in the trail environment.

A good introductory sign *quickly* (in forty or fifty words) orients people to the theme of the trail. It gives a brief prelude to the trail environment and hints at what is awaiting the visitor "inside." Some of the best introductory signs foreshadow or create suspense regarding the trail. In addition, they tell visitors the length of the trail and how long it will take them to complete it. Often, it's a good idea to show an outline of the trail route (or a "bird's eye" view sketch of the site), and if applicable, the locations of one or two key features. Always important is to tell visitors where the trail will take them and where they'll be when they've finished. Ideally, the trail is circular and they'll finish at the same point where they started.

Often, introductory signs are designed in part to welcome visitors to the trail, and to tell them who their host is. Sometimes the welcome is included in the sign's title (e.g., "Welcome to Angel Falls Trail"). Other times, it's built into the first sentence of the text, but be aware that these additional words come at the expense of others if you're following the fifty-word guideline. Usually, a logo or other organizational label is sufficient to identify the host.

Welcome to the Trail of the Little Giants

This trail shows you the little things most people never even notice in a forest—ants, worms, sapsuckers, millipedes and more. You may be surprised at just how big a role they play here.

The trail takes an easy thirty-minute walk and returns you here. Total length is one-half mile.

Figure 9-13. Example of an introductory sign text for a thematic self-guided trail.

Figure 9-14. A simple system for distributing brochures for a self-guided trail. The brochure's text corresponds with numbered posts along the trail. (Photos by Jim Fazio)

Five Steps to Better Conceptual Plans

✔ Familiarize yourself and your team with the trail environment. Get a topographic map and aerial photos if they're available.

✔ Draw a map or outline of the trail showing the locations of important and interesting features, scenic views, etc. Also note areas that should be avoided (such as nests, wildlife trails, eroding slopes, fragile sites, and hazards).

✔ Decide a theme for the trail

✔ Select the stops and develop a "thematic map"

✔ Prepare a sketch or "mock-up" showing how the interpretation at each stop will look. Give the mock-ups to other people to get their ideas. Use them in a funding proposal.

Figure 9-15. Checklist for the conceptual planning of a thematic self-guided trail.

Distributing Trail Brochures

If the trail utilizes a brochure and numbered post system, you can include a supply of brochures in a box attached to the introductory sign, or you can develop some other distribution system. If your area has controlled entrance stations and the threat of vandalism prevents you from leaving a supply of brochures unattended at the trail head, consider giving people the option of obtaining one as they enter the area. There are three possible ways to do this: (1) you can give them a brochure free of charge (perhaps asking them to return it on the way out), (2) you can sell them one for a small charge, or (3) you can ask for a deposit which is reimbursable when they return the brochure. Although it's hard for them to know whether they'll really use it before actually arriving at the introductory sign, giving them a chance to obtain the brochure at the entrance station is much better than simply posting a notice at the trail head telling them they have to go all the way back to the entrance

station or to a visitor center in order to get one. This would effectively eliminate most of the audience you hoped to reach.

Conceptual Planning for Self-Guided Tours

Planning a self-guided tour starts with knowing the tour area. Whether it be a trail, a building, a farm, a highway, a research area or some other setting, you (and preferably a *planning team*) need to become familiar with the area so that you can decide on possible themes for the tour.

As with guided tours, it's a good idea to spend as much time as you can in the area. Travel the route many times, during different weather conditions and at various times of day when the tour will be available to users. If it's an outdoor tour that will be taken by visitors year-round, get to know the area during different seasons and consider changing the tour to capitalize on what's likely to be visible or particularly important during each season. Know what to expect under a variety of conditions, and how things are likely to appear to your audiences. When possible, travel the tour route with people who know it better than you do. Above all, talk to visitors and other people who are representative of the intended audience. They can tell you a lot about what's interesting and important to other people like them.

Having topographic maps and aerial photographs of the area (if they're available) is helpful because they give you a point of view that's impossible to get through other means. Use them to help you locate sites with interpretive potential, as well as hazards and sensitive or fragile areas.

During field work, be sure to record (if possible, photograph) the colors, textures, and predominant materials in the landscape. These records will help designers to blend structures and other developments (e.g., signs, supports, benches, railings, boardwalks, etc.) with the natural environment.

Figure 9-16. A planner prepares the map for a self-guided trail in Ecuador's Cotopaxi National Park. (Photo by Sam Ham)

Decide a Theme for the Trail

It's important to draw a map or (outline) of the tour route, indicating the locations of important or interesting features. This map will help you decide which stops to include in the tour once you've selected a theme. It also allows you to continue working on your ideas for the trail even when you can't be in the field (such as at night or during poor weather).

As you learn more about the area, themes will come to mind. Think thematically: "After people have completed this self-guided tour, I'd like them to know *that* (or appreciate *that*, or think *that*) ..." As we saw in Chapters 1 and 2, completing such a sentence requires you to express a theme. Having done so, potential stops on your tour will begin to become obvious to you—much more so than if you began planning stops with only a vague idea of the message you wanted to communicate.

Develop a "Thematic Map"

Once you have a theme to work with, you're ready to select stops for the trail. Remember, although there may be many interesting features along the trail, you should select only those which will support the theme. Anyway, it's not necessary or desirable to interpret *everything*. Leave some things for people to discover on their own.

Using the map you prepared, decide on a reasonable number of stops that support the overall theme of the trail (see our earlier guidelines for determining the optimal number). Now write a theme title for each one. Try to make each theme title as interesting and as stimulating as possible.

Now draw a new map, this time including only the stops you've selected.

Make Final Decisions Using a "Thematic Map"

Selecting the stops for a self-guided trail is much easier once you've decided on a theme. Draw an outline of the trail on a piece of paper and write the theme at the top. This will be a constant reminder of what the trail is supposed to teach or communicate to people. Remember that even though all the stops have their *own* themes, together they need to support the *overall* theme of the trail.

A thematic map will help you see and evaluate the connection of each stop to the theme of the trail. It also helps you make better decisions about sequence and transitions. As you select each stop, indicate its location on the outline of the trail. Next to each stop write its theme (or theme title if you've already decided it). Once you've indicated all the stops and their themes, your theme map will show you at a glance the conceptual plan for the trail. The plan is easily summarized for a report or proposal: simply write the overall theme, and underneath it, list the themes corresponding to all the stops in the order they'll be encountered (see Figure 9-18).

Figure 9-17. Example of a "thematic map." (Photo by Gerry Snyder)

Write the theme of the trail at the top, and write each stop's theme-title next to the stop it corresponds to. Once you've done this, you've got a conceptual map—a **thematic map**—for your self-guided trail. Read the theme-titles of the stops in the order a real visitor will encounter them. As you read each one, look back at the overall theme and make sure the theme-title really does support it. Ask yourself also whether the sequence of the theme-titles is adequate or whether a different order might be better. Since some features could occur in more than one place on a trail, you may have a lot of flexibility in sequencing the stops. Make adjustments in theme titles and the sequence of stops until you're satisfied with the arrangement. This is your final conceptual plan (see Figure 9-17). (Note that some interpreters may prefer the term "thematic plan" to "thematic map." The terms are interchangeable. What's important is the concept behind them.)

Keep Main Ideas to Five or Fewer

As with any presentation, be careful to keep the number of main ideas presented in the tour to five or fewer. This doesn't mean that the number of *stops* should be limited to five—but simply that the information you use to develop your theme should be organized into five or fewer *categories*. For example, if we decided that the theme of a self-guided farm tour should be that "conserving soil is the key to successful farming," we might plan stops in two major categories: those that demonstrate *good* soil

---

Trail of the Little Giants

Summary of Stops

Theme of Trail: "**Small, unnoticed creatures are an important part of the forest environment.**"

Stop	Theme Title
1	"Small Is Beautiful"
2	"Small Creatures Do Big Work"
3	"Sapsuckers Depend on Ants"
4	"Insects Attack—Birds Eat"
5	"Death Is Natural"
6	"Death Gives Rise to Life"
7	"Worms & Millipedes—Landlords of the Soil"
8	"Moths & Caterpillars—Two Times the Work"
9 (Conclusion)	"Without Little Giants, This Forest Wouldn't Be"

Figure 9-18. How to summarize a thematic map.

management and those that demonstrate *poor or inadequate* soil management. In the first category, we'd include stops that show terracing, catch-basins, banks and slopes seeded with grass, etc. In the second category we'd include stops that show run-off, dry cracked soil, and highly eroded areas. We might even have demonstration plots where food crops have been planted in good and poor soil to show the difference that soil conservation can make in farming success. All in all, we might have twelve or fourteen stops, but they'd correspond to only *two* main ideas—poor soil management and

good soil management. (See Chapter 1 for a review of the "magical number seven plus or minus two.")

Prepare a Mock-Up of Each Stop

Prepare a sketch of each stop as you envision it will look in its final form. If you're developing a brochure trail, include a sketch of both sides of the brochure layout and how it will be folded. If it's a sign trail, include a mock-up of each sign along with a sketch of the kind of signs that will be used (some examples are included in Appendix B). The sketches

Front

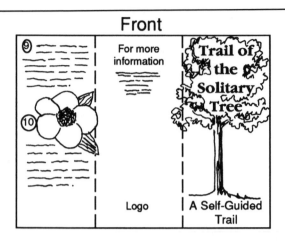

The mock-up of a brochure should include the theme titles, texts, and illustrations for each stop. Place them on the page in such a way that they'll appear in the correct sequence when the brochure is folded. See Chapter 4 for tips on making your own illustrations, and Chapter 8 for principles of layout and design.

Back

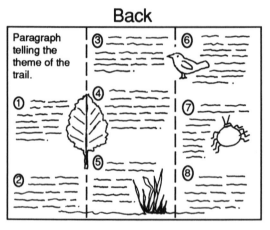

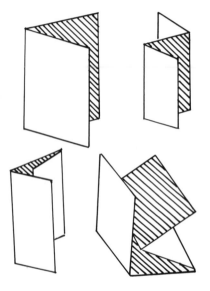

Some ways to fold simple brochures.

The draft of each sign should include the theme title, text, and illustrations for that stop.

Figure 9-19. Example mock-ups for a brochure and sign.

Figure 9-21. Example of a "peep-pipe." (Photo by Jim Fazio)

Figure 9-20. Example of a question-and-answer stop. The answer is provided under the hinged flap. (Photo by Jim Fazio)

can be circulated along with draft texts for comments or approvals. You can also use them to great advantage in funding proposals. Donors are always more likely to finance a project they can envision than one they can merely imagine.

Develop the Trail

With a solid **conceptual design** to guide you, it's time to turn your attention to the physical development of the trail environment. Unless you have the money to spend on expensive brochures or signs, you're probably going to be limited to simple, photocopied brochures or wood-routed signs. Although they might not look as sophisticated as other materials, their rustic appearance may sometimes suit the trail environment *better* than their more expensive counterparts. As we saw

in Chapter 8, communication effectiveness often is more influenced by conceptual design of the message than by the quality of the materials used to convey it. Inexpensive but well-designed brochures and signs will always communicate better than poorly designed, expensive ones. Readers interested in more expensive signs (such as fiberglass embedments, porcelain enamel or metal micro-imaging) should consult Trapp et al. (1991). Good English-language sources on producing interpretive brochures include Fazio and Gilbert (1986), Zehr et al. (1990), and Sharpe (1982). In Spanish, Moore et al. (1989) and Morales (1987) are recommended. A superb English-language summary of criteria for constructing trails and trailside structures can be found in Veverka (1979).

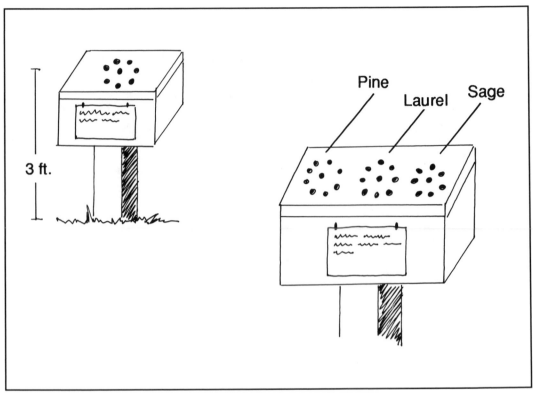

Figure 9-22. Examples of "sniff boxes." (Adapted from Brace et al. 1982, courtesy of U.S. Peace Corps)

Ways to Make Self-Guided Trails More Dynamic

Although self-guided tours lack the personal touch of a guided tour, there's no reason they can't be active and enjoyable. Following are a few things you can do to make self-guided trails more dynamic by actively involving visitors (see Figures 9-20 to 9-23):

1. Ask a question and provide the answer under a hinged flap (Figure 9-20).

2. Install self-quizzing stations that ask visitors about things they learned at previous stops (e.g., tree identification, recognition of animal homes, spotting causes and effects, etc.)

3. Turn a self-guided trail into a "scavenger hunt." On the first page of the trail brochure or directly on the introductory sign, provide a list of immovable objects or features visitors should look for in the stops ahead (e.g., a certain kind of tree, evidence of a certain kind of animal, specific kinds of geological features, a specific viewpoint, etc.) Encourage visitors to find as many as they can. A study by Bitgood and Patterson (1987) found that "cueing" visitors in this way can dramatically increase the amount of reading they'll do.

Figure 9-23. Example of a "tree finder." (Photo by Jim Fazio)

4. A hole in a vertical sign board can serve as a viewing "window" to focus visitors' attention on the feature the sign is interpreting (see Figure 8-12 in Chapter 8).

5. A tree stump or cross section could be used not only to age the tree but to analyze its life. Years of fast and slow growth, fire scars and insect attacks often show in the annual rings.

6. A viewing blind allows people to watch wildlife without bothering them. Saw viewing holes in a piece of painted external plywood and mount it on posts. Relatively dense vegetation is needed on the sides of the board to keep visitors hidden from view as they approach and leave.

7. A **peep pipe** made of a piece of old pipe or large diameter plastic tubing can be mounted on a post and fixed in place so that visitors can look through it at some distant feature being interpreted.

8. **Sniff boxes** are useful if there are plants in the area that have strong or characteristic aromas. Place pieces of the aromatic parts of the plant in a covered wooden box. The top should have a few holes large enough to let the aroma escape. Mount the sniff box on a post or pole.

9. An arrow-window exhibit mounted horizontally on a post can create several stops in one (see Chapter 8). When visitors turn the arrow to point at some distant object, the window in front of them reveals the text related to the object. Objects can include trees, geologic formations, mountains, animal homes, and other features. "Tree finders," a common kind of arrow-window exhibit, specifically interpret different types of trees.

10. Alert people to what's going on around them as they walk, and suggest they look for signs of it. For example, you might challenge them to find a leaf of a certain shape, a type of fruit, or a burrow that's characteristic of a particular kind of animal.

11. Where possible, use foreshadowing and mystery to deepen visitors' curiosity about what lies ahead on the trail. When the rest of the text is short, a brief transition about the next stop could be added without taking the text beyond the sixty-word limit. Occasionally, you might even include a stop whose only purpose is to provide a transition. For example, you could offer a transition like the following in order to foreshadow a major ecological change on the trail:

> "Pause here for a moment. Compare the forest behind you with the open meadow ahead. The environment you're about

to enter is dramatically different from the one you just left. You'll find out just how different at your next stop."

As we saw in Chapter 5, foreshadowing involves hinting at what's to come. A slightly different approach would be used to capitalize on mystery:

"Pause here for a moment. Compare the forest you just left with the open meadow ahead. What do you think causes this difference? You'll walk past the reason on your way to the next stop—see if you can spot it. When you get there, you'll find out whether you were right!"

Remember, when you foreshadow or create a sense of mystery about something, you're making a promise to visitors that you'll complete the picture for them at a later stop. Don't cultivate curiosity and then leave your audience "hanging." Other uses of foreshadowing and mystery are discussed in Chapter 5.

Glossary terms: barrier-free, conceptual design, figure-eight trail, grade (slope), introductory sign, linear trail, loop trail, peep-pipe, sniff box, self-guided tour, stops, switchback, thematic map, water bar.

Talking Trails—Inexpensive Options for Self-Guiding Trail Brochures

Michael Smithson,
Assistant Chief Naturalist
Olympic National Park,
Port Angeles, Washington

Do you have an area or trail you'd like to interpret, but just don't have the staff? With a relatively small initial investment, self-guiding brochures can help you out. A well-written brochure can provide a quality interpretive experience and give visitors a momento of their visit. At Olympic National Park, we have self-guiding brochures for ten different trails. These brochures interpret both the human and natural history of the area and are distributed from waterproof, easily maintained dispensers. Visitors lift the lid of the dispenser, deposit a quarter in a slot in the support pipe and take one of the leaflets. There's a certain amount of loss from individuals who take extra "freebies," but we bring in enough money to cover the cost of reprinting the next batch. All funds are kept in a special brochure donation account managed by the cooperating association.

Cost

The total start-up cost for a two year supply of brochures and a dispenser should be less than one-thousand dollars. The price of each brochure averages around 16 cents and we print 5,000 to 7,500 at a time to reduce production costs. Start-up costs are higher on the first printing because you have to cover the artwork, design, typesetting, and other printer's fees. Subsequent printing is usually much cheaper.

Format

A strong theme is the glue that will hold your guide together. Resist the temptation to write about whatever first appears interesting. Visit the area several times and decide what you would like visitors to understand after they've walked the trail and read your brochure.

You can develop individually numbered stops that are identified with markers, or tell the area's story in a more generalized free-flowing fashion. There are advantages and disadvantages to each style. Visitors tend to stop and read text associated with numbered markers while they're on a trail or at the site. If you choose this format, be sure to pick subjects that are relatively stable. Trees, for example, can be

struck by lightning or blown down in windstorms. Colonies of animals such as marmots can relocate and leave your brochure embarrassingly out of date.

It's easier to write about broader concepts and maintain a flow of ideas in a general brochure or booklet without individual stops, but visitors usually won't take the time to sit down and read it while they're in your area. If you're thinking about creating such a booklet, you might want to develop it to supplement a trail-specific brochure key to numbered stops. That way, after the trail experience, visitors can take the booklet with them for further reading.

Writing

Many of the techniques you use in an interpretive walk can be used in developing your brochure. Try starting off with a good "hook" to capture visitors' interest. You can incorporate questions to help them use the process of self discovery as they explore the area. A common technique is to pose a question at one stop and to answer it a few stops later. Keep the text simple, short and *active*. A voluminous or technical manuscript may satisfy the writer's need to share his or her knowledge, but few visitors will take the time to read it. Have at least two or three people proofread each draft before preparing the final text.

Design

Most of Olympic's brochures are six to twelve pages long with no more than two stops per page. An illustrated identification section for plants and animals or cultural objects can be added in the back. Brochures can be printed in many different sizes. Likewise, they can be folded or stapled in a variety of ways. We use a standard 5-1/2" x 8-1/2" format that easily fits into our brochure dispensers.

Look at other brochures to get design ideas. Desktop publishing programs can help you lay out the brochure, and if you have a laser printer you can produce camera-ready text for the printer. This can substantially reduce layout and design costs, but can be a frustrating experience until you've mastered the intricacies of the publishing software. If you don't have design expertise on your staff, consider contracting out the layout work or recruiting a volunteer to do the job.

Incorporate open space, interesting quotes, bold text "call-outs," and quality pen and ink illustrations into the design. Illustrations generally reproduce better than photographs, although historic prints can be used very effectively. A simplified map of the area helps to orient visitors and guide the flow of traffic along the trail.

All of our brochures are printed on recycled paper. If you only use one

color of ink, printing prices drop dramatically. Experiment with colors besides black. The ink color you decide to use should be dark enough to contrast well with the paper for good readability. Tinted screens behind some illustrations add depth and dimension. You can use the darkest screen of ink for text and a lighter screen for illustrations.

After experimenting with different point sizes for the text, we found the public prefers a larger type size. When given the option, two out of three visitors chose an 18-point large print version brochure designed for visually impaired individuals over a standard 10.5-point text printed for the general public. A number of people walk without their reading glasses and find it easier to read the larger print size when they're standing. Eighteen point text is not practical for all publications, but use at least a minimum of 12-point size type, and larger if possible.

Printing

Shop around for different printers as quality and cost can vary tremendously.

Sometimes it's worth it to pay a little more to avoid production errors and problems. To avoid additional hidden costs, have the printer give you a final written bid before you sign a contract.

Avoid printing brochures through the Government Printing Office unless you're using federal money to complete the project. GPO prints thousands of standard documents without problems, but they contract the work out to the lowest (and often poorest quality) bidder. You have less contact with the print shop and there are restrictions on the type and quality of paper you can use.

Be sure to check the printer's final proof of the brochure before it's ready to go to press. Ask to be present at the beginning of the first printing to check the inking and look for other problems.

Dispensers

We strongly recommend using self-serving "honor system" dispensers over coin-operated dispensers. There is less theft of booklets in the coin-operated type but visitors become justifiably frustrated when these dispensers jam. Honor-style dispensers require less staff time and allow people to return the brochure if they don't want to take it home with them.

Our dispensers are made of steel and have a lockable coin chamber built into the support pipe. We have had only one coin chamber vandalized in over a decade of use. The dispensers can be built by your area's maintenance workers or contracted out to a local welding company. The metal for each dispenser costs less than $100, but the costs increase if you want to upgrade the appearance with a wooden cover. Free plans are available from my office on request.

Evaluation

After you've finished the project, watch how visitors use the brochure. Do they read the text or just look at the illustrations? Are there problems associated with the stops that you didn't anticipate? Make careful notes and hone the design during the next printing.

Accessibility—Facts, Challenges, and Opportunities for Interpreters

Brian C. O'Callaghan
Susan J. Jurasz
Sea Reach Ltd.
Rose Lodge, Oregon

Increasingly, self-guiding interpretive trails designed to accommodate disabled visitors are turning up in our nation's parks and forests. Yet because they're usually located on natural terrain, meeting accessibility guidelines on self-guiding trails can be especially challenging for interpreters. The purposes of this case study are to review the background and rationale behind federal accessibility laws that affect not only trails, but all facilities and programs, to clarify what these laws mean and do not mean for interpreters, and to outline what we believe are the challenges and opportunities facing interpreters in regard to disabled user populations.

Accessibility isn't a new issue. Legal mandates requiring accessibility date back to 1968 and the Architectural Barriers Act (ABA). The ABA required physical accessibility in all construction and renovation projects funded in whole or part by the federal government. Official standards were soon developed, the Architectural and Transportation Barriers Compliance Board

was created, and by 1984, Uniform Federal Accessibility Standards (UFAS) were codified for all buildings covered by the ABA.

In 1973 the Rehabilitation Act was signed into law, and as amended in 1978, Section 504 of the act required program accessibility in addition to physical accessibility for facilities and programs provided with federal funds.

The Americans with Disabilities Act (ADA), which became law in 1990, addresses discrimination against individuals with disabilities in employment, transportation, telecommunications, public accommodations, and even services provided by private entities. The ADA delineates accessibility standards irrespective of federal funding, and although the ADA affects the private sector, public sector interpreters should be aware that the ADA Accessibility Guidelines (ADAAG) are slated to eventually supersede UFAS.

President George Bush characterized ADA as "one of the most comprehensive civil rights bills in history." Indeed, its passage signified the

world's first declaration of equality for people with disabilities and made the United States an international leader on a very basic human rights issue—accessibility.

The world is now watching to see how the U.S. will respond to ADA. How will we remove the physical, social and intellectual barriers built and accepted for decades in our country? Our success or failure in keeping the promises of ADA as the culmination of a long and arduous legislative process will affect the lives of hundreds of millions of people. Accessibility will pose the most significant challenges and present the some of the most exciting opportunities that many interpreters will face in their professional careers.

Who Are the Disabled?

The research supporting the ADA recognized 17.2 percent of the U.S. population as overtly experiencing "a physical or mental impairment that substantially limits one or more of the major life activities... a record of such an impairment, or being regarded as having such an impairment." When this figure is combined with the 32.2 percent that report experiencing a mental disorder some time in their lives, the 1 percent estimated to be cognitively impaired, the 6 percent over the age of

70 with low stamina or impaired coordination, the 10 percent considered temporarily disabled due to accident or disease, and the millions of small and obese people, pregnant women, and the friends and families of all these people, disability must be considered a normal part of human life. Given these criteria, everyone is disabled at some time in their lives, and therefore, everyone stands to benefit from increased accessibility.

The Challenges for Interpreters

The first challenge for interpreters is intellectual. It requires us to replace the old idea that we must somehow accommodate the "average human being" with a new world view in which we attempt to address all degrees of sensory awareness, all types of locomotion, and all levels of physical and intellectual function. This challenge presents a unique opportunity for interpreters to reassess their professional skills, indulge their innate creativity, to experiment, and to solicit the involvement of disabled individuals along with other user groups early in the design phase of a project. To meet this challenge, interpreters must first understand exactly what is meant by "accessibility."

The word "accessible" when used in reference to persons with disabilities is frequently misunderstood and misinterpreted. Under the law, however, it carries a very specific meaning: the UFAS, for example, defines the term as "a site, building, facility or portion thereof that complies with these [UFAS] standards, and that can be approached, entered and used by physically disabled people."

The use of the conjunction, "and" in this definition is important. It means that simply providing physical access is not enough. People must be able to use facilities once physical access has been achieved. In other words, to be truly accessible under the law, programs and facilities must offer persons with disabilities the opportunity to achieve experiences similar to those offered others. This means that programs and facilities must be designed to be approached, entered and used by persons with disabilities. Accessibility means providing the disabled person a place to park, routes of entry and exit, rest rooms, water and all services (including interpretive services) that may be offered other user groups.

The second challenge for interpreters will be defining and then successfully providing the "accessible interpretive experience." This will entail innovation, research and development, and unavoidable risk. The latter stems from the fact that, so far anyway, the only true measure of compliance with federal guidelines is the outcome of a lawsuit. But even this presents an opportunity—to exploit one's creative ingenuity, to experiment with solutions to accessibility problems, and especially to actively and openly involve diverse user groups in the interpretive design process.

When and Where Is Accessibility Required?

One of the most frequently asked questions among interpretive designers is, "when is accessibility required?" A common misunderstanding is that all facilities (such as buildings and trails) have to be completely accessible. This is not the case. People with disabilities, like all humans, possess unique physical and intellectual needs, but their general life experience expectations are the same as the so-called "able-bodied population." Since an accessible facility intends to offer persons with disabilities an opportunity to achieve experiences similar to those offered others, what is important is that facilities are not designed to preclude disabled people from having access to a full range and variety of opportunities that would normally be expected at a particular site or in a particular kind of facility. Therefore, not all facilities and programs will be 100 percent accessible— nor is this desirable. Facilities and programs should, however, provide the highest practicable level of access for persons with disabilities taking into account expectations, experience levels, and the capabilities and potentials inherently offered by a particular site. So do all self-guiding trails need to be 100 percent accessible for visitors with disabilities? No. But should they strive to provide access to fullest extent possible given the inherent characteristics of the site and the experiences it is designed to produce? Yes.

For interpreters, perhaps the greatest challenge posed by the accessibility issue will be that of matching society's general expectations for accessibility with a given site's inherent possibilities and naturally occurring physical barriers. This challenge also presents interpreters one of their greatest opportunities—to test their skills and resourcefulness, to critically examine the purposes behind their facilities and programs, and to rethink their responsibilities as professionals.

Costs Versus Benefits

Accessibility does not have to be expensive. In fact, studies show that its not expensive if it's taken into account in early stages of design. Generally, building accessibility specifications into a new project adds only about 1 percent to the total cost of a project, whereas retrofitting (renovating or rebuilding inaccessible facilities) may add up to 40 percent to the original costs. Since facilities designed with accessibility in mind don't inhibit utilization by other population segments, providing accessibility actually enhances usability of a facility for all people. Accessible facilities and programs cater to the majority, and by doing so, serve the interests of all of us. Accessibility, therefore, is not only the law, it makes good dollars and sense.

References

Beechel, Jacque. 1975. *Interpretation for Handicapped Persons: A Handbook for Outdoor Recreation Personnel*. Seattle, Washington, USA: U.S. National Park Service, Pacific Northwest Regional Office.

Berkmüller, Klaus. 1981. *Guidelines and Techniques for Environmental Interpretation*. Ann Arbor, Michigan, USA: School of Natural Resources, University of Michigan.

Bitgood, Stephen and Donald Patterson. 1987. *Cueing Visitors to Read Exhibit Labels: Effects of Handouts That Ask Questions*. Paper presented at the Southeastern Psychological Association Annual Meeting. Jacksonville, Alabama, USA: Psychology Institute,

Brace, Judith, Ralph R. White and Stephen C. Bass. 1982. *Teaching Conservation in Developing Nations*. Washington, D.C., USA: U.S. Peace Corps, Information Collection and Exchange, Manual M-7.

Cole, David N. and Edwin E. Krumpe. 1992. Seven Principles of Low-Impact Wilderness Recreation. *Western Wildlands* 18(1):39-43.

Fazio, James R. and Douglas L. Gilbert. 1986. *Public Relations and Communications for Natural Resource Manager*. Dubuque, Iowa, USA: Kendall/Hunt Publishing Co.

Grater, Russell K. 1976. *The Interpreter's Handbook: Methods, Skills and Techniques*. Globe, Arizona, USA: Southwest Parks and Monuments Association.

Hammitt, William E. and David N. Cole. 1987. *Wildland Recreation—Ecology and Management*. New York, New York, USA: John Wiley and Sons.

Majewski, Janice. 1987. *Part of Your General Public is Disabled*. Washington, D.C., USA: Smithsonian Institution Press.

Sharpe, Grant W. 1982. Self-Guided Trails. Chapter 14 in Sharpe, G.W.(ed.), *Interpreting the Environment*. New York, New York, USA: John Wiley & Sons.

Tai, Doris B. 1981. *An Evaluation of the Use and Effectiveness of Two Types of Interpretive Trail Media in Yellowstone National Park.* Moscow, Idaho, USA: Masters thesis, Department of Resource Recreation and Tourism, University of Idaho.

Trapp, Suzanne, Michael Gross and Ron Zimmerman. 1991. *Signs, Trails, and Wayside Exhibits—Connecting People and Places.* Stevens Point, Wisconsin, USA: UW-SP Foundation Press, Inc.

U.S. Architectural and Transportation Barriers Compliance Board. 1991. *Americans with Disabilities Act: Accessibility Guidelines for Buildings and Facilities.* Washington, D.C., USA: U.S. Government Printing Office.

U.S. Architectural and Transportation Barriers Compliance Board. 1985. *Uniform Federal Accessibility Standards.* USGPO Publication 1985-494-187. Washington, D.C., USA: U.S. Government Printing Office.

U.S. Forest Service. 1964. *Developing the Self-Guiding Trail in the National Forests.* USDA Forest Service Miscellaneous Publication 968. Washington, D.C., USA: U.S. Government Printing Office.

Veverka, John A. 1979. *Interpretive Trails Manual.* Lansing, Michigan, USA: John Veverka and Associates.

Wetterberg, Gary B. 1982. Self-Guided Auto Tours. Chapter 15 in Sharpe, G.W.(ed.), *Interpreting the Environment.* New York, New York, USA: John Wiley & Sons.

Zehr, Jeffrey, Michael Gross and Ron Zimmerman. 1990. *Creating Environmental Publications: A Guide to Writing and Designing for Interpreters and Environmental Educators.* Stevens Point, Wisconsin, USA: UW-SP Foundation Press, Inc.

Additional Reading

In English:

Countryside Commission. 1980. *Self-Guided Trails.* Advisory Series No. 5. London, United Kingdom: Countryside Recreation Research Group.

Dawson-Medina, Leslie Y. and Cathy Shank. 1987. *Interpretation and Environmental Education: A Practitioner's Handbook.* Washington, D.C., USA: World Wildlife Fund.

Fazio, James R. 1976. *Nature Trails: Guides to Environmental Understanding.* 4-H Leaders Guide L-5-4. Ithaca, New York, USA: Cooperative Extension Service, College of Agriculture and Life Sciences, Cornell University.

Jones, D.K. 1992. The Ambiguities of the ADA. *Identity—The International Magazine of Signs and Corporate Graphics* (Spring).

MacKinnon, John, Kathy MacKinnon, Graham Child and James Thorsell (eds.). 1986. *Managing Protected Areas in the Tropics* (Chapter 7). Cambridge, United Kingdom: International Union for the Conservation of Nature & Natural Resources and the United Nations Environment Program.

McIntosh, Paul A. 1982. Signs and Labels. Chapter 12 in Sharpe, G.W.(ed.), *Interpreting the Environment.* New York, New York, USA: John Wiley & Sons.

Park, D.C. 1989. What Is Accessibility? *Design* (Spring). Washington, D.C., USA: USDI National Park Service and National Recreation and Park Association.

In Spanish:

Berkmüller, Klaus. 1981. *Educación Ambiental sobre el Bosque Lluvioso.* Gland, Suiza: Unión Internacional para la Conservación de la Naturaleza y los Recursos Naturales.

Ham, Sam H. 1992. *Interpretación Ambiental: Una Guía Práctica para Gente con Grandes Ideas y Presupuestos Pequeños.* Golden, Colorado, USA: North American Press/Fulcrum Publishing.

MacKinnon, John, Kathy MacKinnon, Graham Child y James Thorsell (eds.). 1990. *Manejo de Areas Protegidas en los Trópicos* (Capítulo 7). Cancun, Quintana Roo, México: Amigos de Sian Ka'an A.C.

Moore, Alan, Bill Wendt, Louis Penna e Isabel Castillo de Ramos. 1989. *Manual para La Capacitación del Personal de Areas Protegidas* (Modulo C: Interpretación y Educación Ambiental, Apunte 4a). Washington, D.C., USA: Servicio de Parques Nacionales, Oficina de Asuntos Internacionales.

Morales, Jorge. 1987. *Manual para la Interpretación en Espacios Naturales Protegidos.* Anexo 3 del Taller Internacional sobre Interpretación Ambiental en Areas Silvestres Protegidas. Santiago, Chile: Oficina Regional de la FAO para América Latina y el Caribe, 7-12 de diciembre de 1988.

CHAPTER TEN

HOW TO PRODUCE AN INEXPENSIVE SLIDE/TAPE PROGRAM

Audiovisual programs are an important communication medium for natural resource professionals. Because they appeal both to our eyes and ears, they're often entertaining, bringing sights and sounds from the real world to audiences that might otherwise never know them. Although producing an audiovisual program is time consuming, once it exists you can show it time and again without having to rehearse as you would with a talk. If the program is simple enough to operate, you can even send it to be shown unaccompanied by an interpreter. In this chapter, we'll focus on one of the most common and least expensive types of audiovisual programs in environmental interpretation—slide/tape programs.

Types of Audiovisual Programs

Slide/tape programs are just one of many types of audiovisual programs

(Figure 10-1). Other common ones in natural resource fields are videotape presentations, film strip presentations, movies, and booklet-with-tape presentations (see Figure 10-1). Although the latter category has been restricted primarily to storybook applications for pre-literate children (e.g., "listen-and-look" books), it may represent a convenient and innovative medium for certain kinds of school and youth group programs.

Because producing videotapes and motion pictures is so highly specialized and expensive, we won't cover them here. Unless you work for an agency or organization that can afford to hire in-house production specialists, your use of these media is probably limited to borrowing or renting videos and films for special showings. On the other hand, highly effective slide/tape programs, film strips, and booklet-with-tape programs can be produced without a lot of special equipment or expertise. In this chapter, we'll focus specifically on producing slide/tape programs. With only minor adaptation, however, the steps and procedures we'll follow could be used to prepare the other two as well. A film strip is simply a roll of film that contains duplicates of slides that would have appeared in the same sequence in a slide program. The difference is that the film hasn't been cut up into individual slides mounted in frames. A booklet-with-tape program is really the same except that each page of the booklet contains the visual information that would have appeared in the slide of a slide program or a single frame of a film strip presentation.

Why Slide/Tape Programs?

Slide/tape programs are among the most common audiovisual media in natural resource fields. Their popularity is due to their many advantages. Since they're portable, you can take them almost anywhere there's electricity and a screen (or something that can be used as one). An especially important advantage of slide/tape programs is that slides can easily be replaced or updated, allowing continual improvement of a program at little cost. Overall, slide/tape programs are inexpensive compared to other audiovisual media and relatively easy to produce in-house. Like all audiovisual programs, slide/tape programs are consistent—they present their message the same way every time you show them. Even if you're ill or simply can't be there, your presentation goes on just as if you were giving it yourself.

In this chapter, you'll see how easy it is to produce a good, but low-cost slide/tape program. As always, we'll be following a thematic approach. If you're not yet familiar with themes and thematic communication, you should review Chapters 1 and 2 before going any further with this chapter. In addition, you might want to take a look at the section on slides in Chapter 4. Many of the guidelines for preparing and using slides in a talk will apply equally to slide/tape programs.

Many references on producing slide/tape programs are available. In English, Bishop (1984), Podracky (1983), Hooper (1987), Stecker (1987), and Fazio and Gilbert (1986) are recommended. A good summary of basic audio equipment and their applications is contained in Smith-White (1982). Readers interested in more advanced applications or specifically in multi-image production should consult Kenny and Schmitt (1981). In Spanish, Moore et al. (1989), and Morales (1987) offer good discussions about script writing and some general guidelines related to technical production. In addition, Muñoz and Peña (1990) provide a useful summary of audio recording considerations.

Five Steps to Better Slide/Tape Programs

Developing a slide/tape program is similar to developing an illustrated talk. As we saw in Chapter 3, an effective talk requires a theme and a good introduction, body, and conclusion to support it. Once you've accomplished this, you can then find or create slides to illustrate the words you'll be saying. This is precisely the way a good slide/tape program is produced except, of course, that the words the audience hears are coming from a tape rather than from your mouth. Another difference is that along with your voice the audience may hear music and/or sound effects that you've added for dramatic effect.

There Are Many Kinds of Audiovisual Programs	
Type of Program	**Typical Form and Uses**
Slide/tape program	One or more slide projectors that show images synchronized to a sound track recorded on tape. The slides may be changed manually: (1) by someone who has memorized the sequence and timing of the slides, (2) by following a script, or (3) by listening for a noise or tone recorded on the tape at the precise moment each slide should change. Slides can also be changed automatically using a special tape player with slide-synchronization capability. Programs may use: (1) a single-projector showing a single image, (2) multiple projectors that are aligned on the same screen to show a single image, or (3) multiple projectors that are aligned on separate screens to show multiple images simultaneously. Single-projector programs that are manually operated may be shown in a central location such as an auditorium, projection room or outdoor amphitheater, or they can be sent to other people to be shown unaccompanied by an interpreter. Automated and multiple-projector programs usually require someone knowledgeable with the set-up and operation of the equipment.
Videotape	Usually, a video cassette player (VCR) is used to show a videotape on a television monitor. Most common are 1/2 inch tapes in either VHS or Beta format. (In Latin America, Beta is just as common as VHS so be sure to determine which kind you have.) Increasingly common and much more portable are 8 mm video cassettes. Videotapes may be shown anywhere there's a television monitor and a VCR appropriate for the kind of tape you're using. Multiple monitors can be used to show the same tape to more than one audience simultaneously.
Film strip/ tape program	A roll of uncut and unmounted film (usually 35 mm) is shown in sequence on a screen using a film strip projector. The images (or frames) are synchronized to a soundtrack recorded on a tape. Frames can be changed manually: (1) by someone who has memorized the sequence and timing of the images, (2) by following a script, or (3) by listening for a signal or tone recorded on an accompanying tape at the precise moment each image should change. Film strip projectors that change automatically also exist. Film strips may be shown anywhere there is a film strip projector and a screen, but they're usually used in formal academic settings. Slide programs have all but eliminated the use of film strip programs in some countries, but they're still used in many places.

Movie	A motion picture is shown on a screen using a movie projector. Common are 16 mm, 8 mm and Super 8 mm films and projectors. Movies may be shown anywhere there is a movie projector and a screen. They're common in both formal and non-formal education settings.
Booklet-with-tape program	Where slide projectors aren't available, visuals can be reproduced in the form of a booklet. Each page of the booklet serves the same purpose as a slide. Listeners are instructed to turn to the next page by a person following a script or by a noise or signal recorded on the tape. Booklet-with-tape programs are probably best suited for classroom presentations, since battery-powered tape players can be used in places where electricity for slide projectors is unavailable.

Figure 10-1. Examples of audiovisual programs.

Five steps are involved in producing a slide/tape program: (1) script writing, (2) storyboarding, (3) photography and acquisition of existing slides, (4) soundtrack production, and (5) programming (or slide synchronization). Following are descriptions of what you should do and think about in each of these steps in order to produce an inexpensive slide/tape program. Although in a few cases we'll consider some slightly more expensive alternatives, even the least expensive methods can be surprisingly effective.

Step 1: Drafting the Script

Drafting a good **script** is the first step toward an effective slide/tape program. Although you'll probably make changes when you prepare the storyboard and begin pulling together the slides, having concrete ideas about the narration is crucial to selecting strong visuals. Without a script to guide you, you'll run the dan-ger of assembling a collection of pretty slides that don't say much.

As with talks, a script should be built around a central theme with an introduction, body, and conclusion designed to accomplish specific purposes. In Chapter 3, we saw that the "2-3-1 rule" (body, conclusion, introduction) could be used as a guide for developing thematic presentations. This guideline applies equally to script writing for an audiovisual program. Refer to Chapter 3 for a review of the purposes of introductions, bodies, and conclusions and an explanation of the 2-3-1 rule and how to apply it. In addition, be sure to review the four qualities of the interpretive approach presented in Chapter 1. They're *essential* to writing scripts that will capture and maintain a noncaptive audience's attention.

Where to Locate the Theme Statement

An important difference between a "canned" audiovisual program and a "live" talk is that in the latter the speaker can repeat or rephrase things, return to an earlier point, check for understanding, and if necessary, make changes in the presentation based on audience feedback. Audiovisual programs can't do this. They just keep going, even if the audience is confused. Although every part of the script is important, a good introduction is essential to avoiding confusion. Remember that one purpose of an introduction is to reveal the theme of the presentation. In a script, this is especially important because if people in the audience understand the theme clearly from the very beginning, the likelihood they'll be confused later is much reduced. Although there aren't any firm rules about where the theme statement ought to go in an introduction, beginning script writers often find that it helps to put it in the first sentence.

For example, the theme of a slide/tape program on the geologic history of Olympic National Park (located in the northwestern U.S.) was that if people looked in the right places, they could find evidence of the park's unseen geologic past. The program's narration began with the theme statement as follows:

"Olympic National Park is a product of the unseen." (followed by the rest of the introduction)

Theme statements at the end of an introduction can also be effective. The following example comes from a slide/tape program on forest succession. The theme was that forests are ever-changing, and that one must think in terms of centuries to really know what has gone on in a forest. In the following excerpt from the introduction, notice that the final segments give the theme of the program, followed by a transition to the body:

"These trees have seen a lot. If they could talk, they might tell us stories about great avalanches in the mountains high above them, or the grinding of glaciers—one after another—in the valleys below them, the explosive eruption of nearby volcanoes, and the countless billions of seeds that have fallen and failed to take root beneath these ancient giants. Yes, these are the *survivors*. And although they can't speak, their annual rings tell us much of what they've experienced here.

"As you'll see in the next few minutes, change...sometimes *dramatic* change...has been a constant in this old forest, but to truly appreciate it, we must be able to think in terms of centuries." (*Theme sentence*)

"Let's listen now to what these trees are telling us." (*Transition sentence*)

Transitions

The transition at the end of this introduction was important because it let the listeners know that the introduction had ended, and that the story it introduced was about to be told. As we've seen repeatedly in this book, transitions help make sure that listeners know where a presentation is taking them. By doing this, a well-placed transition reduces the work the audience has to do in order to understand what's going on.

In a slide/tape program, the same effect might be achieved without words by using a "black slide" (see Chapter 4). If (at the end of the initial series of slides) the screen had been darkened just as the word "centuries" was said, the audience would have known that the introduction had ended even without the transition. That's because in visual communication, darkening the screen (whether it be a projection screen or a television screen) *always* signifies a change or transition. In a slide/tape program, a dark screen says, "Pay attention, because something is about to change." Because of this, black slides between the introduction and body, and between the body and conclusion are often a good idea. Of course, as we saw in Chapter 4, it's also a good idea to put black slides (or if you prefer, colored translucent slides) at the beginning and end of the program.

Indicating Narrator Inflection

Going back to the example introduction, notice the use of italics in the words *survivors* and *dramatic*. When you read these words, did you put a little more emphasis on them than you did on the other words? Probably so. Use italics, underlining, or CAPITAL LETTERS to identify words that should be stressed when the script is narrated. Doing this as you write not only helps the narrator to read the script as you intended it to be read, it also helps you to write the script with more feeling.

Notice also the ellipsis (...) before and after the phrase,"...sometimes *dramatic* change...". When you were reading

that part of the introduction, did you pause momentarily when you got to each ellipsis? Again, probably so. That's exactly what a narrator would do, too. Use ellipses to indicate pauses in a script, or any place a little extra time is needed between words. If a more pronounced pause is needed, use a double ellipsis (......). For example, if a sentence in the script gives a list of things that you want to show in individual consecutive slides, be sure to leave enough time between each one and the next for the slide to change. Notice the difference in the following examples:

> "Here in the Río Plátano, you'll find virtually every form of life: amphibians, reptiles, insects, mammals, birds, and some of the most unusual plants on earth."

> "Here in the Río Plátano, you'll find virtually every form of life...amphibians...reptiles...insects...mammals...birds...and some of the most unusual plants on earth."

Writing for the Ear and the Eye

When preparing a script for an audiovisual program, imagine that you're speaking instead of writing. In other words, write a script to be *listened* to, not to be read. This is called "writing for ear." If you do this, you'll find that your scripts will be livelier, conversational, and more interesting to listeners. If you've written your script for ear, you'll also find it easier to coach your narrator to read your script well. As we discuss later, this can be particularly important if a radio or television

"Writing for Ear" Leads to Better Scripts and Better Narrations

1. Remember that your audience will hear (not read) your message. Listeners should be able to keep up with what they're hearing without putting out a lot of effort. Readers, on the other hand, can stop, ponder something, or go back and review something if they wish. This isn't possible for listeners; the recorded message keeps right on going.

2. Select your theme and decide on your approach and vehicle if you're going to use one (see Chapter 3).

3. If you're writing a script for an audiovisual program, draft the script before planning the visuals. Although there's always a give-and-take relationship, let your first concern be to write a strong script, and then turn your attention to the visuals. In other words, rather than writing to fit the slides you happen to have on file, let your script be strengthened by the fact that you know your visual approach and creative concept.

4. Decide on the approximate length of the message. For audiences that are standing, one-and-a-half to two minutes is usually considered a maximum length. For seated audiences, fifteen minutes is usually the upper limit, while ten to twelve minutes is a typical duration for slide/tape programs.

5. Outline the script following the "2-3-1 Rule"(body, conclusion, then introduction).

6. Write the draft script:
   a. Don't be afraid to use emotional appeals or a personification vehicle (see Chapter 1).
   b. Consider testimonials, characterizations, oral history excerpts, etc.
   c. Write narrations as though the narrator is having a conversation with the listeners—not lecturing to them or instructing them, but rather *chatting with them*.
   d. Use broken or even incomplete sentences for feeling and meaning. Silence and prolonged pauses (especially at the ends of sentences) can add dramatic effect to the spoken word. Indicate pauses with an ellipsis (…) and longer pauses with a double ellipsis (……).
   e. If the script includes a list of things that need to be shown in separate consecutive slides (e.g., plant or animal species, or a series of locations or features), be sure to plan pauses between the words long enough to allow smooth, unhurried slide changes.
   f. Think about the inflection the narrator should use, and indicate it by underlining, *italicizing*, CAPITALIZING or otherwise **highlighting** different parts of the text. As you're writing, imagine the narrator speaking the words, rather than reading them.

7. Read the draft script aloud many times, practicing inflection and pauses, and playing any prerecorded excerpts at the appropriate moments. Get to know your script. This will help you work with the narrator and others who might be involved. The biggest problem with narrations is that they sound read instead of spoken. Concentrate on this, and practice "saying" your script instead of reading it.

8. If you're not going to narrate your own script, you may need to coach the narrator:

a. Broadcast inflection and narrating inflection are different. Make sure your narrator understands the difference. Your message should sound more like a story than the evening news. Remember, not all broadcasters are good narrators. The best narrators have natural sounding voices that seem to originate from the mouth, not deep in the diaphragm.

b. Many people new to narrating speak too rapidly. Remember that the listeners won't be able to see the narrator's mouth and face. Hearing the words clearly and distinctly is extremely important. Inexperienced narrators often have to speak at about 3/4 of their normal speaking rate. This will seem awkward to them (and possibly to you) at first. But persevere—the results will sound quite normal when the narration and accompanying background sounds are recorded on tape and played back. Listeners usually won't know the narrator personally, and so they won't know that she or he is speaking slower than normal. They'll think the tempo is just right.

9. Record the narration. Play it for others and ask them to tell where it was stiff, too fast, or unnatural. Revise it accordingly.

10. Prepare the final tape.

Figure 10-2. Tips on writing and narrating scripts.

broadcaster is reading the script for you. Most of them have been trained in broadcasting inflection (such as on the evening news), not narrating inflection (such as in a documentary). The two are substantially different. Additional ideas on writing for ear are listed in Figure 10-2.

Writing for the eye is also important, especially when you make changes to the script during storyboarding (Step 2). As you plan or select each slide, you may be able to adjust the narration to capitalize on some feature or quality of it. Or you may be able to add a sentence to set it up better. Sometimes, you may have a creative concept or vehicle that requires a special writing style. Keeping the visuals in mind as you write the script will help you capture this style.

A Word About Personification

Perhaps more than any other communication medium, audiovisual programs lend themselves to the use of personification vehicles. Recall from Chapter 1 that personification is a technique whereby a communicator gives human qualities to nonhuman things in order to make them more interesting to an audience. A few years ago, one of my students produced an emotionally moving slide/tape program in which the narrator was an old and tired cougar. In a whisper-like voice, he explained to the audience that he was the very last cougar in a particular mountain range in the southwestern United States. All the others had left or died from various causes including poisoning, shooting, and advanced age. After telling the audience about the decline of his species, the cougar narrator explained that he, too, was dying. Then the program was over. All of us in the audience were moved. Thanks to the cougar's powerful narration, we left thinking that the extinction of cougars from those mountains was a grave and unnecessary loss. This was the theme the student wanted to leave with us. He succeeded.

Everyone knew the narrator of this program wasn't a *real* cougar. But the facts and descriptions he gave about cougar ecology were scientifically accurate; the mountain range *really did* exist, and there *really were* no more cougars there. A normal, third-person narrator could never have told this story with the same impact. And despite what critics of personification

claim, not one of us left thinking that cougars *really* think and *really* talk like human beings.

Another use of personification was a hat that told a story about seasonal changes. As each new season arrived, a slide of the hat reappeared clad in different apparel (ear muffs, sunglasses, etc.). Another personified vehicle was a talking tree who taught his audience of 4-H kids about forest ecology. In order to show the kids what the narrator looked like, a pair of paper eyes and a smiling paper mouth were attached to a tree trunk and photographed (Figure 10-3). But it's not always necessary to show the narrator in a personified program. The cougar narrator, for example, never appeared on the screen. It was better for everyone in the audience to have his or her own image of what he looked like.

Step 2: Preparing the Storyboard

Once you've drafted a strong script for a slide/tape program, it's time to focus on the visuals. The best way to organize

Figure 10-3. Examples of personified narrators. *Left*: A talking tree (photo by David Shaw). *Right*: Three shells form the face of a character who tells a delightful story about invertebrates and intertidal ecology (photo by Tom O'Brien).

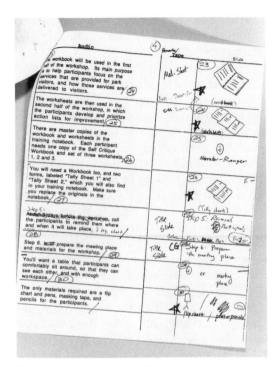

Figure 10-4. A typical storyboard format. (Photo by Peter Slisz)

your thoughts is to develop a **storyboard**. A storyboard is just a visual plan in which you indicate the kinds of slides that would be best to show in each part of the program, and where they should change. As you do this, you'll undoubtedly make small changes in the script to accommodate or capitalize on the visuals you select.

There are a lot of ways to develop a storyboard and none is necessarily better or worse than the others. Like so many things in creative communication, it's simply a matter of what suits you best. Some producers like to use individual note cards. On each card they include a segment of the script and a drawing or description of the visual or visuals that are desired at that point. However, many producers say that separating pieces of the narration on note cards can lead to choppy or segmented programs that lack fluidity. These producers like to indicate slide changes directly on the script, itself. To do this, they divide pieces of paper into two columns. In the left column they type the script; in the right column they make notes about slides. Other producers tape whole sheets of paper to the right margin of each page of the script in order to give themselves lots of space for making notes about visuals. A typical storyboard is shown in Figure 10-4. The circled numbers in the narration show precisely where each slide should change. The numbers next to the slide descriptions in the right column correspond to the numbers in the text.

Planning the Visuals

As you prepare the storyboard, try to put yourself in the place of an audience member. Ask yourself what really needs to be illustrated, and what doesn't. Beginning producers sometimes try to illustrate too many things, as though each word somehow had to be represented on the screen. Be selective, focusing on key images that will come and go as needed in order to give the narration a visual dimension. Most important is to remember that you're looking for slides that will make the words more meaningful. As you plan the visuals, think not only about slides you already have, but about those you might borrow from other people, field photographs you, yourself, could shoot for the program, and those you could create using a **photo copystand** (e.g., pictures from magazines and calendars, shots of logos, covers of documents, graphs, charts, and other visual representations of data, etc.). If you photograph copyrighted material, be sure to obtain permission first, and plan to add a slide at the end of the program that acknowledges the source(s).

Types of Illustrations

In general, there are four kinds of illustrations in most slide/tape programs: **literal illustrations**, **representations**, **graphics**, and **symbolic illustrations**. Slides in any of these categories can occur individually, or in series, depending on what needs to be shown.

Literal illustrations show photographs of things as they really appear. A literal illustration of a particular type of deer, for example, would be a slide of that kind of deer.

Unlike literal illustrations, *representations* show images that relate only in a general way to the ideas being presented by the narrator. That is, they represent the ideas but don't show them directly. An example would be a slide of a park entrance sign that's projected as the park is being mentioned, or a slide of many people at a visitor center as the narrator refers to the popularity of the park.

Graphics usually depict ideas with drawings, charts, tables, figures or words. For example, it's one thing to show a picture of an individual deer, but how do you illustrate the decline in the population of a whole species? A graph showing a downward sloping line over time would work for many audiences. Alternatively, a series of drawings labeled by year could show a progressively smaller group of deer in each slide (first ten deer, then five deer then two deer, etc.). Word-slides, lists, acknowledgements and credits are also examples of graphics. See "Designing Effective Visual Aids" in Chapter 4 for tips on how to create interesting and informative graphics. You should also review the case studies on creating colored background slides and Kodalith graphics at the end of Chapter 4. With just a little forethought, almost anyone can use one or both of these procedures to add professional-looking colored graphics to a slide/tape program.

Symbolic illustrations are "visual metaphors," that use images symbolically related to an idea in the narration. They're useful when you want to illustrate something that can't be seen (like an emotion or the passing of time), or when the ideas you're presenting are too abstract for literal or graphic illustration (for example, the process whereby a whole population of people gradually leaves a town, a few at a time over many years, until all that remain are a few old timers). Trying to illustrate any of these ideas literally would be difficult, and possibly even silly. The passing of time, however, could be illustrated with two or more slides showing people dressed in fashions from different time periods; if the time interval is shorter, a series of slides showing a gradually setting sun or clouds moving past a fixed point could be used; a community on its way to becoming a ghost town could be symbolized by a series of three or four slides of a dandelion with heavy seeds, each one containing fewer seeds than the previous one. (Of course, you blew off a few seeds between each of the photographs.)

As you read the script, think of the four kinds of illustrations. As a general rule, plan to let each slide remain on the screen until it's no longer pertinent to the narration. When this occurs, plan to change to a new slide that would best illustrate the next segment of narration. If a segment of narration is so long that you feel one slide is insufficient, add additional slides related to the subject, or different versions of the same slide—perhaps taken from a different angle—or close-ups of different parts of it (see "Guidelines for Using Slides" in Chapter 4).

Planning for Musical Interludes

A useful technique in slide/tape programs is to occasionally plan music-only segments in the sound track. These **musical interludes** (or "music-ludes" as they're sometimes abbreviated) are usually used in one or more of three ways: (1) to begin the program (usually with a brief series of slides representative of the subject that will be introduced when the narration begins), (2) to end the program (usually with a brief series of final subject-matter slides and credits following the last sentence of the narration), and (3) to reinforce key ideas made in the body of the program (usually between main narration segments, each time with slides that relate back to the ideas you've just presented). As you develop the storyboard, look for places to incorporate music-ludes and plan the slides that will accompany them. Be careful not to make music-ludes too long, especially at the beginning and end of the program. After an introductory slide series of even thirty or forty seconds, an audience may be lulled to the point of being startled by the narrator's first words.

By far, the best way to improve your storyboarding skills is to study the techniques used on television and in movies. In particular, pay attention to how sounds and visuals are used together for dramatic impact. It's true, unfortunately, that being so analytical about a movie or television program can get in the way of your enjoyment, but the pay off is that you'll soon be capitalizing on the same techniques in your own audiovisual programs.

Step 3: Photography and Acquisition of Slides

Once completed, the storyboard represents a list of the slides you'll need. Some will be slides you already have; some will be slides that can you can borrow; and some will be slides or series of slides that need to be created either through field photography or using a copystand. We won't be covering photographic technique in this book since so many excellent guides are available. If you're completely unfamiliar with cameras, you should arrange for someone else to do the photography. If this is the case, be sure to show this person the case studies on colored background slides and Kodalith film at the end of Chapter 4. You can write to the Eastman Kodak Company to get simple instructions.

Although photography is presented here as the third step in producing a slide/tape program, it often continues into the final stages of production. That's because our ultimate choice of visuals often depends on how the **soundtrack** actually sounds, and the final number of slides is ultimately determined by how they're actually synchronized in the final stage of production. Most experienced producers will tell you that even the best planned storyboards are usually changed once the final soundtrack is produced. Often this is because what you thought would work when you wrote your ideas on paper didn't work so well once you actually saw the slides while listening to the soundtrack. There are many possible reasons for this. For example, sometimes music pieces have to run longer or shorter than anticipated, or the narrator speaks a little faster or slower than planned, in both cases affecting the number of slides you'll need. And sometimes your ideas for visuals simply change after hearing the soundtrack. The tone of the narrator's voice, in combination with the music and other background sounds, can create vivid imagery in your "mind's eye." Listening to the soundtrack for the first time may give you a lot of new ideas for visuals that never even occurred to you when you first developed the storyboard. Trust this imagery. It will probably be worth the extra time and effort to make changes in the storyboard and acquire the new slides before presenting the program.

Despite this give-and-take relationship in audiovisual production, knowing in advance what the final visuals will be can help you produce a more dynamic soundtrack. Being able to envision what will be on the screen during any given segment of the program (as well as the number of slides that will be shown) makes recording decisions easier. Especially valuable is knowing in advance how long a given piece of music or sound effect needs to be on the tape. In addition, doing the photography first allows you to make last minute changes in the narration to accommodate or capitalize on what the audience will actually be seeing on the screen.

So which should you do first, soundtrack production or photography and acquisition of visuals? Like so many things in communication, the "best" procedure depends on the nature of a particular program and your personal preference. Depending on the specific program you're producing, you may prefer to produce the soundtrack before doing the photography, especially when the visuals will be relatively easy to obtain or produce. But when even some of the slides will be difficult to find (e.g., specialty slides such as planets, micrography, etc.), or when they'll require special production or a degree of experimentation (e.g., progressive disclosure series or special effects), it's better to have the final visuals in hand first. That way, you can produce the soundtrack to suit exactly the visuals you have, instead of only a vague notion of what they might be.

Step 4: Producing the Soundtrack

Producing a soundtrack can be the most time-consuming part of a slide/tape production. Depending on the complexity of the sounds you want to create, several days of planning and organizing may be necessary. A particularly complicated soundtrack may even take weeks to produce. But fortunately, not all soundtracks have to be so difficult. When all is said and done, what really stands out in an effective soundtrack isn't its complexity, but its simplicity. An engaging soundtrack sounds simple, even if it was difficult to produce; each part of it flows smoothly into the next; combined sounds are heard as one; and audiences are able to listen effortlessly, hearing everything at an appropriate volume and relating it instantly to what they're seeing on the screen. Along with a creative script, a well developed theme and a careful narration, these are the characteristics that distinguish good soundtracks. Simplicity is the essential quality in soundtrack production.

What Equipment Will You Need?

There is no question that producing a soundtrack is easier if you have access to good, multiple-channel recording equipment. My students are lucky. In their interpretation classes they can use professional tape decks, superb microphones, and a number of advanced audio accessories that make things a lot easier for them. Does this equipment make their soundtracks sound better? Of course it does. But are their soundtracks more effective in communicating their themes simply because of this equipment? Absolutely not.

Some of the best soundtracks for slide/tape programs have been produced by people who had only a single cassette tape recorder and an inexpensive microphone. Although the quality of the recording is certainly below professional broadcasting standards, it's quite acceptable for the less-than-acoustically-perfect situations in which the programs are shown (e.g., in classrooms, visitor centers, outdoor amphitheaters, and other settings in which ambient noise can't be controlled). Without exception, what makes the soundtracks effective are the qualities described above. The fact is, with some preparation and simple recording equipment, anyone can produce soundtracks of acceptable quality for most situations.

If broadcast quality is important and you don't have a lot of money, consider asking a radio or television station to help. An experienced recording technician can probably produce a short, simple soundtrack (ten to twelve minutes long with no more than a narration and two or three consecutive pieces of music) in a couple of hours. But be careful. What you may

Figure 10-5. Preparations for an inexpensive recording session. (Photo by Gerry Snyder)

gain from a quick-and-dirty inexpensive production is higher audio quality; but what you may lose is careful communication. If you have the money, it would be better to spend the necessary time with the station personnel to produce a soundtrack that has both qualities. Alternatively, some universities have well equipped interpretive media laboratories that involve students in slide/tape productions as part of their course projects. The students gain a valuable learning experience, and the clients are able to get a high quality product at a much reduced cost. Contact the universities in your area to see if there's a natural resource communication or interpretive media laboratory. If the university doesn't have an interpretation program, try the communications (television and radio) department.

Many interpreters simply don't have the resources to hire professional help of any kind. It's for these readers that the following discussion is intended. We'll be assuming that you have minimum equipment of modest quality, and that you'll have to do your recording in an office or at home. We'll also assume you don't have resources to hire a professional narrator nor to buy a lot of extra music or sound effects.

There are two basic parts of soundtrack production: (1) recording the narration, and (2) recording background sound. With professional recording equipment, we would record these separately (the narration first) and then piece them together later (using a process called mixing). However, since most readers won't have the equipment required to do this, we're going to describe a process in which both are recorded simultaneously. This is called "real time" recording because, as we'll see shortly, the time required to record the entire mixed soundtrack is exactly the length of the soundtrack. That is, a ten-minute soundtrack takes exactly ten minutes to record.

Prepare a Recording Location

To do your recording, you'll need a private and quiet location shielded as much as possible from outside noises such as traffic, telephones, and conversation. Bedrooms, small living rooms, and even closets work well. Hanging blankets, towels or other soft, sound-absorbing material on the walls helps to deaden ambient air noise (the normally inaudible sound of air movement that a sensitive microphone picks up in a room). Avoid rooms with a lot of windows. Besides letting outside sounds enter the room unimpeded, they reflect rather than absorb sound. Curtains help, but they aren't very effective, especially if the windows are large. Bathrooms, kitchens, and other rooms that have plumbing also aren't very good places to record. That's because when water is being used anywhere else in the building it will probably be heard through the water pipes in these rooms. Since fluorescent light fixtures make a humming noise, try to use a room with incandescent lighting.

Prepare a table for the recording session. You'll need a lot of room. Ample work space allows you to move quickly and quietly as you simultaneously narrate, move paper and operate the controls on the recorders you'll be using. The table should be large enough for: (1) your script—including space for the page you're reading and for those you've already read, (2) a microphone—either on a stand or securely tied or taped to an upright that's positioned at the level of your mouth while narrating, and (3) at least two tape recorders—one that will be used to record the soundtrack and additional recorders to play background music and any other sounds you want in the soundtrack. (If you're using a turntable with records as a music source, the controls should be within easy reach.) Be sure to locate everything conveniently on the table. For example, you shouldn't have to stand up to reach the buttons on a tape recorder, and you should be able to sit comfortably in front of the microphone without having to lean forward or to one side in order to speak into it.

Microphones

Many inexpensive cassette recorders have built-in (internal) microphones. The trouble with a lot of them is that since they're physically connected to the tape recorder, they pick up some of the sounds the machine makes when it's running. If at all possible, use an external microphone. Tape recorders with built-in microphones usually have a place to plug in an external one.

Pre-record Music Changes

If you'll be working alone and using several pieces of music, it's a very good idea to first record them on a tape in the desired sequence. That way, you won't have to pause the recorder and switch tapes every time you want a music change. Another alternative is to use separate tape players for each piece of music, but this makes the recording session even more complex unless you have an assistant.

Get an Assistant to Help

If possible, arrange for someone to assist you in the recording session. One of you could be free to concentrate on narrating while the other operates the equipment. Attending to every aspect of the production at the same time you're narrating the script is extremely difficult. One-person productions often have flaws that could have been avoided if another person had been involved.

Rehearse and Set the Recording Volumes

Read and reread the script enough times that you're completely familiar with it. Then, with your assistant's help, practice recording the narration and background sounds. You'll no doubt make mistakes and will need to decide with your assistant how to correct them. Once you're able to do things the way you've planned them, you're prepared to make your first attempt at recording. But be patient. It will probably require more than one "take."

As you practice, you'll need to pay special attention to the volumes of the sounds you're recording. Two kinds of volumes are important, absolute and relative. **Absolute volume** is the recording level of the narrator's voice. Since the narration is usually the loudest sound on the tape, the volumes of everything else need to be established relative to it. It shouldn't be too high or too low. How you establish the absolute volume of the voice is a little different depending on whether your recorder sets recording levels automatically or whether you must set them manually. These procedures are described next.

Manual Versus Automatic Record Volumes

Some tape recorders have an "auto/manual" switch that lets you choose whether the recording level will be set automatically or manually. If you have this option, the automatic setting is probably best to use since it prevents you from under or over recording. If your recorder doesn't have such a switch, you'll need to adjust the recording volume manually in order to set the optimal recording level. To do this, locate the window on your recorder that says, "VU Meter" (VU stands for "volume units"). Ask your partner to adjust the volume control as you read an excerpt from the script. Be sure to position yourself at the microphone and speak into it exactly as you'll be doing it when you're recording. As you read, have your assistant adjust the recording volume until the needle in the VU meter fluctuates near (but only rarely into the red zone). This is your absolute level (for voice recording) and it will remain unchanged throughout the entire recording session.

If your tape recorder doesn't have a VU meter, it automatically sets recording volumes. To set the voice volume, record sample sentences from the script with the microphone at various distances from your mouth. Make note of the distance you're using in each try. Listen to the "takes," and decide which one sounds best. This will be the one that gives your voice its clearest sound without a noticeable "hissing" noise in the background. Use this distance throughout the recording session, and make note of it in case you have to interrupt your recording session. Even the slightest change in the setup will cause noticeable changes in the sound of your voice. You might even use masking tape to secure the microphone in place, and chalk to mark the locations of the chair legs on the floor. This will allow you to record consistently even if you have to leave and come back another day.

Setting Relative Volumes

Having established the recording level for your voice, you now need to determine the proper **relative volumes** for the background music (and other sounds). Practice reading and recording segments of the script as your assistant plays part of each piece of background music or sound effects intended for each of the segments. Experiment by changing and noting the volume of the music in each rehearsal. As before, listen to the sample recordings and make note of which volume setting was best for each piece of music. The best volumes for music pieces will be those in which the music is clearly heard without competing with the narration. Make sure when you're testing the volumes that you include the loudest parts of each song (crescendos, etc.) so that they don't unexpectedly drown out the voice when you're producing the soundtrack, and the quietest parts so you can make sure they'll be heard.

Creating Realistic Sound Effects

Although the best volumes for sound effects (birds, insects, wind, rivers, crackling fires, etc.) will vary depending upon your needs, the most common problem is recording them too loud. Think about how the sounds are really heard in nature, and try to mimic their volume on tape. Mosquitoes that sound like airplanes, and rivers that sound like crashing ocean waves aren't very convincing. Likewise, remember that natural sounds come from all around us, and that they may emanate from several sources. With bird calls, for example, varying the volume of different calls creates the illusion that several birds at different distances (some closer and some farther away) are calling. If your program is taking the audience on an imaginary tour of an area, remember that as they "move" they'll always be getting closer to some sounds and further away from others. Increasing the volume of some sounds while you decrease the volume of others will help create this moving sensation.

Tips for Better Narrations

Contrary to popular opinion, a professional broadcaster's voice (such as a radio or television announcer) isn't always best for a narration. Neither are male voices. I always make my first-year students narrate and produce a short audio program. This gives them and me a chance to hear their voices on tape. Many of them discover that they have a narrator's talent. Before deciding to have someone else do the narration for your program, at least try to do it yourself.

Most of us don't like the sound of our own voices on tape. The reason is that

Keep Unwanted Sounds Out of Voice Recordings

- Don't speak directly into the front of the microphone. Strong breathing, whistling S's, and popping P's will create annoying sounds. It's better to position the microphone a few inches in front of your mouth, and slightly to the left or right, in order to direct most of your breath away from it. If the problem remains, put a thin cloth or handkerchief over the microphone to shield it from your breathing.

- Avoid paper shuffling noises. Best is to attach each page of your script (properly sequenced from left to right) to a small upright bulletin board on the table. That way, you won't have to worry about changing pages and taking the chance of recording the paper movement on tape. If the script is too long to show all the pages at once, lay as many as possible side-by-side on the table to minimize the number of times you'll need to move the paper. When you've finished reading each page of the script, gently slide it to the side rather than picking it up and moving it. This will eliminate the sounds of paper shuffling from being heard. Be sure to leave a space on the table for this purpose.

- Listen critically for unwanted sounds as you're recording. Wearing headphones helps because they allow you to hear yourself as well as sounds you might otherwise miss (e.g., paper rustling, clothing, flying insects, etc.)

- Build a small two-sided "house" for the microphone with foam rubber or couch cushions so that it's protected from room noise above and on both sides. Make sure the open side of the "house" is at mouth level.

- Hang towels, sheets, or other soft fabric on adjacent walls as an extra precaution against unwanted room noise.

- If you do a lot of recording, consider building a low-cost sound-proof booth. Make it big enough for two people, a table for equipment, and a bulletin board for scripts. Cover the walls and ceiling with something that will absorb sound. Some fairly efficient "home-spun" insulators include old egg cartons with tissue paper lightly packed in each cup, used "bubble-wrap," foam rubber, and layers of fabric.

Figure 10-6. Tips for recording quieter soundtrack narrations.

we're not accustomed to hearing ourselves through our ears. When we speak, we hear our own voices after the sound waves have vibrated through our jaw bones and into our ears from the inside. When you listen to your voice on a tape, you're hearing it as other people hear it every day. Even though it may sound odd to you, it sounds quite normal to everyone else.

The effectiveness of a narration has less to do with the inherent quality or tone of the speaker's voice (e.g., how deep or smooth it sounds) than with how he or she says the words and sentences that comprise the narration. Natural inflection, timely pauses, feeling, and sincerity are the qualities that really count in a narration. Deep booming male voices can be boring to the brain even if their tonal qualities are pleasing to the ear. Far more important in narrating are inflection and feeling. If the script sounds like it's being read (or "broadcasted" like the evening news), it will carry a sterile, insincere tone. Scripts narrated with normal speech inflection, rather than the rhythmic rising and falling inflection we associate with reading, sound heartfelt and sincere. It's as though the narrator knows and cares so much about the subject that a script isn't necessary. Narrators who sound like they're reading give the impression that they need to have a script because they really don't know or care anything about the subject. They're simply reading words off a piece of paper. Additional tips on narrating were included in Figure 10-2. Ways to keep unwanted sounds out of voice recordings are listed in Figure 10-6.

Music Selection

More than any other aspect of a slide/tape production, it's the music that will determine the mood and tempo of the program. Studies show that music affects us in powerful ways, including our emotional and physiological states. In this sense, all music is "mood" music, and almost any instrumental piece will go with any narration and slides. The decision of which piece is best is likely to boil down to the mood and tempo you want to establish.

Except for music-only segments, music should not be used to call attention to itself. Its purpose is to complement and embellish the narration. It sets the emotional tone of the narrator's words and suggests a tempo for slide changes. These factors, more than your personal music preferences, should dictate your choice of music for a slide/tape program.

Few guidelines can be offered for selecting music because it's a decision based more on feeling than on logic. Often, music selection is based on the audience or the topic of a program, but this isn't always the case. In most programs, it's a good idea to avoid current or widely popular songs. Besides becoming out-of-date quickly, people may already have strong imagery associated with the songs. If the imagery you offer in your narration and slides isn't consistent with what they already have in their heads, they're likely to find the music inappropriate for the program.

Avoiding vocals (songs with lyrics) is also a good idea, except perhaps when the lyrics are perfect for the message and the narration is temporarily dropped so that the lyrics can be heard well. Using vocals as background music behind a narration creates problems because the singer's voice can easily compete with or even overtake the narrator's words. In most programs, instrumentals are preferred. For a similar reason, you also should avoid selections with widely fluctuating volumes (such as some symphonies). If you're going to be using commercial, copyrighted music in your soundtrack—whether you play it from a recording or live on your own instrument—be sure to get permission first and plan a credit slide to acknowledge the source.

Selecting music that's culturally appropriate for either the audience, topic, or both is important. For example, Andean folk music is used a lot in slide/tape programs in Ecuador and Peru. But it also could be used effectively in North American programs that present topics related to Andean culture. Beginning soundtrack producers sometimes forget that music preference is a common distinguishing characteristic of cultures and subcultures. A frequent tendency among beginning interpretation students, for example, is to produce soundtracks using only the style of music they personally like to listen to at home. This is a mistake unless the intended audience is from the same subculture.

Music variety is often important in soundtracks, especially those that are longer than two or three minutes. In longer programs, it's a good idea to incorporate sharp contrasts in moods—perhaps having some peppy, fast-moving parts followed by slower, laid-back pieces. Some of the best soundtracks change music several times, but there aren't any firm rules for how many times is best. Experiment with different types and styles of music, and don't be afraid to try something new just because you haven't seen it done before. Most of the good ideas about using music in soundtracks are still awaiting discovery.

Tips for Using Music Artistically

Music is art and people expect it to be treated with respect. Because it affects our psychological state, changes in music should be smooth and gradual, not jerky or choppy. Each piece of music in your soundtrack should be handled gracefully, and changes in music should be fluid, not abrupt. Before recording a segment of music, carefully plan how you'll bring it into the soundtrack and how you'll take it out.

Basically, two options exist for beginning a piece of music. You can either let it begin naturally (and at full volume) on the first note or other distinct note of the song, or you can fade it in, gradually making it louder until it's at its proper relative volume.

There are three ways to remove a piece of music. You can use its natural ending, you can fade it out, or you can "stack" it. **Stacking** is fading out the end of a music piece at the same time you're beginning another. The result is that for a second or two both pieces are heard (readers familiar with audio terminology will know this as **sound-on-sound**). If the two pieces don't clash too much, the effect is an artful transition between music and moods.

Stacking is easy if you're working with multiple-channel recording equipment. But even with the simple equipment we're assuming here, stacking is possible with a little practice. A separate tape player is needed for each piece of music. Let's say that the first piece of music is in Tape Player A, and the second piece in Tape Player B. Tape Player B should be in "pause" mode (for reasons we'll discuss shortly) and "cued" (that is, ready to be heard immediately when the tape is set in motion). The person who's operating the equipment needs to know exactly when the transition should begin, as well as the point at which the first piece of music should be completely gone. As the narrator is reading, the first piece of music (Tape Player A) is playing. When the narrator reaches the point where the transition is needed, the assistant releases the pause control on Tape Player B and immediately begins turning up its volume, at the same time gradually turning down the volume of Tape Player A. You'll probably need a few rehearsals to get the timing of the transition just right. But the time is well worth the artistic effect achieved.

Precautions for "Cleaner" Recording

A tape recorder doesn't know which sounds you want on the tape. It records everything, even the noises you make when you're pushing buttons and operating other controls on the equipment. A "clean" recording is free of these and other unwanted sounds. Following are four things you can do to get cleaner recordings.

• Always use a new tape or one that's been completely and thoroughly erased on both sides.

• Make a habit of cleaning and demagnetizing tape recorder heads before every recording session. (Inexpensive kits with instructions are available at almost any store that sells audio equipment.)

• To avoid an abrupt and noisy beginning, allow the tape to run for five or ten seconds in record mode before recording the first sounds of your soundtrack.

• With your free hand, cover your other hand with a piece of foam or a small pillow as you push start and stop buttons on tape players. This will muffle the sound of the machine being switched on and off.

• Use the "pause" control (not the stop button) unless you have to stop the tape to rewind it.

Figure 10-7. Techniques for improving the quality of simple soundtracks.

Importance of the "Pause" Control

Use the "pause" control instead of "stop" whenever possible. When in record mode, using the "stop" button causes the record head to release from the tape. On all but the best recorders this will leave an annoying "click" on the tape at the point the head was released. To avoid these unwanted noises, use the "pause" control. It works like a brake, bringing the tape to a stop without causing the head to release. Of course, if you want to listen to something you've just recorded, you'll have to use the "stop" control so that you can rewind the tape. If this is the case, let the tape continue to run (in record mode) a second or two longer than needed before pushing the stop button. This will put the "click" well after the sounds you recorded. Later, when you want to continue recording, you'll be able to simply record over the click. If you stop the tape too soon, you won't be able to record over it without cutting the end off the previously recorded sound.

Using the "pause" control, you can incorporate break points at different places in the soundtrack to allow you to take a break. Do this by pausing the tape at the end of a song or other logical stopping point (such as at the end of a paragraph that has no music behind it). Pausing is possible only if a moment of silence is acceptable at that particular point in the soundtrack.

Incorporating break points also divides the soundtrack into manageable units. If you make a mistake while recording, you'll be able to resume from the point of the last break point rather than having to start over again from the beginning. If your program is longer than even five or six minutes, you'll be very glad you did this. Real time recording can be nerve-racking because so many things have to be carried out simultaneously and without error. Break points take some of the pressure off.

Music Changes and Natural Endings

There are two places in a soundtrack when a change of music is almost always needed. One is at the end of the introduction; the other is just before the conclusion. In each case, the music change (sometimes accompanied by a darkened screen) serves to signify the end of a major program segment. Psychologically, listeners are being prepared for a shift in focus.

Usually, but not necessarily always, the introduction music is timed so that its natural ending coincides with the last word of the introduction. Likewise, the last music piece is often timed so that its natural ending occurs precisely at the end of the program. In most conclusions, the final piece of music is timed to continue through a final series of slides (summary, "flashback," and/or credit slides) following the narrator's last word. Especially at the end of a soundtrack, the finality of the music's last note helps establish a feeling of completeness and closure that's difficult or impossible to accomplish with a fade out. This doesn't mean you should never use a fade out, but if it's possible to capitalize on a natural ending, you should consider doing it.

Still, there are times when a natural ending just won't work and you'll be forced to fade the music out. In the introduction, no special considerations are necessary. But ending the concluding piece with a fade out requires an extra ounce of patience for many producers. This is because of the long, exaggerated fade out that's needed to avoid "chopping" the end of the music off. If audible music is prematurely or abruptly cut off, the effect is disturbing to an audience. Be patient, slowly decreasing the volume of the music, little by little, until it's completely gone. If the music is even barely audible, it's still too soon to stop the recording. Continue the gradual fade out until the volume control is completely off. The final fade out of a soundtrack is almost always the longest fade out in an audiovisual program.

Using Music to Create Pragnänz

Recall from Chapter 3 the importance of creating pragnänz (unity and completeness) at the conclusion of a talk. Pragnänz is also important in an audiovisual program. As in talks, it can be achieved by linking the conclusion of the program to something that occurred in the introduction. Some producers do this by repeating the introduction's music in the conclusion. This is a common technique in television programs and movies. Pay attention to how music is used the next time you're at a movie or watching a television program. You'll see that many programs utilize a "theme song" that is heard at the beginning and again at the end. In some programs, the same song is used intermittently throughout the presentation. Such songs are referred to as "reoccurring themes." A dramatic technique

Figure 10-8. Examples of inexpensive light tables. (Photos by Peter Slisz)

for achieving pragnänz in the conclusion of a slide/tape program is to show selected slides the audience has already seen ("flashback slides") at the same time they're listening again to the music they heard in the introduction.

Step 5: Programming and Slide Synchronization

The last step in producing a slide/tape program is synchronizing the slides and the soundtrack. This is called **programming**. Depending on the kind of equipment you have, you'll either program the slides manually or with an electronic programmer (a device that allows you to automate a program by recording inaudible slide-change signals on the tape). Since programmers are expensive, a lot of readers won't have one. For this reason, we'll first focus on manual programming and then briefly review the use of electronic programmers. The creative considerations are the same for both.

Manual Programming

There are two basic ways to **synchronize** a slide/tape program manually. One is to indicate slide changes on a script (recall that that's exactly what was done when you developed the storyboard). As the program is shown, you simply follow the script (a small pen light or flashlight will be needed if the room is dark) and advance the slides every time a slide change is indicated on the script.

The second way to synchronize a slide/tape program manually is to record some type of noise or audible signal on the tape everywhere a slide should be changed. Programs with audible slide-change signals used to be common, but they've fallen out of use in a lot of countries because of the availability of automatic programmers. However, the principle is still used with "listen and look" books for children (see "booklet-with-tape" programs in Figure 10-1). The idea is that the child looks at pages in a book that are "synchronized" to a soundtrack on a tape.

The child is told that whenever he/she hears a certain sound (anything from a dog barking to a bell ringing) he/she should turn to the next page. It's possible to synchronize a slide/tape program the same way. The problem, of course, is that unless you have a multiple-channel recorder with independent recording capability on each channel, the signals have to be recorded at the same time the soundtrack is being produced. Besides adding complexity to an already difficult task, the sound may be distracting to audiences when the program is shown. Nevertheless, if these problems can be overcome or tolerated, recording audible slide change signals on the tape may be an acceptable alternative. They still seem quite acceptable for use in primary schools, and in some countries, they may have wide application for other types of audiences.

Electronic Programmers for Automated Presentations

If you have access to a programmer, the operating instructions will explain how to use it. There are many different brands and they're relatively easy to use once you know what the different buttons and knobs are for. Some tape recorders (generally referred to as "slide-synch" recorders) have programmers built into them. They're designed so that the slide-change signals are recorded onto the "B" side (flip side) of a tape. Using a patch cord, a special output from this side of the tape is connected to the projector (or projection system, if more than one projector is being used). In effect, this connection allows the projector(s) to "listen" and respond to the signals on side "B" while

the audience is listening to the soundtrack on side "A."

Other electronic programmers are separate (called "external programmers"). Regardless of which kind you have, it will operate on one of three principles: (1) signal volume, (2) signal frequency, or (3) digital code. Of the three kinds of systems, digital programmers are more complex, more versatile, more reliable, and more expensive. Frequency programmers are intermediate in all these characteristics. Volume-based programmers are no longer manufactured, but a few "dinosaurs" (such as Kodak's original sound synchronizer) can still be found in some places. (NOTE FOR ADVANCED READERS: To use an external programmer, you must have a channel available to record the signals. To do this, leave one channel unused during soundtrack production. If you're using a slide-synch recorder but still want to use an external programmer, you can access the "B" side of the tape using the external synch input on the recorder. During playback, you'll need to use the external synch output.)

The basic procedure of all external programmers is the same. They're connected with a patch cord to an unused channel of a tape deck. As the soundtrack is being listened to, the programmer is used to record signals (one of the three types described above) on to the unused channel of the tape recorder wherever slide changes are needed. When the program is played back, a patch cord is placed between the output of the channel containing the signals and the programmer. The programmer in turn is connected to the projector (or projection system if more than one projector is being used). The channel(s) containing the soundtrack, of course, are played through the speaker.

In this way, the audience hears the sound-track but not the signals. As the tape is played, the inaudible signals cause the slides to change at the desired places in the soundtrack.

Programming Tips

Whether you're recording slide-change signals onto a tape or simply making notations on a script for manual slide changes, it's best to work on a light table. With a light table, you can lay all the slides out in the order you want them, moving your eyes from each slide to the next as you listen to the soundtrack. There's no better way to get to know your program.

Some people prefer to synchronize their programs while projecting the slides on a screen, but in doing so they give up the advantage of being able to see the next two or three slides in advance (a great advantage when precise timing is important). Another disadvantage of projecting the slides during programming is that every time you want to go back to look at something again, you have to reset the slide tray(s). This can add hours to programming a long or complicated presentation. Still, either of the two methods works and you should use the one you're most comfortable with.

Anticipation is the key to smooth synchronization between a soundtrack and slides. If you're using a programmer, be sure to push the slide-change button a fraction of a second before each slide is needed. This allows time for the projector to cycle. If you waited until the slide was needed on the screen before pressing the button, many of your slides would be late in getting to the screen. Anticipation is also important if you're programming

manually. Indicate slide changes slightly in advance of when each slide is actually needed on the screen.

As we discussed earlier, music-only segments (musical interludes) can be a dramatic way to visually reinforce different segments of a slide/tape program. Remember that since you won't be able to key your slide changes to words on the script, you'll have to remember the music very well in order to change the slides correctly. If the program will be shown by people other than you, you'll either have to give them special instructions on when to change slides during the music, or synchronize the program using audible slide-change signals.

If lists of things are included in the script, but there aren't pauses in narration long enough for a slide of each one, don't try to show all of them. It would be better to show a slide of every other one or even every third item.

Pacing is important in a slide/tape program, and it's probably more influenced by the rhythm and tempo of the music than by anything else. Try to match the pace of the slide changes to the pace of the music in each section. Don't speed up the rate of slide changes just to fit a few more slides in.

Presenting a Slide/Tape Program

Before each showing of your program, arrive at least an hour early so that you can check your equipment and prepare the room. Be sure to review the guidelines for using slides that were presented in Chapter 4. Many of them also apply to slide/tape presentations. In addition, you should consider the following procedures for preparing the room and presenting the program.

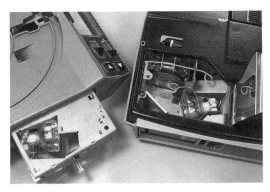

Figure 10-9. Location of bulbs in Kodak slide projectors. (Photo by Gerry Snyder)

1. Arrange the seating so that every seat is a good seat. Some screens reflect images better toward the center of the audience than they do toward people seated on the margins. If this is the case, arrange the chairs so that no one is forced to sit outside of the optimal viewing area.

2. To ensure the soundtrack is heard well, place the speaker(s) in the front of the room (pointing back toward the audience) and as close to ear level as you can get them. Remember, human ears are cupped forward so that they can catch sounds in front of us. Speakers placed behind an audience guarantee the soundtrack will sound muffled.

3. Test your program at least once. If you're going to be changing slides manually, this will give you an opportunity to practice your timing and to verify that all the slides will be projected correctly (see Chapter 4) and in the proper sequence. If the program is automated, a "dry run" will allow you to make sure that the equipment is working properly.

4. From the front of the room, present a brief two- or three-minute introduction before lowering the lights and starting the program. Be sure to mention who you represent and why your work is important. Tell people in advance that you'll be very happy to answer their questions following the program.

5. At the end of the program, allow the last note of the final piece of music to fade out *completely* before you push the stop button on the recorder. As a general rule, it's good to wait two or three additional seconds so you can avoid jolting the audience's emotional state with the mechanical "clunk" of the stop button. And when you do stop the tape, press the button gently.

6. After the program, turn the lights on and return to the front of the room. Present a one-minute post-program conclusion that reinforces the theme of the presentation. Don't just say, "Are there any questions?" If you've brought additional information or brochures, now's the time to give them out. If you have enough for everyone, it's usually best to just hand them to one person and ask that he/she take one and pass the rest to the next

person. While they're circulating you can ask for questions.

7. When the questions have ended, state again that you were pleased to be able to make the presentation, and if applicable, thank the person who invited you. Remind the people one more time who you represent. Invite them to come up afterwards to chat, or to contact you or your office in the future.

8. Conclude the program with a final "thank you," "good night" or other appropriate closing.

How to Handle Projector Problems

As long as there are machines there will be problems with machines. This is certainly true with slide projectors. The best advice is to expect problems to occur and to plan ahead how you'll handle them. Two problems are most likely with slide projectors: burned out bulbs and jammed slides.

Changing the Lamp

Changing the lamp in a Kodak projector is easy. On the newer Ektagraphic-III models you can simply pull out the drawer in the back of the projector, release the lamp and insert a new one. This can be done in a matter of seconds if you have a new lamp nearby. With other models, you'll need to remove the slide tray and turn the projector upside down. Unscrew the lock to the door and open it. Inside you'll find the lamp. In both cases, remember that the bulb is very hot. Be sure to use a handkerchief or rag to grab a hold of it. Avoid placing your fingers

directly on the glass part of the new bulb when putting it in the projector.

Freeing a Jammed Slide

If you show slide programs a lot, sooner or later a slide is going to get jammed in the projector. Unless you know how to unjam it, you won't be able to continue. Fortunately, the procedure is simple (see Figure 10-10): (1) make sure the lock ring is on the tray (it's the plastic ring that keeps the slides from falling out when the tray is turned over); (2) using a coin, turn the screw head in the center of the tray; (3) as you do this, lift the tray up and away from the projector; (4) immediately turn the tray upside down and turn the metal plate on the bottom until it locks in place (don't turn this plate unless the tray is upside down or your slides will fall out one by one); (5) reach into the slot in the projector and remove the jammed slide or push it up from the opening underneath using a small blunt object (Hooper 1987 recommends a wooden ice cream stick for this purpose); (6) set the jammed slide aside, put the tray back on the projector and advance it to the next number in sequence; (7) make sure the tape and the slide are in synch; and (8) resume your presentation.

Multi-Media versus Multi-Image Programs

Although some people use the words interchangeably, **multi-media programs** and **multi-image programs** aren't the same thing. As their names imply, one has to do with the number of communication media utilized in an audiovisual program, and the other with the number of images that are projected. By definition, every slide/tape program is a multi-media

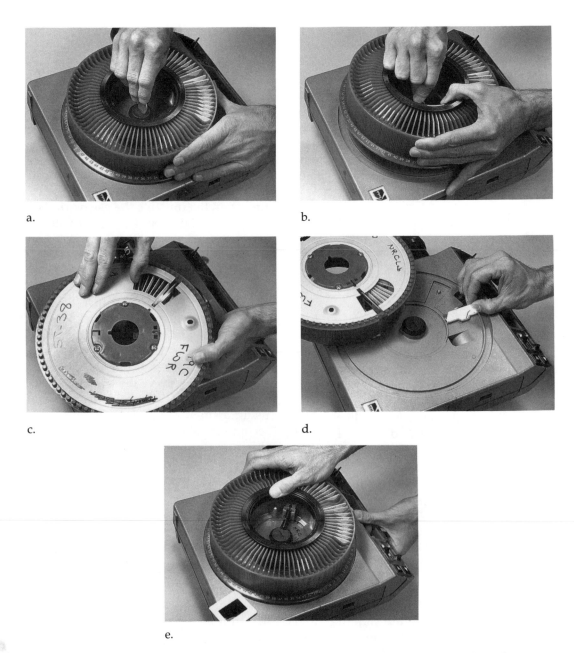

a.

b.

c.

d.

e.

Figure 10-10. Freeing a jammed slide: (a) make sure the lock ring is securely in place, then use a coin to turn the tray-release screw, (b) while turning the screw, pull the tray away from the projector, (c) turn the tray upside down and rotate the bottom plate until it locks in place, (d) remove the jammed slide from the projector, and (e) return the tray to the projector and rotate it to the desired number. (Photos by Gerry Snyder)

program since it involves more than one communication medium—a tape player and at least one slide projector. Multi-image programs are a special type of multi-media program in which more than one image is shown simultaneously to the audience.

The most common types of multi-image programs are slide/tape presentations in which at least two screens are used to show simultaneous images to the audience, or in which multiple images are shown on a single large screen. Multi-image presentations don't have to be complicated. In fact, some of the best multi-image presentations are extremely simple (e.g., two projectors side-by-side focused on two different screens or projecting side-by-side images onto a single large screen). Their effectiveness comes not from being complicated, but because they give their audiences more to look at than single-image presentations do. Since we can absorb visual information so much faster and easier than we can other kinds of information, seeing two or three images simultaneously adds significantly to our understanding without making us work any harder. According to media psychologists, this adds to the entertainment value of an audiovisual presentation. Examples of two- and three-screen multi-image configurations are shown in Figure 10-11. Although planning the sequence of visuals is a little more complicated for multi-image presentations, the procedures for producing them are basically the same as we've been discussing.

There are many ways to capitalize on the extra visual information in a multi-image program. Seven relatively easy techniques include the following:

1. Show parts of a process from left to right. With two images,

a.

b.

c.

Figure 10-11. Example configurations for multi-image audiovisual programs: (a) two projectors are used to show separate images on adjacent screens, (b) two projectors are used to show side-by-side images on one large screen, and (c) three projectors are used to show side-by-side images on one large screen.

a.

b.

Figure 10-12. Three simple multi-image techniques: (a) showing parts of a process; (b) showing multiple distances; and (c) showing a panorama. (Photos by Gerry Snyder)

c.

for example, you might show a bare slope on the left and a mature forest on the right. With three images you might show a bare slope on the left, planted seedlings in the middle, and then a mature forest on the right. You could achieve the same effect with almost any process—for example, a famous person at youth, middle age, and then old age.

2. Show progressive disclosure (see Chapter 4) in which each intermediate step remains in view as subsequent stages are shown. For example, you could show a map on the left screen, and on the right screen the same map with the location of certain features.

3. Show contrast between two or more images. For example,

you might show a person about to drink from a glass of dirty water on the left and the same person about to drink from a glass of clean water on the right.

4. Show multiple perspectives. Simultaneously project slides of the same object photographed from different angles (e.g., from the side, from below, and from above).

5. Show multiple distances (far away, intermediate, and close-up scenes of the same object).

6. Create dramatic emphasis by showing identical images

simultaneously on all screens. For example, two or three side-by-side, identical images of a forest fire, a scenic vista, a water-fall (or almost any object) usually will have more visual impact than a single image of the same scene. If these slides appear on the screen at exactly the same moment, and if they are timed to coincide with a sudden beginning, climax or strong crescendo in the music, the effect is very dramatic.

7. Show panoramas. Simple but acceptable panoramas can be created by carefully photographing adjacent parts of a scene (two photographs for a two-image presentation, three

for a three-image presentation, etc.) and then carefully aligning the projectors so that their images appear to form one large scene. More advanced techniques utilizing three projectors and "seamless masks" can be used, but these are much more costly. Interested readers should consult Kenny and Schmitt (1981) and Eastman Kodak (1981).

Glossary terms: absolute volume, photo copystand, graphic, literal illustration, multi-image program, multi-media program, musical interlude, programming, relative volume, representation, script, slide synchronization, sound-on-sound, soundtrack, stacking, storyboard, symbolic illustration

Slide/Tape Shows— Getting Your Message Across, Even When You Can't Be There

Dave Sutherland, Environmental Education Coordinator

Charles Darwin Station, Galápagos Islands, Ecuador

Rodolfo Tenorio, Director
Guayabo National Monument, Costa Rica

Guayabo National Monument, located in the foothills of Costa Rica's moist Caribbean slope, is famous as the country's foremost pre-Columbian archaeological site. And Rodolfo Tenorio, the administrator and chief archaeologist at the monument, is also well-known for the excellence of his on- and off-site interpretive program. When not actually working on a dig, Rodolfo can often be found interacting with visitors and sharing some of the area's unique natural and human history. He also receives frequent invitations from clubs, schools and other organized groups in nearby communities and other parts of the country to present programs on the monument and the resources it protects. But Rodolfo must balance interpretation with other archaeological and administrative tasks, and frequently has to delegate interpretive functions to other workers at the monument—workers who are not expert archaeologists or trained speakers. Rodolfo explained:

"I initially turned to slide programs because I had too little time to interact with all the visitor groups and travel around to all the speaking engagements. Yet educational outreach is really important: it helps people learn about and respect the features at the monument, and builds support for our preservation efforts."

"Before we developed the slide-tape show, we had this standing exhibit made out of a large painted board with still photos glued to it. We would set it up in banks or schools for people to look at. But only a few people could view it at a time, and it didn't seem to have the impact I wanted. By combining a taped soundtrack with a slide program, I could present an impressive, effective program full of relevant and factual information, in an easily portable form. I could give quality presentations without having to be there myself. If necessary, even one of the workmen from the monument could set it up and run it."

Rodolfo's first step in creating a slide-tape program was to generate a list of objectives. The slide show would be carefully designed to raise public consciousness and interest in the site's archaeological resources, and would help foster an awareness of the growing problem of grave robbing and black market trade of pre-Columbian artifacts. Rather than seeing the ruins as a collection of old rocks or an easy area to plunder, viewers would understand the excavated structures in Guayabo's historical context. The slide program was designed in part to be shown to groups of visitors at the monument before they descended to the ruins, giving them a chance to mull over the information during the walk. At the main archaeological site, more information would be provided to reinforce the slide show. An additional objective was to use the slide program as part of a traveling presentation for groups in local communities and around Costa Rica who were unable to visit the monument themselves. "We could take it anywhere with an electrical hook-up, carrying nothing but the carousel, the projector, a tape player, and a bed sheet for a screen," Rodolfo added.

Once he had decided on his objectives, Rodolfo began preparing a script around the question, "what is an archaeological dig all about?" "I started writing the text before collecting any slides. It's cheaper this way. Then, you know exactly what photos you need and don't have to waste any film. Besides that, the final product is more organized and coherent," he explained. His potential audiences would range from children and illiterate adults to educated professionals. To appeal to all, the program needed to stay under fifteen minutes in length and simplify or define complex archaeological terms.

Up to the writing of the script, there were few production costs other than Rodolfo's time. But subsequent stages were more costly. He needed film and a photographer to compile the slides, as well as narrators and recording equipment for the soundtrack. With few resources at his disposal, these were serious obstacles. He was luckily able to obtain some donations, and support from volunteers.

"Film was expensive. Five rolls of film, thirty-six exposures, yielded only forty high quality pictures. A Kodak dealership donated two of the rolls, and we bought the others with proceeds from T-shirt and pamphlet sales

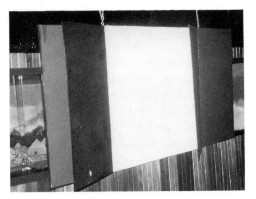

at the monument. Then, I arranged with a volunteer agency for a professional photographer to donate his time and shoot the film to my specifications, based on the script. When the film came back from the developer, we mounted our own slides, saving only the best. By not mounting our rejects, we saved 40 percent of the cost of developing."

Production of the soundtrack was accomplished by a friend of Rodolfo's who worked at a radio station, and thus had access to recording equipment and background music. Several radio announcers helped narrate the script at the station, giving the tape a smooth, professional sound.

When the slides and soundtrack were finally assembled, two obstacles remained. Rodolfo had no slide projector, and no theater to show the program. With his slides and tape in hand, he traveled to the city to make a pitch to the Costa Rican National Park Service. The results: "They were really

impressed, and approved funds for the projector. I was also able to get permission and some funding for a small building to show the slides."

In 1986, when the projector arrived, Rodolfo put away the standing exhibit he had used previously. At first, the slides were shown on a clean bed sheet draped outside at night (weather permitting!), or in the small viewing pavilion. When funds became available, Rodolfo replaced the sheet in the pavilion with a hanging screen made of plywood painted flat white. Two leaves of the screen cleverly fold closed, exposing a green-painted surface which served as a chalkboard. When not in use, the entire screen/chalkboard assembly attached up to a hook in the ceiling.

Currently, a bed sheet is still used as a screen when the slide program is shown away from the monument. Slides are advanced manually at key points in the soundtrack by a park worker familiar with the show. Rodolfo strongly recommends keeping a copy of the script with all of the slide advancements marked in red—in case the slides become jumbled, also new workers can present the show without training.

Rodolfo feels the slide program is largely a success:

"We have changed a few slides over the years, but I can't think of much I would do differently. We have shown this program all over the country. I feel it meets its objectives: it instantly creates interest in the archaeological site. People say, 'Oh, how interesting! I never knew that.' It's hard to say if the program creates a desire to protect cultural resources for archaeological study. I think it does, but of course the risk of such a program is that it may stimulate interest in artifacts, making people more prone to buy them on the black market."

Indeed, Rodolfo is already planning two other slide shows, one on the birds which live in the rainforest surrounding the ruins, and another about the preservation of Costa Rican culture and traditions. When he is unable to acquire a photo he needs (especially of rare birds), he makes slides from book illustrations, calendars, and even post cards, using a homemade copystand.

Rodolfo opened a large box at the side of his desk, and removed an Ektagraphic slide projector which he obviously handled with great care. "One of our biggest problems here is moisture," he said, waving his hand at the rain spattering the windows. "So far, protecting our slides and equipment has been a real challenge. I recently had to send the projector's lens in for cleaning, because fungi were growing inside. It was quite expensive,

and of course we couldn't use the projector in the meantime." A possible solution may be storing the projector in a sealed wooden box with a strong light bulb constantly burning. A similar technique has kept mold from growing in the glass display case that houses a diorama of the ruins.

Rodolfo had several recommendations for others planning to use slide-tape programs as part of interpretive presentations. "Because production of such programs can be costly, objectives should be very carefully thought out before any work is done, to clarify your thinking and to help secure funding." In his case, presenting a completed program to his superiors also strengthened his request for a projector.

"People who work at the area to be featured in the slide program must write the script. They are most familiar with the local resources and with what visitors want to know. The text should be kept short (no more than fifteen minutes per presentation) and should avoid or explain technical terms. I think it is better to complete the text before any slides are assembled. You can cut production costs by actively seeking volunteer labor, by maintaining close ties with organizations which coordinate volunteer activities and even by advertising your needs to visitors. Finally, the messages of the slide program can be cemented by giving visitors a pamphlet or even just a single sheet

> summarizing and expanding on the presentation, which visitors can take with them."

References

Bishop, Ann. 1984. *Slides—Planning and Producing Slide Programs*. Kodak Publication S-30L. Rochester, New York, USA: Eastman Kodak Co.

Eastman Kodak. 1989. *Kodak Sourcebook: Kodak Ektagraphic Slide Projectors*. Publication No. S-74. Rochester, New York, USA: Eastman Kodak Co.

Eastman Kodak. 1981. Kodak Ektagraphic Seamless Slide Masks. *Audiovisual Notes*. Periodical No. T-91-1-1. Rochester, New York, USA: Eastman Kodak Co., p. 5.

Fazio, James R. and Douglas L. Gilbert. 1986. *Public Relations and Communications for Natural Resource Managers*. Dubuque, Iowa, USA: Kendall/Hunt Publishing Co.

Hooper, Jon K. 1987. *Effective Slide Presentations*. Chico, California, USA: Effective Slide Presentations.

Kenny, M.F. and R.F. Schmitt. 1981. *Images, Images, Images: The Book of Programmed Multi-image Production* (2nd ed.). Kodak Publication No. S-12. Rochester, New York, USA: Eastman Kodak Co.

Meilach, Dona Z. 1990. *Dynamics of Presentation Graphics*. Homewood, Illinois, USA: Dow Jones-Irwin.

Moore, Alan, Bill Wendt, Louis Penna e Isabel Castillo de Ramos. 1989. *Manual para La Capacitación del Personal de Areas Protegidas* (Modulo C: Interpretación y Educación Ambiental, Apunte 4a). Washington, D.C., USA: Servicio de Parques Nacionales, Oficina de Asuntos Internacionales.

Morales, Jorge. 1987. *Manual para la Interpretación en Espacios Naturales Protegidos*. Anexo 3 del Taller Internacional sobre Interpretación Ambiental en Areas Silvestres Protegidas. Santiago, Chile: Oficina Regional de la FAO para América Latina y el Caribe, 7-12 de diciembre de 1988.

Muñoz, Milton G. y Bernardo Peña. 1990. *Selección y Utilización de Ayudas Educativas*. Tegucigalpa, D.C., Honduras: Secretaria de Recursos Naturales, Departamento de Comunicación Agropecuaria, Proyecto de Comunicación para la Transferencia de Tecnología Agropecuaria.

Podracky, John R. 1983. *Creative Slide Presentations*. Englewood Cliffs, New Jersey, USA: Prentice-Hall, Inc.

Smith-White, Spencer J. 1982. The Use of Audio Devices. Chapter 11 in Sharpe, G.W. (ed.), *Interpreting the Environment*. New York, New York, USA: John Wiley & Sons.

Stecker, Elinor. 1987. *Slide Showmanship*. New York, New York, USA: Amphoto.

Additional Reading

In English:

Bajimaya, Shyam and James R. Fazio. 1989. *Communications Manual: A Guide to Aid Park and Protected Area Managers to Communicate Effectively with Local Residents*. Kathmandu, Nepal: Department of National Parks and Wildlife Conservation/FAO-UNDP.

Brown, James W., Richard B. Lewis, and Fred F. Harcleroad. 1989. *AV Instruction: Technology, Media and Methods*. New York, New York, USA: McGraw-Hill Book Co.

Bunnell, Pille and Timothy D. Mock. 1990. *A Guide for the Preparation and Use of Overhead and Slide Visuals*. Victoria, British Columbia, Canada: Forestry Canada/ B.C. Ministry of Forests, Research Branch.

Countryside Commission. 1980. *Audio-Visual Media in Countryside Interpretation*. Advisory Series No. 12. London, United Kingdom: Countryside Recreation Research Group.

Eastman Kodak. 1989. *Kodak Sourcebook: Kodak Ektagraphic Slide Projectors*. Publication No. S-74. Rochester, New York, USA: Eastman Kodak Co.

Eastman Kodak. 1982. *Effective Lecture Slides*. Pamphlet No. S-22. Rochester, New York, USA: Eastman Kodak Co.

Eastman Kodak. 1982. Back to Basics: One and Two-Projector Presentations. *Audiovisual Notes*. Periodical No. T-91-2-1. Rochester, New York, USA: Eastman Kodak Co., p. 12-15.

Eastman Kodak. 1981. Visualizing Your Way to a Script. *Audiovisual Notes*. Periodical No. T-91-1-1. Rochester, New York, USA: Eastman Kodak Co., p. 1-4.

Eastman Kodak. 1981. *Some Questions and Answers about Kodak Ektagraphic Seamless Slide Masks (For Three-Projector Panoramas)*. Publication No. S-15-111-AP. Rochester, New York, USA: Eastman Kodak Co.

Eastman Kodak. 1979. Multiply Your Images: How and Why to Get Started in Multi-Image. *Audiovisual Notes*. Periodical No. T-91-9-1. Rochester, New York, USA: Eastman Kodak Co., p. 1-7.

Eastman Kodak. 1973. *Reverse-Text Slides from Black-on-White Line Artwork*. Kodak Pamphlet S-26. Rochester, New York, USA: Eastman Kodak Co.

Grater, Russell K. 1976. *The Interpreter's Handbook: Methods, Skills and Techniques*. Globe, Arizona, USA: Southwest Parks and Monuments Association.

Kuehner, Richard A. 1982. Photography and Interpretation. Chapter 20 in Sharpe, G.W. (ed.), *Interpreting the Environment*. New York, New York, USA: John Wiley & Sons.

O'Neill, Jerome P., Jr. 1979. 101 Ways to Make Copy and Title Slides—Some of Them Good! Part I. *Audiovisual Notes*. Periodical No. T-91-9-1. Rochester, New York, USA: Eastman Kodak Co., p. 8-12.

O'Neill, Jerome P., Jr. 1979. 101 Ways to Make Copy and Title Slides—Some of Them Good! Part II. *Audiovisual Notes*. Periodical No. T-91-9-2. Rochester, New York, USA: Eastman Kodak Co., p. 4-7.

O'Neill, Jerome P., Jr. 1980. 101 Ways to Make Copy and Title Slides—Some of Them Good! Part III. *Audiovisual Notes*. Periodical No. T-91-9-3.

Rochester, New York, USA: Eastman Kodak Co., p. 8-13.

Pennyfather, Keith. 1975. *Guide to Countryside Interpretation: Part II—Interpretive Media and Facilities.* Edinburgh, Scotland: Her Majesty's Stationery Office and the Countryside Commission.

In Spanish:

Asociación Norteamericana de Editores de Facultades de Agronomia. 1970. *Manual de Comunicaciones.* Buenos Aires, Argentina: Editorial Albatros.

Ham, Sam H. 1992. *Interpretación Ambiental: Una Guía Práctica para Gente con Grandes Ideas y Presupuestos Pequeños.* Golden, Colorado, USA: North American Press/Fulcrum Publishing.

Muñoz, Milton G. y Hector R. Fonseca. 1990. *Ilustración de Materiales Escritos en el Sector Rural.* Tegucigalpa, D.C., Honduras: Secretaria de Recursos Naturales, Departamento de Comunicación Agropecuaria, Proyecto de Comunicación para la Transferencia de Tecnología Agropecuaria.

CHAPTER ELEVEN

PROTECTING INTERPRETIVE RESOURCES

Protecting interpretive resources is important, especially if you don't have the money to replace things that become damaged or worn out. Outdoor exhibits, signs, slides, photographs, and video- and audiotapes are among the most important resources to protect because replacing them is usually expensive, time consuming, or even impossible. In this final chapter, we'll consider some simple precautions you can take to protect these interpretive materials. With a little planning and preparation you can greatly extend the life of almost any interpretive resource, especially those that are vulnerable to the damaging effects of temperature and moisture.

Unfortunately, except for information on slide and photograph storage, few good references exist on preventative maintenance for most kinds of interpretive resources. In English, Eastman Kodak (1985) and Pyle (1982) contain useful

information on protecting slides and photographs; Hayman (1991) offers a list of precautions for storing videotapes; and Malbon (1982) offers some general guidelines related to the protection of outdoor structures. The only known Spanish-language source is Moore et al. (1989), which offers excellent advice for storing slides in humid climates. Much of the advice these authors offer is contained in this chapter.

Protecting Outdoor Exhibits and Signs

If you work in a harsh climate, consider building a small roof or shelter for your outdoor exhibits and signs. A shelter can greatly extend their lives in two ways. First, it protects them from direct contact with water (precipitation in the form of rain or snow). Second, it protects them from the damaging effects of direct

a)

b)

c)

Figure 11-1. Examples of inexpensive outdoor shelters for exhibits and signs: (a) posts and sheet metal are used to protect an outdoor exhibit at Guayabo National Monument, Costa Rica (photo by Barbara Ham); (b) two small boards make a roof for trail signs at the Lankester Botanical Gardens, Costa Rica; (c) the top of the roof is made of a split piece of bamboo which grows abundantly in the area. (Photos by Sam Ham)

sunlight. Ultraviolet radiation from the sun is the biggest cause of color fading in both indoor and outdoor exhibits. In humid areas or during rainy seasons, moisture and the repeated (sometimes daily) cycle of wetting and drying causes outdoor wooden structures to deteriorate quickly. Shelters won't completely protect them from decay, but they'll certainly slow the process.

For large exhibits, a roof supported on sturdy posts will normally be sufficient. In areas where the wind blows violently, you may need to reinforce the structure even more. For small signs, a simple shingle angled downward in front of the sign will effectively channel water away from the sign face. (Examples of inexpensive shelters for outdoor exhibits and signs are show are shown in Figure 11-1.)

Various wood preservatives can also be used to protect wooden structures. Some of these were discussed in Chapter 8 (see "Making Inexpensive Outdoor Wooden Signs"). Of these, the preferred brand is called "Wood Pressure." Besides being relatively safe to use, you can paint or stain over it once it's dry. Always be careful when using chemicals to treat wood. Besides being dangerous to you, some can also cause problems for local wildlife. If possible, make posts and frames from a type of wood that's naturally resistant to decay. If the wood is grown locally it will have the added advantage of being inexpensive. In temperate climates, many hardwood species plus redwood (*Sequoia sempervirens*), western red cedar (*Thuya plicata*) and eastern white-cedar (*Chamaecyparis thyoides*) make exceptionally durable posts and frames for outdoor exhibits. Depending on where you live, it may be cheaper to buy "pres-

sure-treated" posts and frames. Ask an expert at a lumber or building supplies store which would be best in your area.

Make Extras and Protect Original Artwork

The biggest expense in making most outdoor exhibits and signs is incurred in producing the first one. Often, you can make a second or third version at a fraction of the cost. If this is the case, make at least one or two "back-ups" and keep them in storage until they're needed. If original artwork was produced, use copies, if possible, and keep the original artwork safely protected for future use.

Protecting Slides and Photographs

Have you ever looked at a slide to see it covered with finger prints, spots or a layer of dust? Have you noticed scratches or even gouges in photographic prints that you hoped to use in a display or exhibit? Have your color prints faded in just a few months? With proper storage and handling, there's really no reason for slides and photographs to deteriorate so quickly. A few precautions and a little common sense will go a long way toward protecting photographic resources, even in harsh climates.

Handling

Finger prints, dust, and scratches are the results of mishandling. If you're not using a slide, print, or negative, put it away in a storage notebook, box, or filing tray. Try never to leave them laying around unprotected, especially if food or drinks are nearby. An otherwise innocent accident could destroy an irreplaceable photographic resource.

Never touch the surface of a slide, print or negative with your fingers. Natural oils in your skin cause photochemicals to breakdown faster, leaving blemishes on the image. Always hold them by the corner. Wearing a thin, soft glove adds extra protection from accidental touching. Many photography stores and laboratories sell special lint-free cotton gloves for this purpose. They're very inexpensive and well worth the investment if you handle slides and negatives a lot.

Storage

All photographic materials "like" cold places. As long as it's dry, even extremely cold environments pose no threat to slides, prints and negatives. Photographic images are made of chemicals, and even though we can't see it happening, these chemicals are constantly breaking down. Over time, the visible result is a faded image. Since cool temperatures slow chemical reactions, they retard the fading process, giving slides, prints, and negatives a longer life.

Heat and humidity are the main threats to photographic resources. Hot temperatures accelerate the breakdown of chemicals, and therefore, the fading of photographic images. Humidity causes two kinds of problems. First, it creates moisture that over time can dissolve the emulsion on slides and prints; second, it creates a breeding ground for fungus and mold.

Where and how you store your slides, prints and negatives determines how long they'll stay in good condition. Eastman Kodak (1985) recommends a temperature of 0° F (-18° C) and a relative humidity of 25 percent as the ideal storage environment—though for most people this isn't very practical. As a general rule, however, always try to keep photographic materials cool, dark, and dry. If you live or work in a building with more than one floor, keep your slide and photograph collections on a lower floor if possible (but not in the basement where stagnant air causes higher humidity). Always locate them away from windows and other sources of light and heat. If it's dry, a closet downstairs would be a good location if nothing else is available.

In humid or even slightly muggy climates, maintaining a dry storage area is difficult. Among the most common inexpensive methods are keeping a small 25-watt lamp on to circulate heat and evaporate moisture, and storing a moisture-absorbing substance (**desiccant**) along with the photographic materials. The safest and most efficient desiccant is silica gel. It can be purchased in bulk quantities at pharmacies, medical and

Figure 11-2. Silica gel is cheap and by far, the best moisture absorber for slide and photograph collections. You can buy it at many camera stores, pharmacies, chemical stores, and places where medical and dental supplies are sold. (Photo by Sam Ham)

Guidelines for Storing Photographic Materials

Regardless of where you store your slides, prints, and negatives, observing the following precautions will extend their useful lives:

- Make sure they're clean before storing them. Dust and oils will gradually degrade them.

- Periodically clean the slides (in humid areas use a fungicide such as ethyl alcohol).

- Protect slides from direct sunlight. Light causes images to fade.

- Keep them away from radiators, hot air vents, and windows. Heat is a leading killer of photographs and slides.

- Avoid humidity over 50 percent (such as in basements, garages and attics). Moisture affects labels, causes cardboard slide mounts and prints to warp, and promotes the growth of fungi, bacteria, and mold on emulsions.

- Color slides, prints, and negatives are especially vulnerable to heat, light, and humidity. Take extra care in protecting them.

Figure 11-3. Precautions for storing slides, prints, and negatives.

dental supplies stores, or at chemical stores; you can also get it in small sealed packets at many camera and photography stores. Some people have recommended using common dry foods such as rice, grain, soda crackers, or even common vanilla wafers as moisture absorbers, but these might not be a good idea in areas where insects or other hungry animals could be a problem. Regardless of the desiccant you use, remember it will lose its absorbency after two or three months. To revive it, put it in an oven at low heat for several hours before reusing it. If you have the money, placing a small dehumidifier in the same room as your photographic collection would be a good investment. If you store your slides in boxes, be sure to keep the boxes inside of plastic bags that are never open for more than a few seconds at a time.

If slides and prints are kept in an air conditioned or atmosphere-controlled building, plastic pages are a good storage system. These can be kept in three-ring notebooks or hanging files and removed a page at a time for quick viewing. Be careful, though, not to use **polyvinylchloride (PVC)** plastic pages. They release a harmful gas that over time can destroy your slides, prints, and negatives. You can smell the gas simply by putting the page near your nose. If it gives off a strong plastic smell, don't use it except for short-term storage (a day or two).

Archival quality slide pages are inexpensive, and since they don't contain harmful gas, are much preferred for long-term

Tips for Keeping Slides Dry

Protecting slide collections from humidity is easy if you have a dehumidifier or an air conditioner. But even if you don't, there are three things you can do to keep your slides drier:

- Allow air to circulate freely in the slide storage area—stagnant air traps moisture

- Keep a small lamp (25 watts) on at all times—the dry heat causes moisture to evaporate quickly

- Keep a moisture-absorbing substance near the slides:
  - silica gel (by far, the best)
  - common soda crackers or vanilla wafers can sometimes be used (but only if insects and other small animals aren't a problem in the area)

Figure 11-4. Three ways to protect slide collections from humidity.

storage of slides. But be careful in storing them. Because they're usually light and flimsy, they can easily slump in a three-ring notebook or file folder. If you use notebooks, store them with the opening edges of the notebook down on the shelf (so that the spine of the notebook is facing up). While this position isn't especially convenient if the notebooks are labeled on the spine, it does help keep the pages smooth and flat, and the spine protects the pages from excessive dust and light. Large notebooks with square or D-shaped rings work best (but C-rings are also acceptable if that's all you can get). If you store the pages in file folders, pack the files snugly (but not tight). If necessary, you can maintain a snug fit by putting a piece of foam rubber or other light packing material behind the files. Experts advise having no more than ten to fifteen pages per file.

"Pull-out" slide files (with drawers or racks for holding slides) are also common. Since they allow air to circulate freely among the slides, they're especially good in humid environments. In drier places, keeping slides in their original boxes is also fine, though not always very convenient. The case study by Francisco Valenzuela at the end of this chapter shows how one person has overcome the problem of storing slides in a variety of climates, including tropical humidity.

Protecting Original Slides

If possible, use only duplicate slides in talks and audiovisual programs. This is especially important for slides that would

Figure 11-5. Three tools for cleaning slides: a blow-brush, anti-static brush, and "canned air."

be difficult or impossible to replace. Besides protecting the original from dirt and finger prints, using duplicates allows you to avoid subjecting originals to the intense heat and light of slide projectors. Over time, slides that are projected a lot begin to lose their color. Keeping originals protected allows you to replace faded slides periodically with "fresh" duplicates that have the same rich colors. Although it's usually more expensive, some people prefer to take two photos of everything when they're taking pictures. This allows them to use one slide for projection purposes and the other to put in storage.

Cleaning Your Slides

If you work in a dry climate, keeping your sides clean is relatively easy because you don't have to worry so much about fungi, mold, and bacteria that require more humid conditions. Although using a fine-bristled brush (sometimes called "camel hair" brushes or "blow brushes") is acceptable, even better is an anti-static brush that neutralizes the static charge on the plastic slide, allowing the brush hairs to easily remove lint and small particles of dirt. You can buy these brushes at most camera stores anywhere in the world. Some people use compressed air, either from a compressor or in a can. Both of these latter methods are expensive, however; and unless you clean a lot of slides almost everyday, they probably aren't worth the expense.

If you work in a humid climate, keeping your slides clean is a little more difficult, but even more important. Moisture allows certain kinds of fungi, mold and bacteria to grow on the slides, actually "eating" the emulsion as they grow and multiply. If they aren't removed

soon after they start growing, they'll permanently damage the slide. An inexpensive way to remove them is to periodically clean your slides (both sides) with a fungicide. Since some fungicides may contain water (which dissolves the emulsion of a slide), be sure to use one that's safe. According to the U.S. National Park Service (Moore et al. 1989), ethyl alcohol can be used without damaging the slide as long as it's done carefully. They recommend dipping a cotton ball or "Q-tip" in the alcohol and very lightly rubbing each surface of the slide using circular motions. After cleaning, use a dry cotton ball to carefully dry the slide. It's important to note that *ethyl* alcohol must be used because it won't leave a residue like other kinds of alcohol. Isopropyl (regular rubbing alcohol) should never be used to clean a slide. Kodak sells a liquid slide cleaner that is safe and highly effective. You can buy it at almost any photography store.

Protecting Video- and Audiotapes

Since both video- and audiotapes contain magnetically recorded information, they require similar kinds of care. The biggest dangers they face are excessive heat, cold, humidity, and magnetic fields. Temperature and humidity can cause physical damage to the tape surface; magnetic fields can erase or garble the recorded information they contain. A room with ideal storage conditions would be well ventilated with a temperature of between 60 to 70°F (16 –21°C) and 40 to 50 percent humidity. Some sources say that up to 80°F (27°C) is acceptable for video-tapes, but according to Hayman (1991) anything over 60°F (16°C) can damage a tape in long-term storage.

Effects of Temperature

Extreme temperatures can damage a tape or even its plastic case. Videotape cases will warp at 130° F (54° C) and the tape itself will start to melt at 160° F (71° C). Although it's unlikely you would encounter these temperatures inside a room or building, temperatures in this range are common inside a parked car on a hot day. If the windows are up, leaving a videotape in the glove compartment or on the seat or dashboard of a car could cause irreparable damage, especially if it were left there for several consecutive days. The same, of course, would be true of tapes left in the trunk of the car.

Cold temperatures can cause tapes to become brittle. Cold can be described as temperatures below freezing, but your tape could easily be exposed to more extreme cold, especially if it's shipped by airplane. Temperatures of minus 40° F (-40° C) can occur in the cargo hold of a high-flying airplane.

Bringing a tape in from a cold environment to a warm one will cause condensation to form on the tape. This moisture can cause a video camera or VCR to malfunction. The same is true of tapes taken suddenly from a warm environment into a much colder one. The best procedure is to never play a cold tape on a warm machine or a warm tape on a cold machine. Always let the tape and the machine reach room temperature before trying to play or record.

Magnetic Fields

Strong magnetic fields can erase video- and audiotapes. In fact, special "bulk" erasers that are specifically

---

A Checklist for Protecting Video- and Audiotapes

✔ Store tapes upright in their cases.

✔ Avoid temperatures above 70°F (21°C).

✔ Keep tapes away from strong magnetic fields.

✔ Don't record at the very beginning or end of tapes.

✔ Repack tapes (by fast forwarding and rewinding) before use.

✔ Avoid keeping videotapes in "pause" for more than three minutes.

✔ Keep tapes out of direct sunlight.

✔ Don't put a cold tape in a warm player or a warm tape in a cold player.

Figure 11-6. Precautions for protecting video- and audiotapes.

designed to quickly erase audio- and videotapes are nothing more than magnetic field generators. It makes sense, then, that accidentally putting a video- or audiotape too close to a magnetic field will have an effect on it. The question, however, is what constitutes "too close." Although there's some variation, tapes located beyond 3 inches (7.5 cm) of a standard **bulk eraser** have been found to be unaffected by the relatively strong magnetic field produced by the eraser. A safe guideline, therefore, would be to keep tapes three or more inches from strong magnetic field such as motors, generators and transformers. Magnetic erasure from a television or loud speaker's magnetic field is extremely unlikely.

Storage

Video- and audiotapes should be kept in their containers at all times to protect them from dust, dirt and physical damage. Store tapes in their containers upright, rather than laying them flat.

Storing a tape flat with other tapes piled on top of it is generally a bad idea because it increases the likelihood that the outside edges of the tape might be damaged by the weight of the other tapes pressing down on it. This is especially important with videotapes since its outside edges contain the control track and audio channels. Any damage could result in an unusable tape.

After a tape has been stored for a while, it's a good idea to fast forward it to the end and then rewind it before playing or recording on it. This repacks the tape and assures more even tape movement when it's being played or recorded on. This is also a good procedure to follow before using a newly purchased tape.

If possible, keep original (master) tapes in storage. Use them only for making duplicates.

Glossary terms: archival quality, bulk eraser, desiccant, polyvinylchloride (PVC).

Storage of Photographic Prints, Slides, and Negatives—If You Value Them, You'll Take Care of Them

Francisco Valenzuela, Recreation Planner
Caribbean National Forest, Palmer, Puerto Rico

There are few moments as depressing as finding photographic materials or equipment ruined due to mold or other environmental conditions. Unfortunately this is a common event almost everywhere and especially in humid areas. But it can be avoided. Carefully protected, organized, and documented photography is an invaluable resource that can be passed on to future generations. This case study shares some of the experience I've gained the past several years managing the photographic files of the Caribbean National Forest in tropical Puerto Rico, and the long-term photographic monitoring program at Mount St. Helens National Volcanic Monument located in the cool, moist northwestern US.

All photographic materials need to be protected from exposure to hazardous environments. There are many methods that can be used, but the following are the methods that have proven best for me.

The Proper Storage Environment
Photographic Prints

Prints have large surface areas that need protection along with the material they are mounted on. Mounted prints should be stored with an over mat to separate them from other prints and with a slip sheet of archival quality paper, polyethylene or mylar over the print. I use polyethylene bags taped closed if the print is going to experience much handling.

When storing prints, high humidity is to be avoided. The relative humidity should be around 30 percent to a maximum of 50 percent. Cold temperatures (below 18 degrees C or 65 degrees F) will prolong the life of prints. Cycling, or fluctuation of temperature and humidity over short periods of time should be avoided. Pick an environment which has stable temperature and humidity year-round if possible.

When shipping prints, they should be sandwiched in the center of two strong sheets of cardboard a few inches larger than the mounted prints and secured in place. Never ship prints framed with glass. Packages should be marked "Fragile" and "Photographs" in large letters.

Negatives

Negatives should be stored in envelopes made of archival paper or in clear or translucent polyester or polypropylene sleeves, or both. They should be filed standing on their edges, and not too tightly pressed.

The ideal climate for black and white negatives is about 15 to 18 degrees C (60 to 65 degrees F) and a relative humidity of about 45 percent. For color negatives, the relative humidity should be 30 percent and temperatures of about 50 degrees F. Maximum temperature for extended periods should not exceed 25 degrees C (77 degrees F), but dry air temperature of 15 to 21 degrees C (60 to 70 degrees F) is acceptable. Cooler temperatures are more beneficial. In humid conditions, each negative filing box should have its own packet of silica gel (or other substance) to absorb moisture. Never store negatives in the darkroom or where photographic chemicals are stored. The chemical fumes can cause rapid deterioration.

Slides

Slides should be kept in the dark until they need to be viewed. They should be allowed to breathe, but not directly open to the room air. Slides can be stored in slide carousels, but these take up lots of room, are expensive, and require slides to be projected prior to selection, which wears out the slide. Plastic slide pages can be used. They are easy to use and can be kept in ring binders or in vertical files. Slide pages made from polyester (mylar), polypropylene, and tricetate are safe.

Specially designed slide cabinets are also an option for large collections and larger budgets.

Excess humidity is hazardous to slides. Beyond 60 percent the emulsion begins to swell, provide habitat for fungi, and undergo chemical changes at a faster rate. Slides are especially sensitive to cycles of temperature and humidity, which together create the greatest rate of chemical change. If you have to choose between the two, however, higher temperature is preferred over higher humidity.

Methods for Creating the Proper Environment

For most interpreters, the optimum photographic storage conditions are impossible to create because of limitations in storage facilities, electrical power availability, and funding. There are also trade-offs between safe storage and storage that is easily maintained and which allows photographic materials to be retrieved easily. This does not mean, however, that your valuable photographs are doomed, but that you will have to accept some wear and loss of quality over time. For that reason, it is important to prioritize which photographs are most deserving of the additional cost and efforts of protection. Take extra precautions with this special set and, if possible, make copies of them.

Air conditioning achieves the proper climate control by removing humidity and providing a cool environment. However, due to high costs, many large offices turn off the air conditioning system during the night and on weekends. This creates the cycling conditions that are so detrimental to photographic materials.

A small room or closet space is usually a better candidate for climate control. This smaller space can be air conditioned more easily and efficiently. But be careful; spaces that have limited air flow can easily become more humid; if the space is even a few degrees cooler than the rest of the building, it can become damp. One way to reduce the humidity in a closet is to leave a light bulb on and increase the relative temperature of the space, thereby reducing the relative humidity. As previously mentioned, higher temperatures are generally preferred over higher humidity. At home I use a small dehumidifier placed in a closet with tightly sealed doors to protect my personal collection of slides, negatives, and equipment. A dehumidifier is more energy efficient and less expensive than air conditioning, and can maintain reasonably constant humidity. The only drawback is that I have to accept a slightly warmer area than would be preferable in my tropical setting. For a cool wet location, this extra heat probably wouldn't be a problem.

Containers that are air-tight can also be used for small collections. Many plastic containers on the market are large enough and seal well enough to store photographic materials. The key in the successful use of these containers is to use some moisture absorbing material to reduce humidity. In my case, I use a reusable desiccant in an aluminum canister to capture the water

vapor. These small highly effective commercial desiccants like silica gel are safe for the photographic materials and provide no food value for other organisms. Once the gel has absorbed all it can, I dry them in an oven, then reuse them. Rice can be substituted for gel but it is about ten times less effective and can provide a food source for unwanted organisms.

The majority of my prints are stored in large wooden boxes with several canisters of desiccant. Use boxes made of untreated wood since wood finishes (like varnish) can emit harmful vapors. Fumes from some oil-based paints can be especially harmful. I use plain wooden boxes since my prints are protected by the polyethylene bags and enclosed in acid-free boxes within the wooden box. I store prints that are often displayed in frames with glass or acrylic inside a wooden box lined with acid-free mat board.

No matter what storage container you choose, it is important to monitor the climate your photographic materials are in. While temperature may be more obvious, humidity is difficult to monitor with the human senses. The easiest and least expensive way to

measure relative humidity is the use of paper or cards that change color indicating the approximate humidity. These are inexpensive enough to place several sheets near the film or prints to more accurately monitor the humidity they are in contact with.

It is helpful to think of protection in layers, each layer providing a specific kind of protection and providing protection if the layer before it fails. The first layer is the building the materials are kept in. It should be weather proof, fire resistant and contain a healthy atmosphere free of pollutants. The building should also be relatively secure from theft. The next layer is the large box, file or cabinet the materials are kept in. Will this layer provide a backup in case the building fails to serve its function? In the Caribbean, Hurricane Hugo ripped the roof off of the building containing many of the Forest Service's photographic resources. Those in strong steel filing cabinets survived the rain, but those that were kept on shelves in a wooden closet molded and were lost.

Inside the large container, it is often a good idea to subdivide the photographic materials into smaller boxes to provide one more layer of protection. Most of the important negatives in our collection are subdivided and kept in acid free cardboard boxes. Slides and negatives are stored in protective, clear polyethylene sleeves or sheets kept in separate binders. This allows safe viewing and handling.

Highly valuable long-term historic photographic resources are kept separate. Normally, we further protect them by storing them in an envelope of acid free paper around a clear protective sleeve. Use of these materials on a regular basis is discouraged, and periodic inspections are made to make sure the environment is constant.

In some countries, many of the methods and materials I've described here won't be practical. My advice is to ask an expert at a local photography store or developer how he/she protects slides, negatives, and prints. It's likely that acceptable alternatives to some of the methods outlined in this case study are being used successfully where you live. If you really value your photographic resources, you can protect them reasonably well, and without a lot of expense.

References

Eastman Kodak. 1985. *Conservation of Photographs*. Kodak Publication F-40. Rochester, New York, USA: Eastman Kodak Co.

Hayman, Randy. 1991. Archiving Videotape. *Audio Visual Communications* 25(3):21-24.

Malbon, A. Sydney. 1982. Buildings, Structures and Other Facilities. Chapter 19 in Sharpe, G.W. (ed.), *Interpreting the Environment*. New York, New York, USA: John Wiley & Sons.

Moore, Alan, Bill Wendt, Louis Penna e Isabel Castillo de Ramos. 1989. *Manual para La Capacitación del Personal de Areas Protegidas* (Modulo C: Interpretación y Educación Ambiental, Apunte 4a). Washington, D.C., USA: Servicio de Parques Nacionales, Oficina de Asuntos Internacionales.

Pyle, Robert Michael. 1982. Collections and Field Notes. Chapter 21 in Sharpe, G.W. (ed.), *Interpreting the Environment*. New York, New York, USA: John Wiley & Sons.

Additional Reading

In English:

Countryside Commission. 1980. *Audio-Visual Media in Countryside Interpretation*. Advisory Series No. 12. London, United Kingdom: Countryside Recreation Research Group.

Eastman Kodak. 1986. *Kodak Color Films and Papers for Professionals*. Kodak Publication E-77. Rochester, New York, USA: Eastman Kodak Co.

Fazio, James R. and Douglas L. Gilbert. 1986. *Public Relations and Communications for Natural Resource Managers*. Dubuque, Iowa, USA: Kendall/Hunt Publishing Co.

Harrison, Anne. 1982. Problems: Vandalism and Depreciative Behavior. Chapter 25 in Sharpe, G.W. (ed.), *Interpreting the Environment*. New York, New York, USA: John Wiley & Sons.

Hooper, Jon K. 1987. *Effective Slide Presentations*. Chico, California, USA: Effective Slide Presentations.

Pennyfather, Keith. 1975. *Guide to Countryside Interpretation: Part II—Interpretive Media and Facilities*. Edinburgh, Scotland: Her Majesty's Stationery Office and the Countryside Commission.

Robl, Ernest H. 1986. *Organizing Your Photographs*. New York, New York, USA: AMPHOTO, Inc.

In Spanish:

Ham, Sam H. 1992. *Interpretación Ambiental: Una Guía Práctica para Gente con Grandes Ideas y Presupuestos Pequeños*. Golden, Colorado, USA: North American Press/Fulcrum Publishing.

Morales, Jorge. 1987. *Manual para la Interpretación en Espacios Naturales Protegidos*. Anexo 3 del Taller Internacional sobre Interpretación Ambiental en Areas Silvestres Protegidas. Santiago, Chile: Oficina Regional de la FAO para América Latina y el Caribe, 7-12 de diciembre de 1988.

APPENDIX A

GLOSSARY OF
KEY TERMS

2-3-1 rule: A guideline for developing sequential presentations such as talks, tours and scripts. According to this "rule," the body should be developed first, the conclusion second, and the introduction last.

Absolute volume: The recording level of the loudest predominant sound (usually the narration) in a soundtrack. All other volumes are adjusted relative to the absolute volume.

Accessibility: The quality of a site, facility, structure, or device that is both conveniently located and free of barriers to the physically disabled.

Active prop: A prop that is actively used or manipulated during a presentation.

Analogous colors: Colors that are adjacent to each other on the color wheel.

Analogy: A bridging technique that shows many similarities between an object of interest and something else that's already familiar to an audience.

Application question: A question that gets people to consider how certain information could apply in different situations.

Archival quality: A characteristic of something that lasts for many years without deteriorating or causing damage to other materials with which it is in physical contact. Archival quality matte frames, art paper and plastic slide storage pages are important interpretive resources.

Arrow-window board: A type of interactive exhibit containing a revolving wheel with an arrow on one side and a small window on the other. When a viewer turns the wheel so that the arrow points to a particular object or topic, the window displays selected information related to it.

Balance: The visual equilibrium that occurs when the visual weights of elements in a design appear distributed equally. Balance may be formal or informal.

Barrier-free: A quality that a facility, installation or area has when it is easily accessible to all people, even those with physical or mental disabilities. See "Accessibility."

Black slide: A slide made of opaque material (such as cardboard or plastic). Black slides are often used during major transitions in talks and audiovisual programs, or when one or more blank screens are desired in a multi-image program. When such a slide is projected, the result is a dark screen. (Thinner or translucent material may be used if a partially illuminated screen is preferred to total darkness.)

Body: The part of a presentation that follows the introduction. Its main purpose is to develop the theme in an organized and interesting way. The body corresponds to the "2" in the "2-3-1 Rule."

Bridge: A figurative description of communication techniques that are used to make new information more meaningful by connecting it to things that are already familiar to an audience.

Broadcast media: Radio and television.

Bulk eraser: A small magnetic field generator used to erase an entire audio or video tape instantly.

Captive audience: Audiences that feel they must or should pay attention to a presentation even if it bores them.

Cause-and-effect question: A question that gets people to think about the causes behind different events, phenomena and objects.

Chalkboard: A hard surface that can be written on using chalk or markers.

Closed question: A question that has a pre-defined number of correct answers.

Cloth board: A type of visual aid consisting of a cloth background (usually flannel, felt, velcro or wool) on which small illustrations are adhered during a talk.

Color scheme: A combination of colors that are selected because they look good together.

Comparison question: A question that asks people to consider the similarities and differences between things.

Comparison: A bridging technique that shows a few of the main similarities and/or differences between an object of interest and something else that

can be related to it. The result is that one or both of the objects becomes clearer in relation to the other.

Complementary colors: Colors that are opposite each other on the color wheel.

Conceptual design: That aspect of the design process that deals with the organization and presentation of the message.

Conclusion: The final part of a sequential presentation. The main purpose of a conclusion is to reinforce the theme. It corresponds to the "3" in the "2-3-1 Rule."

Description/explanation: That part of guided or self-guided tour stop in which important aspects about the object of interest are described or explained to an audience.

Desiccant: A moisture-absorbing substance. For slide and photograph collections, silica gel is the best desiccant.

Emphasis: In visual design, the quality of a design element that draws the viewer's attention. Size, color, shape and location are often used to emphasize design elements.

Entrance: The moment at which an interpreter first encounters the audience in-role during a dramatic performance (such as a living history demonstration or personification performance).

Evaluation question: A question that gets people to express their opinions about something, and to discuss possible choices and judgments.

Event: A short-term educational program of limited duration.

Example: A bridging technique that quickly refers to something that is like or in some way represents an object of interest.

Exhibit: An indoor or outdoor structure that communicates a theme through visual illustrations and written or recorded text. All exhibits are non-sequential (non-linear) communication devices.

Exit: The moment at which an interpreter in a dramatic performance stops playing the role of someone else and returns to his or her real self.

Figure-eight trail: A trail corridor that crosses itself like the number 8.

Flip chart: A type of visual aid consisting of large sheets of paper—usually arranged in sequence on an easel or wall—that contain prepared illustrations and text material for a presentation.

Focusing question: A question that focuses a person's attention on an idea or object of interest.

Foreshadowing: A technique in which an interpreter hints at what is to come later in a presentation. Foreshadowing is often used to create a sense of anticipation in a talk, tour or script.

Formal education: Education programs delivered through the formal school system.

Grade (slope): The steepness of a trail or hill, usually measured in percent increase in elevation per unit of horizontal distance. For example, a trail that increases one meter in elevation over ten meters of horizontal distance would have a grade (or slope) of 10 percent.

Graphics: Drawings, charts, graphs, and other illustrations used as visual aids in oral and written presentations.

Grid technique: A method for enlarging original artwork. One grid is drawn on the original and a larger one on the desired surface. The contents of each cell of the original grid are then drawn in the corresponding cell of the larger grid until the drawing is complete.

Guided tour: Walks, hikes, and other kinds of sequential presentations in which an interpreter leads an audience through a series of pre-planned narrated stops. Guided tours may be conducted on foot, bicycles, boats, trains, planes and other forms of transportation.

Guideline: A general recommended approach to doing something.

Hue: See "Temperature of color"

Illustrated talk: A talk supported by the use of visual aids.

Inference question: A question that gets people to generalize or reason beyond the information they've been given, and to explore possible conclusions and implications.

Information station: Any location that is designed and operated to provide information to visitors.

Interpretation: A communication process in which one person translates a language he/she speaks very well into terms and ideas that other people can understand. It is an educational method that aims to reveal meanings and relationships through the use of original objects, by firsthand experience, and by illustrative media, rather than simply to communicate factual information.

Interpretive approach: A way of communicating that strives to make information enjoyable, relevant, organized and thematic.

Introduction: The first part of a sequential presentation to be heard by an audience. Its main purposes are to capture the audience's interest, reveal the theme, tell how the presentation will be organized, and to establish the vehicle if one is to be used. It corresponds to the "1" in the "2-3-1 rule."

Introductory sign: A forty- to fifty-word sign at the beginning of a self-guided trail that orients visitors to the theme of the trail and entices them to walk it.

Labeling: A communication technique in which new information is presented

to people in the context of some social group they either associate themselves with or disassociate themselves from.

Lacquer thinner transfer: A method of transferring a photocopied original to another background surface by coating the back of the photocopy with lacquer thinner and quickly burnishing it.

Levels: Conceptual parts of an exhibit design that correspond to four purposes: (1) communicating the theme as rapidly as possible, (2) quickly showing the five or fewer main ideas being presented, (3) providing selected information pertaining to each major part of the message, and (4) suggesting to viewers how they can use or act upon their new knowledge. Exhibits designed around these levels communicate their themes to all viewers, regardless of how much time they spend reading the text.

Linear trail: A two-way, "dead-end" trail on which people going one direction encounter people going the other direction.

Linear: Sequential. Linear presentations include talks, guided tours, scripts for audiovisual programs and other presentations that proceed in a pre-planned order from a definite beginning to a definite ending.

Literal illustration: A visual image that shows something as it really appear in nature.

Living history demonstration: A dramatic performance in which an interpreter portrays a real or hypothetical person from the past.

Loop trail: A one-way trail that begins and ends at the same (or approximately the same) point, thus forming the shape of a circle.

Magical 7±2: The maximum number of separate ideas that most people can deal with simultaneously. Since many of us can handle only seven minus two, five is generally considered the maximum number of main ideas that should be presented in a communication program.

Mass media: Communication media such as radio, television, newspapers and magazines that reach many people.

Meaningful: Information is meaningful when we can understand it in terms of something we already know about.

Mechanical exhibit: An interactive exhibit that viewers can manipulate.

Message: The theme of a presentation.

Metaphor: A phrase that describes something with a word or words usually used to describe a very different thing.

Multi-image program: An audiovisual program that shows two or more images simultaneously.

Multi-media program: A presentation that utilizes more than one communication medium. All audiovisual programs are multi-media programs.

Musical interlude: A part of a soundtrack that contains music only.

Mystery: A quality of a presentation in which audience members are actively involved in solving a problem, riddle or mind-teaser. Usually, they're given selected information and told to watch or listen for additional facts that will help them complete the picture.

Noncaptive audience: Audiences that pay attention to a presentation only if they find it gratifying to do so.

Nonformal education: Education programs delivered outside of the formal school system.

Nonillustrated talk: A talk in which no visual aids are used.

Nonlinear: Nonsequential. Exhibits and short publications such as brochures are examples of non-linear presentations. The reader, not the designer, decides the order in which different parts of the message will be read, and whether they will be read at all. Nonlinear communication has no definite sequence and no definite ending.

Nonsequential: See "Nonlinear"

Off-site program: An educational program conducted away from an interpreter's place of work.

On-site program: An educational program conducted at an interpreter's place of work.

Open-ended question: A question that has an undetermined number of correct answers. The focus is usually more on possibilities than facts.

Oral presentation: Illustrated and non-illustrated talks, guided tours, narrated audiovisual programs and other presentations that rely on the spoken word. Oral presentations are linear.

Passive prop: A prop that is shown but not actively used or manipulated in a presentation.

Peep-pipe: A piece of pipe mounted and aimed at some object or feature that can be seen by looking through the hole.

Personal: A quality that information has when it pertains to something we care strongly about.

Personification: (1) a type of communication vehicle in which a story is told from the perspective of a non-human animal, plant or object, or through the eyes or experiences of a non-human narrator; (2) a type of presentation in which an interpreter portrays a non-human animal, plant or object.

Photo copystand: A table with lights and a stationary camera-mount that can be used to photograph titles, artwork, graphics, and small three-dimensional objects.

Polyvinylchloride (PVC): A detectable gas contained in certain kinds plastic pages used for storing slides and negatives. Because the gas is harmful to slides and negatives, PVC pages should be avoided except for short-term storage. Archival quality plastic pages are far superior.

Pragnänz: A German word that means completeness, wholeness and unity. In communication, it's the feeling an audience has when a presentation has come "full circle."

Print media: Those mass media that communicate in written form (magazines, newspapers, billboards, etc.).

Problem-solving question: A question that gets people to think of possible solutions to problems.

Programming: The last step of slide/tape program production in which the slides are synchronized with the tape. Programming may be accomplished manually or electronically. Same as "slide synchronization."

Progressive disclosure: Presenting a series of visual aids such that each one adds additional details to the one preceding it.

Projection method: A technique for enlarging illustrations or transferring text from an original to some other surface. The original image is projected using a slide, overhead or opaque projector, and the enlarged image is traced by hand.

Prop: A real object or physical representation of a real object that is used as a visual aid in a talk.

Quiz board: An interactive exhibit that poses questions to viewers and gives them a chance to test their knowledge. Feedback is always provided.

Referencing: Making specific reference to a visual aid through phrases such as "As you can see in this slide ... ," or "This is a picture of a ... ." Referencing is often unnecessary.

Relative volume: The recording level of a sound in relation to the volumes of other sounds heard at the same time.

Relevant: A quality that information has when we can understand it in terms of something we already know and care about.

Representation: A visual image that relates in a general but direct way to something being described by a narrator.

Roving interpretation: Spontaneous interpretation carried out by personnel traveling through an area (usually on foot, bicycle, or horseback) who greet and chat with the visitors they encounter along the way.

Script: A written text containing the narration for an audiovisual program.

Selective attention: The tendency of people to pay attention to those things they find immediately gratifying.

Self-guided (self-guiding) tour: An interpretive tour in which people lead themselves through a series of pre-planned stops (usually keyed to a brochure, signs or audio messages). Self-guided tours may be taken by people on foot, bicycles, boats, trains, planes, and other forms of transportation.

Self-referencing: A communication technique in which new information is presented to people as they are asked to think about their own experiences related to it.

Sequential: See "Linear"

Shadowing: An experimental technique used in studies on the importance of personal information to human beings.

Sign: An outdoor exhibit usually containing a central theme and only one or two main ideas.

Slide synchronization: Same as "programming."

Sniff box: A box containing an aromatic substance (such as plants with a strong or characteristic odor). Holes are drilled in the top of the box so that visitors can smell the aroma of whatever is inside.

Sound-on-sound: Two or more recorded sounds heard simultaneously from the same source.

Soundtrack: The audio portion of an audiovisual program usually consisting of voice, music or other sounds recorded on a tape.

Speech: Usually a formal oral presentation given in a formal setting.

Stacking: In soundtrack production, a technique whereby the end of one sound is faded out at the same time another sound is being faded in. The result is fluid transition from the first to the second sound.

Staging period: Just prior to the beginning of a guided tour, that period of time in which the interpreter meets, greets and informs audience members about the tour and tour route.

Stop: A place on a guided or self-guided tour at which the audience stops moving in order to hear or read information.

Storyboard: A detailed plan describing the desired coordination between the soundtrack and visual images of an audiovisual program.

Style: An individual's personal approach to speaking in front of groups. There are an unlimited number of effective speaking styles.

Switchback: A sharp ("doubling-back") turn on a trail.

Symbolic illustration: A visual image that relates in an indirect or metaphorical way to an abstract idea that would be difficult or impossible to illustrate literally.

Tactile exhibit: An interactive exhibit that displays objects viewers can touch or handle.

Talk: An informal but well practiced oral presentation. All talks are a type of sequential (or linear) presentation.

Temperature of color (hue): The coolness and warmness of colors depending on their location on the color wheel. Warm colors (like red, orange and yellow) usually advance and look bigger than cooler colors. Cool colors (like blue and violet) usually recede and look smaller than warmer colors.

Thematic connector: That part of a guided or self-guided tour stop in which the stop's relationship to the overall theme of the tour is given.

Thematic map (or plan): A map showing the route of a self-guided tour and the location and theme-title of each stop.

Theme: The central message about a topic of interest that a communicator wants to get across to an audience. It's the answer to the question "so what?"

Theme title: A title that communicates the theme of an exhibit or stop on a guided or self-guided tour.

Topic: The subject matter of a presentation.

Tracing: Copying original artwork using any one of five techniques: tracing with carbon paper, dot tracing on paper, dot tracing on a chalkboard, backlighted tracing, or tracing real-world scenes.

Transition: Simple connectors in a sequential presentation. They tell the audience when the focus of the presentation is going to change from one main point to the next. Transitions are important throughout any sequential presentation, but especially between the introduction and body, and between the body and the conclusion.

Typestyle (font): The style (including shape, size and darkness) of the letters comprising a text. "Font" and "typeface" are sometimes used interchangeably with typestyle.

Unity: Consistency in a visual design. A quality a design has when the elements that comprise it seem to go together.

Value (of a color): The amount of darkness or lightness in a color.

Vehicle: In communication, a contrived scenario or situation that is created by a communicator in order to enhance the entertainment value of the topic being presented.

Visual aid: An illustration that helps to clarify or add interest to written or spoken words.

Water bar: A shallow, downward-sloping channel designed to divert run-off away from a trail corridor.

Written presentation: Exhibits, brochures and most short publications. Most written presentations are nonlinear.

APPENDIX B

MODELS

The following sketches are offered as an aid to readers who must design and build their own interpretive structures and facilities. Most federal and state land management agencies will provide architectural plans for exhibits, signs, amphitheaters, trail structures and other facilities free of charge.

Exhibits and Signs

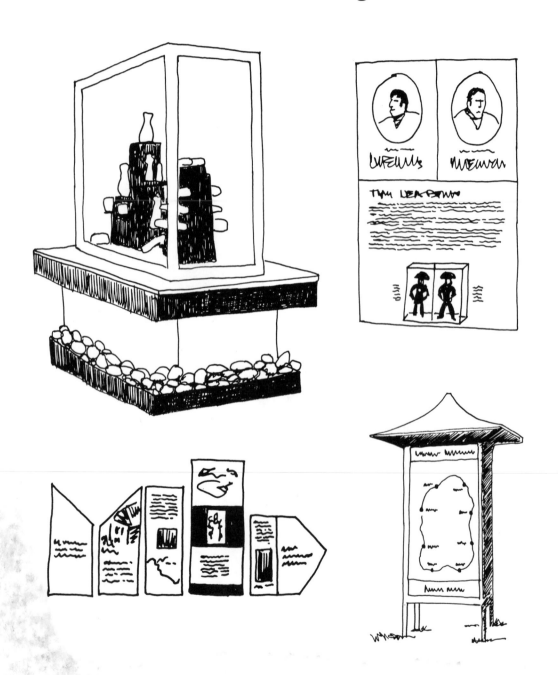

Rustic Outdoor Amphitheaters

Trail Structures

APPENDIX C

LETTERING AIDS

Serif Letters

A B C CH D E F G H I J
K L LL M N Ñ O P Q R
R R S T U V W X Y Z

a b c ch d e f g h i j k l ll
m n ñ o p q r rr s t u v w
x y z á ä é í ó ü
1 2 3 4 5 6 7 8 9 0

¡ ! @ # % ^ & * ( ) _ + -
= [ ] { } ; : " " < > ¿ ? / .

Serif Letters

A B C CH D E F G H I J
K L LL M N Ñ O P Q R
RR S T U V W X Y Z

a b c ch d e f g h i j k l ll
m n ñ o p q r rr s t u v w x
y z á ä é í ó ü
1 2 3 4 5 6 7 8 9 0

¡ ! @ # % ^ & * ( ) _ + -
= [ ] { } ; : " " < > ¿ ? / .

San Serif Letters

A B C C H D E F G H I J

K L LL M N Ñ O P Q R

R R S T U V W X Y Z

a b c ch d e f g h i j k l ll

m n ñ o p q r rr s t u v w

x y z á á ä é í ó ü

1 2 3 4 5 6 7 8 9 0

¡ ! @ # % ^ & * ( ) _ + -
= [ ] { } ; : " " < > ¿ ? / .

San Serif Letters

A B C CH D E F G H I J
K L LL M N Ñ O P Q R
RR S T U V W X Y Z

a b c ch d e f g h i j k l ll
m n ñ o p q r rr s t u v w
x y z á ä é í ó ü
1 2 3 4 5 6 7 8 9 0

¡ ! @ # % ^ & * ( ) _ + -
= [ ] { } ; : " " < > ¿ ? / .

Tracing Grid for Upper Case Letters

APPENDIX D

KEY ORGANIZATIONS IN INTERPRETATION AND ENVIRONMENTAL EDUCATION

Organizations Related to Interpretation in the United States and Canada

Interpretation Canada
187 Old Topsaid Road
St. Johns, Newfoundland
Canada A1E 2B2

Interpretive Management Institute
Mott Training Center
P.O. Box 699
Pacific Grove, CA 93950
USA

National Association for Interpretation
P.O. Box 1892
Fort Collins, CO 80522
USA

North American Association for
Environmental Education
P.O. Box 400
Troy, OH 45373
USA

Professional Guides Association of
America
2416 S. Eads Street
Arlington, VA 22202
USA

Recommended Environmental Education Programs

Acclimatization Series/Sunship Earth
American Camping Association
Bradford Woods
Martinsville, IN 46151
USA

Project Learning Tree
American Forest Council
1250 Connecticut Avenue, N.W.
Washington, D.C. 20036
USA

Project Wet
Idaho Water Resources Research Institute
106 Morrill Hall
University of Idaho
Moscow, ID 83843
USA

Project Wild
Salina Star Route
Boulder, CO 80302
USA

Ranger Rick's Nature Scope
National Wildlife Federation
1400 Sixteenth St., N.W.
Washington, D.C. 20036-2266
USA

International Organizations

Centre for Environmental Interpretation
Manchester Polytechnic
Saint Augustine's
Lower Chatham St
Manchester
United Kingdom M15 6BY

Center for Marine Conservation
1725 DeSales St. NW, Suite 500
Washington, D.C. 20036
USA

Cultural Survival, Inc.
11 Divinity Ave
Cambridge, MA 02138
USA

Ecotourism Society
801 Devon Place
Alexandria, VA 22314
USA

Food and Agriculture Organisation of the
United Nations (FAO)
Via delle Terme di Caracalla
00100 Rome
Italy

FAO Regional Office for Latin America
Casilla 10095
Santiago
Chile

Heritage Interpretation International
P.O. Box 6116, Station "C"
Edmonton, Alberta
Canada T5B 4K5

International Centre for Conservation
Education
Greenfield House
Guiting Power
Cheltenham, Glos. GL54 5T2
United Kingdom

International Union for the Conservation
of Nature and Natural Resources (IUCN)
IUCN-World Conservation Union
Ave. du Mont Blanc
CH-1196 Gland
Switzerland

National Audubon Society
950 Third Avenue
New York, NY 10022
USA

National Parks and Conservation
Association
1701 18th Street, N.W.
Washington, D.C. 20009
USA

National Wildlife Federation
1412 16th Street, N.W.
Washington, D.C. 20036
USA

The Nature Conservancy
International Programs
1815 North Lynn Street
Arlington, VA 22209
USA

New York Zoological Society
The Zoological Park
185th St., and So. Blvd., Bldg. A
Bronx, NY 10460
USA

Organization of American States (OAS)
1889 F Street, N.W.
Washington, D.C. 20006
USA

Sierra Club
777 United Nations Plaza
New York, NY
USA

Smithsonian Institution
1000 Jefferson Dr., SW
Washington D.C. 20560
USA

Unesco
7, Place de Fontenoy
75700 Paris
France

U.S. Fish and Wildlife Service
Office of International Affairs
MIB 3012
1849 C Street, N.W.
Mail Stop 860-Arlington Square
Washington, D.C. 20240
USA

U.S. Forest Service
International Forestry
P.O. Box 96090
Washington, D.C. 20090-6090
USA

U.S. National Park Service
Division of International Affairs
P.O. Box 37127
Washington, D.C. 20013-7127
USA

U.S. Peace Corps
Office of Training and Program Support
Room M-701
806 Connecticut Ave. NW
Washington, D.C. 20526
USA

Wildlife Conservation International
New York Zoological Society
185th St., and So. Blvd., Bldg. A
Bronx, New York 10460
USA

World Wildlife Fund-US
1250 Twenty-fourth St., N.W.
Washington, D.C. 20037
USA

Other International Organizations

CARE International
660 First Avenue
New York, NY 10016
USA

Center for International Environmental
Information
345 East 46th Street
New York, NY 10017
USA

Cities
Rue du Maupas 6
1004 Lausanne 9
Switzerland

Conservation International
1015 18th Street, N.W.
Suite 1000
Washington, D.C. 20036
USA

European Economic Community
Rue de la Loi, 200
1049 Brussels
Belgium

Fauna and Flora Preservation Society
Alfred Brehem Platz 16
6000 Frankfurt am Main
West Germany

International Council for Bird
Preservation (ICBP)-Pan American
801 Pennsylvania Avenue S.E.,
Suite 301
Washington D.C. 20003
USA

International Society of Tropical
Foresters, Inc.
5400 Grosvenor Lane
Bethesda, MD 20814
USA

Peoples Trust for Endangered Species
19 Quarry Stret
Surrey, GU1 3EH
England

RARE, Inc.
19th and the Parkway
Philadelphia, PA 19103
USA

Sierra Club
Office of International Affairs
777 United Nations Plaza
New York, NY
USA

United Nations Environment Programme
(UNEP)
P.O. Box 30552
Nairobi
Kenya

World Environment Center, Inc.
419 Park Ave., Suite 1403
New York, NY 10016
USA

*Regional and National Organizations
in North America, Latin America,
and the Caribbean*

Caribbean Conservation Association
Savannah Lodge
The Garrison
St. Michael, Barbados
West Indies

Caribbean Conservation Corporation
P.O. Box 2866
Gainesville, FL 32602
USA

Caribbean Natural Resources Institute
Clarke Street, Vieux Fort
St. Lucia
West Indies

Centro Agronómico Tropical de
Investigación y Enseñanza (CATIE)
Apartado 7170 CATIE
Turrialba, Costa Rica

Central America
Organization of American States (OAS)
1889 F Street, N.W.
Washington, D.C. 20006
USA

Antigua and Barbuda

Historical and Archaelogical Society
of Antigua and Barbuda
P.O. Box 103
St. John's, Antigua
West Indies

National Parks Authority of Antigua
and Barbuda
P.O. Box 1283
St. John's, Antigua and Barbuda
West Indies

Argentina

Amigos de la Tierra
Anchorena 633
Capital Federal, Buenos Aires
(1170) Argentina
South America

Asociación Argentina de Ecología
Casilla de Correo 1025, Correo Central
Cordoba (5000) Argentina
South America

Administración de Parques Nacionales
Avda. Santa Fe 690
1959 Buenos Aires, (1059) Argentina
South America

Centro Entrerriano del Medio Ambiente-
CEMA
Casilla de Correo 328
Parana, Entre Ríos, (3100) Argentina
South America

Fundación Ambiente y Recursos
Naturales-ARN
Monroe 2142, 1 piso
Buenos Aires, (1428) Argentina
South America

Fundación para la Defensa del Ambiente-
FUNAM
Casilla de Correo 83
Cordoba, (5000) Argentina
South America

Instituto Forestal Nacional-IFONA
Pueyrredon 2446 Capital Federal
Buenos Aires, (1119) Argentina
South America

Barbados

Caribbean Conservation Association
(CCA)
Savannah Lodge, The Garrison
St. Michael, Barbados
West Indies

Ministry of Agriculture, Food and
Fisheries
Graeme Hall
Christ Church, Barbados
West Indies

Belize

Belize Audubon Society
49 Southern Foreshore, P.O. Box 1001
Belize City, Belize
Central America

Belize Zoo and Tropical Education Center
P.O. Box 474
Belize City, Belize
Central America

Ministry of Agriculture, Forestry and
Fisheries
Belmopan, Belize
Central America

Ministry of Natural Resources-MNR
Belmopan, Belize
Central America

Bolivia

Academia Nacional de Ciencias de Bolivia
Avenida 16 de julio No. 1732, Casilla
20068
La Paz, Bolivia
South America

Fondo Nacional para el Medio Ambiente
San Pablo, Piso 7, Of. 701
La Paz, Bolivia
South America

Liga Defensa del Medio Ambiente
(LIDEMA)
Casilla 7000
La Paz, Bolivia
South America

Ministerio de Asuntos Campesinos y
Agropecuarios-MACA
Avenida Camacho 1471
4 piso, Oficina No. 404
La Paz, Bolivia
South America

Brazil

Brazilian Society for Environmental
Protection
Av. das Américas 2300 C40
Río de Janeiro, RJ, CEP 22640, Brazil
South America

Centro de Estudios e Actividades de
Conservacao da Natureza-CEACON
Cx. Postal 20684
Sao Paulo, SP, 01498 Brazil
South America

Fundacao Pro Natureza-FUNATURA
Caixa Postal 02-0186
70.001 Brasilia, D.F., Brazil
South America

Fundacao Brasileira para a Conservacao
da Natureza-FBCN
Rua Miranda Valverde, 103, Botafogo
Río de Janeiro, RJ, 22.281 Brazil
South America

Fundacao Victoria Amazónica
Av. Darcy Vargas, 520
Chapada, CEP 69.050
Manaus, A.M., Brazil
South America

INNATURA-Associacao de Consciencia
Ecológica
Cx. Postal 64649, Shopping Eldorado
Sao Paulo, SP, Brazil
South America

Instituto Brasilero do Medio Ambiente e
Recursos Naturales Renovaveis
Sain Av. L4 Norte-ED, IBDF/MINTER
CEP 70.800 Brasilia, D.F., Brazil
South America

Canada

Interpretation Canada
187 Old Topsaid Road
St. Johns, Newfoundland
Canada A1E 2B2

Colombia

Fondo para la Protección del Medio
Ambiente-FEN COLOMBIA
Calle 72 No. 8-56, piso 9
Bogotá, Colombia
South America

Fundación Natura-Colombia
Calle 90 No. 10-61, OF, 201
Apartado Aéreo 55402
Bogotá, Colombia
South America

Instituto Nacional de los Recursos
Naturales Renovables y del Ambiente,
INDERENA
Diagonal 34 No. 5-18
Apartado Aéreo 13458
Bogotá, Colombia
South America

Costa Rica

Amigos de la Naturaleza
P.O. Box 162
Guadalupe, Costa Rica
Central America

Asociación Costarricense para la
Conservación de la Naturaleza-ASCONA
Apartado 8-3790
San José, Costa Rica
Central America

Centro Agronómico Tropical de
Investigación y Enseñanza (CATIE)
Apartado 7170 CATIE
Turrialba, Costa Rica
Central America

Fundación Parques Nacionales
Apartado 105, Plaza Gonzalez Viquez
San José, Costa Rica
Central America

Fundación Neotrópica
Apartado 236-1002
San José, Costa Rica
Central America

Monteverde Conservation League
Apartado 10165
San José, Costa Rica
Central America

Organización para Estudios Tropicales-
OET
Apartado 676-2050
San Pedro de Montes de Oca, Costa Rica
Central America

Servicio de Parques Nacionales
Sección Educación Ambiental
Ministerio de Recursos Naturales,
Energía y Minas
Apartado 10014-1000
San José, Costa Rica
Central America

Cuba

Comisión Nacional de Medio Ambiente
Av. 17 No. 5008 e/ 50 y 52, Playa
Ciudad de la Habana
Cuba

Secretario Comisión Rectora del Gran
Parque Nacional Sierra Maestra
Calle 42, No. 514 e, 5a. B y 7a., Playa
Ciudad de la Habana
Cuba

Chile

Comité Pro-Defensa de la Fauna y Flora-
CODEFF
Casilla 3675 Santiago, Chile
South America

Corporación Nacional Forestal
Avda. Bulnes 285, Of. 501
Santiago, Chile
South America

Instituto de Ecología de Chile
Calle Agustinas 641, Oficina #11
Santiago, Chile
South America

Dominica

Dominica Conservation Association
(DCA)
P.O. Box 71
Roseau, Dominica
West Indies

Ministry of Agriculture-Forestry and
National Parks Service
P.O. Box 71
Roseau, Dominica
West Indies

Dominican Republic

Dirección Nacional de Parques
Calle Las Damas No. 6
Apartado Postal 2487
Santo Domingo
Dominican Republic

Fundación Natura Dominicana, Inc.
Gustavo Meja Ricart No. 9
El Milton, Apartado 30155
Santo Domingo
Dominican Republic

Fundación para el Desarrollo
Comunitario, Inc. (FUNDECO)
Avda. 27 de febrero
Apartado 366-2, Centro de los Heroes
Santo Domingo
Dominican Republic

Sociedad Dominicana para la
Conservación de Recursos Naturales
P.O. Box 174-2
Santo Domingo
Dominican Republic

Ecuador

Dirección Nacional Forestal-División de
Areas Naturales y Vida Silvestre
Ministerio de Agricultura y Ganadería
Avdas. Eloy Alfaro y Amazonas
A.A. 8543
Quito, Ecuador
South America

Estación Científica Charles Darwin
Santa Cruz, Islas Galápagos, Ecuador
Casilla 17-01-3891
Quito, Ecuador
South America

Fundación Charles Darwin
Colon 535 y 6 de Diciembre
6 piso/Casilla 3891 2 E
Quito, Ecuador
South America

Fundación Ecuatoriana para la
Conservación y el Desarrollo Sostenible
Av. Amazonas 239
P.O.Box 17-12-0310
Quito, Ecuador
South America

Fundación Natura
Casilla 243
Av. América 5653 y Vozandes
Quito, Ecuador
South America

Sociedad de Defensa de la Naturaleza
Pasaje San Luis 104
Edificio Recalde, Of. 401
Quito, Ecuador
South America

El Salvador

Asociación Salvadoreña de Conservación
del Medio Ambiente (ASACMA)
Urbanización Buenos Aires
Calle Masquilishuat #208
San Salvador, El Salvador
Central America

Centro de Recursos Naturales (CENREN)
Cantón El Matazano, Soyapango
Apartado 2265
San Salvador, El Salvador
Central America

Dirección Patrimonio Nacional
Ministerio de Educación, Edificio TVCE
Av. Robert Baden Powell
Santa Tecla, La Libertad, El Salvador
Central America

Fundación Ecológica Salvadoreña Activo
20-30
79 Avenida Norte No. 509
San Salvador, El Salvador
Central America

La Unidad Ecológica Salvadoreña
c/o CESTA, 33 Calle Pte. #316
San Salvador, El Salvador
Central America

Ministerio de Agricultura y Ganadería-
Centro de Recursos Naturales
Cantón El Matasano,
Apartado Postal 2265
Soyapango, El Salvador
Central America

Museo David J. Guzmán
Av. La Revolución
San Benito, San Salvador
El Salvador
Central America

Museo de la Historia Natural
de El Salvador
Parque Saburo Hirao
Final Calle Los Viveros
San Salvador, El Salvador
Central America

Grenada

Grenada National Trust
c/o Grenada National Museum
Young Street
St. George's, Grenada, West Indies

Ministry of Agriculture-Forestry Division
Archibald Avenue
St. George's, Grenada
West Indies

Guatemala

Asociación de Amigos del Bosque
9a. Calle 2-23, Zona 1
Guatemala, Guatemala
Central America

Asociación Guatemalteca de Historia
Natural
Parque Zoológico La Aurora, Zona 13
Guatemala, Guatemala
Central America

Asociación Guatemalteca Pro-Defensa del
Medio Ambiente
20 Calle 19-44, Zona 10, Apartado 1352
Guatemala, Guatemala
Central America

Centro de Estudios Conservacionistas
Avenida de la Reforma 0-63, Zona 10
10101 Guatemala, Guatemala
Central America

Consejo Nacional de Areas
Protegidas-CONAP
Presidencia de la República
7a. Av. 4-00, Zona 1
Ciudad de Guatemala, Guatemala
Central America

Fundación Defensores de la Naturaleza
7a. Avenida 13-01, 2do nivel
Zona 9, Edificio La Cupula 01009
Guatemala, Guatemala
Central America

Fundación para el Ecodesarrollo
y la Conservación
14 Calle "B" 14-24
Zona 10 Oakland 01010
Guatemala, Guatemala
Central America

Ministerio de Agricultura, Ganadería y
Alimentación-Instituto Nacional
Forestal-INAFOR
7a. Avenida 11-63, 6o. nivel
Zona 9, Edificio Galerías España
Guatemala, Guatemala
Central America

Guyana

Guyana Ecological Society
5 Bel Air Promenade
Georgetown
Guyana

Guyana Natural Resources Agency
Brickdam
Georgetown
Guyana

Haiti

Federation des Amis de la Nature, Haiti
Verte-FAN
c/o Institut Pedagogique National
Rue du Docteur Audain
Port-au-Prince
Haiti

Ministere de l'Agriculture-Direction des
Ressources Naturelles et d l'Environment
Port-au-Prince
Haiti

Honduras

Asociación Hondureña de Ecología (AHE)
Apartado Postal T-250
Tegucigalpa, Honduras
Central America

Corporación Hondureña de Desarrollo
Forestal
Apartado Postal 1372
Comayaguela, Honduras
Central America

Escuela Nacional Forestal (ESNACIFOR)
Siguatepeque, Honduras
Central America

Ministerio de Recursos Naturales
Renovables
Apartado Posta 309
Tegucigalpa, D.C., Honduras
Central America

Universidad Nacional Autónoma de
Honduras
Departamento de Biología
Ciudad Universitaria
Tegucigalpa, Honduras
Central America

Jamaica

Jamaica Conservation & Development
Trust (JCDT)
P.O. Box 1225
Kingston 8, Jamaica
West Indies

National Environmental Societies Trust
(NEST)
P.O. Box 1468
Kingston 8, Jamaica
West Indies

Natural Resources Conservation
Authority
53 1/2 Molynes Road
Kingston 10, Jamaica
West Indies

University of the West Indies
Mona Campus
Kingston 7, Jamaica
West Indies

México

Asociación Mexicana de Pro-Conservación
de la Naturaleza-PRONATURA
Apartado Postal #14
53160 Naucalpan, México
México

Biocenosis
Cerrada de Banderillas 25-13
San Jerónimo
10200 México, D.F.
México

Dirección General de Conservación
Ecológica de los Recursos Naturales
Secretaría de Desarrollo Urbano y
Ecología (SEDUE)
Río Elba No. 20-piso 10
Col. Cuauhtemoc
06500 México, D.F.
México

Instituto de Ecología-IE
Apartado Postal 18-845
Delegación Miguel Hidalgo
11800 México, D.F.
México

Pacto de Grupos Ecologistas
Amores 1814/Col. del Valle
03100 México, D.F.
México

Promoción Ecológica Campesina-PROE
Calle San Ignacio #2834, Col. San Manuel
Puebla, Puebla
México

United Nations Environmental
Program-UNEP
President Masaryk 29
5th Floor/Colonia Polanco
México, D.F.
México

Montserrat

Montserrat National Trust
P.O. Box 495
Plymouth, Montserrat
West Indies

Nevis/St. Kitts

Nevis Historical and Conservation Society
Alexander Hamilton Museum
Charlestown, St. Kitts-Nevis
West Indies

Nicaragua

Asociación de Biólogos y Ecólogos de
Nicaragua-ABEN
Apartado 3257
Managua, Nicaragua
Central America

Dirección General de Recursos Naturales
y del Ambiente (DIRENA), MINDINRA
Managua, Nicaragua
Central America

Instituto Nicaragüense de Recursos
Naturales y del Ambiente-IRENA
Km. 12 1/2 Carretera Norte
Apartado 5123
Gob. de Reconstrucción Nac.
Managua, Nicaragua
Central America

Red Regional de Organizaciones
Conservacionistas No Gubernamentales
para el Desarrollo Sostenido de
Centroamérica-REDES
Managua, Nicaragua
Central America

Universidad Autónoma de Nicaragua
Departamento de Biología
León, Nicaragua
Central America

Panamá

Asociación Nacional para la Conservación
de la Naturaleza (ANCON)
Apartado Postal 1387, Zona 1
Panamá, Panamá
Central America

Fundación de Parques Nacionales y
Medio Ambiente-PANAMA
APDO 6-6623, El Dorado
Panamá, Panamá

Central America

Instituto Nacional de Recursos Naturales
Renovables-INRENARE
Paraiso, Ancón
Apartado 2016
Panamá, Panamá
Central America

Sociedad de Amigos de la
Naturaleza-SANA
APDO 286, David, Chiriqui
David, Panamá
Central America

Sociedad Audubon de Panamá
APDO Postal 2026
Balboa, Panamá
Central America

Paraguay

Centro Paraguayo de Estudios
Sociológicos
Eligio Ayala 973, Apartado Postal 2157
Asunción, Paraguay
South America

Fundación Paraguaya de Cooperación y
Desarrollo
Presidente Franco No. 846
Asunción, Paraguay
South America

Dirección de Parques Nacionales, Manejo
de Bosques y Vida Silvestre
Casilla de Correos 3303
Asunción, Paraguay
South America

Sociedad Paraguaya para la Protección de
la Naturaleza-PRONATURA
15 de Agosto #457/Casilla de Correo 2497
Asunción, Paraguay
South America

Sociedad Protectora de Animales y
Plantas del Paraguay
Casilla de Correos 3209
Asunción, Paraguay
South America

Perú

Asociación de Defensa del Medio
Ambiente-ADMA
Av. Universitaria, 318/Correo UV3
Lima 01 Perú
South America

Asociación Peruana Para La
Conservación de la Naturaleza
Parque José de Acosta 187
Lima 17 Perú
South America

Director de Parques Nacionales, DGFF
Natalio Sanchez No. 220, 3er. piso
Jesús María
Lima 11 Perú
South America

Fundación Peruana para la Conservación
de la Naturaleza-FPCN
Chinchón 858-A
San Isidro/Apartado 18-1393
Lima 01 Perú
South America

St. Lucia

Caribbean Natural Resources Institute
(CANARI)
Clarke St, Vieux Fort
St. Lucia
West Indies

Ministry of Agriculture, Lands, Fisheries
and Cooperatives
Manoel Street
Castries, St. Lucia
West Indies

St. Lucia National Trust
P.O. Box 525
Castries, St. Lucia
West Indies

St. Lucia Naturalists Society
P.O. Box 783
Castries, St. Lucia
West Indies

St. Vincent and the Grenadines

Organization for Rural Development-ORD
P.O. Box 827
Kingstown, St. Vincent
West Indies

Ministry of Trade and Agriculture
Kingstown, St. Vincent
West Indies

St. Vincent and the Grenadines
National Trust
P.O. Box 198
Kingstown, St. Vincent
West Indies

Trinidad and Tobago

Asa Wright Nature Center
P.O. Bag 10
Port-of-Spain, Trinidad and Tobago
West Indies

Eastern Caribbean Institute of Agriculture
and Forestry-ECIAF
Post Office
Arima, Trinidad and Tobago
West Indies

Ministry of Food Production, Marine
Exploitation, Forestry and Environment-
Conservator of Forests and Wildlife
Forestry Division
Long Circular Road, St. James
Port-of-Spain, Trinidad and Tobago
West Indies

University of the West Indies
St. Augustine, Trinidad and Tobago
West Indies

United States

Alliance for Environmental Education,
Inc.
Box 1040, 3421 M St., NW
Washington D.C. 20007
USA

Association for Experimental Education
Box 249-CU
Boulder, CO 80309
USA

Coalition for Education in the Outdoors
Box 2000
Park PER Center
Cortland, NY 13045
USA

Conservation Education Association
University of Wisconsin
Green Bay, WI 54302
USA

Environmental Education Coalition
Pocono Environmental Education Center
Box 1010
Dingmans Ferry, PA 18328
USA

Friends of the Earth
124 Spear Street
San Francisco, CA 94105
USA

Institute for Earth Education
Box 288
Warrenville, IL 60555
USA

U.S. Army Corps of Engineers
HQ-USACE
Recreation Staff
20 Massachusetts Avenue, N.W.
Washington, D.C. 20314-1000
USA

U.S. Bureau of Land Management
Recreation Branch
Director 341
Interior Department
1849 C Street, N.W.
Washington, D.C. 20240-9998
USA

U.S. Fish and Wildlife Service
Recreation Management
MIB 3012
1849 C Street, N.W.
Washington, D.C. 20240
USA

U.S. Forest Service
Recreation
P.O. Box 96090
Washington, D.C. 20090-6090
USA

U.S. National Park Service
Division of Interpretation
P.O. Box 37127
Washington, D.C. 20013-7127
USA

World Wildlife Fund-US
1250 Twenty-fourth Street, N.W.
Washington, D.C. 20037
USA

Uruguay

Dirección General de Recursos Naturales
Renovables (RENARE)
Ministerio de Ganadería,
Agricultura y Pesca
Cerrito 322, 2do. piso
Montevideo, Uruguay
South America

Sociedad de Conservación del Medio
Ambiente
Cerro Largo 1895
Montevideo, Uruguay
South America

Venezuela

BIOMA: Fundación Venezolana para la
Conservación de la Diversidad
Apartado 1968, Zona Postal 1010-A
Caracas, Venezuela
South America

Fundación de Educación Ambiental
Edif. Canejo, P.B. Local 3 y 4
Caracas, Venezuela
South America

Fundación para la Defensa de la
Naturaleza-FUDENA
Apartado 70376
1071-A Caracas, Venezuela
South America

Instituto Nacional de Parques-
INPARQUES
Parte Sur, Museo de Transporte
Urbanización Santa Cecilia
Z.P. 1010 Caracas, Venezuela
South America

Ministerio de Ambiente y de los Recursos
Naturales Renovables-Fundación de
Educación Ambiental
Apartado 6623
Caracas 1010-A, Venezuela
South America

Sociedad Conservacionista
Audubon de Venezuela
Apartado 80450

108 Caracas, Venezuela
South America

Universidad Nacional Experimental de los
Llanos Ezequiel Zamora-Programa de
Recursos Naturales Renovables, Unellez
Prog. de Rec. Nat. Renov.,
Mesa de Cavacas
Guanare, Estado Portuguesa, Venezuela
South America

INDEX